EFFECTIVE MANAGEMENT: PEOPLE AND ORGANISATION

Derek Torrington
Manchester School of Management

Jane Weightman
Manchester School of Management

Kirsty Johns
Formerly Manchester School of Management

PRENTICE HALL
New York   London   Toronto   Sydney   Tokyo

First published 1989 by
Prentice Hall International (UK) Ltd,
66 Wood Lane End, Hemel Hempstead,
Hertfordshire, HP2 4RG
A division of
Simon & Schuster International Group

© 1989 Prentice Hall International (UK) Ltd

Printed and bound in Great Britain by
A. Wheaton and Co. Ltd, Exeter

British Library Cataloguing in Publication Data

Torrington, Derek
  Effective management
  I. Title   II. Weightman, Jane
  III. Johns, Kirsty
  658

    ISBN 0–13–244344–9

2 3 4 5 93 92 91 90 89

ISBN 0-13-244344-9

CONTENTS

PREFACE

This book is a successor to *Business of Management* by Derek Torrington and Jane Weightman, which Prentice Hall published in 1985. That was a satisfying venture, but we felt that changes beyond simple up-dating were needed when the time came to consider a second edition, so those familiar with *Business of Management* will find much that is little altered, some new material, some radically altered and some omitted.

Our objective remains that specified in our 1985 preface:

> Management textbooks do not impress students unless they seem practical, but practical books are of little value without a satisfactory theoretical framework. We have tried to write a practical book that will gain the assent of practising managers as a realistic explanation of what they are doing, but which will also be convincing to students: 'this could be your life'. We have been careful to examine not *management*, but *managing*, seeking not detachment from, but identification with, the life that managers lead and the problems they face.

Kirsty Johns has joined us as co-author to give a greater breadth of experience and to add substance, especially in the areas of problem-solving, decision-making, budgetary control and management information systems.

Completely new chapters are: 5, The management functions of the business; 6, Strategy and policy-making; 8, Managing change and 22, Management information systems. Most of the others have undergone varying degrees of development, including some amalgamations and much retitling. Some of our more abstruse illustrations have been removed, but we have an additional feature for most chapters entitled 'Putting It Into Practice'. There are a number of practical examples centred round named individuals. These are all actual incidents we have encountered, but we have excluded the name of the organisation, partly because most of the individuals were anxious to remain anonymous and partly to avoid the distraction from the issue that naming the organisation could introduce. We have worked hard at trying to reduce to the minimum the language and assumptions that suggest managing is an exclusively male activity.

We trust that the text will prove relevant and readable to those facing the problems and opportunities of managing in the 1990s.

Our thanks go to Pat Loftus for hours at the word-processor, to Maggie McDougall, Cathy Peck and others at Prentice Hall for their unwavering support and efficient production. Most of all we appreciate the comments of those who have used the book, whether as students or tutors or as practising managers.

School of Management
UMIST
P O Box 88
Manchester M60 1QD

Derek Torrington
Jane Weightman
Kirsty Johns
January 1989

that are available, and the difference between different types of managerial role. In reading books about organisation, or participating in management courses, managers and aspiring managers frequently find the material fascinating but insufficient, as it deals with what they see that others *ought* to do rather than what they personally *can* do.

Review Topic 1.1

To what extent are managers in control of the areas of the organisation for which they are responsible, and to what extent are they at the mercy of external factors?

Numbers and changing circumstances of managers

Some ten per cent of the working population are now in management jobs. This does not include the many more who have a management dimension to their work without them being regarded as managers.

The management career is changing also. In the expanding organisations that were the norm of industrialised societies until the middle 1970s, there was at least the assumption that most managers would eventually be promoted to senior posts, and middle management positions were used as training posts for senior management. This was never really true, but it was believed widely enough for it to become a valid operating assumption. Increasingly middle management is a whole career for many people, and a respondent in one of our research studies described it as 'terminal management'. In another very large and *expanding* company we obtained comprehensive manpower information of the average age at which managers reached the grade at which they eventually retired. For senior managers this was between 46 and 53, but for middle managers it was between 43 and 48, so when middle managers retire they have been in their final grade for longer than senior managers, with all the problems of frustration and lack of fresh opportunity. Another twist to this situation is the age at which people are put in management posts. No longer do young people graduating from university, for instance, aim to be in a management position by the time they are thirty; they expect it within months. Any visit to a supermarket will confirm the number of people holding significant management responsibility in their early twenties, so the time spent 'in the middle' may well be increasing for many people.

Also the job of the manager is typically described in terms of the job of the chief executive delegated in different-sized parcels to others and therefore similar to his. In fact the job of the chief executive is quite different from all other management jobs and it is unrealistic for managers at other levels to model their behaviour on that example.

Organisational size. Management and management ideas have both developed during the last fifty years against a background of increasing organisational size and an expanding number of jobs classified as managerial, bringing greater problems of co-ordination and communication and an emphasis on the administration of stable environments rather than dealing with the risks and uncertainty which are the reality of the modern organisation. Middle managers have been identified as the administrators of the stable state and with a vested interest in resisting change. White (1981) conducted a study in a south coast electrical company and explained middle managers' resistance to innovation by the fact that they are structurally dissociated from the satisfactions of ownership, technically dissociated from the process of production and socially dissociated from the work force.

The move to ever-increasing size has halted, especially in the number of people employed. Most large organisations have reduced the number of employees and many have decentralised their management operations so that only a small number of matters are reserved for resolution at the centre while operating units are managed with increased autonomy. A further aspect of this trend is that managers are finding their sphere of operations to be more compact. Some forecasters also think that the number of small, independent companies will increase. At the same time there is the growth of the employment complex, like the airport, shopping centre, or construction site or science park, where a large number of independent organisations share a common location, facilities and some aspects of co-ordination.

The move to specialisation slackens. With increasing organisational size came specialisation, much encouraged by two sets of interest groups: professional bodies and academic institutions. Professional bodies exist to serve the interests of those who share a specialised bit of the management action, such as purchasing or personnel. Once created, the professional body then has to strengthen and expand that specialised interest in order to exist itself. Higher education adopted management with enthusiasm during the 1960s and 1970s in order to meet the demand from large numbers of students seeking entry to the apparent joys of managerial life and a company car. The essence of academic study is specialisation within academic disciplines, so both universities and the professional bodies have an interest in the specialist manager. Between them they provide the most common entry ticket: qualification, so that people coming in to management have a developed specialisation.

One of the effects of the economic recession in the 1980s appears to have been a move away from specialisation towards flexibility. The self-justifying specialised function that Parkinson (1957) caricatured so vividly is losing ground so that individual managers are rediscovering a need to operate in all areas of the business, which was regarded as the prime attribute of those who first experienced business school training.

PART I

MANAGEMENT AND THE MANAGER

Managers of the 1990s have a job to do which is considerably different from that of their predecessors – and yet they still have the same job to do! This introductory section of the book sets management and the manager in their contemporary context, as well as tracing the development of management ideas from antiquity to the present. The reader sees the unchanging nature of the management role as well as the changes it has undergone. There is also an analysis of how management work is constituted, how management functions and managers' jobs differ, and what they all have in common.

1

INTRODUCTION TO MANAGEMENT

Mankind survives and operates through organisation. Organisation is needed to provide us with our motor cars and cultural amenities; our health care and education; our consumer goods and information services. For all these things we have to work together – to organise. We also *are* organised. Organisational life is the setting in which most of us spend our working hours and at least part of our leisure. A day at the office may well be followed by an evening with the amateur dramatic society or a weekend with the hockey team.

This book concentrates on the role of manager in contemporary organisation. It is about management as a job to be done by people with a wide range of specialist responsibilities. It is not just about those who are ultimately in charge, but mainly about those who cope with bits of organisational functioning rather than with the grand design. We try to get inside the mind of the individual manager and answer questions like: How do I understand what is going on around me? Why do people behave this way? When is my undertaking organised differently from the one in which my neighbour works? How do I cope with this situation? Do I understand the structure properly? Can I make a better contribution? Am I secure? How do I resolve this problem? How do I get things done? How do I meet my responsibilities?

Although there has been some reaction against very large scale and impersonal bureaucracy, working in concert rather than working alone seems to be a pervasive feature of our lives. The feats of David Livingstone or Francis Chichester are famed because of the courage and skill of individuals triumphing over formidable obstacles, but when Neil Armstrong walked on the surface of the moon it was the triumph of thousands who had contributed to the co-operative venture of the NASA space programme. Marie Lloyd or Harry Lauder were solo performers of great popularity, but the contemporary rock star travels with an entourage of thirty or forty people, all of whom are needed to put together the eventful performance. Individuals will continue to make great contributions to society on their own, but the major achievements that are often needed come from managed organisations; not only factories, offices and commercial undertakings, but hospitals and research centres, government departments and charitable bodies, schools and colleges. For every novel representing the creative output of an individual there will be a hundred newspapers representing the creative accomplishment of a managed team. Management is not just a job done by people called 'managers'; it is an aspect of the job done by all those who have to cope with the problems and opportunities of organisation: social workers, editors, ward sisters, chefs, housewives, engineers, school teachers, clergymen, administrators and many more.

There are many challenges to mankind that require a management contribution for their resolution. We have to learn to manage problems such as atmospheric pollution and the shortage of energy; technological innovation and the obsolescence of traditional skills; poverty in the third world and unemployment in the west. Few of these problems have a simple solution requiring no more than the necessary political will, and few of them depend on the intuitive insight of an individual. Managed activity is needed both to produce the solutions and to implement the programmes for those solutions to be put into operation.

Trewatha and Newport (1982) quote the late President J.F. Kennedy, writing in 1963:

> Much of the free world's success in using its human resources fully and with dignity can be laid to enlightened and progressive management . . . It is to managers who grow with the needs and resources of their time that we must continue to look for the new ideas and their implementation to meet the challenges of the future.

THIS BOOK AND THE CONTEMPORARY MANAGEMENT SCENE

We have written this book in the hope of meeting a number of needs, based on work we have been doing with managers and management students in the last few years.

Managerial uncertainty. Large numbers of people have management jobs, or jobs with a management component, and most of them seem uncertain of what they are doing. For some this is caused by disappointment on finding out how little managers can achieve. Believing that managers make decisions, solve problems and shape the future, they find in practice that their scope is limited and that only a portion of their time is spent in these exciting activities. Other people are frustrated by problems of structure or policy within their organisation that they feel helpless to remedy. We have, however, found the most common reason to be uncertainty about simple things, like the nature of managerial work, the basic methods of working

In this book we include a chapter on the main areas of management specialisation in contemporary business, but the main thrust is to deal with the things that most managers do. It is, for example, about influencing people, but not about marketing; it is about selecting team members, but not about personnel management. Similarly it is about the majority of management work; not about the top manager making strategic decisions, but about the work of other managers in influencing those decisions and making them work.

We concentrate on the job to be done, with methods that can be applied. We attempt to give reasoned arguments for those methods, demonstrating the logic of doing something and helping to analyse which methods are appropriate for which settings. Too often only the academic or only the practical is available. Where a bridge can be made between the two, a more forceful method is developed, as it has to stand the test of both logic and use.

Review Topic 1.2

Think of one or two methods of managing that are *only* academic and one or two that are *only* practical. What are their shortcomings?

MANAGEMENT: JUST ONE PART OF THE SAGA OF HUMAN ORGANISATION

Having briefly looked at the prevailing situation we take a glance back towards antiquity, as management is no more than one facet of the long-running saga of human organisation. Our understanding of contemporary management phenomena is enlightened and placed in perspective by looking for some of the ways in which the process evolved.

The Egyptians

The modern nation state evolved 4,500 years ago and was brought into being by the building of the great pyramids at Giza, near Heliopolis in Egypt. The pyramids exercise a strange fascination over the minds of modern men and women. We marvel at the largest stone structures in the world, each containing enough stone to build a wall all the way round a country the size of France. The technological achievement of building with such precision and durability was extraordinary, but the reason for their being built is even more intriguing. Mendelssohn (1974) has argued that the great pyramids were built as a method of creating an integrated human community the size of a state. Previously man had lived in communities no larger than a tribe or village, but the increasing size of the Egyptian population required a larger-scale pattern of organisation in order to make optimum use of the resources of the Nile, the sole source of water to irrigate the land on which the food was grown. Not only was the water seasonal, with inundation followed by drought, but the level varied from year to year, as is mentioned in the Old Testament prophecy of Joseph about seven fat years being followed by seven lean years.

For the people to be fed there had to be co-operation, not just between families and within the local village, but between villages that were widely dispersed. That sort of co-operation depends on social organisation to bring about commitment, obedience and sacrifice for the sake of benefit. People learn to co-operate because they want to; no system of imposing authority on the unwilling can operate unless either the majority are willing or the leaders have exceptional coercive power at their disposal.

The pharaohs had power to coerce that any modern despot would envy, but Mendelssohn believes that this was insufficient for the purpose, so the pyramid project was a means of reinforcing their authority through willing co-operative endeavour of the peasantry.

For three months each year 100,000 to 120,000 men were gathered together on the Giza plateau to co-operate on this immense task. These men left their families and their homes for three reasons. First, the pyramids were great projects on which to be engaged, providing an experience quite different from the limited routine of village agriculture. Secondly, the resurrection of the pharaoh, after a suitable burial, was essential to the afterlife of the common man. You ensured your own afterlife by contributing to the appropriate interment of your pharaoh. Thirdly, the surrounding system of social organisation provided the pharaoh with centralised stocks of grain for distribution during the lean years.

This project achieved a number of outcomes:

A civil service infrastructure. If 100,000 men were to work on the arduous physical labour of cutting and manhandling blocks of stone weighing fifteen tons each, they had to be not only organised, but fed and housed. This required a large number of administrators and a bureaucratic system.

A sense of nationhood. The workers developed a sense of commitment to, and membership of, the nation as well as their family and village, because of the common task on which they were engaged. Patriotism was born.

Dependence on the centre. The pharaoh had the grain. So the common people were economically dependent on him for survival, and the central administration acquired a steadily increasing hold over the population as a whole.

Hierarchy. The organisation and co-ordination of such a large labour force produced a hierarchy of authority as the logical means of integrating dispersed effort. There is an echo of this in an often quoted passage from the Old Testament where Moses, having led the exodus of the Jewish people out of their bondage in Egypt, is counselled by his father-in-law Jethro to set up a system of delegation that must have been very similar to that which they had experienced at the hands of the pharaoh:

> Search for capable, God-fearing men among all the people, honest and incorruptible men, and appoint them over the people as officers over units of a thousand, of a hundred, of fifty or of ten. They shall sit as a permanent court for the people; they must refer difficult cases to you but decide simple cases themselves. In this way your burden will be lightened, and they will share it with you. (New English Bible, Exodus, Chapter 18, verses 19–22)

The pyramid project provided the pattern for the nation state, which was not only successful in Egypt, but was taken as the pattern for succeeding nations and other large-scale organisations like armies and the Roman Catholic Church. In turn it became the pattern of schools, hospitals, local government and business.

The principle was simple and logical, and it worked because the task facing the organisation was relatively simple once the original design and technological work had been done. After that the project required small expertise and huge labour.

The main features of the pyramid organisation are to be found in all large-scale contemporary enterprises. The hierarchy and the 'civil service infrastructure' of central administration binds the dependent employee to the corporation. Wages, salaries and fringe benefits have replaced the stock of corn and the employing organisation may well be one in which the employee takes great pride, but the company pension scheme for support in the afterlife of retirement is a poor substitute for the eternity with Osiris that the pharaoh could offer. Furthermore the modern-day corporation will seldom have a single undertaking for its employees of the simplicity of pyramid building. So the pattern of human organisation that has been with us since antiquity is no longer sufficient.

The Sumerians

The earliest civilisation known in the fertile crescent of the Middle East was that of the Sumerians, slightly before the early Egyptians. Their main contribution is that they invented writing, because their priests kept business and legal records on clay tablets.

Woolley (1963) excavated extensively in the area of Ur of the Chaldees and demonstrated how priests in Sumer achieved great power. The ordinary Sumerians did not anticipate the blissful afterlife that was the expectation of the Egyptian pyramid-builders; they expected it to be at best a dismal reflection of their time on earth and their apprehension led them to offer constant propitiation to the Gods. The agents of this propitiation were the priests, who were the only ones able to carry out the ritual. The ritual involved sacrifices with the quality of the propitiation being related to the volume of sacrifice that had been made. It was also the priests who kept the records of what sacrifices had been offered and by whom.

Records were the basis of control and became the avenue to an élite position of power. As organisations have developed and evolved, the need for centralised information has remained and carried with it the power to control. The main contemporary examples are the accountancy profession and the computer, which are used to control complex organisations, and which are shrouded in mysteries which their practitioners use to maintain their exclusive access to the data banks.

The Florentine

As the western world grew up the ideas and methods produced by the Egyptians and Sumerians were refined in the Greek city states, the Roman Empire and the Roman Catholic Church, described by one pair of contemporary management writers as 'the most effective formal organisation in the history of western civilisation' (Koontz and O'Donnell, 1976).

A novel and original contribution came in the writings of a disgraced Florentine civil servant of the late fifteenth century. Niccolo Machiavelli served as secretary to the Florentine Republic from 1498 until 1512, when he was dismissed and imprisoned on the charge of conspiring to overthrow the Medici family, who had returned to power. When he was released he started writing, but his classic *Il Principe* was not published until 1532, five years after his death. In this book Machiavelli makes a clear distinction between ethics and politics, which brought him long-running notoriety, although many statesmen have followed the spirit of this concept by not allowing objection on ethical grounds to interfere with political and diplomatic goals. It is an easier notion for managers to accept, as they can argue that social responsibility is drawn from them by legislation, government policy, employee resistance, union power or consumer choice, so that their task is to get on with running the business as effectively as possible within those constraints.

The main interest in Machiavelli's ideas lies in his analysis of how the prince (or leader, or manager) meets his obligations. These have been resurrected for the management audience by Jay (1967), but the original in modern translation (Machiavelli, 1981) is so lucid and so constantly relevant that it is eminently accessible, as well as short. The main points are:

Cohesive organisation. The prince should maintain the cohesiveness of his organisation by binding to him his friends and those on whom he will depend. This will involve giving them rewards for their contribution and making sure that they know what the prince expects and what they can expect from him.

Mass consent. However cohesive the power stucture of the organisation, the prince has to maintain the consent of the governed, as this is the source of his authority. Not only does it give him authority over the governed, it also gives him authority over his 'courtiers'.

Leadership. Cohesive organisation and mass consent can only be achieved if the prince is a leader and example-setter for his people, being wise and tempering necessary justice with mercy.

Review Topic 1.3

Think of contemporary examples of cohesive organisation, mass consent, leadership and toughness, as defined by Machiavelli.

Toughness. There will be attempts to unseat the prince, so he must have the toughness to resist any such attempts and be ruthless with the instigators.

This cool appraisal of what is involved has given our language the word *Machiavellian*, to mean cunning, amoral and opportunist. It is interesting that the word 'management' is derived from the Italian sixteenth-century word *maneggiare*, meaning to control or train, especially relating to horses. The conception of the manager as devious was developed further when the job emerged as a distinct entity in the nineteenth century:

> At this point the concept of 'manager' was a neutral one, even pejorative. Thus, Robert Owen, writing in 1811: 'My intention was not to be a *mere* manager'. 'We rely not upon management or *trickery*, but upon our own hearts and heads' (Jowett, 1881). 'Talent for *intrigue or management* usually counts for more than debating power' (Bryce, 1888). In the more refined employments – the colonial and civil services – there were no managers but 'administrators'. (Mant, 1977, pages 21–22)

The Industrial Revolution

Slowly the patterns of human organisation began to evolve and the role of the leader was clarified, but then came the watershed of the Industrial Revolution which was to transform first Britain and then the rest of Europe and the United States into industrialised nations. Hitherto the practice of management had been confined to church, state and army; the job of prelate, prince or officer. Now the great institutions of commerce and industry were born, and the traditional leaders of society had no place in them – wanted no place in them – so we acquired a new occupation and a new class – the bourgeoisie:

> The bourgeoisie has created more massive and more colossal productive forces than have all preceding generations together. Subjection of nature's forces to man, machinery, application of chemistry to industry and agriculture,

steam navigation, railways, electric telegraphs, clearing of whole conti-
nents for cultivation, canalization of rivers, whole populations conjured out of
the ground – what earlier century had even a presentiment that such
productive forces slumbered in the lap of social labour? (Marx, 1848, page
147).

The wealth of technological innovation at this time brought great economies of scale and the invention of power-driven machinery transformed
the production process. The capital cost of the new equipment was beyond
the individual worker so that he had to move out of his home and into the
factory, where the machines could be economically located under one roof
and efficiency could be enhanced by skilled co-ordination of employees'
work.

Marglin (1971), using extensive examples from the weaving industry,
argues that it was the discipline and supervision of the labour force in the
factory that was most important in reducing costs as there was greater
labour input, less embezzlement and patents were easier to monitor. Also
by increasing the division of labour the entrepreneur had an essential role
as integrator, controlling the process and quantity of output, as the worker
was now selling his labour rather than a product.

In 1800 James Watt and Matthew Boulton built a new factory to make
steam engines and introduced aspects of practice that were to form the basis
of production organisation for more than 150 years:

Flow of work. Having estimated the demand for their engines, Watt and
Boulton laid out their factory for a smooth flow of work between the various
operations and equipped it with machines that were timed so that the
expected output would match as closely as possible the anticipated demand. At the same time the jobs of individual employees were broken down
and analysed to estimate their contribution – the beginning of time and
motion study.

Wages. Wage payment arrangements were developed to be consistent with
the requirements of each job. As many jobs as possible were paid on a piece
rate basis so that income was linked to output, and weekly rates were paid
for those jobs where such measurement was not feasible.

Records. Detailed records were developed for cost accounting, so that there
was control of direct and indirect costs, enabling the managers to identify
areas of inefficiency and high productivity. With this information the
managers were able to control the operation by trying to raise the efficiency
of those areas where it was defective and adjusting the payment system.

The flow of work had been one of the organisational problems of the early
Egyptians, the keeping of records for control had been developed by the

Sumerian priests, but the elaboration of wages as an impersonal means of motivating employees rather than the leadership ideas of, for instance, Machiavelli, was a new departure and a new breeding ground for the development of middle management expertise.

We return to a historical perspective in the next chapter, when we examine the work of management analysts that began in the twentieth century, but we conclude this introductory chapter by offering a definition of what we mean by management.

A WORKING DEFINITION

Probably the best-known definition of management is that of Mary Parker Follet, who described it as 'The art of getting things done through people'. This is neat but insufficient, as the emphasis is solely on getting other people to do things, without giving due weight to other tactics and resources. It also implies that the 'other people' are subordinates, although they are frequently peers, outsiders or superiors in a hierarchical sense.

The sales manager aiming to increase sales may achieve that by getting the salespeople to work harder or more effectively, but he may also achieve the objective by altering the advertising policy. We suggest five headings for the dimensions of management as a job to be done:

1. Managers have conflicting *goals*. They have to meet production targets at the same time as keeping costs down. They achieve profit margins but also satisfy the needs of subordinates. They seek to use economic methods of production but also satisfy environmental controls. They are always seeking for a balance to ensure that one goal is not attained at the expense of another.
2. Managers are held *responsible* for results, not only their own results, but also the results of others. The branch bank manager is held responsible for everything that happens on his premises. If there are mistakes, he takes the blame from his superiors, from his staff and from the customers, all of whom have a touching faith in his ability to satisfy their various expectations.
3. Managers work in *organisations*, with all the resources, opportunities and frustrations that such settings provide. The complexity of the organisation provides a wide range of skills and facilities that can be deployed, but it also requires co-operation, synchronisation and communication. Enabling the complex organisation to perform is a crucial part of the manager's job that makes it distinctive from some other leadership functions like, for instance, captaining a cricket team.
4. The stable state for managers is *uncertainty*. There will be planning and procedures to reduce the level of uncertainty, but the unexpected

problem, the unprecedented situation, is the realm of the manager. Generally the operators in an organisation are able to cope with predictable situations as a result of their training, information and authorisation, but have to call on managerial assistance to deal with the unfamiliar, either because the manager has more technical understanding and experience or because the manager has an element of hierarchical authority to take certain decisions which have not been delegated to the operators.

5. Managers work with and through other *people*. Here we are not quite back to Mary Parker Follet, because the people are not only subordinates but also organisational peers, customers, clients, suppliers and many other outsiders who make up the network of contacts that the manager uses to make the job effective. In the 1980s it is a very varied, changing constituency that the manager has to manage.

The initial letters of the key words above produce the mnemonic GROUP, and increasingly managers find all those five aspects of management are being mediated through groups (see Fig. 1.1). There is the group decision-making of boards of directors and senior management teams, planning conferences in advertising and the media, autonomous working groups in factories, joint production committees in industrial democracy exercises, selection panels, suggestions committee meetings, staff meetings and all the other ways in which managing becomes a corporate activity rather different from the emphasis on individuals that until recently was the sole focus for management work.

Fig. 1.1　Five dimensions of the manager's job.

SUMMARY PROPOSITIONS

1.1 Although managing the work of organisations is a widespread activity, many managers lack understanding of their role and knowledge of simple methods that can be used in managerial work.

1.2 The main dimensions of the manager's job are that they have conflicting goals, are held responsible for results, work in organisations, cope with uncertainty, and work with and through other people.

1.3 Management is but one aspect of human organisation, which can be traced back to the beginning of civilisation.

REFERENCES

Jay, A., *Management and Machiavelli*, Penguin Books, Harmondsworth, 1967.
Koontz, H. and O'Donnell, C., *Management: A Systems and Contingency Analysis of Management Functions*, McGraw Hill, New York, 1976.
Machiavelli, N., *The Prince*, Penguin Books, Harmondsworth, 1981.
Mant, A., *The Rise and Fall of the British Manager*, Macmillan, London, 1977.
Marglin, S., *What Do Bosses Do? The Origins and Functions of Hierarchy in Capitalist Production*, Harvard University Department of Economics, 1971.
Marx, K., *Communist Manifesto 1848*, quoted in Bottomore, T.B. and Rubel, M. *Karl Marx: Selected Writings in Sociology and Social Philosophy*, Penguin Books, Harmondsworth, 1979.
Mendelssohn, K., *The Riddle of the Pyramids*, Thames & Hudson, London, 1974.
Parkinson, G.N., *Parkinson's Law*, John Murray, London, 1957.
Trewatha, R.L. and Newport, M.G., *Management*, 3rd edn, Business Publications, Plano, Texas, 1982.
White, O., 'Why won't managers co-operate?', *Industrial Relations Journal*, March/April 1981, pages 61–72.
Woolley, L., *Digging Up the Past*, Penguin, Harmondsworth, 1963.

2

THE DEVELOPMENT OF
MANAGEMENT THOUGHT

This chapter sketches the main developments in understanding the management job over the last hundred years. This helps us to understand what is going on now and what will be happening tomorrow. The job of the manager is steadily evolving, and understanding the range and nature of the modifications that have taken place so far helps us to do the job better. The analysis in the two following chapters deals comprehensively with the current situation.

As the industrial revolution continued through the nineteenth century the social impact was enormous. People left the land for the cities in such numbers that the population of Manchester, for instance, increased from 30,000 to 300,000 in less than sixty years. Yet this was at a time when social change proceeded at a snail's pace when compared with the hectic speed of the present day. It is also notable that similar large-scale migrations from the land to the cities have been taking place in the less developed countries of the world in the latter part of the twentieth century. Cities like Cairo, Addis Ababa and Mexico City have experienced dramatic growth with almost identical consequent problems.

The migrations of the industrial revolution found cities quite unable to cope with the increased demands on housing, water, sanitation and other facilities. The poverty and hopelessness of rural life was replaced by the dehumanised nature of existence in the squalor surrounding the factories. The social problems created by the industrial cities were not initially seen as undesirable. William Wilberforce is known today as the man who brought an end to the slave trade, yet he was able to say of his own countrymen:

> The more lowly path of the poor is allotted to them by the hand of God. It is their part dutifully to accept its inconveniences and faithfully to discharge its obligations.

Gradually such diverse characters as Lord Shaftesbury, Friedrich Engels and Charles Dickens began to rouse the national conscience on this issue, and the early sociologist Seebohm Rowntree gave substance to the need for change with such chilling statistics as finding the average life expectancy in parts of London to be only 23 years.

THE PHILANTHROPISTS

Seebohm Rowntree was not only a renowned sociologist; he was also chairman of the family confectionery company for sixteen years. Together with several other wealthy and influential entrepreneurs, he began innovations in management practice that were in reaction to the brutal conditions of most factories. Welfare officers were appointed, canteens and social clubs were introduced and a range of employee benefits provided. Cadbury Schweppes remains one of Britain's largest and most efficient businesses. Lord Leverhulme built Port Sunlight for his workers in Ellesmere Port and Unilever today is a world-wide operation.

These men set a pattern of benevolence combined with prosperity, but there are two aspects of this era that are especially relevant today. First, they concentrated on the context in which people worked rather than on the work itself. Secondly the innovations were those of paternalists, who knew best. When introducing a profit-sharing scheme that few businesses could match seventy years later, Lord Leverhulme wrote in 1913:

> Seven pounds is a lot of money, and it will not do you much good if you send it down your throats in the form of bottles of whisky, fat geese for Christmas and sweets for the children. If you leave the money with me, I will use it to provide those things that make life pleasant, houses, schools and hospitals. Anyway I am not disposed to allow profit-sharing in any other circumstances.

Although there has been some change in attitude, there remains a balance to be struck on both dimensions. If people are working without reasonable pay and conditions they will not be productive, but the nature of the work itself is equally important for managers to consider and is often neglected. To some extent people at work need and welcome leadership, but few respond positively to being patronised.

SCIENTIFIC MANAGEMENT

Perhaps the best-known name among management pioneers is that of the American Frederick Taylor, who was able to introduce considerable increases in productive efficiency by questioning traditional work practices and finding the one 'best way' in which each job should be done. Having determined the best way the job should be done, Taylor selected appropriate employees, trained them in the method and required them to perform the job in the precise, described manner. Like Watt and Boulton, Taylor linked individual wages to individual output. So higher productivity brought higher wages and increased profitability.

Although much criticised, he introduced the concepts of management of work rather than simple custom and practice, and some of his key innovations – selection, training and job analysis – still form the basis of modern personnel management. Also his approach to problem-solving has served as a model for succeeding generations of managers. Although Taylor is the outstanding figure of scientific management, other contributors were Henry Gantt, who invented the planning and control tool known as the Gantt chart, and Frank and Lillian Gilbreth, who developed time and motion study with such effectiveness that they were able to increase the number of bricks a man could lay in an hour from 120 to 350.

ADMINISTRATIVE MANAGEMENT

Taylor analysed work from the perspective of the supervisor, but his contemporary, Fayol, evolved a top management theory. Henri Fayol is one of the few management pioneers who was neither British nor American. He was the French managing director of a mining company and defined five functions of management: planning, organising, commanding, co-ordinating and controlling. He also produced no fewer than fourteen different principles of management and made possible the teaching of management as an academic subject by producing a viable conceptual framework. A typical Fayol principle was his fourth – unity of command:

> For any action whatsoever, an employee should receive orders from one superior only. (Fayol, 1949, page 24)

Reading Fayol today it is not easy to see the scale of his contribution as his assertions are mainly commonplace. Also his theories stemmed only from his own experience and observation, without any research data for further validation. The fourteen principles have been derided as 'proverbs' being so vague as to have no practical value to the practitioner. It has been argued that he was concerned only with the inner structure of organisation rather than its operating context, and – like Taylor – regarded the employee as a mindless robot to be manipulated only by financial incentives.

A contemporary of Fayol, Mary Parker Follet was the first to consider the organisation in its context and modified the universalism claimed by Fayol by her 'law of the situation' that was a forerunner of contingency theory.

Although not an original thinker, Lyndall Urwick can be said to have summarised the whole of the work of the original theorists to produce a logical arrangement or general system of administration. As with the precision of Taylor, here too was to be seen the conviction that the employees have to be adaptable to the requirements of the organisation:

In good engineering practice design must come first. Similarly, in good social˙ practice design should come first. Logically it is inconceivable that any individual should be appointed to a position carrying a large salary, without a clear idea of the part which that position is meant to play in the general social pattern of which it is a component, the responsibilities and relationships attached to it and the standard of performance which is expected in return for the expenditure. (Urwick, 1943, page 43)

Although no disciple of Fayol, the German sociologist, Weber, influenced this school of thought by his analysis of bureaucracy. He was not a practitioner but somene who had studied economics, religion and political science before turning his sociological insights to organisations. He argued that the market structure of western societies required business organisations to be highly structured, or *bureaucratic*, with the following qualities:

Role definition. The duties and responsibilities of organisation members are clearly defined.

Hierarchy of authority. There is a clear chain of relationships with all members knowing precisely to whom they are responsible and who is responsible to them.

Rules and procedures. The organisation operates according to an elaborate system of rules determining the way in which each member should perform. Records should provide precedents to be followed so as to ensure consistency.

Qualification for office. People are appointed to positions on the basis of merit that is formally attested and subject to systematic selection and training.

Impartiality. Members of the organisation discharge their duties without heat or partiality, motivated by the prospect of moving up the hierarchy, as well as by a sense of duty.

This has proved to be a very accurate account of how many organisations have functioned, especially the large and complex, but there is a tendency for rules to become an end in themselves and for personal initiative to be discouraged.

THE HUMAN RELATIONS MOVEMENT

A number of researchers set out to redress what they saw as an imbalance in the work of Taylor and Fayol, by taking greater account of the mind as well as the body of the employee.

The most famous member of what came to be known as the human relations school of management thought was Elton Mayo, who conducted an experiment at a Philadelphia textile mill in which rest periods were introduced with the result that productivity increased sharply, morale improved and labour turnover dropped. Mayo reasoned that the rest periods helped to lessen the effects of two key problems: fatigue and monotony.

The next step was a series of studies at the Hawthorne Works of the Western Electric Company, which were to continue for eight years and provide a seminal work for management researchers. The main conclusions were:

Work pacing. The pace at which employees produce is one set informally by the work group.

Recognition. Acknowledgement of an employee's contribution by those in authority tends to increase output, as do other forms of social approval.

Social interaction. The opportunities provided by the working situation for social interaction between fellow workers, especially if they could select for interaction those with whom they were compatible, enhanced job satisfaction and sometimes influenced output.

Grievances. Morale is improved by providing scope for employees to air their grievances.

The Hawthorne effect. Changes in working arrangements often lead to an improvement simply because of the effect of their novelty and the workers concerned being at the centre of attention. This discovery was made because of the methodological confusion of the Hawthorne studies.

Here was a change in emphasis away from the precision of Taylorism. Workers were no longer the extension of the machine responsive only to the electric current of financial incentives; instead they were seen as individuals and members of a social group, with attitudes and behaviours that were the key to effectiveness. The focus, as with Taylor, was on the supervisory task, but another contribution from this period took up the strands of Fayol.

Chester Barnard was an executive of considerable, varied experience who was dissatisfied with earlier theoretical explanations and produced his own. He regarded the executive as having the task of maintaining co-operative effort, which was achieved through three functions. First, he established and maintained a system of *communications*, largely by means of informal organisation and careful selection of organisation members. Second, *essential effort* was won from members by inducing them to identify with the business. Third, *purpose and objectives* had to be formulated, via a system of delegated authority, so that each individual was responsible for some segment of the overall enterprise. Suffusing all that he said was the theme that authority could only be effective when accepted. This was not the image of managerial power and infallibility that had been in the minds of Taylor and Fayol, but Machiavelli had spoken of the need for mass consent and the manual workers of twentieth century America were not as compliant as the factory workers of nineteenth century Britain. Management was rediscovering some of the eternal verities about human organisation.

THE MANAGEMENT THEORY JUNGLE

The period following Mayo and Barnard has been one of uncertainty and conflicting views in developing management ideas often represented by the latest fashion rather than some systematic development of well-founded theories. With the increased status and academic respectability given to the use of scientific method, social scientists in the field of management have often divided problems into manageable units so they can carry out an academically viable study. For example, the comparison of two payment systems can be carried out empirically; whereas the general question of gaining the compliance of workers cannot. This division of problems is also reflected in the diversity of schools or approaches found in management literature. The *quantitative approach* was developed after the Second World War, during which mathematical modelling had been used to solve some of the operational problems of warfare. Techniques of operations research have been devised which have had great success in dealing with problems of production planning, warehousing and materials. The advent of the computer has boosted this field of work in defining objectives and constructing models for the solution of complex problems. The contribution to management effectiveness has been considerable, not only in the particular problems for which it has been able to provide optimal solutions, but also for its spin-off in management thinking generally by encouraging an orderly approach to problem-solving and measuring performance.

The *behavioural approach* has moved in so many directions that it is difficult to contain it under a single, general heading. The main thrust is obviously in studying how managers get things done through people, but some advocate an understanding of the individual as a means towards more effective management and others see management as a social system of interdependent groups.

> The recognition of the organised enterprise as a social organism – made up in turn of many social organisms within it, subject to all the attitudes, habits, pressures and conflicts of the cultural environment of people – has been

helpful to both the theorist and the practical manager. Among other helpful aspects are the awareness of the institutional foundations of organization authority, the influence of informal organization and such social factors as those Wight Bakke has called 'bonds of organisation'. (Koontz and O'Donnell, 1976, page 58)

The behavioural approach has produced invaluable insights relating to communication, motivation and leadership.

Continuing in the tradition of Fayol is what can be described as the *process approach*, in which management is viewed as a process of interrelated functions. It has the great appeal of providing a framework for systematic study and analysis, with variations of Fayol's five functions: planning, organising, commanding, co-ordinating and controlling. There follows the temptation to derive management principles from the functional process, and this is one of the main reasons for criticism of the approach. A typical principle is that managerial responsibility is absolute. Managers cannot escape from responsibility for the activities of their individual subordinates: they can delegate authority but not responsibility. To many commentators this is a statement of value rather than fact, is of little practical help, is not always feasible and attributes an unhealthy degree of social superiority to the manager.

Forty years after Mary Parker Follett had first spoken of the law of the situation, research studies were undertaken to demonstrate the situational nature of management, which became known as *contingency theory*:

The basic idea of the contingency theorists is that the nature of the organiza- tion's technology, its size, its legal incorporation, the character of its markets, and other factors confront the organization with some opportunities as well as constraints and problems and therefore set the tone of the organization's adaptation as revealed by its structure. The idea is an elaboration of the biologist's functional view of the adaptation of living forms to the environ- ment. For example, elephants have trunks to enable them to feed from their great height, and apes have prehensile fingers and toes to enable them to swing from trees. Contingency theory indicates the kinds of structure that may be appropriate responses to each of several different organizational contexts or situations. (Khandwalla, 1977, page 236)

Contingency thinking was earlier applied to studies of leadership and has demonstrated the impracticability of seeking universal principles. The best type of organisation structure, leadership style and method of control depends on the particular features of the situation. There are further references to this later in the book.

In the United Kingdom the development of *industrial relations* activity since the 1950s has had two main effects on the work of managers. First it has modified the view that the manager is the only focus for managerial activity and decision-making. The plurality of legitimate interests in the organisation has been recognised to the extent that management is now seen as a process through which managers and others seek to bring those varied interests into balance.

This had led to the second effect, the extended use of procedures: not simply administrative procedures as ways of obviating decision-making for situations where a formula has already been worked out, but also control procedures, like grievance and discipline, whereby management and employee delimit the scope of each other's activities by specifying the range of freedom of action each has.

Rose (1975) has argued that the various schools have continued to develop in an evolutionary manner. This has the attraction of integrating everything currently known and the latest product is the best. However, there seem to be fundamental differences in the basic assumptions of some schools that have not yet been reconciled or integrated. This has been well described by Burrell and Morgan (1979) who argue that some contrasting assumptions could never be reconciled.

A BURST BUBBLE?

In some ways the development of management ideas now seems to have gone too far, in making of management something far more elaborate and mysterious than reality dictates, particularly in Britain and the United States where the management movement has flourished much more than in other industrialised nations. The fields of academic study that have expanded recently, and which have a direct bearing on management education, are organisation theory, organisation behaviour and – to a lesser extent – industrial relations and marketing. Those studying organisations have shifted the emphasis away from how managers manage organisations towards how people perform in organisations. As students from developing countries have flocked to the business schools of Britain and the United States, the relevance of Anglo-Saxon models to other situations has been shown to be small, especially with the rise as economic competitors of countries like Japan and Western Germany, that do not seem to have a management movement at all.

> The puzzle, then, is to understand why we downgrade so many of the jobs that really matter whilst building around the idea of 'management' a plethora of myths, shibboleths and incantations which our most successful competitors seem able to do without. (Mant, 1979, page 3)

This is further developed in Fores and Glover (1978).

Review Topic 2.1

Why do we build around management a plethora of myths, shibboleths and incantations, while downgrading so many of the jobs that really matter?

The national wish for economic prosperity and the individual wish for employment offering status and material benefits have combined to impute great significance to the arts and sciences of management, so that the number of management jobs in the economy is increasing more than other types of job and the number of people seeking management training now exceeds the number pursuing training for careers in, for example, teaching.

THE CONCEPT OF EXCELLENCE

The suggestion that the bubble of management theory has burst is supported by the extraordinary popularity of a recent study by two American consultants, Peters and Waterman (1982). After studying forty-three companies that were 'excellently managed' according to a range of criteria, Peters and Waterman concluded that the success was not due to anything more elaborate than being 'brilliant on the basics' and working hard at fundamental aspects of management. Academics immediately found fault with their analysis for all manner of reasons, but the authors remained undeterred as their book sold over one and a quarter million copies. This does not prove that they are right, but it does prove that they are convincing and managers, like everyone else, model their actions on prescriptions in which they believe will help them rather than on analyses which do not convince.

Peters and Waterman derived eight attributes of the management style of their excellent companies, as follows:

1. *Bias for action.* A preference for doing something rather than waiting for further analysis.
2. *Keeping close to the customer.*
3. *Autonomy and entrepreneurship.* Breaking a corporation into small units, each thinking independently and competitively.
4. *Productivity through people.* Enabling all employees to appreciate the importance of their personal participation and enabling them to share success.
5. *Hands-on, value-driven.* Keeping everyone in touch with the main task of the business.
6. *Sticking to the knitting.* Remaining in a line of business that the people are good at.
7. *Simple form, lean staff.* Uncluttered organisation charts, with the minimum number of levels in the hierarchy and few people at the upper levels.
8. *Simultaneous loose–tight properties.* A climate in which there is dedication to the central values of the company combined with tolerance for all employees who accept the values.

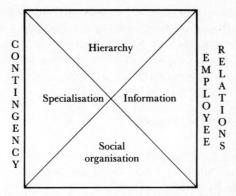

Fig. 2.1 The central methods of management and their modifiers.

Perhaps we have become too much concerned with the grand design and lost a necessary emphasis on management-as-a-job-to-be-done. With that in mind, what are the lessons of the past? What are those aspects of management work that can be seen through a number of studies and pieces of experience that have been reviewed in this chapter?

First of all there are four central activities or methods of operation which form the core of all management operations (see Fig. 2.1).

1. *Hierarchy*. Since the pyramid-building project, hierarchy has been used to distribute power, to centralise control and to provide the basic pattern of social organisation for those employed in the organisation.
2. *Information*. The Sumerians established, and the industrial revolution pioneers developed, the storage and use of information as a means of making organisation work.
3. *Specialisation*. As organisations grow in size the need for specialisation and economies of scale increase, and in turn that specialisation expands the need for management to co-ordinate the activity of specialists. The work of Taylor is the principal contribution to this type of practice.
4. *Social organisation*. The human relations movement demonstrated the importance of social organisation in the face-to-face group of working colleagues as an additional feature to traditional hierarchy.

Those four means to an end are fundamental and universal, although the emphasis will vary and the degree of development of the fourth much reduces the significance of the first.

There are then two important *modifiers* of those four central methods:

1. *Contingency*. Management theory could be more precise if its fields of activity were more uniform, but the infinite variety of situations in which management is practised requires specific methods to be tailored to specific situations.

2. *Employee relations.* There is a constant challenge from below in the hierarchy to the legitimacy of management actions, and this challenge can be channelled through formal organisation so that management decision-making cannot be unilateral but has to be the outcome of negotiation.

SUMMARY PROPOSITIONS

2.1 Some recent developments in management thought have confused rather than clarified our understanding of management, imputing to it an unjustified mystique.

2.2 There are four central activities or methods of operation forming the core of all management operations: hierarchy, information, specialisation and social organisation.

REFERENCES

Burrell, G. and Morgan, G., *Sociological Paradigms and Organisational Analysis*, Heinemann, London, 1979.

Fayol, H., *General and Industrial Management*, Pitman, London, 1949.

Fores, M. and Glover, I., *Manufacturing and Management*, HMSO, London, 1978.

Khandwalla, P.N., *Design of Organizations*, Harcourt Brace Jovanovich, New York, 1977.

Koontz, H. and O'Donnell, C., *Management: a Systems and Contingency Analysis of Managerial Functions*, McGraw Hill, New York, 1976.

Mant, A., *The Rise and Fall of the British Manager*, Pan Books, London, 1979.

Peters, T.J. and Waterman, R.H., *In Search of Excellence*, Harper & Row, London, 1982.

Rose, M., *Industrial Behaviour: Theoretical Developments since Taylor*, Allen Lane, London, 1975.

Taylor, F.W., *The Principles of Scientific Management*, Harper, New York, 1947.

Urwick, L.F., *The Elements of Administration*, Pitman, London, 1973.

3

MANAGEMENT JOBS

Management covers a range of jobs more diverse than many other general occupational titles. The title 'doctor' or 'teacher' describes a job where all job holders have a common core of activity that is substantial and generally acknowledged, no matter how varied the specialisation. Managers have a common core to their activities that is more vague: a general concern with directing and controlling affairs, lacking a clear knowledge base, the mastery of which enables the job holder to produce acceptable performance. The uncertainty is increased by the range of activities in which management is undertaken. The combination of an imprecise core of activity and knowledge and such a diversity of applications make categorisation difficult. The most familiar methods of differentiating between management jobs are to classify them according to *function* or *level*, and a consideration of those methods forms the bulk of this chapter. There is also an account of the research carried out by Rosemary Stewart in the United Kingdom and Henry Mintzberg in North America that have advanced the understanding of management work substantially.

DIFFERENTIATION BY FUNCTION

One of the most familiar ways of organising management jobs is to label them according to function, so that the pre-fixed title indicates the area of the organisation's activities in which the manager specialises, e.g.:

- General manager
- Operation manager
- Marketing manager
- Personnel manager
- Accounting manager

There are many other specialisations; we find managers of purchasing, research, management development, distribution, data processing, public relations, warehousing and so on. This method is extensively used, even in situations where the fundamental activities of production and marketing do not exist. The different units of the British National Health Service, for instance, have been in the charge of management teams with the following membership:

- Medical officer
- Nursing officer
- Finance officer
- Administrator
- Works officer

This method is designed to fit the classic methods of functional organisation that we consider in Chapter 9, but functional labels are also used in matrix and other types of organisation, although the emphasis will differ.

This method of labelling assumes that a job holder is a specialist first and a manager second, so that a nursing officer qualifies as a nurse and works in that specialism before becoming a director and controller of nursing affairs. Management is represented as an aspect, of a wide variety of jobs which have their main substance and justification in an area of specialised knowledge or skill that is deployed within the employing organisation. It also links the activities of the manager with those other employees who share his specialised knowledge. The marketing manager is a linking pin between all marketing personnel and other organisational members: he is the voice of marketing and responsible for its people. It is this sort of classification that makes sense of management education, in which students typically study functional areas, and is sustained by professional bodies. In the United Kingdom there are institutes that act as qualifying associations for specialists in accounting, marketing, operations, personnel, purchasing and other functions. The degree of control these bodies exercise over their professions or quasi-professions varies, but they all represent a vested interest in functional affiliation by individual managers. This functional type of classifying management jobs is further discussed in Chapter 5.

In the first example we gave of functional management, the general manager was the odd man out: this specialisation is in co-ordinating affairs in general, acting as a mediator between the specialisms. Some methods of organisation have a number of general managers who act as the only manager in relatively small units, sometimes as a result of geographical distribution of activities. The picture of functional management is therefore only complete when we include the *non-functional* manager. The retail bank has a single manager, as do many shops, distribution depots and small factories. The project manager in a matrix organisation is a form of non-functional manager.

DIFFERENTIATION BY LEVEL

A more significant form of management differentiation is that of the level at which the manager operates, because we now see the effect of the *hierarchy*. There may be any number of levels in a hierarchy, but we can identify four levels at which the nature of the management job differs: top, senior, middle and supervisory (see Table 3.1). Some readers may feel that this labelling is no more than attributing different amounts of status to people, but we will see that there are substantive differences in the type of jobs done by incumbents.

Top managers

Many top managers are senior managers as well, so our account in this section only includes part of the work of such executives, the other part being set out in the next section. Top managers have few, but enormous, responsibilities, such as occasional major changes in direction: to introduce a new product, or not; to export to Chile, or not; to close a factory, or not; to dismiss the chief executive, or not. These activities are usually undertaken by the Board of Directors or comparable body with a broad legal responsibility to safeguard the shareholders' interests and the long-term interests of the company. The principal top manager is the chairman, and his most important task is likely to be the appointment, with directorial colleagues, of the managing director or chief executive and other key senior appointments. When *The Times* and *Sunday Times* newspapers were bought in 1981 by the Australian entrepreneur Rupert Murdoch, quite elaborate

Table 3.1 Management jobs classified by level

Level	Main characteristics
Top managers	Relatively detached from the organisation; few, but very important, responsibilities; spend most of their time with outsiders and with peers, very little with subordinates.
Senior managers	Head up functions or operations; concerned with policy formulation and implementation; work tends to be hectic and frequently interrupted; often out of the office; spend time dealing with outsiders, peers and subordinates.
Middle managers	Work mainly within the organisation and are concerned with making the organisation work; can be line or staff; work mainly with peers and senior managers.
Supervisory managers	Relatively detached from the management hierarchy, but vitally concerned with the main activities of the organisation; busy, frequently interrupted and constantly switching between jobs; spend most time with subordinates, some with peers and little with superiors or outsiders.

arrangements were made to vest the authority of appointing the editor in the hands of external, independent directors. The editor could not be dismissed without their concurrence, although they could not stop him from resigning. A director is not, as such, an employee or servant of the company. Their accountability is to the shareholders or owners. They are not, however, precluded from holding employment in the company by this directorship, and many board members are also full-time employees, discharging duties of senior managers, which we come to shortly. Also, a very small proportion of directors are employees holding more humble positions in the hierarchy, usually termed worker directors.

The value of top managers lies in their relative detachment from the organisation and its employees. They will probably be involved with several companies, giving them a range of current operating experience that full-time employees in a single undertaking will lack. This relative detachment and independence will also enable them to handle more easily some of the difficult decisions that have to be made. If a project has to be discontinued because it is no longer viable, many senior managers will be so involved with that project, for sentimental, career or status reasons that they will be committed to protecting it. But an independent director could view it more dispassionately. Many organisational changes involve making employees redundant. Senior managers frequently know the employees personally and have great difficulty in facing up to this operational necessity, so that the detachment of the top manager can be an invaluable element in the discussions that have to take place.

Top managers spend most of their time with outsiders and with peers; very little with subordinates.

Senior managers

Senior managers are those who head up *functions*, such as marketing or personnel, as we saw at the beginning of the chapter; or they head up *operations*, factories, branches, depots or other units that are relatively self-contained with a number of functions being co-ordinated. While it is important to distinguish between top managers and senior managers, any neat distinction is made difficult by the fact that so many top managers are also senior managers. A way of clarifying the distinction is to say that senior managers are concerned with both *policy formulation*, in conjunction with top managers; and *policy implementation*, in conjunction with subordinates.

Hugh Parker (1970) gives the following list of functions concerned with policy formulation:

1. To establish the longer term objectives of the company, and the basic strategies for their attainment.
2. To define the specific policies (finance, personnel, marketing and the like) to be followed in implementing the company's strategies.

3. To decide the organizational structure of the company's management, and to appoint individuals to fill key positions in it.
4. To develop management planning, information, and control systems appropriate to the organizational structure of the company, and to use these systems effectively to ensure control by the board at all times over the results produced by the executive management.
5. To take decisions on 'such matters' as the Articles of Association may reserve to the Board (e.g. payment of dividends, disposal of corporate assets, appointments to the board), or that the board in its own discretion decides not to delegate (e.g. capital projects above a certain amount, diversification into a new business).

Defined like this policy formulation is a collective activity where senior managers with specialist responsibilities and interests meet with each other, and with top managers who do not hold specific portfolios, to decide matters that can best or only be satisfactorily determined by consensus between them. A policy to resist the use of consultants, for instance, might be an aspiration of the personnel managers, but they could not make that effective unless they could obtain the understanding and consent of senior management colleagues to make it work. A plan to change advertising policy away from national newspapers to television would be for the marketing managers to devise, but they too would need to convince colleagues of its wisdom.

Policy formulation has the predominant emphasis on *decision-making* but includes the element of control, mentioned by Parker, to ensure that decisions are being put into operation.

In policy implementation the senior manager changes activity away from deciding what should be done towards putting the decisions into practice: they become *executives* working with those who share specialist concerns, knowledge and skills, whether that specialist interest be in a function or an operation. Implementation also involves constant activity in a boundary role on behalf of members in the specialist group, as the senior manager enlists the help of people elsewhere in the organisation or outside it, seeks clarification from other specialists, and mediates demands on the specialist area from outside.

Studies of the work of senior managers (for instance, Carlson, 1951; Mintzberg, 1975; Copeman *et al.*, 1963) all confirm that the senior manager's job tends to be a very hectic one, dealing with peers, outsiders and subordinates. Many of the matters to be dealt with are urgent and there are frequent interruptions: Copeman and his colleagues found an average of three visitors and four telephone calls each hour. Senior managers are frequently out of the office and spend the majority of their working time talking to people.

Middle managers

Middle managers are creatures of medium to large organisations, as only in those situations are there enough people to generate hierarchical layers between senior managers and supervisors. It tends to be a difficult role because of its potential artificiality. It is not sufficiently senior to have a broad task of co-ordination nor significant decision-making powers, and it is not closely in touch with the urgencies of the organisation's main activity, like making machine tools in a factory or caring for patients in a hospital.

The basic artificiality of their *management* work provides the main problem, not only for many middle managers, but also for their organisations. It is the organisation and its bureaucracy that 'feed' the middle managers. Too few of them can enjoy the satisfaction of bringing off a sale, or manufacturing an excellent item, or acquiring a useful subsidiary, even though they may help towards such achievements. Many middle managers find their satisfactions within the organisation and its operating complexities.

In 1956 William H. Whyte coined the term 'organisation man' to describe people who became over-preoccupied with, and dependent on, the organisation of which they were part. The following year Parkinson (1957) produced his devasting critique of administration, with particular reference to the British civil service. Both pointed to the way in which those holding middle management roles live in a world which takes on a life and purpose of its own, quite distinct from the purposes of the undertaking in which they are supposed to be engaged. Some discussion in the United States even reached the point of regarding organisational growth as a denial of individual freedom. The worst predictions of the organisation man syndrome have not been realised, but middle managers remain more concerned about organisational mechanics and process than products. This makes them vulnerable when the foundations shake.

Dickson (1977) found middle managers in a nationalised industry displaying low morale and lack of commitment as they steadily lost decision-making duties, and Marshall and Cooper (1979) found middle managers to be under greater pressure than their superiors and having less satisfaction. If an organisation goes out of business or sheds personnel, displaced middle managers frequently find that their chances in the labour market are poor because all their expertise has lain in making one organisational system work and knowing how to get through the administrative jungle.

Middle managers' jobs can be either line or staff. *Line* jobs are those where subordinates are directly involved with the main product of the organisation, such as section manager in a margarine plant or editor of a television programme. *Staff* jobs are those in parts of the organisation providing supporting services for others, like management services, personnel or the company secretary. There has been a trend to an increasing number of staff rather than line jobs in middle management. Child (1978, page 52) studied the employment records of the tyre company Dunlop between 1948 and 1977 and concluded that resources were moving from the productive to the non-productive sector within organisations as well as across them, suggesting an increase in middle management staff jobs. Since Child's study many organisations have reorganised, and it has been these middle managers who have been most vulnerable to being made redundant.

Child went on to argue that, instead of dividing economic activities into manufacturing and non-manufacturing, we should distinguish between activities which produce marketable outputs and those that do not. For example, some public services, such as education, medicine and road tolls, are potentially marketable, and within manufacturing there are staff functions that are not directly productive.

Middle managers have a wide variety of jobs and roles. Some have large numbers of subordinates, while others have none. In one research investigation we spoke to an army major with 130 subordinates, but we also spoke to a management services consultant, a project manager and a senior nursing officer who did not have any subordinates. Some will share the same work as their subordinates, but have additional administrative duties, such as deputy heads and heads of departments in schools. Others will do quite different work, like the project manager mentioned above, who co-ordinates the work of engineers, designers, suppliers and customers. Middle managers of all types spend a great deal of their time operating procedures and responding to the requests, queries, demands and initiatives of others rather than generating their own work.

Horne and Lupton (1965) analysed the working lives of sixty-six middle managers and found that they spent most of their time exchanging information (page 26)(see Table 3.2).

Table 3.2 Horne and Lupton's analysis of the working lives of middle managers

Activity	Percentage of time
Giving, seeking information	42
Giving, seeking advice	6
Giving, confirming, reviewing decisions	8
Giving, receiving, confirming instructions	9
Co-ordinating, reviewing plans	11
Seeking, preparing explanations	15
Other activities	9

The promotion to middle management often leads to people allowing their previous, technical expertise to wither. The salesman gives up seeing customers, nurses no longer give bedside care and engineers leave technical problems to others. This is because they are 'too busy' with meetings, paperwork and other administrative tasks; learning the way of life that Mant sceptically calls 'clean and gentlemanly'. There are problems in abandoning previous expertise or involvement with the main task of the organisation; problems for the individual managers, for their subordinates and for the organisation.

Early in their careers middle managers acquire a body of knowledge and technical skill to qualify and practise as pharmacist, engineer, teacher or whatever specialist career was followed. The jobs could not be done without that knowledge, and more specific information could always be obtained to solve an unexpected problem so that an answer could always be found.

When they cross over to the better paid, higher ranking (and logically more skilful) activity of managing, they expect the new activity to have a similar body of expertise: reliable, explicit and accessible. All they find is a ramshackle collection of humdrum tasks that any literate school-leaver could easily accomplish, but their earlier training makes it almost impossible for them to believe that there is not more to management than this, so they look for the solution to a non-existent mystery. To some extent they find what they are looking for in management development. The constant stream of books, lectures, seminars and symposia from the behavioural science entrepreneurs offer neat packages of answers, rapidly replacing one management myth with another, and the clientele for such placebos is almost exclusively middle management.

As few middle managers are lazy they often set up activities to justify their positions, producing administrative controls and requests for information that are not needed other than to build the individual middle manager more securely into the administrative system of the undertaking. Thus begins the political activity of the middle manager, that is discussed more fully in Chapter 10.

The problems for the subordinates of these middle managers are expressed in the complaint heard frequently in organisations that the manager has lost touch with the task and is making unrealistic demands and unreasonable decisions because he is out of date with current problems. Although much of this grumbling will be no more than the jaundiced view of those who resent the greater privilege of those immediately 'above' them, the loss of technical skills by a middle manager does not help and leads to a situation in which subordinates are expected to comply with managerial requests on the basis of the manager's *position* of authority, whereas compliance based on experience and expertise is both easier to comply with and does not need the support of power and control of resources. This question of authority is explored more fully in Chapter 16.

One of the main problems for the organisation of middle managers abandoning their technical expertise is the loss of the experience. All too often they are promoted out of work connected with the main task of the organisation at the very stage where they have sufficient experience to work confidently and be at their most effective. Our own study (Torrington and Weightman, 1982) found British organisations encouraging middle managers with proven expertise in a technical specialism to abandon this in favour of very general, and usually strightforward, managerial and administrative duties:

> We also found that middle managers often did administrative work, that is work following procedures, because they were unsure what their managerial work was. We consider the main managerial work of middle managers to be dealing with the uncertainties associated with the difference between plans and reality and establishing networks within the system to get things done. (Torrington and Weightman, 1988).

Jones *et al.* (1981) found similar difficulties in their extensive study of the nursing profession. The conclusion is that middle managers should maintain as much contact with, and practise in, their technical specialism as they can, even though this might appear to increase their workload. This will increase the respect of their peers and subordinates and will make them less vulnerable at times of redundancy, more marketable and less dependent on organisation-specific skills.

Senior managers might consider changing the balance in the demands they make of middle managers, giving greater weight to current performance rather than an assessment of nebulous and imprecise personal qualities. At present middle managers are often caught in a trap:

1. They need to justify their *performance* in achieving results to their superiors in order to keep their jobs and meet current organisational requirements.
2. They need to justify their *personal qualities* as socially acceptable members of management to their superiors to gain promotion.
3. They need to justify their *performance* to their subordinates and peers to obtain their support and collaboration.
4. But if they justify their *personal qualities* ('I have a way with the chaps',) to their subordinates, they are seen to adopt a personal superiority and aloofness that inhibits the support and compliance of subordinates.

Logically we can expect the number of middle management posts in organisations to decrease in the future with the growing sophistication of information technology that is available to senior managers and the increasing complexity of operational tasks that are making necessary more regular contact directly between senior managers and those at the operational level. Whether the number of middle managers increases or contracts, Nancy Foy sounds a word of warning:

> Many middle managers have stopped thinking of themselves as developable. Turning them back on may be one of the most important steps towards revitalising organisations . . . their power is immense, based on deep knowledge of how the organisation really works; thus, while they may not be able to bring about change themselves, they nonetheless have tremendous capacity to block changes other people want, to paralyze an organisation, consciously or unconsciously. (Foy, 1981, pages 28–9)

Supervisory managers

The largest number of managers are supervisors or first-line managers, with a range of titles like foreman, office manager, ward sister, sergeant, chief clerk, superintendent, charge hand, leading seaman, head steward, floor manager, leading chef. In any organisation most employees report to a supervisor, who is responsible for assigning tasks to them, overseeing their work, making sure it is done satisfactorily and dealing with all complaints and queries. It is a job that has suffered much recently.

> For half a century or more first-line supervisors, especially those in manufacturing and clerical work, have seen their roles shrinking in status, in importance and in esteem. Where a supervisor was 'management' to the employee only half a century ago, he or she has now, by and large, become a buffer between management, union and workers. And like all buffers, the supervisor's main function is to take the blows. (Drucker, 1977)

Unionisation of the workforce has led to shop stewards and other employee representatives steadily bypassing the first line of management in order to raise with middle and senior managers issues that lie beyond the competence of the supervisor to deal with ('we want to see the organ grinder, not the monkey'). There is also a widespread feeling among supervisors, that senior managers are reluctant to confirm that supervisors are used as expendable front-line troops in skirmishes with organised employees. Either they can be used to test out an initiative that senior managers can then repudiate if it does not work, or they are used to delay things while their senior managers try to decide on a plan of campaign.

Most top managers have previously been senior managers and nearly all senior managers have been middle managers, but few top, senior or middle managers have ever been supervisors. The supervisory post is often the career culmination for people who start in an operative post, so that in many organisations the management hierarchy starts in the lower reaches of middle management. There are exceptions: nursing, teaching and the police service are all occupations in which the only feasible starting point for a career is at the bottom. Marks and Spencer provides one of the best known examples of a career progression style that involves the potential manager starting at the bottom and working up from there. In most employment, however, it is rare for people to work their way up from supervisory positions. This has some interesting effects:

1. There is a clear gap between the management hierarchy or pyramid and the supervisory grades.
2. Supervisors come to rest in their supervisory position. It is the end of the road, so that their main objective soon becomes the maintenance of the status quo; they are seldom bidding for promotion.
3. Those in middle and senior positions frequently lack the ability to judge the fine detail of the actual job that the organisation exists to carry out. In the earlier section of this chapter about middle managers we saw the tendency for their technical skills to become outdated; here we are referring to the problem of them not being able to make a judgement because of never having had 'coalface' experience. This has led to such problems as production engineers specifying equipment that is technically appropriate, but inappropriate to the skills and expertise of production employees. Many industrial relations disputes and difficulties with technological innovation begin for just this reason.
4. The supervisory role has been largely neglected in the whole management development circus. Management courses seldom have relevance to supervisory, first-line duties, although there are some separate courses for supervisors.

There is a dearth of recent studies of supervisors, but some of long standing (Guest, 1956; Mahoney, 1965) show that the supervisor's life is remarkably similar to that of the senior manager in that it is likely to be busy, frequently interrupted and constantly switching between jobs, as they deal with the immediate and the urgent. Unlike the senior manager, they spend most time with subordinates, some with peers and little with superiors or outsiders.

AN ALTERNATIVE APPROACH TO CATEGORISING MANAGEMENT JOBS

In organisations where the differentiation of top, senior, middle and supervisory does not fit neatly – such as matrix, differentiated and ad hoc structures (see Chapter 9) methods that might be more appropriate and helpful have been devised by Mintzberg (1973) and Stewart (1976). Here we give an account of Mintzberg's method and the alternative method of Rosemary Stewart.

Mintzberg studied management job holders in North America and

Fig. 3.1 Mintzberg's managerial roles.

subsequently listed ten management roles (see Fig. 3.1) that were present in the jobs of all managers, although the proportion varied with different jobs. He argues that managers derive status from the formal authority they have over the units, departments or activities with which they are identified. Because of this position they are involved in interpersonal relations with subordinates, peers and superiors, who provide the manager with the information he needs to make decisions.

Review Topic 3.1

If salary, conditions of employment and security were all equal, would you rather be a top manager, a senior manager, a middle manager or a supervisory manager? What are the reasons for your choice?

Interpersonal roles. These help keep the organisation running smoothly. The *figurehead* role is where the managers have certain ceremonial duties to perform, like taking a customer to lunch or greeting a visitor, where they represent the unit or activity for which they are responsible. As *leaders* managers are dealing with subordinates and enabling them to perform well and meet objectives, while the role as *liaison* requires them to deal with people outside the unit, either peers within the organisation or customers, suppliers and others outside.

Informational roles: Mintzberg regards as the most important aspects of the manager's job those activities which are concerned with giving and receiving information. As *monitors* managers seek to be well informed about events relating to this section of the organisation. They gather and store information that will be useful, by questioning subordinates, tapping a personal network of contacts and scanning unsolicited information that comes in. As *disseminator* the manager distributes information to subordinates that would otherwise not be available to them. This, of course, is a crucial aspect of the manager/subordinate relationship and the main source of the trust or mistrust existing in that relationship. As *spokesperson* the manager passes on information collected to people outside the unit or outside the organisation. A large part of this role is keeping the boss informed, but other aspects might be advice to a customer about a product or information to a supplier about modifications that are required before delivery.

Decisional roles. In these cases the manager makes use of the information received to make decisions. The *entrepreneur* is trying to make changes because a new idea is worth pursuing, that it will develop the area of activity and responsibility. *Disturbance handler* is not initiating change but coping with the result of situations that cannot be controlled: a customer goes bankrupt, the warehouse is burned down, someone is away sick or any one of the thousand situations that have to be managed to prevent the disturbance reducing the effectiveness of the unit. The role of *resource allocator* is when the manager decides where and how the resources of the unit, including managerial time, will be deployed. The final decisional role is that of *negotiator*, where the manager is doing deals with those people and interests whose consent or co-operation are needed by the manager's organisation but where there is no formal authority *over* them: union representatives, suppliers wanting to change their pricing, local authority officials seeking better employment opportunities, and so forth. Negotiating is an important activity for managers, as only they have the information that negotiating requires and only they have the necessary scope of authority to make realistic decisions about progress in negotiations as the information available to the two parties separately is gradually exchanged and organised. As the proportions of the roles varied from job to job, Mintzberg (1973, pages 126–9) concluded that there were eight types of managerial job:

> *The contact man*, who is a figurehead and liaises with outside agencies.
>
> *The political manager*, who spends a lot of time outside the organisation trying to reconcile conflicting forces that affect it.
>
> *The entrepreneur*, who seeks opportunities and implements change in the organisation.
>
> *The insider*, who tries to build up and maintain internal expectations by 'fire-fighting.

The real time manager, who tries to build up and maintain a stable system over time.

The team manager, who is preoccupied with the creation of a team which will operate effectively as a cohesive whole.

The expert manager, who advises other managers and is consulted on specialised problems.

The new manager, who so far lacks the contacts and information to be any of the other seven.

The Stewart method of classifying management jobs

Rosemary Stewart is a British research worker who has spent twenty years studying management work and who produced an original classification method in 1976. She regarded the main weaknesses of the function/level mode of classification as being the assumption of similarities rather than a search for differences. She studied the behavioural rather than the technical content of managers' jobs and asked questions about the demands that the job made on the manager's behaviour. After detailed examination of the demands made by 252 jobs she produced a novel typology, the bare outline of which we reproduce here as it enables the readers to think about their jobs in a fresh way, and to understand better the constraints and opportunities available to them. (pages 15,16):

Hub jobs have necessary contact with subordinates, superiors, peers and others above and below them in the hierarchy. This was the most common type of job among the managers studied and had a dominant man-management component. (*116 jobs*)

Peer dependent jobs were those where there was less 'vertical' demand and much dependence on winning the co-operation of peers. They were much found at the boundaries of the organisation (*63 jobs*)

Man-management jobs were those concerned primarily with the vertical type of working relationship, having contact mainly with superiors and subordinates. (*52 jobs*)

Solo jobs were those of managers who spent a large proportion of their time working alone on assignments. (*22 jobs*)

The full account of Dr Stewart's work and results of her investigation are to be found in Stewart, R. *Contrasts in Management*, McGraw-Hill, Maidenhead, 1976. Further development of both methods and ideas are to be found in Stewart, R. *Choices for Managers*, McGraw-Hill, Maidenhead, 1982.

Review Topic 3.2

Of the eight types of managerial job listed by Mintzberg, which is most like the one you have now? Which would you like to be? What are your reasons?

SUMMARY PROPOSITIONS

3.1 Management jobs are of such a variety that precise definition is impracticable.

3.2 The most familiar methods of classifying management jobs are according to function and organisational level (see Fig. 3.2).

3.3 The research of Rosemary Stewart and Henry Mintzberg has provided novel ways of classifying management jobs that enlarge our understanding of the variety that is comprehended by the term 'management'.

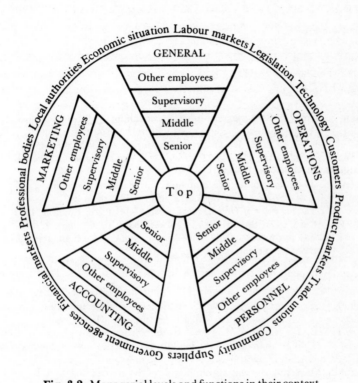

Fig. 3.2 Managerial levels and functions in their context.

PUTTING IT INTO PRACTICE

Consider the role of middle management – defined as anyone working with people both above and below them in the hierarchy, who have a management component to their work. Fill in Table 3.3.

Table 3.3 Management assessment form

	Difficulties	Strengths
For the organisation		
For their superiors		
For their subordinates		
For themselves		

REFERENCES

Carlson, S., *Executive Behaviour*, Strömbergs, Stockholm, 1951.

Child, J., 'The non-productive component within the productive sector', in Fores, M. and Glover, I. (eds), *Manufacturing and Management*, HMSO, London, 1978.

Copeman, G., Luijk, H., Haneka, F., *How the Executive Spends his Time*, Business Publications, London, 1963.

Dickson, J., 'The plight of middle managers', *Management Today*, Dec. 1977.

Drucker, P.F., *Management*, Pan Books, London, 1977, page 243.

Foy, N., *The Yin and Yang of Organizations*, Grant McIntyre, London, 1981.

Guest, R., 'Of time and the foreman', *Personnel*, May 1956, pages 478–86.

Horne, J.H. and Lupton, T., 'The work activities of middle managers', *Journal of Management Studies*, February 1965, pages 14–33.

Jones, D. *et al.*, *The Role of the Nursing Officer*, Department of Health and Social Security, London, 1981.

Mahoney, T., 'The jobs of management', *Industrial Relations*, Feb. 1965, 97–110.

Marshall, J. and Cooper, C.L., 'Work experience of middle and senior managers', *Management International Review*, vol. 19, 1979, pages 81–96.

Mintzberg, H., *The Nature of Managerial Work*, Harper & Row, London, 1973.

Mintzberg, H. 'The manager's job: folklore and fact', *Harvard Business Review*, July–August 1975, pages 49–61.

Parker, H., 'Managing the managers: the role of the board', in Mann, R. (ed.), *The Arts of Top Management*, McGraw Hill, Maidenhead, 1970, page 31.

Parkinson, C.N., *Parkinson's Law*, John Murray, London, 1957.

Porter, L. and Ghiselli, E., 'The self-perceptions of top and middle management personnel', *Personnel Psychology*, vol. 10, 1957, pages 397–406.

Stewart, R., *Contrasts in Management*, McGraw Hill, Maidenhead, 1976.

Stewart, R., *Choices for Managers*, McGraw Hill, Maidenhead, 1982.

Torrington, D.P. and Weightman, J.B., 'Technical atrophy in middle management', in *Journal of General Management*, Summer 1982.

Torrington, D.P. and Weightman, J.B. 'Middle management work', in *Journal of General Management*, 1988.

Whyte, W.H., *The Organisation Man*, Simon & Schuster, New York, 1956.

4

MANAGEMENT WORK

Having, in the last chapter, distinguished between different types of management job, we now examine what managers do, and especially what different types of manager have in common.

The work of management has to be assumed from the activities of managers, which are mainly talking, reading, writing, telephoning, using electronic hardware, driving cars, waiting for aircraft, attending meetings and so on. We have to infer the nature of management work from these activities, as well as distinguishing it from the work of people not called managers; and distinguishing it from other work done by managers that is technical, such as selling, budget preparation, design engineering or whatever their specialist area happens to be.

There are five main ways of trying to understand management work. First one can study the behaviour of managers by asking them to fill in detailed *diaries* of how they spend their time or by observing their behaviour over a period. Classic examples of this type of study are Carlson (1951), Stewart (1967) and Mintzberg (1971). Secondly, one can read the *autobiographies* of successful managers and leaders who try to pass on what they found worked in their experience, their prescriptions of how others can replicate the success that they have enjoyed. Statesmen and generals are the best known providers of this type of material, but examples of successful managers' writing are Sloan (1967), Harvey-Jones (1988) and Edwardes (1983).

A slightly different version of this is where a person with a successful business career attempts an explicitly management book. Examples are Barnard (1938), Brown (1971) and Townsend (1970). A third method is to *interview* managers about what they do. Examples of this approach are Marshall and Stewart (1981), Kotter (1982) and Torrington and Weightman (1982, 1988).

Fourthly one can look at *management textbooks*. These make implicit assumptions about the nature of management work by choosing to include some subjects but not others, partly because some aspects of management are more suitable for written treatment than others. Most textbooks employ the conventional categories of management work suggested by Fayol: planning, organising, controlling, commanding and co-ordinating. The fifth method is a detailed, *empirical study* of a particular area of management, which can provide a great deal of information about specific aspects such as motivation or leadership.

None of these is sufficient alone. Diaries are very revealing, but many managers are reluctant to compile them and to reveal themselves in what they regard as an unfavourable light. The problem of objectivity is also present with autobiographies, together with the fact that the very successful usually have the benefit of some exceptional personal qualities or good luck that were the main determinants of their success, and enabled them to operate in an idiosyncratic way that others would find hard to emulate. Interviewing managers introduces the detachment of the interviewer to achieve a more objective account than simple self-reporting, but the manager being interviewed is the sole source of information. Textbooks have the drawback that their purpose is to provide appropriate material for study, so there will always be a selection for emphasis on that which it is easiest to handle in written form. This is one reason why textbooks have always had such a large proportion devoted to decision-making. Empirical study is always partial and tends to isolate the subject being examined from the context in which it was undertaken.

The most fruitful way of trying to understand management work is to blend insights from all these sources.

HOW MANAGERS SPEND THEIR TIME

In 1981 Roger Mansfield and his colleagues reported on a detailed survey carried out in the previous year among 1,058 British managers, widely spread geographically and between different types of organisation. One question to the respondents was the amount of time spent on work each week. Remembering the problem of self-reported information that has already been mentioned, the figures suggest that managers spend about the same amount of time working as manual workers on overtime: see Table 4.1.

Other evidence suggests that managers at middle and lower levels spend less time on work (Horne and Lupton, 1965) and chief executives seldom stop thinking of their jobs (Carlson, 1951). This can, however, give no more than a very general picture as these replies are affected by some uncertainty in the minds of the respondents regarding what does and does not constitute management work. Is reading the *Financial Times* work or pleasure?

Undoubtedly the activities of most managers are characterised by brevity, variety and fragmentation. For example, Mintzberg (1973) found that the chief executives he studied made contact, on average, with fifty-two

Table 4.1 Weekly hours spent working by British managers in 1980

Hours per week	Percentage of sample
less than 30	0.7
31–40	14.1
41–50	44.3
51–60	27.7
61–70	10.5
more than 70	2.7

(Mansfield *et al.*, 1981)

people each day. Only ten per cent of tasks took an hour or more and more than 50 per cent of tasks took less than nine minutes. This differs sharply from the specialisation and extended periods of application to a single task that characterise most non-managerial jobs.

Managers spend much of their time, between 50 per cent and 80 per cent, in conversation with others (Guest 1955, Stewart 1967 and Mintzberg 1973). Stewart found that they spent an average of 41 per cent of their time with subordinates, 12 per cent with superiors and 47 per cent with others. Mintzberg has similar results and suggests a preference among managers for spoken rather than written material and for current information and live action rather than considered reports.

Review Topic 4.1

With how many people do you make contact in each working day?
What percentage of your daily tasks take more than one hour?
What percentage of your daily tasks take less than nine minutes?

How much of your time do you spend with subordinates?
How much of your time do you spend with superiors?
How much of your time do you spend with others?

Are there any of those numbers or percentages you would like to change?
If so, why?

Mintzberg (1975) uses this sort of evidence to argue that managers are not in fact devoting their time to planning, decision-making and the other types of reflective activity which the textbooks suggest. If, however, we take account of what is being said in all these face-to-face encounters and telephone conversations, often decisions are being taken and plans being laid, although the independent observer may regard the process as lacking system and thoroughness. Similarly the business lunch has considerable potential content in terms of information exchanged, discussion and agreement on actions to follow, even though some may consider it a wasteful and self-indulgent method for managers to conduct their affairs by.

These studies tell us that managers spend much of their time in conversation with a variety of people and they are frequently interrupted, but why do managers work in this way?

DIFFERENT TYPES OF MANAGEMENT WORK

There are three distinct strands in the work that managers do: *technical*, *administrative* and *managerial*. In Chapter 3 we introduced the importance of technical skills for managers especially at the middle levels. The technical work of a manager is that work done, not because of being a manager, but almost in spite of that fact; work concerned with the main task of the organisation, section or department, and it is probably the work of at least some subordinates as well. It is the head teacher teaching children in the classroom, the chief designer working at a drawing board, or the garage proprietor tuning the engine on a customer's car.

This technical work involves the manager using the skills and knowledge acquired through qualifications, training and experience. Many of these technical skills could be transferred to all other organisations where they are used, like the examples quoted in the last paragraph, or they may be specific to the particular organisation in which the manager works, such as understanding precisely how Shell's polymer functions in practice, or how Coca-Cola is made. We suggested in Chapter 3 that managers abandon these skills at their peril, as they can then lose touch with the main task of the department or organisation, although the management development process in many British organisations appears to encourage managers to let their technical skills atrophy.

Administrative work is concerned with organisational maintenance, while managerial work is taking initiatives. The one is carrying out official, often regular, duties authorised by others, such as the organisational superior or a committee; the other is conducting and controlling organisational affairs with the freedom to create precedents. Much of 'management' literature is about administrative activities with its emphasis on administering the stable state rather than the unstable, uncertain world faced by many managers.

One aspect of the managerial/administrative distinction is intuitively described by many managers when they talk about the scope that a person has to make mistakes or exercise discretion. The greater the discretion, the greater the managerial content of the job and the more one is setting rather than following precedents. This is reflected in the timespan theory of discretion advanced by Elliott Jaques (1970), who postulated that all jobs had a prescribed content and a discretionary content. The first were those elements of work over which the job holder has no authorised choice, while the second was that area of work where the job holders chose how to do their

work. Jaques used this to describe *all* work, not just managerial work, and
devised the concept of the timespan of discretion:

> The maximum period to time during which the use of discretion is authorised
> and expected, without review of that discretion by a superior. (Jaques, 1970,
> page 21)

It is the greater range of discretion open to managers, and especially the
greater length of time that will elapse before the effect of mistakes is known,
that is one of the distinctive characteristics of management work.

This administrative/managerial distinction can also be expressed in
terms of novelty and comfort. Like many human activities, managerial
work is active, extrovert and novelty-seeking, concerned with initiating and
taking risks by setting precedents. Administrative work is a quieter activity,
introvert and providing the comfort of familiarity and dealing with what is
known. It keeps the system going by maintaining things in working order.
Scitovsky (1976) discusses how a number of psychologists have offered the
opinion that the novelty/comfort balance in human beings is always in a
state of change, according to the situation in which they find themselves.
The behaviour of those facing bereavement is often characterised by actions
that are so prosaic as to seem bizarre, like needing to go to the hairdresser or
to go shopping, and deciding to decorate the back bedroom or work on the
car. This is not callousness but seeking the comfort of the familiar at a time
when the crises are too great to bear.

When managers are faced with too many difficult problems and uncertain about what to do, they may take great comfort in filling in timesheets,
record cards or other routine administrative tasks. The executive briefcase
is partly a badge of office ('I am important') but also contains a supply of
administrative comforters to go with the indigestion tablets. The first-class
compartments of intercity trains are full of managers travelling to meetings
and passing the time by 'catching up on their reading' or 'checking through
the figures'. On the other hand, when the routine paperwork becomes
too oppressive a manager may seek some stimulus to get the adrenaline
flowing: they go looking for novelty or excitement. Much of the by-play of
organisational politics described in Chapter 10 comes from this need for
challenge.

The career development circus has been one of the means whereby a
manager's needs to initiate has been met. Young men and women identified
as having high potential have taken the opportunity to change jobs fairly
often, perhaps seven or eight times by their early thirties. When they reach
their peak the number of job changes drops sharply; and if that coincides
with the time of life when the heyday in the blood is tame, humble and
waiting upon the judgement, then the manager may welcome a shift in
emphasis towards more administration of the stable state and less hectic
excitement. Not all managers, however, age at the same rate or at the same

time. Furthermore the career development move has become harder to accomplish with the contraction of the managerial labour market and this presents a new problem for aspiring managers and for the organisations in which their careers get bogged down. It is difficult to keep initiating new solutions to old problems and there is the danger that the creative drive of the enthusiastic young manager may be redirected into the more destructive aspects of organisational politics or away from organisational concerns altogether, so that the manager's working life is one of lack-lustre organisational maintenance during the day with creative energies channelled into selling life insurance in the evenings, writing crime novels or running the local operatic society.

Review Topic 4.2

In your job have you got the balance right between technical, administrative and managerial work?

THE DISTINCTION BETWEEN MANAGEMENT AND OTHER WORK

Most other jobs have an immediate inbuilt purpose and logic. The schoolteacher faces the classroom of children waiting to be occupied, the machinist has a pile of cloth waiting to be made into shirts, the chef has customers waiting for food to be cooked and the postman has a satchel full of letters to deliver. The job is clear in its logic, which is to translate a demand from the system of the organisation into activities or tasks to be undertaken by the job holder.

Managers have some aspects of their jobs that are like this: the in-tray full of papers, the incoming mail to be dealt with, the outgoing letters to sign, the telephone to be answered. These are responses, mainly administrative, to demands from the system of the organisation. An activity of a manager is to read letters that arrive in much the same way as the activity of a postman is to deliver the letters in the first place. *How* the manager responds to the letter will be one aspect of how management work differs from other work, as it is likely to involve some aspects of problem-solving and decision-making with features of co-ordination and command. It is still, however, reacting to a situation and responding to the initiatives of others. Managers we have studied usually describe these activities – mail, paperwork, answering the telephone, dealing with enquiries – as time-consuming and unsatisfying. They prefer those activities where they impose their own logic on a task rather than the task having its own logic which is imposed on the manager. They prefer 'making things happen' or being proactive instead of reactive.

Managers enjoy the degree of autonomy which they have in being able to control the details of their working programme by the use of their personal diary. Every Christmas one of the favourite 'executive presents' is the desk diary in hand-tooled leather, which is a status symbol because it declares the flexibility that managers have. Not for them the precisely controlled and timetabled day: they organise their own daily and weekly programme. Although many demands are made on their time, the individual manager usually reserves the right to agree that something can be 'fitted in' to the schedule, on which much time is spent reviewing, re-ordering and projecting. Most other workers have a daily schedule or just do what they are asked to do as it occurs, but managers have a greater range of discretion, so that they exercise choice (*pace* Rosemary Stewart) not only in *what* they do and *how* they do it, but also *when* they do it.

Another aspect of this range of choice is the degree of responsibility which managers carry. 'That is my decision . . .' is a typical statement by managers asserting and taking pleasure in their power. 'That is my responsibility . . .' is the statement of managers asserting their duty, but also declaring their status by setting themselves apart from the ordinary people who merely hew wood and draw water, leading simple lives unburdened by any sense of duty. The responsibility may be for the results achieved by subordinates, for the decisions reached by the manager or for other aspects of the quality of work, like the satisfaction of colleagues with the performance and contribution. The managers certainly have more scope than others for organising their own work and changing the nature and direction of these activities, either through delegation or through initiating changes *vis à vis* other members of the hierarchy. This contrasts with non-managers, who have virtually no choice, despite the programmes of job enrichment and job enlargement that have been popular.

In different ways managers assert and cherish their independence and autonomy, being free from close supervision, having duties that are not repetitive and not too specialised.

THE CORE BEHAVIOUR OF MANAGEMENT

Can we now produce a list of job dimensions that can characterise a job as managerial, no matter what title it carries?

Several systems have been developed to grade jobs within organisations. One that is highly regarded is the Hay-MSL system of job evaluation, which is based on an assessment of three elements in a job: knowhow, problem-solving and accountability, each with subdivisions, as can be seen in Fig. 4.1.

The purpose of this and similar systems is obviously to determine which jobs are the more valuable to the organisation and therefore which merit a

1. *Know how*
   (a) Technical, professional.
   (b) Managerial.
   (c) Human relations.

2. *Problem solving*
   (a) Environment in which the thinking takes place;
       from routine to completely unstructured.
   (b) Challenge; from repetitive to creative.

3. *Accountability*
   (a) Degree of discretion; freedom to act.
   (b) Value of the areas affected by the job.
   (c) The directness of the impact of the job.

Fig. 4.1 The Hay-MSL system for assessing the content of management jobs.

higher level of pay. This approach has the value that it indicates some of the areas of work that are widely accepted in organisational circles as being managerial. The system defines what management is and then makes possible the assessment of individual jobs to determine how they compare with the model.

An attractively simple approach to defining the core behaviour of managers has been provided by Kotter (1982). In a study of general managers in the United States he concluded that they all had two activities in common: setting agendas for action, and setting up networks to implement those agendas.

He used the word *agenda* in the sense of a list of items to be dealt with, so that it becomes a way of putting into practice all the range of decisions that are made, such as policy, plans, strategies and agreements. Each of those is an occasional, cerebral act. Setting agendas is the constant activity of managers as plans and ideas are put into operation. 'Increase sales turnover by 25 per cent over the next twelve months' is a splendid general statement of policy, but the manager responsible will set up a series of agendas to bring out the desired result. Some hard bargaining with union officials may produce an agreement 'to introduce a new scheme of job evaluation', but that will be no more than a general declaration of intent until a manager puts together an agenda of what to do, what to do first, what to check, whom to deploy, whom to ask, when to aim for as a completion date, and so on. The organisation may have a corporate plan, but the individual managers responsible for achieving the results of the plan will each have a series of agendas, evolving, developing and extending, as the plan becomes a reality.

Review Topic 4.3

What agendas and networks are you currently operating? Is there any way in which you could extend and improve any of your networks?

These variegated frameworks for action are created by a process of thinking out possibilities, constant questioning and aggressively gathering information, with the questioning aided by a shrewd knowledge of the business. Choices are made both analytically and intuitively as careful calculation is combined with skilled guessing to move into action. The agendas are seldom written, although many lists are jotted down on the backs of envelopes, and may be either vague or specific, according to the subject matter.

Agenda-setting is one way in which managers impose their will on the situation around them; the other is by setting up and maintaining *networks* through which the agendas are implemented. These are quite different from the formal structure, although no substitute for it. Networks are a reflection of the need for political activity that is discussed in the next chapter. The individual manager identifies a large number of people, both inside the organisation and outside, who will help in implementing agendas, as well as being sources of information to go into agendas. The popular picture of the manager constantly making telephone calls is an expression of the network process of 'having a word with' contacts: the people who help to get things done by speeding something up, providing information, jumping a queue, endorsing a proposal in committee, checking data, arranging for the manager to meet someone and – of course – doing jobs. Networks are peopled partly by subordinates, but by a large variety of others, including those who have some respect for the manager, those who are dependent on or under obligation to the manager. Position in the hierarchy is crucial to having a good network, but so is expertise and social skilfulness. Methods used to set up networks include using disarming candour, doing small favours for others, being a 'nice guy', building a team of willing subordinates and generally shaping the relationships among the people in the network.

Enterprises often begin life as a partnership between two people, one of whom is better at agendas and another who is better at networks. Henry Royce was a brilliant engineer who could see clearly the 'agenda' of what was needed to create high-quality motor cars, but it was Charles Rolls who was able to set up and sustain the 'network' of business contacts that was to make Rolls-Royce a long-running success story. One activity emphasises analysis, imagination and planning; the other emphasises social skill and political judgement. All managers do both, but the most effective are those with equal skill in both areas.

THE MANAGEMENT JOB

We have been describing various ways of classifying managerial work as a means of understanding the range and variety of the managerial role. We have carefully avoided a definition of management or of manager because any definition tends to exclude as many jobs as it includes. Perhaps the most realistic approach is that of Rosemary Stewart in starting her research:

> We used the word 'manager' very broadly to include anyone above a certain level, roughly above foreman, whether they were in control of staff or not. There was no need to be more precise because we were interested in studying the jobs that our companies called managerial, and which formed part of the management hierarchy for selection, training and promotion. (1976, page 2)

Her investigation included jobs with titles like mill accountant, assistant treasurer, chief draughtsman, nutritionist, deputy chief architect, veterinary officer, and buyer. This is not because some jobs were included incorrectly, but because the essence of management appears in so many different jobs.

Some jobs have all the elements of management that have been considered in the last few chapters, yet the job holders are never described by that term and would probably not welcome its use about what they do. Only recently have head teachers begun to describe themselves, on occasions, as managers and the use of management ideas is quite widespread in nursing, but town clerks, solicitors, estate agents, orchestral conductors, film directors and choreographers are just a few of the job titles that carry a large management element; so there are some managers who are not called managers.

We have seen so far that managers, whether with that title or not, have a subtle and varied job, although the core behaviours of making agendas and operating networks is so simple that the detractor is inclined to say that the manager's job has been inflated out of all proportion and that any subtlety and complexity is around the job rather than in what managers actually do (see Fig. 4.2). In the remainder of this work we set out the details of what makes the management job so much more demanding and rewarding than it first appears, as those with the flair, common sense and experience to be in management positions combine the elements we have described to achieve equilibrium by getting all the components in a degree of balance. This is summarised in Fig. 4.3.

In understanding management work, however, we must always remember:

> Management is a much less tidy, less organised, and less easily defined activity than that traditionally presented by management writers or in job descriptions. (Stewart, 1976, page 125)

Fig. 4.2 Managerial work and the core of management behaviour.

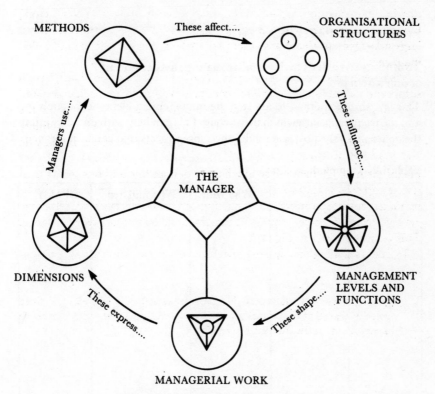

Fig. 4.3 The dynamics of management.

SUMMARY PROPOSITIONS

4.1 Management work differs from most other types of work in being more varied and staccato, involving extensive interaction with others and responsibility for initiating change.

4.2 The work managers do has three distinctive strands: technical (which is non-management), administrative (which is maintaining the system) and managerial (which is being able to change the system).

4.3 Compared with most other jobs, managers exercise choice in what they do, how they do it and when they do it.

4.4 The core behaviour of management is setting agendas for action and setting up networks to implement the agendas.

4.5 Some jobs have all the hallmarks of being managerial, but are never described in that way.

PUTTING IT INTO PRACTICE

Administrative drill to determine management content of one's own job

This is a simple method to analyse the management elements of one's job and the frequency with which they occur. This can help with understanding the demands of the post and modifying those aspects that can be improved.

Table 4.2 A sample diary sheet

Time	Activity	Who with	Who initiated	STAMP

Account for Time Spent.

1. Keep a diary for at least one week of exactly how time at work is spent. See Table 4.2 for a sample diary sheet.
2. The form is a basis that could be modified to your personal situation. Fill it in as events take place, rather than by recalling what has happened. Every time you switch attention from one subject to another, or from one person to another, that is a *change of activity*: and you start a new line. A meeting counts as one activity.
3. Read through the notes about how to analyse the results before starting to record.

Analysis of Diary. This record of exactly what you have done can be used in a number of ways. Here are some suggestions:

1. How many hours did you spend working each day and in the whole week?
2. What percentage of your time is spent with people?
3. How much of this time is spent with superiors, subordinates, others inside the organisation, people outside the organisation?
4. What is the average length of time you spend on an activity and, on average, how many activities do you have in a day? To what extent is your work characterised by brevity, variety and fragmentation, as suggested by Mintzberg?
5. What percentage of your activities is initiated by yourself, your boss, subordinates, others in the organisation, outsiders or by standard procedures? What proportion of your activities are you initiating?
6. What do you do most and least?

Outcome of analysis. By looking at the descriptions can you sort the activities into categories, viz:

1. Mainly technical.
2. Mainly administrative, e.g. routine paperwork, getting typing done.
3. Mainly managerial, e.g. influencing others, resolving conflict.
4. Mainly social.
5. Mainly personal.
6. Others, e.g. don't knows, mixture.

How satisfied are you with the distribution? What can you do to improve it?

REFERENCES

Barnard, C.E., *The Functions of the Executive*, Harvard University Press, Cambridge, Mass., 1938.

Brown, W., *Organization*, Heinemann, London, 1971.
Carlson, S., *Executive Behaviour*, Strömberg, Stockholm, 1951.
Edwardes, M., *Back From the Brink*, Collins, London, 1983.
Guest, R., 'On time and the foreman', *Personnel*, No. 32, pages 478–86, 1955.
Hales, C.P., 'What do managers do? A critical review of the evidence', *Journal of Management Studies*, 1986.
Harvey-Jones, J., *Making it Happen: Reflections on Leadership*, Collins, London, 1988.
Horne, J. and Lupton, T., 'The work activities of middle managers', *Journal of Management Studies*, vol. 2, pages 14–33, 1965.
Jaques, E., *Equitable Payment*, Heinemann, London, 1970.
Kotter, J., *The General Managers*, Free Press, New York, 1982.
Mansfield, R., Poole, M., Blyton, P., Frost, P., 'The British manager in profile', *BIM Survey 51*, British Institute of Management, London, 1981.
Marshall, J. and Stewart, R., 'Managers' job perceptions', *Journal of Management Studies*, vol. 18, Nos. 2 and 3, pages 177–90 and 263–75.
Mintzberg, H., 'Managerial work: analysis from observation', *Management Science*, 1971, vol. 18, 97–110.
Mintzberg, H., *The Nature of Managerial Work*, Harper & Row, London, 1973.
Mintzberg, H., 'The manager's job: folklore and fact', *Harvard Business Review*, July/Aug, 1975, page 49.
Sloan, A.P., in J. MacDonald (ed.), *My Years with General Motors*, Pan Books, London, 1967.
Scitovsky, T., *The Joyless Economy*, Oxford University Press, 1976.
Stewart, R., *Managers and their Jobs*, Macmillan, London, 1967.
Stewart, R., *Contrasts in Management*, McGraw Hill, Maidenhead, 1976.
Torrington, D.P. and Weightman, J.B., 'Technical atrophy in middle management', *Journal of General Management*, 1982.
Torrington, D.P., and Weightman, J.B., 'Middle management work', *Journal of General Management*, 1988.
Townsend, R., *Up the Organization*, Michael Joseph, London, 1970.

5

THE MANAGEMENT FUNCTIONS OF THE BUSINESS

Managers have to develop and maintain the business: they have to be both entrepreneurs and housekeepers. This argument is advanced very clearly by John Harvey-Jones (1988) in reflecting on a successful period as Chairman of ICI. We saw a similar dichotomy in the chapter on management work, with the need for precedent-setting, initiative and creativity in managerial work and the concomitant need for keeping things running smoothly in administrative work. We see it also in the functions of the business. Marketing and research, for instance, are primarily development functions, creating fresh opportunities and leading growth by introducing new ventures. Operations and purchasing are primarily housekeeping functions, keeping things running smoothly, controlling costs and maintaining quality. Functions are rarely entirely concerned with either development or housekeeping. Marketing includes the maintenance activities of after-sales service as well as the business expansion of sales promotion and advertising; purchasing will find new suppliers and better prices as well as ensuring regular deliveries.

Two of the major functions are more equally balanced between development and maintenance, with the difference in emphasis indicated by their labels. Finance and accounting is a function which raises the finance needed by the business and creates development opportunities by that entrepreneurial activity, but it also 'keeps the books', providing control data and monitoring expenditure. The personnel and human resources function has a key responsibility in maintaining smooth running, through dealings with unions, handling discipline and grievances, counselling, training, recruitment and job evaluation, but there are also the development activities of organisational culture, management development, negotiating agreements and personnel strategy.

In this chapter we describe the main management functions; general management, marketing, operations, personnel and human resources, finance and accounting, with a concluding comment on public service agencies.

THE GENERAL MANAGEMENT FUNCTION

General management has changed from being primarily inward-looking (managing the organisation) to outward-looking (doing the business of the organisation) with a heavy emphasis on entrepreneurialism and the need for every organisation to create its own opportunities for growth and continued relevance. There is always a customer to satisfy, whether it be the vegetarian finding too little choice on a restaurant menu, the eighteen-year-old deciding which university to attend, the buyer of a fleet of company cars, the librarian being confronted with allegations of racial bias in the book stock, or many more examples. Wherever the organisation is operating, the last decade of the twentieth century is undoubtedly the age of the consumer and general management has reflected this change of emphasis.

General management and change

The late 1970s and 1980s were a period of concern with development that bordered on obsession in many businesses; entrepreneurialism was often no more than opportunism, and lack of investment led to an inability to fulfil the promise offered by bright ideas. This era was bounded by two influential books. The first was by Robert Townsend (1970), a successful businessman, who regarded his achievements as being based on strong individualism and impatience with organisational maintenance. There were certainly other factors that explained his specialised success story, but the picture of the manager as swashbuckling hero cutting a swathe through bureaucratic controls was as appealing to legions of managers under tight financial controls as romantic fiction is to the lovelorn. The remarkable success of the book was due more to the attractiveness of the ideas than to the accuracy of its diagnosis.

The second book was by the well-known consultant Tom Peters (1988), one of the advocates of corporate excellence. He went so far as to advocate chaos, saying that success comes to those who thrive on chaos – or constant change – rather than to those who seek to eliminate it. This book says little that Townsend did not say eighteen years previously, although the examples are more diverse, so why is it still being said? We believe there are two reasons. First it is a message for every *management* but not for all *managers*; secondly, few entrepreneurs continue to have good ideas.

Many managers are in jobs where maintenance of smooth running is the paramount need, however tedious. These are the customers for the Robert Townsend ethic as they see a vision of a better life for themselves, but their colleagues in the organisation want them to carry on producing widgets, so that other people within the same management can use their profitability to finance new ventures. All managements need to innovate, but that innovation requires many individual managers to stagnate – at least for a time.

Some people have enough imagination, drive and luck to bring off an effective innovation. They are promoted and prosper through the lifespan of their achievement, but very few people indeed can repeat their success, and even fewer can do it more than once or twice. Unlike athletes, managers rarely retire at the peak of their powers, they remain in office and rest on their laurels. Hierarchy does its deadly work.

> There is nothing more difficult to execute, nor more dubious of success, nor more dangerous to administer than to introduce a new order of things; for he who introduces it has all those who profit from the old order as his enemies, and he has only lukewarm allies in all those who might profit from the new. (Machiavelli, 1984, page 21)

In another twenty years, books will still be written repeating the same basic message about the need for change and flexibility. One of the main tasks for general management is to sustain both change and stability, organisational development and maintenance.

General management and strategy

A further change has been a move towards more considered decisions about what the business should be doing and the range of strategic choices available. Tobacco companies have devoted considerable energy to reducing their dependence on tobacco products by diversification into a number of other industries. In the late 1980s banks and building societies suddenly extended their interests into estate agency. One obvious choice is therefore acquisition of other companies.

A further possibility is to sell off parts of the business – divestment – in order to concentrate resources elsewhere. This sale may be to another conglomerate or to employees. Management buy-outs have had a considerable vogue, many with remarkable success, as responsibility for the success or failure of the business has moved into the hands of those with the greatest degree of personal commitment.

Diversification comes not only from acquisition but by internal or joint development. The introduction of new models or new products is an everyday occurrence and many organisations grow and thrive as a result of this type of initiative from within their own resources. Others find opportunities for development by working in partnership with other businesses. Airlines and hotels find it helpful to work together in providing package holidays. Time-share holiday home developments usually have a building contractor as one of the partners in a joint development.

As was indicated in Chapter 3 diversification of interests and overall strategy is one of the main activities of top managers.

Review Topic 5.1

The way this chapter opens makes the position of employees seem one of little
influence over their personal affairs with jobs and careers that are at the mercy
of decisions taken according to a whole array of strategic considerations. How
can managers prevent the problems of unsatisfactory job performance that this
can bring with it?

THE MARKETING FUNCTION

A classic definition of marketing is:

> The process in a society by which the demand for economic goods and
> services is anticipated or enlarged, and satisfied through the conception,
> physical distribution and exchange of such goods and services. (Wills, 1976)

The reality has much to do with the orientation of the business and the
attitudes of the people who comprise it. The increased importance of
marketing is *the* most significant business development of the 1980s, as the
emphasis has shifted finally and inexorably away from making things for
people to buy, towards finding what people will buy – even though they are
probably unaware of their need – and then supplying it. Philip Kotler (see
Fig. 5.1) illustrates the centrality of the customer in the affairs of the
business by showing how marketing used to be one of several, equal
functions of the business, but has now become the medium through which
customer need is translated to all other functions.

Central to marketing is the concept, the original idea or bee in the bonnet
that is mulled over, knocked into shape, discussed, re-shaped and eventual-

Marketing as an equal
function

Customer as controlling
function and marketing as
integrative function

Fig. 5.1 Evolving view of marketing's role.

ly launched as a new venture. Holiday camps, pocket calculators, super-markets, timeshare holiday apartments, credit cards, microwave ovens, unit trusts and word processors are a few marketing concepts of recent years. There was a potential need or market that some imaginative person not only thought of but also found a way of meeting. The concept can start close to the source of supply or the development of technology or they can begin by an idea of what would sell. Examples of the first are optical fibres and colour sensitive thermometers. Optical fibre was a technological development for which people thought of imaginative applications; colour sensitive thermometers were a chance by-product of space technology. On the other hand package holidays and credit cards were ideas of market potential that were turned into viable concepts. This necessary emphasis on imagination and flair puts the marketing function close to the central strategic activities and an increasing number of chief executives come from a marketing background.

Marketing planning is the disciplining of the innovator, the process of applying cool analysis and calculation to creative fervour so that the ideas are not only turned into reality, but turned into a reality that pays its way and survives the first flush of enthusiasm. This is the activity of working out sales targets and pricing, calculating the budget, commissioning advertising, preparing sales promotion material and ensuring sources of supply from the operations function (Stapleton, 1982).

Market research is another device to temper creative enthusiasm.

> Market research is the way industry does reconnaissance. It seeks to provide knowledge of customers, how they behave and to what they respond, and the current and expected state of the market. (McDonald, 1983, page 227)

It consists of a series of investigative devices to measure potential sales and to sample reaction to existing and proposed products. If a new product is selling well, the market researcher may be able to discover what the aspect is that appeals to customers, who the customers are and how they are making their purchases. It is then possible to modify design, packaging, distribution, advertising and price to enhance sales further. The most common market research method is the questionnaire administered to a sample of the buying public, usually in face-to-face interviews, although postal and telephone surveys are also used. A refinement is to establish a panel of consumers whose attitudes or behaviour are tested periodically to assess changes in buying. The best known example is the metering of volunteers' television sets to indicate when the sets are switched on and the programme that is being watched. There is no point in conducting market research and then ignoring the results, although the extent to which the results are used will vary. One successful entrepreneur proudly claims to have commissioned four different sets of market research until he got the answers he wanted. This degree of confidence is what prevents marketing from become exclusively a matter of scientific (or quasi-scientific) measurement, but not all marketing experts are in a position to take such risks.

Test marketing is a development of conventional market research whereby a new product is tried out in a series of selected areas to determine a potential level of sales and the impact of the innovation on other lines. This makes possible a number of modifications before the final product launch.

Sales promotion is providing incentives to customers to buy your product: special offers, price-cutting, coupons, vouchers, competitions, free gifts, endorsements from glamorous people and special 'media events'. This aspect of marketing has certainly become very hectic and now extends to unlikely areas like the privatisation of public corporations.

Pricing is as calculative as sales promotion is superficial. Theories of pricing are central to the study of economics but have little impact on pricing policy in marketing as they deal with general explanations of price movements rather than pricing for competitive advantage. The unanswerable question of how to maximise your return in both the long and the short term is a matter of determining a price which will raise or sustain sales without reducing margins. This is not a simple – or complicated – calculation of costs and numbers, it is a tactical decision requiring shrewd judgement and a slice of luck (Gabor, 1977).

THE OPERATIONS FUNCTION

When interest in management ideas was largely centred in manufacturing industry, this function was known as 'production'. The broader term of 'operations' makes it possible to encompass a wider variety of activities as operations management is the management of systems that provide goods or services:

> An operating system is a configuration of resources combined for the provision of goods and services. Bus and taxi services, motels and dentists, tailors and mines, fire services and refuse removers, retail organizations, hospitals and builders are all operating systems (Wild, 1980, page 7)

Wild also classifies operating systems into four types (*ibid*, pages 8–17). *Manufacturing systems* are those in which something is physically created, while *transport systems* are those where the location of people or things is changed even though their physical characteristics remain the same. *Supply systems* are those in which ownership is changed, while *service systems* treat or accommodate something or someone. Many undertakings fit into two or more of these categories, but the operating system retains its distinctive integrity and the word 'system' is the key to making the process effective as:

> A system is a collection of interrelated components that performs tasks and has goals pertaining to the entire system. (McClain and Thomas, 1985, page 21)

Operations management is much concerned with the co-ordination and integration of the work done by differing groups and individuals, with the requirements of the system being paramount. The system is only made viable by the precise interlocking of the work done by the different elements. There is less interest in the individualistic concern with flair and initiatives of the marketing people and the emphasis on autonomy and personal choice that is so lauded by personnel specialists.

Operations management requires the intelligent anticipation of the resources, time and action to meet objectives in circumstances which are uncertain and restrictive. It is a never-ending, iterative process which includes forecasting, capacity planning, inventory management, purchasing and supply, scheduling and network analysis. There has recently been a growth of methods to improve and maintain quality, including the idea of quality circles, which locate responsibility for enhancing quality in groups of people who actually do the work. At the same time they provide those people with the opportunity to take a greater degree of control over what they are doing rather than having their activities prescribed by others.

The link between operations and marketing is operations control. This is a development from production control and often retains that title, especially with the tendency for businesses to extend use of the term 'product' to items not traditionally labelled that way, like insurance policies and unit trusts. Operations control translates demand data into a programme to deliver the products required and then turns production capability into product availability. This has been an area of great interest to those running management information systems using advanced information technology, because of the potential to manipulate data fast and accurately as well as transmitting it instantaneously over great distances. The best-known examples of recent years are in the newspaper industry, where the translation of ideas into laid out pages of newsprint has been made simpler and more efficient. Another example is in retailing, where machine reading of bar codes prints the price and description of the item on the customer's bill at the same time as adjusting the figures of stock level in the warehouse and re-order level in the purchasing office. Appleby (1987, page 313) considers that this type of development has the following implications for the future of operations:

1. A different kind of manager and a higher ratio of managers and supervisors to operators.
2. Shift working.
3. New skills, especially in complex machine maintenance.
4. Different payment schemes.
5. A smaller workforce, with need for redeployment and training.
6. Improved working conditions.

Rosemary Stewart's study of how managers spend their time found production managers to be a distinctive group, with working days even more fragmented than those of other managers. They also spent more time with their subordinates and less with people outside their own department. In contrast sales managers would try to get special treatment for their customers without concern about the effect on other sections of the business. Since the time of her original fieldwork, the marketing orientation of operations staff has increased markedly, but the basic tension between satisfying the customer and keeping the operation running smoothly always produces problems of communication and understanding (Stewart, 1986, Chapter 7).

THE PERSONNEL AND HUMAN RESOURCES FUNCTION

The personnel and human resources function of the business will provide the necessary support and leadership for many of the features of management work described in this book. It is likely to possess extensive expertise on the job of managing with people. Seldom will it be described with the cumbersome title we have given it. 'Personnel' is the usual and adequate shorthand, but the dual title has important implications.

Personnel management

This is the traditional title which everyone has come to understand over fifty or sixty years. It is indeed that aspect of management which is most widely understood by the general public outside the life of organisations. Personnel work is directed mainly at the organisation's employees, finding and training them, arranging for them to be paid, explaining management expectations of them and justifying management's actions to them. Personnel specialists are concerned with the satisfaction of employees' work-related needs, dealing with their problems and trying to modify management policy and actions that might otherwise provoke an unwelcome employee response.

The personnel function of management is present in all management work and an integral part of all managers' jobs, but in all but the smallest organisations it is partly undertaken by specialists to ensure consistency of treatment and to operate those systems – like performance appraisal or job evaluation – that only have value when run on a company-wide basis. These specialists are never totally identified with the management interest, as they lose effectiveness when not able to understand and articulate the views of non-managerial employees. Equally they do not *represent* the employees' views, as their standing in the eyes of employees depends on their ability to represent the management. For this reason they are always to some extent in between the two, mediating the needs of each to the other.

Implicit in personnel management are the complementary ideas that, first, employees need some looking after while at work; and, second, that they only make the organisation work properly when their needs are being met.

For most of the period following the Second World War, personnel managers grumbled about their lot, voices crying in the wilderness of management indifference that they were not appreciated, undervalued, underpaid and had no power. The legitimacy of their complaints faded during the 1970s, at least as far as pay and power were concerned, because managements became anxious about negotiations with unions and dealing with employment law. Research shows that personnel management is a board level responsibility in nine organisations out of ten, but:

> Personnel managers still worry about how they are perceived by their colleagues; obtaining the long-sought goal of recognition at the highest levels . . . but how far is their authority acknowledged by other managers? (Mackay and Torrington, 1986, page 18)

The difficulty is that the authority of personnel specialists lies in their ability to be people specialists, and few of us readily concede to others greater skill in dealing with people than we have ourselves. There is also the problem of not being totally identified with the management interest, which makes some managers keep personnel specialists at arm's length.

Human resources management

This is a concept of the late 1980s representing a major shift of emphasis in the employment of people. The starting point is not with the organisation's employees, but with the organisation's needs for human resources, which is a subtle but important distinction. There is less concern with the conciliation, motivation and propitiation of employees as a potentially uncooperative *cost*, and more concern with providing people – who may or may not be employees – with the scope, autonomy and objectives to enable them to deliver what the organisation needs. Instead of being a cost, they become *assets* in which to invest, thereby adding to their inherent value.

The human resources management approach ties in with another developing feature of employment, *core and periphery workforces* (Atkinson, 1984). The core workforce comprises those people on whom the future of the business absolutely depends, possessing specialised skills and knowledge that are constantly needed. The periphery workforce is those whose contribution is important but not difficult to replace, and who are perhaps not constantly needed. Those in the core are carefully selected, trained and bound in to the organisation with attractive fringe benefits and career prospects. Those on the periphery are likely to be engaged on one of a variety of contractual arrangements; part-time or temporary employment, freelancing, subcontracting, consultancy and so forth. The organisation's commitment to the second group is low.

Not all organisations adopt this type of division and those who do usually have a large core and a small periphery, but the approach marks a significant break from the tradition that the work of organisations was done by employees of that organisation, with full-time, permanent employment being the norm. Human resources management manipulates the balance between core and periphery, ensuring thorough nurturing of those in the core and clear contractual terms for those in the periphery, with interesting possibilities for moving between the two categories. Core employees are often recruited from a peripheral category and core employees sometimes move to the periphery. Many is the company director who has resigned but remained – for a time – as a 'consultant'.

Many personnel departments have been retitled 'human resources management' simply because is sounds fashionable, with no other change taking place. Our argument is that organisations need both strands in their people management specialism – both maintenance and development.

FINANCE AND ACCOUNTING

The finance and accounting function carries out three main activities. First, it raises the financial resources that the organisation needs, secondly, it controls the use of those resources within the organisation by monitoring of budgets and thirdly, it ensures the probity of the organisation's financial affairs in complying with company law. The first is a development activity; the other two are aspects of organisational maintenance.

Sources of funds vary. The bulk will come from invested funds, either from the public purse or from individual and institutional investors, although additional resources are available from banks, which loan money in order to derive an income. Any call for extra finance will need careful evaluation and justification of the case, especially estimates of when the investment will yield a return (Merrett and Sykes, 1973).

Most companies need a portfolio of capital projects and financial commitments with a variety of starting and finishing points and with varying timespans. Investment appraisal techniques help managers identify profitable projects before committing expenditure. Careful planning is vital – the profit-earning capacity of the business may be affected for a long time by the acquisition of long-term assets such as buildings, plant and equipment, and current assets such as stock. Such decisions involve large sums of money, are not easily reversible, and commit the organisation and its employees to long-term types of activities. Managerial judgement is still required in the interpretation of financial data. A more qualitative criterion than mere financial advantage to the organisation may be needed, for example, in the decision about new medical or welfare facilities. Financial analysis highlights the quantitative areas in a proposal, and focuses attention on those areas where judgement needs to be exercised. The accountant can show the relationship between project cost and expected return, but many financial planning decisions are management, not accounting decisions.

Controlling the use of resources is through budgetary control and cost accounting, that is described in Part V of this book. Ensuring the correctness of financial affairs is mainly through producing annual accounts that are then independently audited and published in line with the requirements of the Companies Acts to indicate to the shareholders how their money is being used (Reid and Myddleton, 1982). Central in these publications are the profit and loss account and the balance sheet, accompanied by a statement of the taxation position. A further requirement is the Director's Report, which contains many items including the directors' shareholdings, charitable and political donations, a review of the year and a statement about future plans. All of these statements are considered by the auditors to ensure that they are consistent with each other.

It has been suggested (Putnam, 1980) that the accounting system is often the weakest bit of most business systems. Cost accounting is a complex area, and one which gives rise to much confusion and misunderstanding. Management uses cost information for the purpose of control and decision-making. The costs incurred by the different parts of the organisation have to be compared with each other and with their pre-determined estimates, as part of management control. Management also has to take logically based decisions about selling prices, product profitability and business expansion, using comparative cost information to assist. One of the major problems to the non-specialist is that various cost accounting techniques may be used in the business at any one time. For example, for manufacturing control, budgetary control in conjunction with total absorption and standard costing techniques might be used, whereas for management decision-making, marginal costing methods might be more appropriate. Problems on which decisions requiring financial information have to be made may be, for example, estimating the effect of closing one unit of the organisation or of purchasing a component from outside instead of manufacturing it internally. (See Harvey and Nettleton 1983 for more details on managerial accounting and finance.) Whilst financial information is vital to management control and decision-making, too much complicated information, which is expensive to produce, is often of little value and an organisation should consider this in reviewing the financial information it produces.

Review Topic 5.2

The Businessman's Diary

January: we explored,
At our meeting of the Board,
Why the year we'd just completed
Mustn't ever be repeated.

February: all agreed
Strategy is what we need
To liquidate the Chairman's fear
On the current fiscal year.

March: unanimously moved
Action plan should be approved;
Especially in view of costs
Of three months we've already lost.

April: Finance Chief reviews
Prospects for our revenues;
Generally sad prognosis;
Sales Director under notice.

May: the Marketing Director
Senses he may now detect a
Movement in the market place,
If Production can keep pace.

June: the growth of finished stock
Suggests the forecast's all to cock,
Uproar as the meeting ended;
Half-year divided suspended.

July: bank a little pressing;
Chairman ill and convalescing;
Plant on strike, but no one worries
Considering the inventories.

August: Marketing explain
New promotional campaign;
Quiet confidence prevails,
Possibly excluding Sales.

September: quarterly accounts
Suggest the wages cheque may bounce;
Chief Accountant wins reprieve –
Kept a little up his sleeve.

October: budget overspent;
Cut the price by ten per cent;
Advertising decimated;
Overheads re-allocated.

November: temporary pause;
Fire at main competitors,
Sales beyond all expectations,
Directors cancel resignations.

December: All the Board excited;
Rumours Chairman to be Knighted;
Letters to employees linking
Success with new strategic thinking.

(Ralph Windle, 1981)

PUBLIC SECTOR AGENCIES

It is obviously incomplete to discuss business functions without considering public sector agencies, where the service principle dominates the profitability principle, even though the service provided to the consumer may be the same. Health Care, for instance, may be provided by the National Health Service or by the British United Provident Association, and pupils may be prepared for GSCE at local authority schools or independent schools. There are also many features of running the business that are identical or very similar:

> All large organizations face the same general management problems and perform the same functions, regardless of whether they are in the profit-seeking or nonprofit sector. All must develop (1) an appropriate product and/or service mix, (2) the ability to market successfully, (3) a workable organization structure, (4) effective personnel management techniques, (5) a capacity to finance their operations, and (6) an efficient production process. (Megginson *et al*., 1983, page 555)

The Training Commission is not a profit-making organisation, but it uses financial resources and there is a need for it to be cost-effective in its operation. The Departments of Health and of Social Security have to ensure that the range of benefits provided are those appropriate to the needs of the clientele and are known to those members of the population eligible for the benefits. The Passport Office, like any other business, needs an organisation and communications structure that will enable it to perform its functions reliably and efficiently.

John Child (1978) demonstrates how Dunlop, a private sector, profit-making business had distinct organisational norms operating in different parts of the business, according to whether the section was generating income or expense.

The key differences about public sector operations are the public nature of their governance. The independent auditors and evaluators of private sector companies are either 'professionals', with background and values similar to those of the people whose work they are judging, or they are consumers of the product. In the public sector there are those elements plus a more general representation of the public interest, which is essentially amateur rather than professional, and with more diverse background and values than those whose performance they are monitoring. This theoretically leads to more openness and accountability in management operations, although in some cases it simply leads to more subtle and devious manipulations of the decision-making processes.

There are many horror stories about panel interviews in the public sector, and these provide a clear illustration of the public nature of management in the public sector, and some of the problems it brings. The objective is not only to appoint the 'right' person, but also to do it in a way that is seen to be 'right'. Interview panels tend to be large and made up of people who are as anxious to score points off each other as they are to consider the applicants. Worried about the unpredictability of such unwieldy decision-making, the professionals try to suborn the democratic process by pre-determining the decision.

Richard was an education advisor with general responsibility for advising on the appointment of headteachers in his metropolitan borough, although decisions on appointments were made by school governors. For one headship there were thirty-five applications, which were initially considered by Richard and his colleagues, Frances and Henry. They agreed that Sylvia was the most appropriate candidate. She was well-known on the advisory network and had exactly the right track record. Few other candidates were worth considering. Several looked good on paper but the advisory network sent back warning signals about each of them. Feeling it was important to ensure Sylvia was appointed, Richard discussed all the applications with the Chairman of Governors and agreed a short list of three that included Sylvia and two 'dummy' candidates. At the interview Sylvia failed to impress one or two members of the panel and one of the other candidates was appointed.

Perhaps Richard acted unwisely as well as improperly, but this is an illustration of how well-meaning professionals try to short-circuit the public processes to achieve what they regard as right decisions. Although the example is in employee selection, there are many more from all aspects of management decision-making.

Any business is made up of a number of specialist functions, but every manager shares some responsibility for every function: operations managers are concerned about service to the customer, personnel managers are concerned about working within budgets and marketing managers are involved in the performance appraisal of their personnel. The differences are necessary for us to understand so that we can fit together a viable organisation with the requisite expertise available. Those differences then have to be managed so that the whole enterprise works as an integrated undertaking rather than a range of loosely-federated units.

SUMMARY PROPOSITIONS

5.1 All management is about both developing and maintaining the business.

5.2 General management co-ordinates activities and ensures the growth and continuing relevance of the business.

5.3 The marketing function generates demand for the products of the business.

5.4 The operations function deploys resources to provide the goods and services of the business.

5.5 The personnel and human resources function provides expertise, analysis and support in managing with people.

5.6 Finance and accounting manage both the input of necessary funds and the maintenance of monitoring procedures to ensure the wise use of those funds.

5.7 Public sector agencies may provide the same products and services as private sector businesses and many of their functions are very similar, but managers have a different ultimate accountability for their deployment of the resources under their control.

REFERENCES

Appleby, R.C., *Modern Business Administration*, Pitman, London, 1987.

Atkinson, J., 'Manpower strategies for flexible organisations', *Personnel Management*, August 1984.

Child, J., 'The non-productive components within the productive sector' in Fores, M. and Glover I. (eds), *Manufacturing and Management*, HMSO, London, 1978.

Gabor, A., *Pricing, Principles and Practices*, Heinemann, London, 1977.

Harvey, D.A. and Nettleton, M., *Management Accounting*, Mitchell Beazley (Core Business Studies), London, 1983.

Harvey-Jones, J., *Making it Happen*, Collins, London, 1988.

Kotler, P., *Marketing Management: Analysis, Planning and Control*, (4th edn), Prentice Hall, Englewood Cliffs, New Jersey, 1980.

Machiavelli, N., *The Prince*, Penguin Books, Harmondsworth, 1981.

McClain, J.O. and Thomas, L.J., *Operations Management*, 2nd edn, Prentice Hall, Englewood Cliffs, New Jersey, 1985.

McDonald, C., 'Market research' in Lock, D. and Farrow, N., *The Gower Handbook of Management*, Gower, Aldershot, 1983.

Mackay, L.E. and Torrington, D.P., *The Changing Nature of Personnel Management*, Institute of Personnel Management, London, 1986.

Megginson, L.C., Mosley, D.C. and Pietri, P.H., *Management: Concepts and Applications*, Harper & Row, New York, 1983.

Merrett, A.J. and Sykes, A., *Finance and Analysis of Capital Projects*, Longman, London, 1973.

Peters, T.J., *Thriving on Chaos*, Macmillan, London, 1988.

Putnam, A.O., *Management and Information Systems: Planning, Developing, Managing*, Pitman, London, 1980.

Reid, W. and Myddleton, D.R., *The Meaning of Company Accounts*, Gower, Aldershot, 1982.

Stapleton, J., *How to Prepare a Marketing Plan*, 3rd edn, Gower, Aldershot, 1982.

Stewart, R., *The Reality of Organisations*, Pan Books, London, 1986.

Townsend, R., *Up the Organization*, Michael Joseph, London, 1970.

Wild, R., *Operations Management: A Policy Framework*, Pergamon, Oxford, 1980.

Wills, G.S.C., 'Marketing' in Kempner, T. (ed.) *A Handbook of Management*, Penguin Books, Harmondsworth, 1976.

Windle, R., *Boardroom Ballards*, Bertie Ramifications Ltd, 1981. More recent material of the same genre is available in Windle, R., *The Bottom Line*, Century Hutchinson, London, 1985.

PART II

POLICY, PLANNING AND DECISION-MAKING

The most powerful aspect of the management role is to make decisions on major issues. The success or failure of any undertaking will be determined by the policies which are shaped for its future and the strategies set within that policy framework. Solving problems and making decisions are tasks that can be aided by a series of well-tried methods that have proved successful in a range of different situations. One of the most difficult aspects of strategy is making plans that will implement change successfully.

6

STRATEGY AND
POLICY-MAKING

There is some confusion in the world of management about the distinction
between strategy and policy, although strategy is usually related to planning and policy commonly linked to shaping everyday affairs. Strategy is
what is to be achieved and policy is the framework within which the
activities will be conducted. The management process is then the implementation of the strategy within the framework of the policy.

Stoner (1986) provides contrasted definitions:

> [Strategy is] . . . the broad program for defining and achieving an organiza-
> tion's objectives; the organization's response to its environment over time.
> (page 695)

> A policy is a general guideline for decision-making. It sets up boundaries
> around decisions, including those that can be made and shutting out those
> that cannot. In this way it channels the thinking of organization members so
> that it is consistent with organizational objectives. Some policies deal with
> very important matters, like those requiring sanitary conditions where food
> or drugs are produced or packaged. Others may be concerned with relatively
> minor issues, such as the way the employees dress. (page 91)

An example will help illustrate the distinction. Multiparts is a company in a
highly competitive segment of the computer peripherals business. To meet
expansion requirements they have decided to open a new sales and service
centre in Bradford and they are anxious to start trading from the new centre
without alerting their competitors to the move. This bare *strategy* is then
filled out with decisions on how many people are needed, with what skills
and with what facilities. A further set of decisions determines the type of
premises, the range of services within the premises and the moves needed to
locate and employ the necessary people, the sequence in which they are to
be engaged and the employment costs of each category.

Alongside there will be *policy* decisions on whether or not vacancies in the
new centre will be made known to existing employees, what methods of
recruitment and selection will be used, what type of remuneration package
will be offered and how legal obligations in matters such as health and

safety and employment rights are to be met. Many of these matters will have been resolved beforehand, as policy is a continuing framework for a range of activities, even though each new activity tends to throw up policy considerations that have not occurred previously.

THE NATURE OF STRATEGY

Because of its association with decision-making and objectives, strategy is generally viewed as a sexy, top management activity. The grim comparison with nuclear weapons makes the point. *Tactical* weapons kill thousands, but *strategic* weapons can kill hundreds of thousands. Strategic decisions in business are the ones that really matter. They do not, however, only involve top managers. In Chapter 9 we describe the organisational feature of decision-making complexes involving teams of advisers and analysts who rough-cut the decisions for managers to make. The support teams provide the expertise, the information and the analysis, while their leaders add the elements of flair, judgement, boldness and political skill to make the decision – and then make the decision work.

In his study of general managers, Mintzberg (1973a) decided that strategy-making was probably the most crucial part of his subjects' work, and:

> One clear conclusion emerges from my study: the manager . . . is substantially involved in every significant decision made by his organization. This is so because (1) as formal authority the manager is the only one allowed to commit his organization to new and important courses of action, (2) as nerve center the manager can best ensure that significant decisions reflect current knowledge and organizational values, and (3) strategic decisions can most easily be integrated by having one man control all of them (page 77)

He further distinguished three modes of strategy formulation (Mintzberg, 1973b):

1. The *entrepreneurial mode* is where a single strong leader makes bold and risky decisions, relying heavily on intuition and personal experience. The organisation is able to move swiftly and decisively in pursuing its aims, always seeking new opportunities to exploit. Strategy is uncomplicated and shows no sign of modification to accommodate a variety of interests and points of view.
2. The *adaptive mode* is where managers react to situations as they develop. Instead of the bold and dramatic leaps forward of the entrepreneurial mode, there is a gradual progression of small moves, aimed mainly at defending the organisation against the competitive initiatives of others. Thus described, the adaptive mode sounds pusillanimous, unattractive and doomed to failure. In practice the lack of a single powerful leader

has advantages as well as drawbacks. There may not be dramatic leaps forward, but neither are there dramatic leaps in the wrong direction. Influences on decision-making are spread widely with many people having some stake and producing an element of flexibility. It is an approach which is often called 'muddling through'; it may not be exciting but it avoids spectacular failure.

3. The *planning mode* is the most generally attractive, as it involves a systematic approach to strategy by which the top managers use their decision-making complexes and their own analysis to study the market and other aspects of the environment in which they are operating, and then use that as a framework in which they will deploy their experience, imagination and creative discussion to produce a plan for the future. Risks are calculated risks, intuition and flair are directed at matters that have first been fully explored and bounded by investigation and analysis. Bold leaps forward may be in the dark, but they are at least towards the light.

Seldom do we find only one mode of strategy formulation in an organisation. The entrepreneurial mode is usually the method adopted at the beginning of a business, when there is strong reliance on the guts and vision of a founder or founding team. Some management buy-outs make initial rapid strides forward as a result of confident, committed managers (mortgaged up to the hilt) suddenly replacing an uninterested, muddling through management. In very large, long-standing businesses there have been recent moves to set up new venture divisions, whereby a small team are partly insulated from the adaptive norms and encouraged to set up new ventures within the corporate fold.

Other variations in mode will be due to the nature of the functional activity. Marketing departments tend to be strong on planning, and most of the best examples of a planning approach to strategy come from marketing. Personnel departments have traditionally been adaptive, although the human resources movement which we consider in Chapter 5, seeks to replace that with planning. For research and development to bear fruit, it is usually necessary to foster an entrepreneurial mode, with individual researchers following their hunches in their own idiosyncratic way. There are other mixtures with, for instance, some parts of purchasing being entrepreneurial while others are adaptive.

Quinn (1980) demonstrates that the fusion of the three modes, especially planning and adaptive, is often found in organisations following a practice that he calls *logical incrementalism*, whereby the top management has a clear plan and set of objectives for where the organisation should be moving, but is unable or unwilling to impose that plan rigidly on everyone else. Moving the organisation in the way they think it should go is then a series of nudges and shoves. If a section begins moves in a direction that is consistent with the overall strategy, then top management reinforces those developments by allocation of resources or some formalisation and extension of the corporate plan in that direction. When a section begins moves in a direction inconsistent with the overall plan, then top management may adapt, by modifying their plan or waiting, or they may take an entrepreneurial approach by trying to change the new initiative. The advances are logical, but in small, incremental steps.

> **Review Topic 6.1**
>
> **Consider one or two organisations of which you have experience and decide which strategy formulation mode they are in. Is it the right one? What circumstances might make a change necessary?**

There are also dangers in overemphasis on strategic planning, which is a clear sense of direction and focus on where the business is going. Although obvious, this simple clarification and possible change in emphasis can have a profound effect as, for instance, when the Canadian Pacific Railway management decided that they were not in the business of running a railway but in the business of transportation. From that clear sense of direction can stem specific objectives, the collation of necessary information, the anticipation of problems and the assessment of strengths, weaknesses and opportunities.

There are also dangers in overemphasis on strategic planning, which can become the purpose of the business rather than an aid to running the business. Thought is no substitute for action, plans are not an alternative to operations and analysis can aid but never replace judgement. The strategy development process is one in which top management decision-makers tend to surround themselves with young, sharp thinkers. The young advisors focus on the ideas and aspirations of their bosses and this can insulate the bosses from the everyday realities of the business. There is the possibility of becoming so rational in decision-making that only safe courses of action are pursued and opportunities lost or elementary errors made. In the 1960s a British company went to considerable trouble to estimate the future home demand for refrigerators. Their forecasting and strategy were accurate, with one exception: they developed production facilities to meet the total demand, allowing no scope for competing companies.

Currently the advantages probably outweigh the disadvantages for most types of business, but there are notes of caution being sounded by those who feel that entrepreneurial flair can be stifled by over-preoccupation with analysis (for example, Peters and Austin, 1985).

THE NATURE OF STRATEGY IN MANAGING WITH PEOPLE

Because of the emphasis on analysis and precision there is a tendency to concentrate on economic data and overlook the way in which people and their values can influence the implementation – or failure to implement – a chosen strategy:

> Corporate strategy is . . . concerned with what people *want* organisations to do . . . the aspirations, expectations, attitudes and personal philosophies which people hold. (Johnson and Scholes, 1984, page 116)

This can affect strategy in different ways, depending on both the aspirations and expectations of those inside the organisation and of those outside. A move for an organisation to trade on Sundays would, for instance, partly depend on the attitudes of customers to opening on Sundays and partly on the attitudes of employees. Customers might boycott or move their custom elsewhere; employees might refuse to work on Sundays unless paid double or triple time. The level of this feeling might be insignificant in relation to other benefits, or it might be sufficient to warrant the abandonment of the strategy.

Some of the constraining values are made manifest in law, while others have to be sensed by the management in interpreting a number of signals from those interested in what the organisation is doing. With the increasing number of pressure groups expressing various types of social concern, there are many issues of management strategy that come under public strategy, from the dumping of nuclear waste and the handling of radioactive emissions to the methods of selling timeshare apartments. One reaction to this public interest has been the establishment of codes of conduct for businesses in specific industrial sectors, such as the Association of British Travel Agents and the National House Builders Registration Council.

Inside the business the values to constrain strategy are manifest most obviously in trade union organisation, but also in professional groupings (like surgeons in hospitals or pilots in an airline) and coalitions of interest which develop, particularly in response to perceived threat. This type of internal issue is dealt with in our chapter on organisational politics. The recent interest in organisational culture is an attempt to get a closer fit between the values of the various stakeholders in the business and the objectives of that business. Strategy is one expression of how that fit is achieved; policy is another.

WHY BOTHER WITH POLICIES?

Often managers regard policies as encumbrances, curtailing their necessary freedom of action to make difficult decisions in rapidly changing circumstances. Here is a typical comment from a stock allocator in a retail chain:

> Policy is just an excuse for a jack-in-office to tell me what I can not do and to slow down the implementation of what I have to do. My section is expanding

fast and we have agreement for the recruitment of two new girls. We have the budget, we are hellishly busy, but we can not recruit yet because of 'policy'. I have had to send explanatory memos to three different people at head office, my draft advertisements have been sent back for revision because I used the word 'her' once. I know that was a mistake, but as a woman I get really pissed off when some middle-aged male ticks me off in a sarky way for breaching the equal opportunity policy. We want to get on and do things. Policy just holds you back.

Policies are problematic for the policy-maker as well. If your policy does not work, you are incompetent; if your policy works but is unpopular, then your enemies try to undermine it; if your policy works and is accepted, you will have little chance of changing it. Why bother? Why not treat each case on its merits? Here are some reasons:

1. *Policy can introduce change.* Many aspects of organisational life are bounded by precedent, which is the *de facto* policy when there is no other guideline. In the field of industrial relations precedent, or custom and practice, has been so influential as to be regarded as a set of rules (Flanders, 1967, page 70), carrying as much weight as collective agreements and being extremely difficult to change. In all areas of employment and management practice there is a strong tendency for things to be done the way they always have been done and any individual manager will find this dependence on precedent hard to fight. Getting agreement to a new policy is the best way of breaking out of that relevance on past practice.

2. *Policy makes a manager's position clear.* If the amount of responsibility to be carried by subordinates is to increase, there need to be clear guidelines for the delegation of that responsibility. When policy is explicit it becomes a significant element in making that delegation possible. Also managers regularly seek endorsement of their strategies from colleagues, by getting their budgets approved or their plans accepted. In making this type of bid a statement of policy on how, as well as for what, the money is to be used increases the strength of the case.

3. *Policy can make the management's position clear.* Members of organisations increasingly want to be supplied with information, especially about management intentions for the future regarding security of employment and career prospects. Policy statements on notification of vacancies, trade union recognition, consultation on redundancy and so forth partly meet those expectations.

4. *Policy can produce consistent managerial behaviour.* Policy provides a useful discipline for managers as they have to behave in a consistent way, avoiding capricious changes in direction and bewildering their colleagues. Consistent behaviour is not the same as creative action and any manager needs both. Some grumble about the need to behave consistently, feeling that it blunts their creative drive, but they soon find that a

policy framework prevents them from wasting time and energy working out new solutions to problems that have already been solved, and enables them to concentrate initiative and imagination where they are really needed.

5. *Policy shapes the response to imposed change.* Frequently organisations are faced with changes being dumped on them from outside, and managers then await policy guidance so that they know what to do. When a new piece of legislation is introduced on, for example, closed shop ballots, managers will receive information about what the legislation intends, but they will await an organisational initiative before taking any action. 'How are we going to respond to this change?' If there is no policy guidance, there will be no management initiative until a crisis occurs.

6. *Policy can reduce dependence on individuals.* In Chapter 9 we examine different types of organisation structure and culture. The entrepreneurial form described there is heavily dependent on the person at the centre, with all initiative stemming from the centre and the actions of individual managers bounded by their reliance on precedent and guessing what the spider at the centre of the web wants. When that ceases to be a viable way of operating, policy development is a way of making the functioning of the business less dependent on that single source of power, wisdom and judgement. At a more prosaic level organisational functioning can become over-dependent on 'treasures' and 'founts of wisdom':

> Mary is marvellous at controlling the debtors. She keeps it all in her head and we'd be lost without her. She really is a treasure.

> Frank has a system all of his own, which no one else can understand – he makes sure of that! – so he is the fount of all wisdom on salaries.

Splendid individuals are no substitute for sound policies.

Review Topic 6.2

To what extent can sound policies be a substitute for splendid individuals?

THE NATURE OF POLICY IN MANAGING WITH PEOPLE

Although policies are to be found in all parts of the business, we focus here on those relating to the employment and deployment of people, which have a variety of names, such as personnel policy, human resources policy, employment policy, and industrial relations policy, although manpower policy appears to be the most widely used. The danger of slack thinking in this area is demonstrated by Sheila Rothwell:

> Too often . . . policy is in reality a set of free-floating personnel policies, often developed in the '60s and '70s, most of which continue regardless,

unconnected with each other or the business plan. For example, ruthless redundancies may take place (when a long-term gradual reduction in line with business needs might have been implemented relatively painlessly) while benefit policies encouraging long service remain in existence. (Rothwell, 1984, page 31)

In examining policy statements from companies, one is baffled by their infinite variety and frequent meaninglessness.

It is our policy to offer attractive terms and conditions of employment, to be a fair employer of highly-motivated people within a successful business.

This exemplifies the danger of policy statements that are so bland that they merely state the obvious. How many companies do not want highly-motivated people, and how many do not want to run a successful business? For that matter, how many would publicly state their intention to offer *unattractive* terms and conditions? This trap is caused by two problems, first the reluctance to be tied by specific commitments and secondly the need to give scope for individual managers to interpret policy for application in particular circumstances rather than having their hands tied completely.

No action will be taken if an officer is up to five minutes late in arriving for duty. Those arriving beween six and fourteen minutes late should fill in form L2, have it countersigned by the supervisor and lodge it at the Personnel Office before 12 noon. Those arriving more than fourteen minutes late should report to the supervisor, who will deliver a verbal warning.

As well as being apparently designed for a robot penitentiary, the problem with that excerpt from a *policy* statement is that it is not policy at all but procedure, which is the drill to implement some part of policy. We have a separate chapter on procedures and it is always helpful for the manager to distinguish clearly between these two quite different ways of making things happen.

Increasingly policy frameworks are being introduced that avoid the rigidity of collective agreements without involving the license of unfettered managerial judgement. This can improve manpower utilisation at the same time as providing scope for individual employees to have some flexibility in their personal working arrangements.

Despite the decline in trade union assertiveness in the 1980s, very few organisations have withdrawn recognition and most have a series of formal agreements and regular dealings with union officials. This is an area where policy cannot be avoided and where it is most valuable: the alternative being reliance on custom and practice.

Custom and practice may arise . . . from management acceptance of informal unilateral work practices developed by work groups or from an isolated management decision which employees regard as binding on future decisions in similar circumstances. (Salaman, 1987, page 37)

Gradually companies are developing radical employee relations policies which are designed to alter the fundamental nature of the employment relationship away from a conflict base to a co-operative base, involving strategies on employees in the management decision-making process and harmonisation of employment conditions between different categories of employee. (See, for example, Roberts, 1985.)

A special type of policy is on equal opportunity. Logically this type of equality is an integral part of all other policies, but legislation and the activities of pressure groups have tended to single out the area as one needing separate treatment, laying strong emphasis on policy as the way to bring about change. The strength of this emphasis can be measured by the fact that a survey of manpower and personnel policy statements from forty different organisations showed that approximately half of all the words were on this topic. In five cases the equal opportunity policy was the only one.

Whatever the policies may be, they need to be related to the corporate plan or strategy, so that the policy frames actions that are going to take place instead of actions that used to take place.

FORMULATING AND IMPLEMENTING POLICY

Copying another organisation's policy is attractive as it has presumably proved successful in that context, so why bother re-inventing the wheel? Unfortunately it may be the wrong type of wheel, even though the principles may be exactly right. Like most aspects of effective management, policy formulation requires diligence, care and time. If a policy is adopted independently of issues relevant to the organisation, and not seen by members of the organisation as relevant to those issues, then commitment is unlikely and failure is probable.

Policy is valueless without action to make it work. There will be no action without a commitment to both the policy and to the measures to implement the policy by those who can make it work. Those who can make policy work are not only managers holding key positions, however essential their commitment is. A policy decision that all vacancies will be filled only after internal advertisement will not succeed until prospective applicants know, understand and believe in the change, so that they apply for posts instead of disregarding the advertisements in the belief that it is only 'going through the motions' and that the appointee will be approached and asked to apply after the formalities have been completed.

Arthur Chisholm is the personnel controller in a mail order company with a majority of women workers. Believing that more women should progress to supervisory and management positions, he prepared a draft policy statement on equal opportunity that was discussed with shop stewards, fellow managers and the Equal Opportunities Commission. All accepted the statement and it was duly put up on noticeboards. After a year there was very little change and Arthur's attitude was of some mild irritation that he had taken a lot of trouble to no avail, also: 'Well, at last we've got it, so I'm covered if there is any criticism. Nobody can say I didn't try and we will carry on regardless.'

It is convoluted reasoning to regard a policy as satisfactory when it has had no effect. Arthur Chisholm could have advised Pontius Pilate.

We suggest the following outline procedure for formulating and implementing policy.

1. *Identify the topic.* Events make a specific policy initiative timely. The equal value modifications to the Equal Pay Act produced a flurry of policy moves relating to job evaluation and payment, and there are many examples of legislation stimulating policy formulation. Another type of event making the time ripe for a particular topic is management strategies, like a decision to introduce shiftworking or extend the range of the performance appraisal scheme. Other events calling for policy clarification are unexpected changes, uncertainties about the future and questions from managers asking how they should approach a particular matter. There is little prospect of a successful initiative unless there is stimulus to give it priority in people's eyes.

   As well as being identified as timely, the policy topic must also be clearly defined. If appraisal interviews are being introduced, is this part of a policy on selection, or promotion, or staff development, or performance assessment?

2. *Win provisional support.* Policies need supporters. Key allies recruited early start the processes of both political commitment to the idea and practical contribution to the policy itself. Preliminary consultation and testing of reaction may cause the initiative to be abandoned or deferred, but if it is worth pursuing its value will become clear at this stage. The supporters of the policy need to confer both with those having sufficient political influence in the organisation to make eventual acceptance likely, and with those having sufficient expertise to offer constructive suggestions.

3. *Decide the key elements.* A policy will succeed or fail because of its two or three central features. In working out the arrangements for personnel travelling overseas, for instance, the class of air travel, the style of accommodation and the level of maintenance allowance will be crucial features of its success. Careful consultation at this stage ensures that the policy is developing in a way that deals with real issues rather than academic issues.

4. *Work out the details.* Policies always require interpretation, and interpretation hinges on the details. In observing the processes of international

negotiations it is interesting to see how key elements and details interact. In sorting out how to organise the world after the Second World War, Churchill, Roosevelt and Stalin had several historic meetings and sessions were of two types. First were the 'three-only' meetings where the three men met alone with interpreters to decide the broad measures, then there were the full meetings of all the advisers to sort out the details. These took much longer and many matters agreed by the leaders in outline were referred back because of problems with detail. More recently negotiations on the limitation of nuclear weapons seem to follow a similar path. Details of policy require as much care and consultation as the key elements.

5. *Win agreement.* Policy can only work with commitment. Following on the careful consultation and advice so far, there is a policy statement that has supporters of its key elements and details. That support has now to be extended to win the agreement of most, if not all, of those affected.

6. *Implement and publicise.* If the policy is to work it must be understood by those affected by it. Some of this will have been achieved by the stages of formulation, but now many others will have to be briefed, with their questions answered and their understanding developed. Not everyone will welcome the initiative as it will involve them in changing some aspect of what they do.

> Sometimes it seems as though a great many talented people are wasting an awful lot of time . . . they develop sensible, well-thought out policies that would make their company one of the most progressive and highly respected of employers. And then they see their efforts continually frustrated and subverted by a management team that seems determined to ignore most of what the personnel department does. (Brewster and Richbell, 1982)

Why do they 'seem determined to ignore . . .'? That apparent determination needs to be deflected and one means towards deflection is making sure that people are briefed so that they understand as well as know about the policy.

7. *Have the procedures ready.* Policy is implemented by procedures and drills. If a new safety policy has an element requiring the completion of an accident reporting form, the form must be ready and available at the same time as the policy is promulgated.

8. *Monitor the outcome.* Innovations require nurture. In the early stages there will be accidental or deliberate breaches of the policy's intentions. Some people will forget what they are supposed to be doing, others will run into problems that had not been envisaged. If these problems can be picked up and resolved quickly, the policy will be strengthened, otherwise inconsistent strategies will develop from various quarters and the necessary reasonable consistency will be lost.

Soon the policy will need to be updated to suit changing circumstances and to create fresh opportunities. Having broken the mould of custom and practice it is important that another mould does not set too hard, inhibiting change and curbing initiative.

DOES IT HAVE TO BE WRITTEN DOWN?

So far everything in this chapter has implied that the policy is written and publicised. The obvious reasons for this are to meet the main objectives of policy-making that have been set forth, but many managers hesitate to put policy in writing for fear of being trapped with a commitment to actions which later become difficult to sustain. Your reaction may be 'Well, they would, wouldn't they?' but whatever we say in the last paragraph about up-dating, written commitments are difficult to change and are sometimes formulated without sufficient thought for the future. Reluctance to put things in writing can produce behaviour that is devious or difficult to understand. Did President Reagan authorise the sale of armaments to Iran in 1986 or not? The widespread belief that President Nixon *did* authorise the Watergate break-in is based largely on an interpretation of what he *did not* say on the so-called Watergate tapes.

Review Topic 6.3

Which of the following policies do you think should be written down;
1. A policy of not using certain newspapers for recruitment advertising because of their party political allegiance.
2. A policy not to purchase goods and services from specific suppliers because of their apparent support for a particular political regime, like apartheid;
3. A policy of senior managers receiving a higher standard rate of subsistence while travelling on company business than other managers.

There is a case for some policies not to be written down, partly because the issues that will shape the policy have not become sufficiently clear so that there is no more than a tentative policy to deal with the present, and partly because some policies are confidential and their disclosure could disadvantage the business. A policy *not* to recognise a trade union, for instance, is not likely to be publicised. Brewster and Richbell (1982) make an interesting distinction between policies which are 'espoused' and those which are 'operational'. The first are officially endorsed usually in writing; the second are the policies which managers actually follow. Sometimes there is no difference between the two, there are often slight variations and occasionally marked differences, but it is only the operational policies that are of value. Those that are espoused but not operational are either ignored or become a basis for criticising managers who are not doing what they should do.

SUMMARY PROPOSITIONS

6.1 There are no clear, generally accepted definitions of the difference between policy and strategy.

6.2 Normally strategy is linked to planning what to do, while policy forms the framework within which everyday matters are carried forward.

6.3 Modes of formulating strategy are either entrepreneurial, adaptive or planning.

6.4 Strategic planning can improve the effectiveness of a business by clarifying direction and improving the rationality of decisions, but it may impede entrepreneurial flair.

6.5 The benefits of clear policies are that they increase the likelihood of introducing change, clarify issues, engender consistent management behaviour and make the organisation less dependent on individuals.

6.6 Policies that are copied uncritically from other organisations are rarely effective, as they were designed for a different situation.

6.7 The steps in formulating and implementing policy are identifying the topic, winning provisional support, deciding the key elements, working out the details, winning agreement, publicising, having the procedures ready and monitoring the outcome.

6.8 Policies are not always in writing, either through being only partly developed or through being confidential.

PUTTING IT INTO PRACTICE

Obtain a policy document relating to some aspect of managing with people in an organisation. This could be one published where you work, part of the company handbook of a business to which you once applied for employment, or part of the annual statement to shareholders.

1. What is the policy intended to achieve?
2. How successful is it likely to be? Why?
3. How could it be improved? If you can think of ways to improve it, why did the authors not do it that way in the first place?
4. Rewrite and develop the policy, together with the associated outline procedures, as suggested in section 5 of this chapter.

REFERENCES

Brewster, C.J. and Richbell, S., 'Getting managers to implement personnel policies', *Personnel Management*, Dec. 1982.

Flanders, A., *Collective Bargaining: A Prescription for Change*, Faber & Faber, London, 1967.

Johnson, G. and Scholes, K., *Exploring Corporate Strategy*, Prentice Hall International, Hemel Hempstead, 1984.

Mintzberg, H. (a), *The Nature of Managerial Work*, Prentice Hall, Englewood Cliffs, New Jersey, 1973.

Mintzberg, H. (b), 'Strategy-making in three modes', *California Management Review*, vol. 16, no. 2, 1973, pages 44–53.

Peters, T. and Austin, N., *A Passion for Excellence: The Leadership Difference*, Random House, New York, 1985.

Quinn, J.E., *Strategies for Change: Logical Incrementalism*, Irwin, Homewood, Ill., 1980.

Roberts, C. (ed.) *Harmonization: Whys and Wherefores*, Institute of Personnel Management, London, 1985.

Rothwell, S., 'Integrating the elements of a company employment policy', *Personnel Management*, Nov. 1984, pages 30–3.

Salaman, M., *Industrial Relations: Theory and Practice*, Prentice Hall International, Hemel Hempstead, 1987.

Stoner, J.A.F. and Wankel, C., *Management*, 3rd edn, Prentice Hall, Englewood Cliffs, New Jersey, 1986.

7

PROBLEM-SOLVING
AND DECISION-MAKING

When Crawford drove to the beach for some sun and swimming, he found
that the car park adjacent to the beach cost £2 a day, while the car park at
the top of the hill overlooking the beach cost 30p for the first two hours and
10p for each subsequent hour. He drove uncertainly from one to the other
before settling for the first, adjacent to the beach. He found it was full, so he
had to go to the hilltop car park anyway.

That sort of elementary dilemma is typical of the situations managers
face and is the reason why we combined problem-solving and decision-
making in a single chapter. Although Crawford could 'quantify' his decision to some extent by calculating how long he would stay, other aspects of
the situation could not be so readily assessed: How long would it take him to
walk down the hill? How long to walk back up? How tired would he be after
swimming? Would he still find a space on the beach if he parked on the
hilltop? Did he want to come back to the car before the end of his visit?
Could he park in the shade? Many managerial dilemmas have so many
considerations that there is only the time or effort available to resolve the
question on the basis of balancing one or two. Also the decision to be made
is often similar to tossing a coin. It is difficult to see that one alternative is
markedly better than the other; so why not toss a metaphorical coin rather
than spend hours calculating? Finally, there is not always a choice available, because of some external constraint that was not initially apparent.

There are problems, of course, which do not require subsequent action
for their solution, such as crosswords or quiz games, but they are of less
relevance in management. Managers good at solving these types of conun-
drums and brain-teasers are not necessarily those good at the action and
change implied by problems requiring decision-making. The well-known
'lateral thinking' proponent De Bono (1985) suggests that a more action-
based problem-solving is often done by employees on their way up the
hierarchy, whilst the job of senior managers is to practise the more strategic
and conceptual thinking associated with larger-scale decisions. Whichever
way you look at the different types of problems and decisions requiring the
manager's attention, it is clear that an organisation may need different

types of people to perform these different functions.

Managers need time to think, to deliberate and to conceptualise. Too often matters urgent drive out matters important. Problems are often solved by the easiest, most obvious and familiar route, when perhaps they should become opportunities for change. The manager is often concerned solely with the removal of risk rather than increased risk and workload. In this way, a bypassed opportunity may become a problem in itself some time in the future. The product group which reacts to lower profits by immediately reducing advertising spending is solving one problem in the short term by getting the books to appear more healthy, but may be creating more problems later, by which time events may be more difficult to put right. The high-risk solution may be to increase advertising expenditure in order to tap into a different potential market and increase turnover. This is not to say that all problems are more complex than they initially appear to be. There is often a temptation to change the pressing job to be done (implementing a straightforward decision) into a less pressing one (finding a different problem to solve). Making a few long-serving staff redundant at the same time as rationalising one part of the business may be the obvious, albeit painful, solution to a changed business environment. Redoubling the number of working parties, consultations and market research in order to avoid any redundancies may achieve nothing and may be very costly. Part of the art of management is not to see problems where they do not exist, and not to dither so that something that is straightforward becomes problematical through prevarication.

It will be obvious by now that this area of a manager's work is often the least easy to describe. Problem-solving is rarely a spectacular or exciting activity, but it is one that is ignored at the organisation's peril. Success in decision-making can rarely be guaranteed, but there is scope for improving our ability to avoid failure.

Review Topic 7.1

John Adair (1985), suggests that 'thinking is the preliminary work of weighing up the pros and cons for each course of action. A decisive person is one who has the power to stop thinking and start acting. How do you stop yourself thinking and start yourself acting?

CRISES, PROBLEMS AND OPPORTUNITIES

Mintzberg, Raisingham and Theoret (1976) provide a helpful distinction between crises, problems and opportunities facing managers. A *crisis* is a sudden, unexpected event requiring immediate action. The canteen is burned to the ground, someone makes a bid for the company equity, the marketing director resigns, or some similar quite unexpected event requires a rapid decision or set of decisions. A *problem* is something of which there is warning in that it becomes apparent gradually, through clues from various sources, and is not initially clear-cut. Examples would be poor morale among the staff of the organisation, the influence of a competitor, or uncertainty about product quality. An *opportunity* is the chance to do something that is created by a single event and often needing swift action (opportunities are 'grasped' or 'seized' rather than 'taken', or 'missed' rather than 'ignored'). A small change in tax laws provides opportunities for the person shrewd enough to see how that can be exploited, a spell of bad weather provides an opportunity to sell umbrellas. Crises often also provide opportunities, and some languages use the same word for both. The example of the crisis caused by the resignation of the marketing director may provide an opportunity for reshaping the organisation and distribution of responsibilities.

Crisis, problem and opportunity all have in common the need for a decision to be made and all are *unprogrammed decisions* that are not dealt with by routine, procedure or habit. Some events that have all the hallmarks of crisis can be classified as *programmed decisions* in that they have been anticipated and the appropriate action prescribed. If a factory catches fire and is destroyed, the managers will have moved through a series of programmed decisions, as there will have been a procedure to be followed in the case of fire. When those procedures prove inadequate to prevent the disaster, there is a whole series of unprogrammed decisions to be taken. Most people have plans to deal with the onset of misfortune, but few have procedures to deal with the aftermath if the preventive routines fail.

REACTING TO PROBLEMS

We have seen that problems become apparent rather than suddenly popping up in sharp outline and this requires a manager to make a preliminary decision about how to react to the emerging problem. If it is spotted early; what should be done now? There are various choices:

1. *Dealing with it.* In most cases managers will deal with the problem themselves, by finding out further information, pondering it, defining the problem more clearly and deciding between alternative ways of dealing with it.
2. *Passing it on.* Just because a manager perceives a problem, it does not necessarily have to be dealt with. It may lie outside their competence and responsibility, so that things may be made much worse if the manager tries to deal with it. It can be passed to a superior if it is too big to be dealt with, it can be delegated to a subordinate if the subordinate will have better detailed knowledge of the situation and will thus be able

to handle it more effectively (as well as being resentful if the problem is taken away); or it could be passed to a peer, elsewhere in the organisation. Deciding what to refer is a matter of nice judgement.

A general rule of thumb appears to be that one passes down as many as possible and passes up as few as possible:

> When confronted with an important problem requiring a decision, a manager must determine if he or she is responsible for making the decision. Here is a general rule that can be of help: The closer to the origin of a problem the decision is made, the better. This rule has two corollaries: (a) Pass as few decisions as possible to those higher up, and (b) pass as many as possible to those lower down. Usually, those who are closest to a problem are in the best position to decide what to do about it. (Stoner, 1982, page 168)

Referring a problem to a peer elsewhere in the organisation can be seen as avoiding proper responsibility, but failing to do it can cause ructions. An example might be dealing with the problem of an employee who is suspected of stealing. Should this be done by the immediate superior, or should it be referred to the security people or to the personnel department? If it is referred to security and the suspicion is groundless the working relationship with the suspect has probably been destroyed. If it is not referred and the suspected employee then has time to remove confidential documents of great value to a competitor, then the manager has contributed to that loss by negligence.

3. *Taking advice.* A variation of the first alternative is for managers to deal with the problem themselves, but defer action until advice is taken from those with specialist knowledge or skills that help to understand the problem. This can also be preliminary to deciding to refer the problem elsewhere.

4. *Working party.* Remitting a problem to a working party or similar group for consideration is fraught with difficulties and dangers. The issue can be 'blown up out of all proportion' and made more difficult to deal with rather than easier. Despite this, there are clearly situations in which a complex problem can only be approached satisfactorily by convening a group of people with varied expertise to examine the matter from different perspectives, providing that they all have the degree of commitment that will obviously be needed to solve what is such a difficult problem.

One of the critical factors in successful companies identified by Thomas Peters and Robert Waterman was a 'bias for action'. They suggest that in big companies the all-too-reasonable and rational response to complexity is to co-ordinate things, study them, form committees, ask for more data. Over-complex systems make companies unresponsive. Successful companies do have working parties for specific problem-solving and decision-making tasks, but they are 'task forces that last five days, have a few members, and result in line operators doing something differently, rather than the thirty-five person task force that lasts eighteen months and produces a 500-page report'. (Peters and Waterman, 1982, page 120.) Many organisations (whether commercial companies or non-profit making units such as schools) are increasingly holding working party discussions off-site, in some other congenial location. By convening a discussion group away from the hubbub, telephones and daily crises of the working place, problems are more easily concentrated on and a creative atmosphere more readily produced. Such activities must not be arranged indiscriminately, however. Unless some positive benefit is detected, the rest of the organisation will dismiss them merely as opportunities for a day off and a free lunch.

5. *Consultants.* Most managers at some time will find themselves acting as informal consultant to colleagues struggling with a problem. Increasingly, however, companies are formally calling in external consultants to help with problem-solving within the organisation. The effectiveness of these experts is heavily dependent on how well thought-out are their terms of reference. The managers calling in such outside agencies should decide beforehand whether they wish the consultants to be sounding-boards, thereby helping the managers reach an understanding of the problem and reach their own conclusion. Alternatively (and there is a continuum in between these two), the consultants may be called upon to provide their own expert knowledge, so that it is the consultant who identifies options, sets criteria and makes recommendations for action. A competent consultant will probably use a mixture of techniques, depending on the balance of the remit. Sometimes probing and listening is the best thing, sometimes recommending or prescribing is appropriate.

6. *Ignore it.* An even more 'dangerous strategy' for a problem is to ignore it on the assumption that something will turn up to deal with the difficulty or that the passage of time will make it obsolete. This seems to most enthusiastic managers a shabby strategy and not facing up to the demands of the job. It is interesting, however, to think of what happens when you go on holiday. During your absence a number of problems will emerge and when you return you find that some of them have been dealt with by other people, but only because you were away. Other problems await your urgent attention, and others have stopped being problems at all. Managers will not survive long if they ignore all the problems that occur, but with some it is a wise strategy to leave the matter to resolve itself.

THE PROBLEM-SOLVING PROCESS

Table 7.1 illustrates a straightforward problem-solving process and is adapted from Stoner (1982). There are four stages.

Stage one. Definition and diagnosis

As problems emerge, rather than presenting themselves with sudden, sharp clarity, they first need to be defined. Is it the right problem? Is declining sales turnover a problem of pricing, or quality, or delivery times, or poor advertising, or an inappropriate product line, or something else? Getting to the correct problems among various possibilities is the first aspect of definition. The second is to question whether it is a problem at all. A taken-for-granted assumption in management circles for many years was that one should try to reduce staff turnover; if a large proportion of the employees left the organisation this was 'a bad thing'. The assumption was underpinned by calculating joining costs, leaving costs, training costs, advertising costs and so on. Although these could be calculated and added up to provide a hefty sum, there was no consideration that turnover among staff employees could also avoid some people lingering on in dissatisfaction, could introduce new blood, could save on payroll costs through having some people at the bottom of pay scales instead of everyone being at the top, and could open up career opportunities for younger employees. Changes in the labour market have recently tended to produce an opposite assumption: that turnover is much needed to prevent a growing sense of frustration. The most useful approach to defining a problem correctly is to assess it in terms of what the organisation is trying to achieve and the extent to which the

Table 7.1 The problem-solving process

Stage one	Stage two	Stage three	Stage four
Definition and diagnosis	Generating alternatives	Deciding between alternatives	Implementation
Define problem	Generate alternative solutions	Consider available resources	Check availability of resources
Test definition	Defer judgement	Evaluate alternatives	Check understanding of those involved
Specify appropriate solution		Select most appropriate	Implement
			Monitor

(Adapted from Stoner, 1982, p. 170)

achievement of those objectives is being hindered by the existence of the supposed problem.

Review Topic 7.2

Small, everyday decisions are often of the 'Yes, let's . . .' or 'No, I think not . . .' type.
How many small decisions did you make yesterday at work and at home?
How many big decisions did you take, affecting future action over the next six months?

If the problem can be satisfactorily defined, it is then necessary to determine what would be an appropriate solution. If, despite the comment in the last paragraph, staff turnover is accurately defined as being too high, what would be a satisfactory solution? An example could be where a department has an establishment of fifty posts and an annual turnover of 200 per cent, made up like this:

Total number of posts	50
Semi-permanent job holders	25
Unsettled job holders, each staying an average of only three months	100

There is an underlying stability of 50 per cent, as twenty-five of the posts are held by people whose attachment to the company is settled. Without defining the problem satisfactorily the solution may be inappropriate, such as blanket attempts to persuade everyone to stay longer. These could be wasteful and might unsettle the semi-permanent job holders, who had not previously realised there was anything wrong. What is the problem here? Do we want the short-stay employees all to stay a little longer, or some of them to stay a lot longer, or is it a reasonable mix already? If short-stay employees were to stay for an average of six months instead of three, labour turnover would halve. If ten of the short-stay employees were to become semi-permanent and the remaining fifteen posts still occupied by people staying only three months, the turnover would drop to 120 per cent. Different strategies would be involved according to how the problem was defined. It is always necessary to diagnose what has caused a problem by obtaining information, analysing it and – probably – discussing it with others.

Review Topic 7.3

One of G.K. Chesterton's characters remarked that 'it isn't that they can't see the solution, it is that they can't see the problem'. What techniques can be used to prevent this happening?

By now the manager knows the problem, what is wanted is to achieve a solution and know how the problem has been caused. Now on to stage two.

Stage two. Generating alternatives

The more complex the problem is, the more alternative solutions there are likely to be. The more intractable a problem has proved to be, the more alternative solutions are needed for consideration. The second stage is one of looking for alternative strategies, possibly using the brainstorming method, or one of the other techniques that have been devised. One system is that of the Americans Kepner and Tregoe (1982) who first promulgated their method in 1965. Better known is the lateral thinking approach, described by Edward de Bono (1982) which enables people to generate new ideas and to escape from old ones by attempting radically different methods of thinking and approaches. He proffers an intriguing example:

> In a singles knock-out tennis tournament, there are 111 entrants. What is the minimum number of matches that must be played? It is easy enough to start at the beginning and to work out how many first-round matches there must be, and how many byes. But this takes time. . . . Instead of considering the players trying to win, consider the losers after they have lost. There is one winner and 110 losers. Each loser can lose only once. So there must be 110 matches. (de Bono, 1982, page 7)

Lateral thinking claims to do more than develop alternative solutions to problems, it can be a useful approach at this phase of the problem-solving process.

It is important to defer judgement on which solution is best until a number have been propounded. If alternatives are considered as they emerge, that act of consideration and evaluation can inhibit the generation of more alternatives. Either there is an early commitment to one that sounds attractive, and the effort of shifting one's allegiance is too great, or subsequent alternatives are conceived within the constraint of meeting only the shortcomings of what has already been proposed.

Stage three. Deciding between alternatives

When a range of options have been laid on the table for consideration, there is the stage in the process of choosing between them. There are two interrelated questions to be asked for each alternative. Can we do it? Will it work? First is the question of whether or not the strategy can be put into operation with the resources that are available. Many possibilities cannot be used because there is not the time, or manpower, or finance to mount them. Also some strategies might tackle the problem but cause others, equally or more serious. The second question of whether or not a proposal will work concerns whether or not it meets the criteria set in stage one of being an appropriate solution to the problem defined.

Sometimes there is a clearly preferred solution that is not immediately apparent, but which becomes unequivocally right through the problem-solving process. More often there are a number of inadequate solutions and the decision between alternatives is much more difficult.

Stage four. Implementation

Because problem-solving is fun, people often lose interest once the nut is cracked, just as many of the people who complete crossword puzzles cannot be bothered to send up for the prize. The road to bankruptcy is paved with the gravestones of those who solved problems beautifully, but did not make the solutions work. Aspects of implementation are making sure that the necessary resources are available and that those who are to be involved in the implementation understand what they have to do and will do it. Later the managerial problem-solver has to monitor developments to see if the solution is working. Unless the solution to the problem was so obvious that the ratiocination described here was superfluous, there must be a good chance that the solution will be different from that anticipated; so the monitoring of implementation and its effects is essential.

AIDS TO PROBLEM-SOLVING

A problem-solving technique which many companies, including Wedgwood, IBM and STC, have successfully used is *quality circles*. This is where small departmental groups of five to ten volunteers meet regularly, primarily in order to resolve quality-related problems in that department. They look, not at large-scale problems, but those niggling local issues which are within members' scope to resolve but about which management may not be aware. Members need to be trained regularly in data collection methods, presentation and meeting skills. The group may use brainstorming techniques to generate ideas. The types of solutions this type of group might generate could include identifying some paperwork in the accounts department which was lessening its effectiveness, re-siting the riveting machine in a finishing unit to facilitate movement and flow, or rationalising quality-sampling techniques in a continuous flow process whilst still ensuring top quality.

Some problems can be solved by mathematical modelling, providing that all the significant variables can be isolated and analysed in order to determine the optimum solution. One of the best known techniques of this type is the formula for determining an *economic order quantity*, so that material for steadily moving stock is ordered at the frequency and in the quantities that are most economical and efficient. The method of doing this is shown in Carter (1982, page 136).

DECISION-MAKING

Many decisions that managers have to make are limited in their problematic component, and the challenge is not the intellectual question of what should be done, but other questions such as: Who should decide? What will be the reaction of the employees? How do we make it work? It is important to emphasise the aspect of decision-making that requires confidence, courage and skill in winning commitment from others. An elementary rule is that people will support that which they have helped to create, and this proposition supports the process of consultation and participation, but not all decisions are susceptible to such treatment. When action must be taken quickly, there is no time for consultation and a need for someone to say firmly 'We will do this'. When decisions are going to be unpopular, some aspects may require consultation and others may call for straight executive action. An example might be the decision to close a factory, which has within it a series of components. There is first the business decision that the factory is to be closed because demand for the product has collapsed or because the costs are too high. There is the employment decision about what should happen about the employees generally, and there is the set of individual decisions about each employee personally. There is usually extensive consultation about the second of those three and less about the first and third.

Aids to decision-making

One useful aid to decision-making is the *decision tree*. A decision tree is a means of displaying the flow of possible courses of action in the form of a branching network. A large decision is broken up into a series of smaller decisions which can be made more easily, by examining the expected benefit at each decision point. The advantage of a decision tree is that it helps managers lay out familiar information in a manner which leads to systematic analysis, and consequently better decisions. It is not a method which provides definitive answers, but it clarifies the issues on which a decision will finally have to be made. A decision tree could, for example, be used to help the production and purchasing managers decide whether to make a spare part within the factory, or to buy it in ready-made outside.

Another very simple, but effective, decision-making aid is the *checklist*. A list is made of all the factors which might be important to, or have an influence upon, the decision. The problem is thus given shape, and potentially important dimensions are highlighted. Checklists may be made more sophisticated by ascribing relative values to the different factors: for example is return on investment more important than market size and if so, how much more important? An example of a checklist is given in Chapter 12.

In addition to paper and pencil techniques, there are many *computerised decision support systems* available. They are systematic devices which co-ordinate data, models and statistical techniques and turn them into a basis for action. Their main advantage is that they are interactive, allowing the managers to apply their judgement at various points whilst taking the drudgery out of the mathematical calculations. An example could be a computer programme which helps line managers identify the recruitment patterns or training activities needed to provide the skills which it is estimated the organisation will require in, say, five years' time. As with many of the aids above, they do not make the actual decision but they do help to make the elements of the decision clearer.

Review Topic 7.4

Try jotting down factors you consider important to your family in the decision about the location of your next summer holiday.

Most decisions require the manager to come to terms with uncertainty, to cope with it, to eliminate it wherever possible, and to live with it efficiently when not possible. *Good quality information* can help lessen uncertainty. Any decision involves making a choice between alternatives, and is accompanied by attendant risk regarding the consequences of any action. Avoiding making a decision does not, in most cases, eliminate this risk, it merely ignores it. The decision-maker must weigh up the costs of each alternative against the benefits by selecting a solution that gives the optimum pay-off. Information is thus an essential decision-making tool.

Decision-making is rarely a totally rational process. Emotion, power politics, the influence of others, individual values, the search for a satisfactory compromise, lack of time, the pressure of action – all these work against the manager following a systematic decision-making path. Logical processes can indeed help with unblocking a problem, as we have tried to show in this chapter; so can creativity exercises; equally, asserts John Adair (1985), can that sixth sense, *intuition*. He says (page 99): 'Encourage intuition in yourself. Become more aware of it. Be more receptive to its often faint whisper. Always subject it, however, to evaluation. Granted that safeguard, intuition can save you a great deal of time in decision making.' Intuition is no substitute for information but can sometimes save the day in situations when information is limited, uncertainties abound, time is short and when the penalties for getting it wrong are not severe.

Review Topic 7.5

Wrong decisions are often made, not due to stupidity, carelessness or ignorance, but due to the way information is handled. Can you think of a problem you tackled in recent weeks, the solution to which you would now, with hindsight,

change? Could you have had access to any information which would have improved that decision at the time? Why was it not available to you?

PLANNING

Another activity which involves decision-making is planning. If managers are to lead working teams, they must know where they are heading. They must constantly be thinking ahead and deciding what goals to aim for and the best means of reaching them. However, planning is not extensively used in practice. Managers tend to feel dominated by plans, especially when they are prepared by someone else. If there is too much planning, people feel hemmed in and they lack scope to deviate or express individuality. Initiative is hampered because unplanned activities are not regarded as legitimate. Planning must therefore be used as a framework, not as a straitjacket. When things do not go according to plan, the plan must be re-appraised and changed if necessary. Without any sort of plan whatsoever, the organisation is reactive rather than proactive, and opportunities may be overlooked and lost.

Various elementary aids to planning include the following:

1. *Gantt charts*. These are visual displays of the planned order of activities over a period which allow for continuous monitoring and control. Such a chart may, for example, be used for scheduling jobs to be assigned to individual production employees.
2. *Network planning*. This identifies the chain of events that will determine the overall length of an activity. This 'critical path' can then receive special attention to ensure that things go according to plan. A sample critical path diagram appears in Putting It Into Practice.
3. *Linear programming*. This is a tool widely used in operations research to decide how scarce resources should be allocated to keep costs at a minimum or to maximise return, especially in areas such as production planning and transport logistics. A simple graphic method may be used to show clearly the relationship between two variables to non-numerically minded colleagues. Where the factors of a problem are more complex, solutions based on more sophisticated linear programming techniques using matrix algebra, such as the Simplex Method, have to be used. These methods are highly repetitive and highly suited to computerisation.
4. *Goal planning*. This is a simple device which avoids the difficulty of splendid ideas being too difficult actually to put into practice. See Chapter 8, Putting It Into Practice which shows how the method is developed.

Other methods of operational planning include *milestone planning* and *time series analysis*. All these techniques are aids to decision-making. They provide the manager with procedures for the processing of data and the application of judgement. The chief value of techniques such as critical path analysis is that it encourages managers and their teams to set out a situation in such a way as to permit thorough examination of the problem, and the effect of possible solutions and outcomes. Information has to be collected from all sources likely to be engaged in the activity and then fitted together. In this way, project and people are bound together in a flow of information-gathering and feedback that in itself will lead to better planning. Operational plans should not be locked away in the manager's desk. They should be openly displayed on the office wall or workshop noticeboard and continuously updated. In this way, supervisors and staff will develop confidence in the plans and their relationship to their actual work.

PROBLEMS, DECISIONS, PLANNING AND THE COMPUTER

Increasingly, the complex problems facing managers can be passed through other channels for initial evaluation. The range of mathematical models and computer applications is such that specialist departments or those with specific management information functions can handle the variables in the first instance, thus presenting their colleagues with a summarised statement of the situation. These managers are then able to deploy their judgement, intuition, experience, political nous, courage or simple authority to decide on the interpretation of the information and the subsequent action to be taken. This requires managers to define and formulate their problems in precise terms for their advisors or their desktop computers, which may well be one of the major benefits of the computer in management.

The most elegant models and sophisticated statistics can, however, become the purpose of the exercise rather than tools to be used in achieving the purpose. There is now available in organisations a wealth of data and much opportunity to manipulate that data. If handled sensibly, management planning and decision-making should become more effective in this environment; if not, such facilities may reduce management to an unwieldly game of figures and scenarios. There is little point having elaborate plans if there is no monitoring, or if problem-solving and decision-making are neglected. The most brilliant plans are of no value if there is inadequate will to make them happen. People will only commit themselves to what they believe to be right and worthy, with a reasonable chance of success. The more a decision or a plan requires people to see things in a fresh light and to alter their familiar ways of working, the more difficult they will be to convince, no matter what the computer printout says.

SUMMARY PROPOSITIONS

7.1 Thinking is an essential part of problem-solving and decision-making, but not to excess. Many decisions for managers to make are simple, requiring speed, firmness and conviction rather than careful analysis to find the right answer.

7.2 Alternative ways of reacting to a problem are dealing with it, passing it on, taking advice, referring to a working party, or ignoring it.

7.3 The four stages of the problem-solving process are definition and diagnosis, generating alternatives, deciding between alternatives and implementation.

7.4 Techniques such as decision trees, checklists, computerised decision support systems, good quality information and intuition are only decision *aids*, not decision *makers*.

7.5 There are many simple techniques that aid planning. It is important to know about and use these, but more important is to know when the planning and co-ordination of people, information and resources over a period of time is needed.

7.6 Planning should be the servant of the manager, not the master.

PUTTING IT INTO PRACTICE

Who should make the decisions?

Analysing where and at what level in the organisation decisions are made can tell you something about the prevalent culture of the organisation.
   Are decisions in your department made by:

1. The person with the highest power and authority?
2. The person whose job description carries the responsibility?
3. The people with the most knowledge and expertise about the problem?
4. The people most personally involved and affected by the outcome?

   Would you do it any differently?

                                                          (Adapted from Handy, 1981)

The four steps in planning

1. *Goals*. What are you trying to do? What objectives are you trying to reach? What are the priorities? Without asking and answering this type

of basic question there is a danger of trying to achieve too much and of uncertainty in execution. It is only if goals are brought into reasonable focus that managers can deploy resources effectively. This is particularly important where resources are scarce or time is short.

Sally Ann Nield was a social worker having great difficulty in coping with her workload, so that there were many complaints and she was suffering considerable strain. Her section leader asked her to sort out her priorities so that she could clear some of the backlog. Sally Ann could not acknowledge that any one activity took preference over any other. She was not willing to concentrate on the preparation of social enquiry reports for a day if that meant deferring something else. As a result her affairs became even more muddled and she eventually left the career for which she had trained.

2. *The present position.* How far are you now from reaching the goals you have identified? What resources are available? This definition of the starting position and state of readiness begins to eliminate those features of operations that are not a problem and to direct attention to those areas where action is needed.

3. *Aids and hindrances.* What factors can help to achieve the goals and what might cause problems? This is scanning the future to see what is likely to change the present position for better or worse. When General Eisenhower was planning the D-Day landings in the Second World War, a crucial factor was the weather. He and his advisors had the most detailed and comprehensive weather reports they could obtain, but so did the Germans. The significance of judgement (and perhaps of luck) in the implementation of plans was shown by the fact that both sides knew the weather was expected to remain clear, but not for long. General Eisenhower decided that the landings must therefore proceed before the weather broke. His counterpart on the other side of the Channel, Field Marshal von Rundstedt decided that the allied landings would be postponed until the weather improved.

4. *The plan.* The final step is to work out alternative series or programmes of action and eventually choose the one that seems most appropriate as a way of reaching the objective, taking account of the opening situation and the way in which the future is expected to develop. This activity often has contributory elements for verification, like test marketing, design prototypes, computer simulations and other ways of trying out the plan to test the likelihood of it being successful.

The critical path diagram

The responsibility for drawing up a planning schedule in diagrammatic form will rest with a few people. Copies of the diagram are distributed, however, along with work orders, to all supervisors and all those involved in the project should know what is represented.

Sub-tasks which are necessary to complete a project are called activities and each activity is represented by an arrow to indicate whether it is consecutive or concurrent. For example

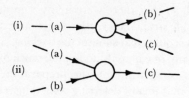

Fig. 7.1 Consecutive and concurrent activities in a diagram.

Fig. 7.1 (i) means that (a) must finish before (b) and (c) can start, and Fig. 7.1 (ii) means that (a) and (b) must be completed before (c) can start. The point in time when a specific activity is commenced or finished is called an event, represented by a circle indicating the end of one activity and the start of another. Events are numbered in order to identify activities.

Example. If we were to take a 'simple' problem, such as buying and moving into a house, we would identify the activities, determine their logical sequence and interdependence, assign times to each activity and then draw the critical path diagram. The result may look something like Fig. 7.2 (timings omitted).

Fig. 7.2 A simple diagram.

Activity

1–2 Decide the price and type of house.

1–3 Decide the area where it is to be situated.

3–4 Inspect different houses.

4–5 Make and obtain acceptance of an offer.

5–6 Obtain a mortgage.

6–7 Apply for gas, electricity, phone services.

6–8 Measure house for carpets, curtains.

6–9 Exchange contracts.

7–10 Services arranged.

8–10 Buy carpets, curtains.
9–10 Complete contract.
10–11 Move in.

The critical path is identified only after the 'float' for each activity has been calculated. Float is spare time, the excess of available time over necessary time for each activity. The critical path is the path which has the least float. The process of calculating floats is explained in most books which examine critical path analysis in detail.

REFERENCES

Adair, J., *Effective Decision Making*, Pan Books, London, 1985.
de Bono, E., *Tactics: The Art and Science of Success*, Fontana, 1986.
de Bono E., *Lateral Thinking for Management*, Penguin Books, Harmondsworth, 1982.
Carter, R., *Business Administration*, Heinemann, London, 1982.
Handy, C.B., *Understanding Organisations*, Penguin Books, Harmondsworth, 1981.
Kepner, C.H. and Tregoe, B.B., *The Rational Manager: a Systematic Approach to Problem Solving and Decision Making*, McGraw Hill, Maidenhead, 1982.
Mintzberg, H.A., Raisingham, D. and Theoret, A., 'The structure of "unstructured" decision processes', in *Administrative Science Quarterly*, June 1976, pages 246–75.
Peters, T.J. and Waterman, R.H., *In Search of Excellence*, Harper & Row, New York, 1982.
Stoner, J.A.F., *Management*, 2nd edn, Prentice Hall, Englewood Cliffs, 1982.

8

MANAGING CHANGE

Change is one of the catchwords of the 1980s, and an ability to manage change is a prime requirement of management success. To some people, change means excitement and the thrill of being part of the action and keeping up with trends. For others, change feels like a threatening, imposed dismantling of the stable order of things with a great deal of uncertainty which is frightening. The common saying is that change is now an everyday part of our lives. There is a useful distinction between four broad types of change experience.

First is *imposition*, where the initiative comes from someone else and we have to alter our ways of doing things to comply with this external requirement. This undermines our sense of security in being able to handle what we know, and we worry about the implications of what is now required. The initiative comes from someone else, so that we can only respond, and our response will be limited because someone else has already set the parameters. New rules, new laws, changes in working practices are all examples of this category.

Second is *adaptation*, where we have to change our behaviour or our attitudes at the behest of others. Acquiring different attitudes can be extremely difficult, as the persistence of racial prejudice demonstrates, and we are likely to feel uncertainty about our ability to become the new type of person. This is probably the main reason people retire early, as they lack the confidence to change the values and behaviours in which they have come to trust.

In contrast, *growth* is much more attractive. Now we are not responding to the demands of others, but to the opportunities for becoming a person of greater competence, poise and achievement.

The fourth type of change experienced is *creativity*, where we are the instigator and in control of the process, bringing into being that which we have envisaged. Most of us are probably resistant to the first, uncertain about the second, delighted with the third and excited by the fourth. Whoever is pulling the strings is most likely to overcome the difficulties of one and two by ensuring that three comes first!

Whether we are trying to get others to change, helping others to handle change, or trying to cope with change ourselves, it is worth taking some time to think it through. We need to think about what needs changing and how the change is to be implemented.

Review Topic 8.1

The philosophers have only interpreted the world in various ways, the point is to change it.

Karl Marx, 1818–1883.

Why is it difficult to move from analysis to action?

WHY CHANGE?

The first indications to some that change is necessary are that things do not seem to be working quite as well as they used to. Too much time is spent patching up, filling in or dealing with crises. For example, the biscuit production line which is constantly stopping or over-flowing onto the floor needs something changing. The hotel receptionist who finds rooms over-booked on several occasions clearly needs to change something. The Deputy Headteacher who is at school from 7.30 in the morning until 7.00 at night at least three days a week might want to change something to get life better balanced. These indicate changes that an individual might initiate.

Another indication of change ahead is the rumblings heard in head office, the community, parliament, at conferences or from customers. Gradually it is felt something should be done and guidelines are issued, codes of practice agreed on or laws passed. For example, laws passed on the sort of polyurethane that can be used in furniture will mean changes for manufacturers and importers. Codes of practice about late night opening before Christmas mean changes for shop workers and their managers. New customs arrangements with the EEC mean understanding the guidelines about the new documentation and ensuring that everyone involved also understands them. The public services particularly have to deal with this imposed change and decisions are taken at a political level about such matters as the content of education in schools, priorities for the health services or whether money is to be spent on nuclear or conventional weapons for the armed forces. All of these imposed changes need careful implementation as they invariably meet resistance where people have not been involved in deciding what to change.

A third reason for expecting change is the desire to keep up to date with new products and services to offer as old ones become outdated. A much quoted model of the life of a product is that developed by the Boston Consulting Group which is well described in Stewart (1983, pages 19–24), see Fig. 8.1.

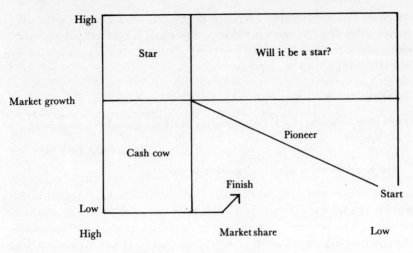

Fig. 8.1 The product life cycle.

Products start off from innovation and creativity (see Chapter 16) with not a lot at stake at the pioneer stage. The next stage is a question mark to indicate whether it is a future star or not and is at the risk-taking stage. The third stage is when there is rapid growth in the market and the product is a star. The fourth stage is when the product has an established position in the market but is no longer increasing its share of the market. The final stage is when the product makes little money and has no further prospects. Each stage requires a different sort of managing in order to anticipate a different sort of change ahead.

Review Topic 8.2

The most striking of all impressions I have formed since I left London a month ago is of the strength of this African national consciousness . . . The wind of change is blowing through this continent.

Harold Macmillan, 3 February 1960, Cape Town

Why is acknowledging that change is inevitable so difficult for well-established people and organisations?

WHAT NEEDS CHANGING?

Whatever the reason for change, deciding what has to be changed is often a difficult step. Because the how of change is seen as complicated, the what is often given less attention. For example, what needs to change in the biscuit production problem may be because of technical difficulties with the conveyor belt, such as rollers being worn out or mis-matched with the new ovens, or the operators are not following the correct procedure for mixing the ingredients so the biscuits are too brittle and, consequently, fall off more easily. Or the staff may feel aggrieved over the new shift system and not be as vigilant as previously about problems on the line. Similarly, the hotel receptionist may need to improve the booking system, the percentage of 'no-shows' may need to be worked out again and reassessed or the staff may need training to fill in the official booking forms, not just give over keys. The Deputy Headteacher may need to assess the work in a day and what is being done that does not need to be done, what can be done by others and what are the priorities of the job.

All these are examples of the fact that any reason for change may need several things changing. There may be *technical* changes required in the product, machinery or building. There may be changes in the *systems* of procedure, monitoring, communication, budgeting required. Changes in the *organisation* of the department or unit may be necessary. There may also be changes necessary in our *personal* beliefs, behaviour or work. We also need to decide whether we want more, different or better of these and whether that is possible.

HOW TO COPE WITH CHANGE

In Chapter 4 we mentioned how the work of managers is a balance between those activities that give us comfort and those that give us novelty. The stimulation of novelty and change usually means we put more effort into something. However, if the stimulation becomes too great we become less able to make a useful contribution. This can be summarised graphically, see Fig. 8.2. It is at this point that stress is experienced with all the feelings of increased ambiguity and the possibility of failure is seen.

Toffler as long ago as 1970 recognised that we can cope with a lot of change, pressure, complexity and confusion if at least one area of our lives is

Fig. 8.2 Effect of stimulation and effort.

relatively stable. He suggested these stability zones were all important. The main kinds of stability zones are as follows:

1. Ideas   – moral, religious, political.
2. Places   – home, town, pub, offices.
3. People   – spouse, parents, old college friends.
4. Organisations   – rotary, church, employer.
5. Things and habits   – routines, possessions, cars.

We all need at least one of these secure. Working out where our stability zones are and maintaining them helps to cope with stress in other areas. For example, the salesperson who enjoys travel, new food, new ideas, new films, books and people, who is impatient with tradition and seeks novelty, often has been in the same job for years or has a group of long-lasting friends or a good, close marriage.

Ed Schein (1978) has coined the phrase *career anchors* to suggest that there are distinct categories of stability zone at work that individuals will evaluate themselves on. Each of us will have one of these as most important in our lives. The five career anchors are:

1. *Managerial competence.* Individuals seek out and value opportunities to manage. They have a strong motivation to rise to positions of managerial responsibility.
2. *Technical/functional competence.* People enjoy the technical activity, for example, finance, engineering, marketing, nursing.
3. *Security.* The anchor for some who look for a stable career situation, job security, a decent income and a reasonable pension.
4. *Creativity.* For those who want to build something entirely their own such as a new product, process, theory, company and fortune.
5. *Autonomy and independence.* People value being free from constraints and pursue their own life and work style.

Stewart (1983, pages 108–12) suggests various strategies for keeping one's balance during a time of rapid and unsettling change.

1. Know what to keep stable, for example, stability zones.
2. Calm one's physiology for controlling the pace at which we work and using the pause by breathing slowly for a second or two. Meditation can help here.
3. Ask for help. It can bring new insights, new companionship, new learning. Beware of becoming an advice junkie who never gets to the action, but advice from one or two carefully chosen people can either tell you what to do or so clarify the problem the solutions suggest themselves.

HOW TO MAKE CHANGES

How to get changes effected is the concern of most managers. Sometimes it is to get imposed changes accepted. Sometimes it is to get agreement that change is necessary but the solution is still to be found. Sometimes it is persuading individuals to change their ways to comply with the norms of the organisation. As Pettigrew (1985) argues, change is not just a rational choice of events but has to be seen in its cultural and historical context. His study of ICI suggests that a sequence of episodes was involved in the dramatic changes at ICI:

1. There were rational arguments for change with a concentration on political influencing of events.
2. There was an emphasis on efficiency whose advocates became powerful.
3. There were exceptional men who were able to foresee what ICI needed and persuade people to follow them.
4. There were extreme circumstances of plants being outmoded.
5. There was the untidiness of chance events, people, materials, resources and circumstances generally.
6. There were the forces in the environment such as economic and political climate, oil prices, competitors building/closing plants, legislation effecting pollution and health.

Pettigrew argues that change occurs because of a mixture of these; the problem is gaining legitimacy for the change proposed.

He suggests (page 434) a model for effecting change:

1. The development of concern by a subset of the organisation.
2. Acknowledgement and understanding of the problems with possible causes and alternatives by others.
3. Planning and acting to create specific change.
4. Stabilising the change including rewards, information and power to appropriate individuals to sustain the change.

Review Topic 8.3

Change is not made without inconvenience, even from worse to better.
Samuel Johnson, 1709–84.

Detailed discussion about organisation level changes is in our chapter on policy making and strategy (Chapter 6), the specific arguments about technical changes are in our chapter on innovation and creativity (Chapter 15) and discussion about changing the behaviour of individual performers is in our chapter on staff development (Chapter 13).

INFLUENCING OTHERS TO CHANGE

How does one persuade those we work with to change in the desired way? The research literature suggests there are several questions that need to be answered.

What is in it for them?

If the person can see that the new behaviour, procedure, technology will make their work easier, more interesting, more fun, they are likely to be enthusiastic. If they cannot see any benefit they are likely to resist it; or they will appear to change in order to test it or show loyalty but the change disappears ere long. The chapter on motivation and influence (Chapter 17) has detailed evidence about the importance of meeting a felt need for people to want to act.

Have they had a say in the change?

If people help to create a new scheme they are more likely to be committed to making it work (see Chapter 11 for details). There needs to be a genuine opportunity to participate in the introduction, design, execution, feedback and evaluation of any and all aspects of the new programme. However, retaining the option not to change is rarely included in the consultation process. An example of sham consultation was a questionnaire sent to all members of a head office whose top managers had decided to re-locate. The questionnaire asked whether they would like to go to another central London, outer London, M4 corridor or North West location. They answered (a) domestically and (b) for the business. Seventy per cent wanted a London location domestically and fifty per cent a London location for the business. The planning permission for the new headquarters in the North West was published on the front page of a local North West paper the same month, suggesting that the decision had already been made. Is it surprising that senior staff wondered why staff felt abused!

Is it clear what change is envisaged?

If we are trying to persuade someone to change we need to have a clear vision of what we want to achieve. This vision needs to be practical, with a clear explanation about why, what and, possibly, how, it is to be done. It needs to be put in terms that are understood by the other. Too often a rather confused picture is given because the change is not well thought out. This is perfectly sensible if the other person is to be included in deciding if a change is necessary and if so, what. It is quite inappropriate where the change is decided and we want to influence them to co-operate. Frequently we try to communicate an idea which is at the edge of our own understanding, particularly where the idea or change has been handed down from on high.

Are there guidelines for managing change?

There are lots of books and pamphlets giving guidelines on how to manage change. One we found useful is based on research in schools by Loucke-Horsley and Herger (1985) quoted by Fullan (1986, page 79). They base their guidelines on seven steps:

1. Establishing the project.
2. Assessment and goal setting.
3. Identifying a solution.
4. Preparing for implementation.
5. Implementing the project.
6. Reviewing progress and problems.
7. Maintenance and institutionalisation.

We discuss these processes further in Chapter 15. They give the following wise advice.

1. *Acting* is better than *planning*. Protracted needs assessment can be worse than none at all.
2. The Head is not *the* key to school improvement. Although the Head is important, so are many other people . . .
3. Thinking you can truly create ownership at the beginning of a project is ridiculous. Like trust, ownership and commitment build and develop over time through the actual work of improving a school.
4. Help and support given teachers after planning and initial training is much more crucial for success than the best (pre-implementation) training money can buy.
5. Coercion is not always bad. A firm push, coupled with lots of help, can launch a project on a path to success.
6. New programmes and practices imported from somewhere else may offer a viable, cost-effective . . . alternative to major development efforts.

SUMMARY PROPOSITIONS

8.1 Change may be imposed, to improve current performance, or to keep new products and services coming.

8.2 We may need to change the technical aspects, the systems, the organisation or our personal behaviour.

8.3 To cope with change ourselves we need to keep something stable.

8.4 Change is not just a rational process but involves the culture of the organisation.

8.5 To influence others to change we need to think what is in it for them.

PUTTING IT INTO PRACTICE

Drill for goal planning

1.   Decide what particular goal you want to achieve, or change you want to make.
2.   Write down the criteria you will use to judge whether the goal has been met.
3(a) Fill in the list 'Strengths and Needs' (see Table 8.1). Write these as concretely as possible so you can tell when you have met a need and it becomes a strength.
 (b) Goal.

Table 8.1 Strengths and needs

Strengths	Needs
1. Time	
2. Place	
3. Money	
4. Materials	
5. Co-operation of . . .	
6. Agreement of . . .	
7. Expertise	
8.	
9.	
10.	

4.   Take one of your needs that is particularly difficult to achieve. Break it down into smaller objectives on the form in Table 8.2.

Table 8.2 Goal planning analysis

Need			
Objective	Method	Target date	Date done

REFERENCES

Fullan, M.G., 'The management of change', in Hoyle, E. and McMahon, A. (eds), *The Management of Schools*, Kogan Page, London, 1986.

Loucke-Horsley, S. and Hergert, L.F., *An Action Guide to School Improvement*, Association for Supervision and Curriculum Development, Andover, Mass., 1985.

Pettigrew, A.M., *The Awakening Giant: Continuity and Change in ICI*, Blackwell, Oxford, 1985.

Schein, E.H., *Career Dynamics: Matching Individual and Organizational Needs*, Addison Wesley, Reading, Mass., USA, 1978.

Stewart, V., *Change the Challenge for Management*, McGraw Hill, London, 1983.

Toffler, A., *Future Shock*, Pan, London, 1970.

PART III

ORGANISATION AND EFFECTIVENESS

The effectiveness of the business will depend on the mechanisms through which the policies are put into action. The members of the organisation have to be deployed, and their activities co-ordinated, in a way which combines slick, administrative efficiency with methods that tap and make the most of the full human potential to breathe life and purpose into the systems. Organising the work to be done is one of the most fascinating of all the jobs a manager has to do.

9
ORGANISATION STRUCTURE AND CULTURE

A popular misconception of organisation structure is of integrated precision in human action:

> What you may expect to see – but don't – is an animated organisation chart – a pyramid of little boxes, each sitting astride seven others, and seven more under each of those seven, and seven more, and so on. Perhaps too, you expect to see each of the top boxes occupied by a faceless figure in a gray flannel uniform and the lower boxes occupied by figures, also faceless, in overalls. Each figure is busily pushing levers to make other figures turn and jump in unison until the whistle blows, when they all stop together. (Leavitt, Dill and Eyring, 1973, page 3)

For some this is a glimpse of nightmare, while for others it is a vision of perfection, taking the comfortable Victorian view of class structure – a place for everyone and everyone in place – and adding to it the feature of specialised, interlocking tasks.

There are difficulties about this view. First, it is not true; no organisation operates with that degree of mechanical precision. Secondly, attempts to achieve precision of that type are ineffective as employees are not sufficiently uniform in their abilities and experience to fit neatly into boxes and are seldom willing to be constrained to that degree. Thirdly, the rigidity of the arrangements inhibits change and makes the organisation inappropriate for new challenges from the environment and the opportunities provided by technological change.

In the 1970s distaste for the formal structure became so great that there was a tendency to throw the baby out with the bathwater as enthusiasm for anti-structure developed. Face-to-face relationships were to replace formal reporting as the norm and the purpose of the organisation was no more than to service the freewheeling activities of its members. That vogue has altered but the feasibility of the rigid structure has been shown as dubious. A more common view is now of structure as being necessary, but ideally sufficiently flexible as a system to enable bits of the structure to be altered or removed so that the remaining bits can adapt to change, rather than having the entire edifice collapse. There is much more emphasis on communication between people and groups in the structure, and an acknowledgement that it is the people in the structure, individually and collectively, who achieve results: procedures can do no more than enable people to achieve.

One feature of this change in emphasis has been to increase interest in organisational culture, the characteristic spirit and beliefs in an organisation, demonstrated, for instance, by the values held in common by all members on how people should treat each other, the nature of working relationships that should be developed and views of change. It is appreciated that features of the working environment like these have a more profound effect on people's behaviour than the formal structure of reporting relationships.

Managers pick up this idea of culture and apply it in two ways. First there is the approach epitomised by Handy (1985), which advocates understanding what the culture is so that you work with it rather than against it, using the strengths of the organisation to enable you. A second approach is to attempt to change an unproductive culture and make it more appropriate to the prevailing situation. Peters and Waterman (1982) and Schein (1985) have been used by managers in efforts to break out of a situation in which all action seemed to be bound by precedent, or inward-looking, or with strong feelings of them-and-us, alienation and lack of commitment. The new type of culture to be developed is likely to have 'requisite' values such as service to the customer, ready acceptance of innovation, high consensus and co-operation. The other features of culture that will deliver these requisites vary considerably, although openness, informality and social skill training are often common elements. The changes are likely to be brought about by an emphasis on leadership, although leadership is also being reconstructed, as we shall see in chapter 16. Trade union organisation is likely to be marginalised and life becomes uncomfortable for those who have lost – or never found – enthusiasm for the job.

THE ELEMENTS OF ORGANISATION STRUCTURE

Organising requires a combination of *differentiation* and *integration*. First, the arrangements for individuals' jobs have to be set up so as to differentiate what the job holder has to do from what everyone else is doing. Secondly, integration is achieved by co-ordinating the activities of individuals so that the total task of the business is undertaken satisfactorily.

Methods of differentiation and integration vary according to the predictability of what has to be done. Waiters in a restaurant have their activities integrated by a tightly specified system for taking orders from customers, passing those orders to the kitchen in strict sequence, taking completed orders to the table and then clearing the table. Their activities are differentiated by two definitions of territory. The kitchen is the territory of the chef, not the waiter, and each waiter has a set of tables to service. Their activities are further differentiated in their dealings with the customer, where they have considerable latitude to use personal, idiosyncratic social skills to persuade the customer to spend money, not complain, be quick and come again. The only uncertainty is the behaviour and reaction of the customer. In contrast, jobs in social work or marketing, for instance, have greater unpredictability and a constant flow of new problems. This type of situation produces frequent re-definition of job boundaries, great individual autonomy and a tendency to flexible networks of working relationships rather than rigid hierarchies. The four essential building blocks for organisations are *job descriptions, the structure of working relationships, decision-making complexes* and *operating procedures*, all of which can be used to ensure the attainment of objectives.

Job descriptions are not popular among managers, especially when they are contained in lengthy typewritten documents lost in filing cabinets, and all too often the job description is the epitome of stifling, irrelevant bureaucracy. However, each member of an organisation has a job to do and some understanding is needed, by themselves and their colleagues, of the content and boundaries of that job. Much is achieved by the job title. Titles like managing director, electrician, chef, telephonist, newsreader and window cleaner all describe what the job holder does in a way that will meet most organisational requirements. Other titles are less readily understood as descriptions of job content – despatcher, clerical assistant, organisation development adviser and manager, external relations, for instance. Also all jobs need some clarification at the boundary. What are the limits of responsibility held by this person? Do areas of influence overlap?

The job description is a problem for managers. It is a basic, essential requirement for allocating people to jobs and work to people in a way that can be understood and be used to avoid gaps and duplication, but there is always the risk that it becomes a restriction that people fight against or a defence behind which they hide when there is a need for change or when the unpredicted is encountered.

Review Topic 9.1

Why is the job description a problem for managers and how can the problem be overcome?

An excellent use of job descriptions is for a group of managers with interrelated jobs to write out their own, according to an agreed format, and then exchange copies with each other before meeting to discuss gaps and overlaps. This requires each one of them to work through the various parameters of their jobs and then explain aspects on which others ask for clarification. The draft documents will probably be thrown away after the discussion, but the process of which they have been the central part will have been invaluable in producing a mode of working that is more effective than any that could be achieved by other means.

The structure of *working relationships* is most commonly expressed in the organisation chart or 'family tree', which sets out the membership of the various working groups or departments and how they interconnect. This describes the hierarchy and the system, expressed by that hierarchy, for distributing power through the organisation. As a tool of old-fashioned 'classical' organisation theory it has been criticised as limiting the scope of individuals, emphasising subordination and rank and producing conformist, narrow thinking. It remains necessary to provide general guidance on where to find expertise and information, to legitimise the formal aspects of authority and to provide one of the means of resolving disagreements: the crossover point in the hierarchy. When two or more people cannot agree on a course of action, such as the interpretation of policy on an issue, one of the ways of resolving it is to 'go upstairs'. If the head of mathematics and the head of english in a school meet a point of fundamental disagreement about the distribution of timetable hours between their respective subjects, they may well resolve that by seeking a judgement from the head teacher. It is not the only way of resolving such problems, but is one of the possibilities.

The hierarchical emphasis in organisation charts can be modified by the presentation device of drawing them laterally rather than vertically. They still describe the grouping of activities and the distribution of power.

Some decisions in organisations are made by individuals, others are made by groups. The scope of decisions to be made by an individual will be contained either in the job description or in the position on the organisation chart. Decisions to be made collectively are allocated to *decision-making complexes*. The obvious example is the board of directors who make certain decisions by majority vote, and those decisions cannot be made in any other way. Other decisions are reserved for particular committees or councils, sometimes as specified in collective agreements with employee representatives. These are called decision-making complexes rather than decision-making groups because the process of reaching decisions goes beyond the face-to-face discussion to include the collection and presentation of data. This is a significant feature of jobs done by people outside the decision-making group and sometimes is the sole activity of committee secretariats.

Just as the organisation chart is the main expression of power distribution, the composition and operation of the decision-making complexes can be another basis on which organisation members channel their interests in obtaining access to power.

Operating procedures are ways in which decisions are implemented and the standardised means whereby the everyday activities of organisation life are conducted. The sundry administrative routines range from the drill that is followed in determining who has time off with pay to attend funerals, to the elaborate routine of consultation that is required in authorising a purchase order for a new piece of equipment. John Child (1984, page 8) includes in this grouping two further aspects, first the specification of working routines for how tasks are to be performed and secondly the determination of performance standards, such as level of output or quality of performance, when the methods of doing the job cannot be precisely tied down.

THE ENTREPRENEURIAL STRUCTURE

Most organisations start life as an *entrepreneurial* structure (see Fig. 9.1) in that they are brought into existence to extend the capability and a capacity of an individual, who has discovered a way of meeting potential customer or client need, but cannot achieve results without assistance. The two essential components of any dictionary definition of the word 'entrepreneur' are risk and initiative. The fact of having had the initiative and taken the risk gives the entrepreneur such dominance in the evolving organisation that everything depends on him and most activities of other members are either replicating or mirroring what the entrepreneur is doing. The initiative shown usually includes a powerful ingredient of expertise or specialised knowledge that nobody else can supply, and which is the secret of success. Erle Stanley Gardner was a writer of crime novels that were so successful that he was able to employ a team of writers who wrote large parts of later novels according to his outline or formula, while Mr Gardner provided the vital ingredients of the formula, the characters and his own name. The popular singer has a small entourage of acolytes (interestingly they are

Fig. 9.1 Entrepreneurial organisation structure.

usually called managers) whose duties are to enable the performer to do well: they have no function or purpose apart from that. Eddie Land invented the Polaroid lens and later the Polaroid camera, so that all the members of his organisation centred their activities on his inventive genius.

The questions about entrepreneurial structures are to decide where such structures are appropriate and how practicable it is to maintain that form with increasing organisational size. Most people are employed in organisations that do not depend absolutely on the continuing, irreplaceable contribution of a single entrepreneur. The large oil companies, most public sector undertakings like the National Health Service or the Civil Service, high street banks, schools, colleges, airline companies, insurance companies have a quite different type of drive to their activities. Other types of organisation appear to need, however, the strong centralisation of the entrepreneurial form to be effective. Where there is the need to move fast and take major decisions requiring flair and skilled judgement rather than a measured weighing of alternatives, then the entrepreneurial form is maintained.

There are many examples of entrepreneurial structure at the micro-level in larger organisations. The passenger aircraft in flight has a pattern of routine organisation that is decentralised: all members of the crew are trained and self-confident in discharging their specialised tasks, but at any hint of danger the crew members look to the captain for precise instructions which they will obey without discussion or argument. The routine of the hospital operating theatre is similar. There is not time for all those involved to confer about the most appropriate course of action while the patient bleeds to death. There is common consent to the need for someone to make decisions quickly, even if they turn out to be wrong. Larger scale activities that have this same need are the printing of daily newspapers, running a fashion house, much of merchant banking and some marketing operations. It is interesting that some other types of operation that are in many ways similar to journalism actually operate on a different, highly consultative basis. Advertising campaigns and magazine editing have been complex activities drawing upon and merging the expertise and insights of a team rather than imposing the ideas of a single person. These situations require strong leadership to avoid the pitfalls of 'groupthink' that can come from trying to satisfy all participants, but the lack of immediacy provides the opportunity to work at getting the best possible formula.

The entrepreneurial form is attractive to many managers because of its emphasis on individual power and risky competition.

> There are a few rules and procedures, little bureaucracy. Control is exercised by the centre, largely through the selection of key individuals, by occasional forays from the centre or summonses to the centre. It is a political organization in that decisions are taken very largely on the outcome of a balance of influence rather than on procedural or purely logical grounds. (Handy, 1989 page 89)

THE BUREAUCRATIC STRUCTURE

Bureaucracy is the most common form of organisation and has been used, as we saw in the opening chapter, in various forms for most of human history. It is only recently that the word has taken on the unattractive overtones that turn 'bureaucrat' into a term of abuse.

The principle of bureaucratic organisation is that jobs are grouped according to some common feature and then ranked in a conventional hierarchy of responsibility to distribute power between organisation members. The most common grouping is *function*, with a marketing hierarchy, an operations hierarchy and so on (see Fig. 9.2). An alternative is the *geographical* grouping, where there is a factory hierarchy and another for the London office and a third for the warehousing and distribution centre. In bureaucracy employees focus on their roles in the organisation rather than on the relative power of individuals.

> Bureaucratic structures are characterized by an advanced degree of specialization between jobs and departments, by a reliance on formal procedures and paperwork, and by extended managerial hierarchies with clearly marked status distinctions. In bureaucracies there tends to be a strictly delimited system of delegation down these hierarchies whereby an employee is expected to use his discretion only within what the rules allow. (Child, 1984, page 7)

In its extreme form bureaucracy gives rise to the sort of picture mentioned at the opening of this chapter, but is more usually a necessary and

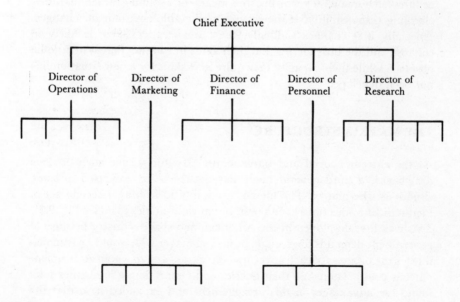

Fig. 9.2 Typical bureaucratic organisation structure.

agreeable environment for people to work in, providing that the nature of the organisation's task is appropriate to this organisational form. The working routine is predictable and understood, jobs are defined so that individuals know what they are to do and how to do it, and efficiency derives from rational allocation of work and responsibility rather than individual flair and judgement. Standardised performances are required and it is a form of organisation that is reasonably equitable and proof against corruption.

A useful example is retail banking or the work of building societies. Here the operations have to be standardised, not only in all branches of the same bank but also between competing banks, so that customers find the system easy to deal with. The work of bank clerks and, in a different way, bank managers requires knowledge, skill and accuracy, but it must be carried out strictly in accordance with the rules and there is little scope for individuality apart from one's manner in talking with customers and manual dexterity in counting banknotes. Bureaucracy provides scope for economies of scale and extensive specialisation at the expense of flexibility and product innovation. Their predictability provides a secure environment for the employee and a clear line of safe career progression.

Bureaucracy has recently acquired a bad name for a variety of reasons. It has been pointed out that it is not always efficient, especially in times of rapid change and with increasing complexity of organisational tasks. It is also criticised as pushing people to clone-like uniformity instead of developing individual ability and potential. The inflexible and immutable procedures of bureaucracy can become means of avoiding rather than discharging responsibility. If the secure, predictable environment changes, especially if it changes suddenly, the bureaucratic system is likely to collapse and the bureaucrats find their skills in running that system to be obsolete, while their capacity to acquire new skills for a new situation has not been developed.

THE MATRIX STRUCTURE

As the entrepreneurial and bureaucratic structures have such obvious drawbacks, a third general mode has been evolved and used in some situations: the matrix. The method is simply to overlay a second set of hierarchical connections over a first, but at right-angles to it (see Fig. 9.3). This was first developed in the American aerospace industry because of government demands for a single project manager who would be responsible for the progress of each government contract and to whom government officials could channel all their queries and instructions Companies soon found big advantages in this arrangement and expanded it so that the project manager was not only a communications link but also a direct

Fig. 9.3 Typical matrix organisation structure.

superior of employees in different functional groups, although these employees would also still report to their functional superiors. This was directly flouting Fayol's dictum about unity of command that we saw in the second chapter, to say nothing of the New Testament observation that a man cannot serve two masters. Despite this, the form proved popular because it provided a measure of individual autonomy and formalised the necessary, informal lateral lines of communication that are developed by people coping with interrelated problems.

An example could be the making of a television programme, which will require a range of specialist skills, such as set-building, make-up, special effects, design and engineering. The necessary specialists are a part of their functional area and have a place in that hierarchy, but they will mainly work on attachment to a particular programme. The attachment may be for a few weeks, like preparing for a Royal Wedding; a few months like a cricket season; or several years on a magazine programme. Whilst attached they are part of that programme team and thus have a dual link. For technical expertise they refer to their functional grouping, but for regular direction and control they are responsible to the producer of the programme. In this way individuals have full scope to use their expertise and judgement and to organise their contributions, the project team leader has 'his own man' as a full-time member, and yet there is the backup of the functional organisation if additional resources are required and as somewhere for the team member to return to and identify with.

For the matrix to succeed there has to be depth of skilled personnel, so that a person can be allocated full-time to a project, and the operating context of the organisation has to be appropriate to the mode of working. There are still likely to be problems in dealing with resource allocation, as the project manager may want more people than the functional manager deems necessary and all too often the project manager wants a particular person whom the functional manager wants to deploy elsewhere. A further difficulty is with the specialist personnel themselves who have the benefit of independence but lack opportunities to develop specialised expertise, as they have to work on a variety of tasks. They will develop flexibility and experience but may not deepen their specialist skills. This can also lead to uncertainty about career progression and occupational identity. Do you stay with the functional career path or do you try and become a project manager? The administrative costs can be high due to a multiplication of hierarchies that tends to increase overheads as more and more people establish the inescapable need for private secretaries, personal assistants, larger offices, more telephones and computer facilities. The level of conflict requires managerial time for its resolution and an increased amount of political behaviour can lead to excessive paperwork as people make out their case in seventeen copies.

The matrix organisation does, therefore, need time and care in its creation, balancing the power of the two axes and working out a basis of trust and understanding among the key participants. It is not something to work out on the back of an envelope during a train journey; it requires extensive consultation and discussion, progressive implementation over several months and attention for several years as it settles down and moves towards effectiveness. Davis and Lawrence (1979) suggest three stages of matrix evolution. First *temporary overlay*, during which project teams are created only for special and immediate needs; secondly *permanent overlay* in which project teams are established as a continuing form of organisation working across the functional hierarchy; and thirdly the *mature matrix*, at which point the project lines of authority and influence are brought into balance with the functional lines.

Useful guidance on matrix management is in Galbraith (1977) and in Kingdon (1973).

Mintzberg (1979, Chapter 21) uses the term *adhocracy* to describe a variant of the matrix organisation, where the work is complex and innovative, such as theatre companies and some computing specialists. Such an organisation is one in which there are many highly trained specialists with an organic structure that always remains flexible, and which tends to be very big in the middle. Organisations of this type have problems in balancing work loads between individuals and groups and in managing the conflict that such a diverse group of people generates.

DIFFERENTIATED STRUCTURES

It should not be assumed from the foregoing that an entire organisation must follow the same organisational pattern. The structure of organisation follows the requirements of the environment and the needs of organisation members rather than the whim of highly placed individuals seeking control, so that appropriate structures will vary from one part of the undertaking to another. Fig. 9.4 shows the main types of organisational structure. The sales manager will be properly concerned about satisfying customers' demands today, while the R&D manager will be more interested in the development of products for the future. It is unlikely that the same form of organisation structure would suit both situations. A hospital will have within it an operating theatre in which surgeons conduct their high dramas in a way that has to be centralised and autocratic to cope with the crises on the operating table, but the same hospital will have a psychiatric unit requiring a different approach.

The pattern of the organisation could, therefore, have a tightknit entrepreneurial structure at the centre and bureaucratised functions or a matrix elsewhere. Bureaucracies can have within them small entrepreneurial organisations, as some large companies have set up such small groups to

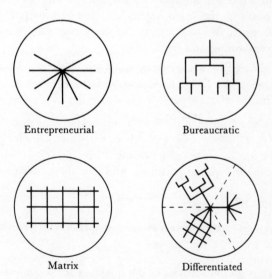

Entrepreneurial   Bureaucratic

Matrix   Differentiated

Fig. 9.4 Main types of organisational structure.

develop new business ventures. What is crucial in organisation differentiation is that the different structures are independent of each other in their operations. The entrepreneurs must be relatively free of set procedures and the bureaucrats must be able to escape the power-play needed by the entrepreneurs.

The seminal work on this aspect of organisation is by Paul Lawrence and Jay Lorsch (1967) working in the United States. They demonstrated that companies operating in an unstable, unpredictable environment had the greatest variations in organisational structure and style and those in the predictable environments had little differentiation. They also established that the high-performing companies in both situations had a higher degree of *integration* than low-performers. Whilst it is essential for subunits of an organisation to be independent in their operations if their styles are different, it is also essential that their operations are integrated.

THE SPAN OF CONTROL

One idea that has fascinated management analysts for decades is the span of control – what is the optimum number of subordinates for a manager? The idea of an optimum number has been so ridiculed in recent years that interest in it has waned, but we resurrect it here because it includes some of the detailed decisions that have to be taken by managers about how work should be organised and how bits of the organisation fit into the overall structure. Decisions about job descriptions and working relationships, for example, will affect the number of subordinates and will determine the number of posts in the organisation and the relative steepness of the hierarchy, with all the implications of cost, communication problems, potential overmanning and inefficiency.

> No executive should attempt to supervise directly the work of more than five, or at the most six, direct subordinates whose work interlocks. (L.F. Urwick, 1974)

To Urwick the feature of the work interlocking was important, as that required the executive to resolve problems more often. Such a pattern of 1:5 or 1:6 may be appropriate when looking at the question from the point of view of how the individual performs, and it is the pattern found in most

Review Topic 9.2

How useful is the idea that there is an optimum span of control for an individual manager?

hierarchies, but another aspect of the question is the amount of management and managers that such a norm builds into an organisation and the

Table 9.1 A comparison of management structures

Rank and grade		Manufacturing	Retailing
Senior	1	4	4
management	2	9	
Middle	3	16	8
management	4	40	–
Supervisory	5	55	12
management			
Total managers		114	24
Total other			
employees		1500	600

degree to which it introduces the inefficiencies of over-management. Table 9.1 compares two actual organisations, one manufacturing and one retailing, but both part of large conglomerates. At first glance the disparity is enormous, even though both have ratios of managers to others that exceed the 1:5/6 suggested by Urwick, but there are a number of factors to explain the differences. The manufacturing operation is technically sophisticated, requiring a range of technical expertise, it is physically more widely distributed and shifts are worked over twenty-four hours for five and a half days a week. The retailing unit does not have to buy or advertise and has a relatively simple operation, even though it is carried out with great skill.

However necessary the larger number and proportion of managers in the manufacturing organisation, there is both extra cost and administrative burden caused by the number of managers and levels: more secretaries, more memoranda, more necessary communication, more problems with role definition and boundary, less scope for subordinates to exercise responsibility, and a larger salary bill. There is obviously a potential benefit in *increasing* the average span of managerial control if this has the knock-on effect of reducing the number of levels in the hierarchy, which Child (1984, page 59) claims to be typically four in the organisation employing up to one hundred people, rising to six when one thousand people are employed and seven or eight in the organisation with ten thousand people. Among the factors that can be examined to enable a widening of control spans to flatten the hierarchy are the following:

1. *Standardising the work to be done.* If the work to be done by the managed can be standardised, then the need for supervision will decline as individual employees are working to a standard, clearly understood procedure for which they will require little instruction and guidance. There is a narrow line separating the constraining standardisation of the many mindless tasks that are to be found in mass production and the liberating

standardisation that can be found in skilled jobs, like that of the craftsman or travel agency booking clerk, where the standard is set for the output rather than the details of method.

2. *Autonomy.* Closely related to the methods of standardisation are the methods of providing autonomy, whereby supervision is virtually removed from the work of those sufficiently and experienced to be able to do their own management. One version of this is the converse of Urwick's point about work that interlocks. Where there is close interaction between the work of people or departments, that interaction needs careful management to keep the varied activities in balance. Whether that is done by managers or by the people themselves, it is still a time-consuming activity. If the interlocks can be removed, then the management requirement can reduce.

3. *Specialist advisers.* Theoretically the use of specialist advisers or departments eases the management burden in the line, by taking over responsibilities for activities such as safety, personnel or quality control. The introduction of these services should allow spans of control in the middle of the hierarchy to widen, although it means more departments for senior managers to co-ordinate. Such specialists can also develop standard procedures to simplify general administration. Specialists are, however, a dangerous drug as they are always likely to increase rather than reduce the managerial burden: the tail wags the dog. Information is called for, forms are required to be filled in and the specialist becomes aloof and didactic rather than genuinely easing managerial loads in the line. This is often because the detachment of the specialists enables them to be uninterested in everyday problems, but also it can be because the position of the specialist adviser is always precarious and they feel a need to make themselves necessary by becoming a part of the administrative system of the undertaking and thus being 'indispensable'.

Quite apart from the possibility of increasing the span of control and the number of levels in the hierarchy, managers have to guard against the strongest pressure of all in the organisation towards increasing the number of levels, namely the managers themselves. When a hierarchy is established the members of the hierarchy want to go up it, so they are always looking for openings higher up and can often make out the most convincing case for a new opening that does not already exist.

In a medium-sized chemical plant there was a plant manager, four production superintendents reporting to him and twenty-two supervisors: a clear three-level hierarchy. Safety was the responsibility of the personnel manager, but the plant manager was anxious to be in charge of his own safety arrangements and eventually won a battle with the personnel manager to appoint his 'own' safety officer. This involved not only a flurry of administrative activity in redefining the limits of responsibility between the personnel manager and the plant manager, it also required redefinition in the three-level hierarchy of the plant. The safety officer reported to the plant manager, so the four superintendents wanted to know whether he ranked above or below them (which was partly a coded question meaning, 'Does he get paid more than we do?'). It was confirmed that he 'ranked' below superintendent but above supervisor, which produced a problem in the personnel department, where the safety officer was on a supervisory scale. It also introduced a new level and within two years six of the supervisors had been promoted to the new position of senior supervisor, ranking equal with the safety officer.

This same tendency has been seen as groups of people have sought 'improved career prospects'. Nurses in the National Health Service used to have vague career prospects beyond the clear and well understood posts of ward sister or charge nurse. After that there was deputy matron and matron. When the case for career advancement was made, those two vaguely defined and amorphous levels became four: nursing officer, senior nursing officer, principal nursing officer and divisional nursing officer.

Concern about the span of control led the Lockheed Corporation to devise a means of evaluating managerial posts in order to decide the number of subordinates for whom the job holder could be held responsible. This was used in 1961 to reduce the number of management levels in several sections of the undertaking. It has not proved to be a popular method in other organisations and is thus little more than a footnote to the development of management ideas, but some readers might be interested in the account of the method provided by Barkdull (1963). Child (1973) accounts for the growth of specialists' numbers in organisations as being related to the size, dispersion, technical complexity and number of divisions in the organisation. Howells (1981) made a comparative study of the Marks and Spencer chain store and the Civil Service. He found distinctive styles of decision-making with Marks and Spencer putting very little on paper and emphasising decision-making by individuals, whereas the Civil Service put a lot on paper and used committees to make decisions. Howells considers that the Civil Service operates in this apparently laborious way because of the complex decisions that have to be made with less clear criteria and operating with external accountability. This demonstrates how both environment and product influence formal organisation structures.

CULTURE

The culture of the organisation needs to be understood because a mismatch of action and culture can produce ineffective action. There are a number of examples of organisations taking resolute action to modify and develop a part of their culture. Allied Dunbar used an approach based on three key beliefs ('commitment to service', 'demanding and caring' and 'positive management') to deal with a period of rapid growth (Carby and Stemp, 1985), and Schein's methods were used by the Sheffield City Works Department to produce a major shift in culture (Kilcourse, 1985).

The most penetrating analysis of organisational culture is by Schein (1985), who distinguishes between the need for an organisation to develop a culture which enables it to adapt to its changing environment (pages 52–65) and, at the same time, to build and maintain itself through processes of internal integration (pages 65–83). He suggests that there are primary and secondary mechanisms for the culture change process. The primary mechanisms are as follows:

1. What leaders pay most attention to.
2. How leaders react to crises and critical incidents.
3. Role modelling, teaching and coaching by leaders.
4. Criteria for allocating rewards and determining status.
5. Criteria for selection, promotion and termination (pages 224–37).

The difficulty with emphasising leadership is the implication that a organisation can only succeed when led by a great person, on whom everything depends and to whom everyone else responds. Some of the most productive organisational cultures avoid that extreme interpretation of leadership by tolerating a plurity of views and styles that make for a lively community, and handling the conflict that invariably ensues through discussion and meetings. Organisational culture is the concern of all organisational members and developing that culture is most effective when a majority of members agree on and own the changes that they all want to bring about. That degree of consensus is rare, but it remains a necessary, practical objective to aim for.

Schein's secondary mechanisms for the articulation and reinforcement of culture are as follows:

1. The organisational structure.
2. Systems and procedures.
3. Space, buildings and façades.
4. Stories and legends about important events and people.
5. Formal statements of philosophy and policy (pages 237–42).

This introduces a greater variety of possible strategies, and it is interesting that formal statements are placed last. All too often the attempt to develop some aspect of culture actually begins with a formal statement of policy, and sometimes cultural inertia is attributed to the lack of such a statement. In fact, such statements are only useful in summarising and expressing what is achieved by other means.

Without a shared sense of mission all organisations lose their essential integrity and become no more than a collection of people who would rather be somewhere else, because they lack effectiveness and conviction in what they are doing. The effective organisation has a few central values about which there is a high degree of consensus. Those are supported and put into operation by simple rules and clear procedures, which are subordinate to the values. The organisation that depends principally on rules for its cohesion is in the process of decay.

SUMMARY PROPOSITIONS

9.1 The four elements of organisation are job descriptions, the structure of working relationships, decision-making complexes and operating procedures.

9.2 The most common forms of organisation structure are entrepreneurial, bureaucratic and matrix.

9.3 Although undertakings may adopt more than one form of organisational structure, integration will be an element of their operations that will influence the success of their business.

9.4 Tendencies in organisations to being over-managed can be partly mitigated by increasing the managerial span of control and reducing the number of managerial levels.

9.5 The behaviour of people in an organisation, and the effectiveness of their combined activities, is crucially determined by the culture of the organisation.

9.6 Organisational culture must be understood by managers, and can be changed.

PUTTING IT INTO PRACTICE

Drill for tackling problems of organisation

Table 9.2 gives a preliminary drill for deciding how to approach problems of organization and similar issues, with the advantages and disadvantages of each.

Identifying problems of organisation

To identify problems of organisation one must have some criteria against

Table 9.2 Drill for tackling the problems of organisation

Approach	Advantage	Disadvantage
1. Use one's own judgement	Reinforces one's role as the person in charge	No testing for the accuracy of diagnosis
2. Ask for guidance from one's hierarchical superior	Tests own judgement against that of person with wider view, who shares responsibility	Might make superior's view of own judgement questionable; advice from superior difficult to ignore
3. Consult with key subordinates	Several views expressed and those consulted become partly committed to eventual solution	Spreads uncertainty about existing arrangements, which *have* to be changed
4. Survey attitudes of all subordinates	Comprehensive expression of opinion from all those most directly concerned, with anonymity of survey method ensuring reasonable frankness of views	Some subordinates will feel that they are being asked to solve problems that are the proper domain of the manager, who is showing incompetence by asking subordinates
5. Consult peers	Co-ordinating views with those from other units and perspectives in the organisation	Some peers may regard consultation as sign of weakness and indecision. May influence competition for resources
6. Seek external advice	Tests own judgement against that of person with experience in a variety of organisation settings, who is detached from one's own	Advice could be expensive and advisor does not carry responsibility to temper advice

which to judge the various features of the organisation being studied. There is a dearth of absolute standards in this field, but the following is a list of statements that are *generally valid* on the basis of the extensive research about organisations that has been carried out. They are useful as broad criteria, but should not be taken to have any more reliability than that.

1. *Size of organisation unit*
   (a) As organisations grow they tend to become more bureaucratic, with a taller hierarchy.

   (b) Large units tend to have problems of morale among members low in the hierarchy or remote from the centre.

   (c) Increasing organisational size provides career progression moves (mainly for middle and senior managers) and the facilities of specialist departments.

   (d) Small working units tend to have high morale among members.

2. *Age of organisation unit*

   (a) As a unit grows older it will become more stable (otherwise it would not have survived) and the conventions of customs and practice will become strong.

   (b) As units grow older their structures become less flexible but their goals more flexible.

3. *Setting of organisation unit*

   (a) A unit cannot operate independently of its setting and many of the norms, procedures and practice will be dictated by the setting.

   (b) The unit will be able to make its strategic objectives more ambitious if the setting is buoyant or competitive or both.

   (c) The unit will tend to be innovative, and its members creative, if the setting is changing and being challenged.

4. *Job descriptions*

   (a) All organisation members need some definition of their role and tasks, especially where their activities interlock with, or overlap, those of other organisation members.

   (b) Job descriptions written for them by others can cause members to ignore the descriptions or to use them as a means of limiting their contribution.

   (c) Job descriptions written by members themselves can stimulate creative thinking about the members' roles and working relationships.

5. *Structure of working relationships*

   (a) Different forms of organisation structure are most appropriate for different settings.

   (b) Entrepreneurial structure is most appropriate in situations of rapid change or constant crisis, or where the unit is not performing well in comparison with competing units.

   (c) Bureaucratic structure is most appropriate in situations of relative stability with readily-measurable performance standards and/or public accountability.

   (d) Matrix structure is most appropriate when responsibility for action has to be devolved to individual specialists so that they can work on their own account with peers having different qualifications of a comparable standard.

   (e) Differentiation of structure is most appropriate when an organisation has diversity of objectives and methods of operating in the subunits, which can operate with reasonable independence of each other providing that there are co-ordinating mechanisms.

(f) Diversified organisations need co-ordination. This can be achieved by using various forms of face-to-face meeting to develop trust and understanding; by using the crossover point in the hierarchy when a 'ruling' is needed; and by using co-ordinators to assist in finding solutions to major disagreements.

6. *Span of control*
   (a) There is no universal, optimum number of subordinates for a manager.
   (b) Increasing the number of subordinates reporting to an individual manager can reduce the risks of over-management.
   (c) The hierarchy may be flattened by standardising the work to be done, increasing the autonomy of individual employees and providing specialist advisers or departments to support managers in the line.
   (d) Managers may seek to steepen the hierarchy and narrow the span of control in order to improve their own career prospects.

7. *Pitfalls of organisational change*
   (a) It is not possible to predict precisely the outcome of any particular organisational change: there are always unintended consequences.
   (b) Individual organisation members sometimes seek changes which would satisfy their personal needs but which would not necessarily satisfy the needs of the organisation.
   (c) The presenting symptoms may not necessarily be due to problems of organisational structure.

More detailed suggestions about identifying problems of organisation can be found in Khandwalla, P.N., *Design of Organizations*, Harcourt, Brace Jovanovich, New York, 1977.

An alternative approach is that developed by Roger Harrison, who looks at the culture of the organisation. His scheme for finding how compatible an individual is with a particular type of organisation structure can be found in Handy's *Understanding Organisations*, pages 214–21.

REFERENCES

Barkdull, C.W., 'Span of control: a method of evaluation', *Michigan Business Review*, vol. 15, 1963, pages 25–32.

Carby, K. and Stemp, P., 'How Hambro changed its name and much more besides', *Personnel Management*, Oct. 1985.

Child, J., 'Parkinson's progress: accounting for the number of specialists in organisations', *Administrative Science Quarterly*, Sept. 1973, pages 328–48.

Child, J., *Organization: a Guide to Problems and Practice*, 2nd edn, Harper & Row, London, 1984.

Davis, S.M. and Lawrence, P.R., *Matrix*, Addison Wesley, Reading, Mass., 1977.

Galbraith, J.R., *Organization Design*, Addison Wesley, Reading, Mass., 1977.

Handy, C.B., *Understanding Organizations*, 2nd edn, Penguin Books, Harmondsworth, 1985.

Howells, D., 'Marks & Spencer and the Civil Service: a comparison of culture and methods', in *Public Administration*, Autumn 1981, pages 337–52.

Kilcourse, T., 'How culture can be the key to management development', *Personnel Management*, Dec. 1985.

Kingdon, D.R., *Matrix Organisation*, Tavistock, London, 1973.

Lawrence, P.R. and Lorsch, J.W., *Organization and Environment*, Harvard University Press, 1967.

Leavitt, H.J., Dill, W.R. and Eyring, H.B., *The Organizational World*, Harcourt Brace Jovanovich, New York, 1973.

Mintzberg H., *The Structuring of Organizations*, Prentice Hall, Englewood Cliffs, New Jersey, 1979.

Peters, T.J. and Waterman, R.H., *In Search of Excellence*, Harper & Row, London, 1982.

Schein, E.H., *Organisational Culture and Leadership*, Jossey Bass, San Francisco, Calif., 1985.

Urwick L.F., 'V.A. Graicunas and the span of control', *Academy of Management Journal*, June 1974, pages 349–54.

10

ORGANISATIONAL POLITICS

The idea of behaving politically is one that managers do not readily accept for themselves. This is partly because of the immediate association of the word 'political' with national and local government, but also because the word carries connotations of insincerity and deviousness, and managers disparage these qualities in their colleagues (not themselves being guilty of such behaviour) and deplore the extent to which they detract from the main tasks of the organisation in which they are employed.

When Shepherd Mead wrote his book *How to Succeed in Business Without Really Trying*, he described the activities of his central character who achieved power and influence through *appearing* to do the right things whilst actually doing very little: image without reality. This idea was so unthinkable in the context of American business that it could only be expressed by making the whole thing a joke. It is a very funny book, but it became a best-seller because it also had the qualities of the good horror story, near enough to reality for the readers to thank their lucky stars that they were not such unprincipled persons; at the same time as working out how close each of their colleagues came to the model.

Much of management development activity in recent years and the underlying emphasis of organisation behaviour punditry is that openness in one's behaviour brings results as relationships with colleagues become more candid and constructive through stripping away the veneer of posturing and guile that otherwise masks integrity. The attractiveness of candour and integrity are so obvious that it may seem strange to bring discussion of politics into a book about management. Why should managers understand politics?

POWER IN ORGANISATIONS

The formal structure of the organisation, as described in Chapter 9, is a map of working relationships that are official and is the main device for distributing power among organisation members. The formal distribution is not the only determinant of the power held by individuals: it is the main factor in providing people with resource power, but not power from other sources. Dalton (1959) conducted a detailed study of the power structure in a large American manufacturing plant and included a grading of the relative influence wielded by different members of the management. In many instances this did not correspond with their position in the hierarchy. An example was the relative influence of a plant manager, Stevens, and his assistant, Hardy:

> In executive meetings Stevens was clearly less forceful than Hardy. Appearing nervous and worried, Stevens usually opened meetings with a few remarks and then silently gave way to Hardy, who dominated thereafter. During the meeting most questions were directed to Hardy. While courteous, Hardy's statements usually were made without request for confirmation from Stevens. Hardy and Stevens and other high officers daily lunched together. There, too, Hardy dominated the conversations and was usually the target for questions. This was not just an indication that he carried the greater burden of minor duties often assigned to assistants . . . for he had a hand in most issues, including major ones. (page 23)

Hardy apparently was more strongly motivated than Stevens towards acquiring power and probably had more skill.

The amount of power can also vary according to the problems that are paramount for an organisation at a particular time, so that power accrues to those organisation members or sections who are coping with critical organisation problems.

Harry Denton was an order clerk in a company that supplied portable, battery-operated equipment for use in coal mines. Harry's job was to deal with all the orders that came in for the batteries, ensuring that the goods were despatched and invoiced. He was so quietly efficient that he got on with his job year by year and was left alone. Then there was a nationwide selective strike by a union that sought to bring industrial action to support its case by calling out on strike its members in some companies where the interruption of supply could be particularly effective. Harry's company was one of those where strike action was called because of the importance of the batteries that Harry despatched. Suddenly Harry was a man of great influence in his company, taking part in meetings with directors and senior managers much concerned about how many batteries were in stock, how many were in depots, how many in transit, how many orders pending; all questions to which Harry, and only Harry, knew the answers. He was an unassuming man, not seeking promotion or other personal advantage, but he had been trying for years to get a small change made in the warehouse administrative routines, and had been asking for months if he could have a direct telephone connection to the vehicle loading bay. Both requests were now agreed and dealt with in a few hours. Harry Denton had suddenly acquired power because of the critical organisation problem with which he was dealing.

Another factor governing the political activity of managers is the degree of their dependency on others. A management development officer, for instance, is more dependent on his colleagues than the chief accountant, as he has to convince them of the value of his activities and persuade them to participate in his training activities and co-operate in identifying training needs. Managers in dependent positions have to spend more time in building relationships with their colleagues and worrying about breakdowns in communication and understanding.

Kotter (1978) examined the situation of two managers. X was a plant manager whose main dealings were with only four groups: the company president, plant employees, customers and suppliers. He had high dependency on the president and the customers, but only medium dependency on employees and suppliers. Y was a hospital administrator with six high dependencies and seven medium dependencies. Kotter found that Y spent 80 per cent of her day in activities relating to power and influence over others, but X spent only 30 per cent of his time on that sort of activity (*ibid.* page 30). This matches some of Rosemary Stewart's conclusions, reported in Chapter 3, about the different types of management job, one of which is peer dependent.

Having reviewed these aspects of the importance of organisational politics it is useful to take note of the following definitions of Pfeffer (1981):

> Organizational politics involves those activities undertaken within an organization to acquire, develop, and use power and other resources to obtain one's preferred outcomes in a situation in which there is uncertainty or dissensus about choices. (page 7)

Power is a property that exists in any organisation or system; politics is the way in which that power is put into action.

THE PLACE OF POLITICS IN MANAGEMENT

Dahl is one of the political theorists who helps us to an understanding of organisational politics, as he points out that political behaviour stems from conflicting aims:

> If everyone were perfectly agreed on ends and means, no-one would ever need to change the way of another. Hence no relations of influence or power would arise. Hence no political system would exist. Let one person frustrate another in the pursuit of his goals and you already have the germ of a political system; conflict and politics are born inseparable twins. (Dahl, 1970, page 59)

Any organisation has within it limited resources for its members. Organisation members compete with each other for promotion in developing their careers. On an everyday basis they will be competing for resources in material terms: a bigger departmental budget, more space, newer equipment, more staff, and greater influence over the direction of the general organisational policy. This competition causes the nature of political activity to vary according to the state of growth or decline that the organisation is in. With growth there is the opportunity for all members to 'win' the above sort of competitions. If the organisation is stagnant, then the person who gets a bigger amount of resources can only do this at the expense of someone else, so the arguments may be more bitter. If the organisation is declining, the political activity will often be less sparkling because of the demoralising effect of decline and possibly the greater anxiety to stick together in adversity. In the stable situation politics cause some to win while others lose, but the dynamics of that situation and the range of external considerations should cause the winners to be those who have a stronger substantive case. Only in growth is there likely to be a situation in which all are winners.

It may be that political behaviour often involves being devious and cunning, but the substance of political activity is the manipulation of *power*. Those who understand the subtleties of power in relationships are better able to get things done than those who ignore them:

> The graveyards of history are strewn with the corpses of reformers who failed utterly to reform anything, of revolutionaries who failed to win power . . . of anti-revolutionaries who failed to prevent a revolution – men and women who failed not only because of the forces arrayed against them but because the pictures in their minds about power and influence were simplistic and inaccurate. (Dahl, 1970, page 15)

Organisations have power as one of their crucial dimensions, and only by understanding how power is distributed and deployed can members of organisations get things done. The innovative idea or the accurate diagnosis is insufficient without the means for their implementation. This is considered further in Chapter 15.

Here are some of the ways in which organisational politics are important.

1. *Competition*. Members of organisations compete with each other. They compete for more attractive posts further up the hierarchy and for opportunities to develop their careers and express their individual interests. The most important aspect of competition is for resources, which are always scarce in relation to the needs of organisation members and where one person gets the extra resources only at the expense of someone else who does not.

2. *Performance measurement*. There are few objective means of measuring performance of those holding managerial and administrative posts

because of the interdependence of their activities. An author writes books, the sales of which are a measure of their worth; a batsman scores a certain number of runs; a tennis player wins or loses a match; a research scientist can discover a new cure for a crippling disease; but the manager embedded in the complex web of relationships of a contemporary organisation is bereft of such objective criteria for determining personal success and failure. They therefore have to win friends and influence people by impressing their superiors with their personal qualities and loyalty, by building an empire of subordinates or by making alliances with colleagues.

3. *Job mobility.* Political behaviour is encouraged by job mobility. In many large organisations job mobility is a requirement for all those with career aspirations, who are moved from post to post and often from location to location for most of their working lives. Geographical mobility has become less attractive with the tightening of the labour market and the development of career expectations among women, who may be very reluctant to abandon a satisfying and well-paid job in Birmingham to follow a husband to Aberdeen, where they may find their employment prospects to be poor and their husbands to be even more preoccupied than before with their own careers. Although less attractive , geographical mobility still features strongly in the organisational life of many high-flying young managers and movement within the organisation structure is very common. This means that it is even more difficult for the mobile manager to show depth of accomplishment in any one position, and he feels the need to impress and manipulate the perceptions of those around him. After moving from Birmingham to Aberdeen his wife will be left even more to her own devices because he has to spend so much time winning friends and influencing people in the strange, new business context, to make sure that he is eventually promoted away from Aberdeen.

4. *Style of leadership.* There has been a gradual change in leadership style in recent years which has changed the nature of politics in many organisations. The entrepreneurial form which was described in Chapter 9 is an overtly political situation as there is high concentration of power in the centre. Modern management thinking in bureaucratic and matrix structures has become more democratic than autocratic, and much of this book is devoted to winning consent rather than simply telling people what to do. Going along with this has been the increasing impracticality of an individual manager being able to get approval for a programme of action simply by selling the idea to the boss: there is more dependence on committees, task groups and alliances. Not only does this require the deployment of what could be called the skills of diplomacy (tact, skill and cunning in dealing with people to win their support for your aims) it also tends to produce underhand, Watergate-type behaviour among

managers who are uneasy with a democratic style.

5. *Political context*. All organisations operate in political contexts. They are concerned with national political movements, international events that could close an export market or jeopardise the supply of a raw material, and with the volatility of the stock market. The salesperson trying to land an order has to establish where in the customer's organisation the authority to purchase lies. Is this the right person? Some companies depend on changes in government policy for an improvement in their business, and those in public sector organisations are closely concerned with national political thinking.

Review Topic 10.1

The English philosopher and essayist Francis Bacon (1561–1626) made the comment 'It is a strange desire to seek power and to lose liberty.' Are the two necessarily connected in organisational life?

There are four main sources of power for the individual or group to garner in order to exercise political influence: resources, skill, motivation and obligations. The most obvious is the control of *resources*. Those who control what others need are in the position of relative power. We have seen this in the early historical developments, where it was the granaries of the pharaoh that gave him the power to weld together the nation state of Egypt. The power of a contemporary government resides largely in the system of taxation and state spending, and the power of the British crown lies largely in the accolades of social esteem which only the monarch can bestow, whether it be an earldom or a telegram for your diamond wedding. The resources which managers control are similar. They may not be able to ennoble their subjects, but they do offer or withhold promotions. This is why most public sector employment has rules and procedures to ensure that at least the appearance of the process whereby people are appointed to posts is 'democratic', so as to prevent any individual wielding too much power. Equally managers influence the level of earnings which people can receive, and employees have worked hard in their collective organisations to reduce managerial power over the pay-packet. Incremental pay scales are a further device for prising power away from managers, and unions invariably resist 'merit' payments for individuals with as much resolution as managers display in trying to introduce them.

Most of the comments in the previous paragraph relate only to the power of superiors over subordinates, but another battle over resources takes place between peers, and that is the share of the budget, the staff, the time of the committees that make decisions, and all those other ways in which the relative power of functions or departments is mediated and altered. It would be quite inadequate to regard power through control of resources as being solely the exercise of power *over* subordinates. It is also power *vis-à-vis* peers and power *against* superiors.

Whatever resources you have you still need *skill* to deploy them. The best-loved aspects of patriotic folklore are those in which one's country-men won battles against the odds. The Battle of Britain retains pride of place in the annals of the Second World War, partly because of the turning point it marked, but mainly because it seemed as if skill and courage outwitted an enemy with more planes and pilots. Control of resources is not sufficient to be powerful, because the political system is only brought into being as a result of competitive bids for power. Neustadt (1960) has compared the effective use of power by three consecutive American presidents, Roosevelt, Truman and Eisenhower. All held the same office with the same resource control, yet achieved different degrees of success because of the varying skill with which they exercised their control.

6. *Motivation.* This can also explain why one manager has more power than another, even though they both possess the same resources and skills. Some seek power much more enthusiastically than others and use their resources to try and get it; others use their resources and skills for different purposes. This can be either due to varying degrees of personal need for power or the feeling that only by obtaining power can the manager's function be effective. Personnel managers have long tended to be politically active (whilst often deploring 'political behaviour' in others) because of the belief that they could only be effective by achieving influence over their colleagues through having power to deploy. Accountants seldom have this worry.

Another reason for individuals having varying amounts of power is the *obligations* owed by 'dependents'. The dependent may be a subordin-ate hoping for a favourable report at the next annual performance appraisal; it may be someone on an equal footing who is under an obligation to the manager for past favours; or it may be a superior who requires the particular skill of the manager with no satisfactory alterna-tives being available. The more of these debts a manager has to call in, the more powerful he will be.

TECHNIQUES USED TO OBTAIN POWER

There are further aspects of power and authority to be discussed in Chapters 16 and 17; so we conclude this chapter by reviewing some of the methods that can be used by individuals seeking to achieve power in organisations.

1. *Alliances.* Individuals collaborate in their power search with those who

have interests sufficiently similar for an alliance to be mutually beneficial. The managers of manufacturing and personnel may form an alliance to block moves by a marketing manager to scale down production and buy in more ready-made materials, for instance. The benefits of an alliance are the obvious ones of having someone else on your side, together with their resources, skills and motivation; the drawbacks are the degree of commitment which you have to contribute. Also alliances cannot be readily discarded; in discarding an ally you probably make an enemy.

2. *Lobbying*. Falling short of the alliance is the process of drumming up support on a particular issue – 'I hope I can rely on your support for this . . .' This is much used in getting one's way with committees, as is described in Chapter 11, but is also appropriate for all the minor dealings that take place throughout the working day.

3. *Doing favours*. There are various ways in which people with some power use that to provide services for others and therefore extend their power with the person they have helped. This is a time-honoured way of ensuring the loyalty of subordinates, who feel grateful to the superior who has been benevolent and whose benevolence may be used again. It is also a method to be used with peers and superiors, who are put in the debt of the person providing the favour. There is a need to be cautious when using one's own power to elevate another, as the person elevated may then be wary of his erstwhile helper.

> Whoever is responsible for another's becoming powerful ruins himself, because this power is brought into being either by ingenuity or by force, and both of these are suspect to the one who has become powerful. (Machiavelli, 1981, page 44)

4. *Being present*. It is the powerful person who can afford to be away. At one extreme post holders may find that they do not have a job to come back to; it is so much easier to dispossess someone who is absent. More common than that is the need to be present when significant decisions are made. Such decisions usually involve the balancing of conflicting interests in competing for resources or advantage. Each interest will have its spokesperson and the interest that is absent will not be heard, so that the decision will seldom be favourable to that interest, unless there is some other aspect of power – like a veto – which can be exercised afterwards to nullify the decision that has been reached.

5. *Cornering resources*. Empire builders reason that their importance to the organisation is in direct proportion to the number of subordinates in their sections. That conclusion may be very dubious, but at least the number of subordinates can be measured, whereas contributions to organisational objectives cannot be.

6. *Being indispensable*. A variant on cornering resources is to make oneself

indispensable. This is done either by being a lone, but essential expert, or by being an essential part of administrative, decision-making procedures. Safety officers often have influence as a result of their familiarity with health and safety legislation, which no one else except shop stewards finds very interesting, but the expertise is essential to the organisation. Personnel officers trying to establish a personnel function usually aim to break in on well established procedures. A typical initiative is to get a ruling that in future recruitment advertisments will have to be placed by the personnel officer, and not by anyone else, or that all management dealings with full-time union officials will be made only by the personnel officer.

7. *Reciprocal support for a patron.* Peter (1969) pointed out that it is much better to be pulled up in an organisation than to push yourself up. Political power can be enhanced by having a powerful patron. Those appointed to newly created posts nearly always define their influence by confirming to whom they report: 'I am directly accountable to the Chief Executive' or 'I am part of the Manufacturing Division but have direct access to the M.D.' Some people have difficulty in finding such a patron and Jennings (1967) has coined the odd word *visiposure* to describe the need first to be in a position to see enough potential patrons to pick one but secondly to be in a position where a potential patron can see you. The first is visibility, the second is exposure; visiposure is both. Once the patron is found support will only be given to the acolyte if the acolyte helps the patron to achieve objectives. Patrons enhance one's power but also exact fealty.

The remorseless logic of Machiavelli described the nature of the relationship between the patron and the patronised.

> To keep his minister up to the mark the prince, on his side, must be considerate towards him, must pay him honour, enrich him, put him in his debt, share with him both honours and responsibilities. Thus the minister will see how dependent he is on the prince; and then having riches and honours to the point of surfeit he will desire no more; holding so many offices, he cannot but fear changes. (Machiavelli, 1981, page 125)

8. *Being able to cope with uncertainty.* The customary routines of formal authority structures, centralised control and circulating memoranda shelter people inside the organisation from the outside world, which is not controlled in the same convenient way. The outside is, however, a hard and urgent reality for the organisation, so that those who can cope with the demands of the environment in which the organisation operates are those towards whom political power tends to flow (Salancik and Pfeffer, 1977). It is the uncertainty of the demands from outside that gives political influence to those who confront them, and anyone dealing with organisational affairs that are uncertain acquires some power.

Michel Crozier (1964, page 154) studied the work of plants in France where tobacco was processed and commented on the extraordinary power that was wielded by the maintenance engineers. The entire process was highly mechanised and predictable, so that the activities of every member were in a smooth routine. The only thing that could go wrong was for a machine to break down, yet that caused a complete disruption to the system. Because of this the only people who could put the machinery right (the maintenance engineers) wielded power out of proportion to their formal status.

This sort of power fluctuates. When the office photocopier breaks down the service engineers are much reviled, because of not being there. When they arrive they are greeted with warm smiles and cups of tea for this brief time of glory. When the photocopier works once more they are quickly forgotten or asked to move their car as it is blocking the car park. Small wonder that they seem to move so slowly in actually conducting the repair. The greatest worry for those who specialise in being able to cope with uncertainty is the fear of not being able to do it. The service engineer who has brought the wrong tools or cannot diagnose the fault suffers all the horrors of the fallen idol.

Review Topic 10.2

We have listed eight techniques to obtain power. Which have you used and which others do you think you will use in the future?

MAINTAINING BALANCE

In closing this chapter we revert to the problem that was posed at the beginning: how can we advocate behaviours that are so obviously devious and unattractive? Also, how can we set discussion about political behaviour alongside the widely canvassed behaviours of openness that are the basis of much contemporary management development?

The answer is that neither politics nor openness are the total solution. An appreciation of organisational politics is an essential part of managerial effectiveness and some political behaviour is required of every manager. When the Polaris missile system was developed in the United States it was hailed as a remarkable achievement for rational management techniques. PERT was devised and has subsequently been used in many other applications. Harvey Sapolsky (1972) studied the project as a case history of success and came to the conclusion that PERT was as effective *technically* as rain dancing (page 246) but that it was effective *politically* because of the reputation it gave the special projects office for efficiency, and that overall Polaris was a political rather than technical achievement in management terms:

> The success of the Polaris program depended on the ability of its proponents to promote and protect Polaris. Competitors had to be eliminated; reviewing agencies had to be outmanoeuvred; congressmen, admirals, newspapermen and academicians had to be co-opted. Politics is a system requirement. What distinguishes programs in government is not that some play politics and others do not, but rather, that some are better at it than others. (Sapolsky, 1972, page 244)

Extremes of 'politicking' are destructive, as well as distasteful, and openness can mitigate such extremes. We must not overlook, however, that power is what the French political scientist Maurice Duverger has called 'Janus-faced'. Janus was the Roman god of doorways and passages, who was always depicted as facing both ways. Power is essential to the process of social integration, yet it divides people and produces conflict. For an organisation to work at all there has to be a distribution of power within the structure to get things done. Yet that very distribution is divisive and produces stress on the structure and members of the organisation. It is when that stress becomes too great that effectiveness declines.

Finally, how can one judge whether an individual manager is going too far in political behaviour? A useful test is to think back to the distinction mentioned in Chapter 4 between setting agendas for action and using networks to implement the agendas. Political behaviour is potentially useful when it is deployed to put agendas into action. It is counterproductive when it is deployed only to build and maintain networks.

Too much network and not enough agenda is associated with the type of person who is more concerned with *being* a manager rather than getting on with the job. The manager who underemphasises networks and concentrates on agendas can be inward looking and fail to take politics seriously, but we have found more examples of managers who spend so much of their time 'networking' that they forget to do the job. We recently found an example in a very large multinational company where a manager dealing with a major customer relied on a gentleman's agreement rather than on a contract with serious results.

SUMMARY PROPOSITIONS

10.1 Power is an inescapable part of management in organisations.

10.2 Four aspects of power are resources, skill, motivation and costs.

10.3 Techniques used by individuals and groups to obtain power include alliances, lobbying, doing favours, being present, cornering resources, being indispensable, reciprocal support for a patron, and being able to cope with uncertainty.

10.4 Openness, as advocated in most management development programmes, can mitigate the extremes of political behaviour which
would otherwise become destructive.

PUTTING IT INTO PRACTICE

Make a list of the various parts of your job. Which would you consider has a
political aspect? Which has little political content? Make a list of the
technique to obtain power. Beside each, list the advantages of using it,
for oneself and for the organisation as a whole. Now list the disadvantages of
each for oneself and for the rest of the organisation.

REFERENCES

Crozier, M., *The Bureaucratic Phenomenon*, Tavistock, London, 1964.
Dahl, R., *Modern Political Analysis*, 2nd edn, Prentice Hall, Englewood Cliffs, New
    Jersey, 1970.
Dalton, M., *Men who Manage*, John Wiley, New York, 1959.
Duverger, M., *The Study of Politics*, Nelson, London, 1972.
Hickson, D.J. *et al.*, 'A strategic contingencies theory of intraorganizational power',
    Administrative Science Quarterly, June 1971, pages 216–29.
Jennings, E.C., *The Mobile Manager*, University of Michigan Press, 1967.
Kotter, J.P., 'Power success and organization effectiveness', *Organization Dynamics*,
    Winter 1978.
Machiavelli, N., *The Prince*, Penguin Books, Harmondsworth, 1981.
Neustadt, R.E., *Presidential Power: the Politics of Leadership*, John Wiley, New York,
    1960.
Peter, L.J., *The Peter Principle*, Morrow, New York, 1969.
Pfeffer, J., *Power in Organizations*, Pitman, Marshfield, Mass., 1981.
Salancik, G.R. and Pfeffer J., 'Who gets power, and how they hold on to it',
    Organizational Dynamics, Winter, 1977.
Sapolsky, H.M., *The Polaris System Development*, Harvard University Press, 1972.

11

TEAM WORKING AND COMMITTEES

The teams of people at work are varied in the degree of involvement with each other that team members have. The members of a choir or a team of dancers have to work together with split-second precision, subordinating all aspects of their own personality to a tightly controlled, collective activity. Those working on machine paced production lines have equally specific and inflexible operations to perform, but with less skill and variety being offered in the routine they follow. A group of sales representatives introducing a new brand of photocopier all follow a similar selling routine and are selling an identical product, yet they spend most of their time alone and are physically dispersed from each other. The people running a hotel have duties that interrelate closely, but with very different skills and conventions. However varied the nature of working teams, the one thing they have in common is a desire by all members that the team should succeed. The desire of an individual to succeed personally at the expense of team success is dangerous.

It is unrealistic always to seek team spirit and commitment to management objectives. Some groups of working people may mistrust or not accept management objectives, yet will still be able to make the specific contribution that managers require of them. Studies of conflict demonstrate that groups whose interests diverge can still find an accommodation that will satisfy both, just as the Russians are able to purchase large quantities of surplus North American grain to supplement the poor yield of their own harvests at the same time as vigorously opposing the economic system that produces the abundance.

THE REASONS FOR WORKING IN TEAMS

Working via a group of people rather than via individuals has many problems. Groups tend to work slowly and present the difficulty of producing compromise solutions that may be too timid for the problem they are designed to tackle, but managers and administrators persist in convening new groups or working parties. Company reorganisation is a commonplace of industrial and commercial life, and the essence of this activity is regrouping of individuals and the reallocation of managerial responsibilities. Whatever the reservations, the way in which groups operate, and the way in which group membership is set up, are both obviously regarded as crucial to management and organisational effectiveness. There are three reasons for this.

First, a group approach is usually best when the problem to be faced is unfamiliar and difficult or risky, without a clear procedural basis for action. Secondly, a group approach is needed when a range of skills and understanding has to be deployed in concerted endeavour, individual skill being insufficient. Thirdly, there is the shrewd view that 'people will support that which they have helped to create'. If action is to follow decision, then action will be taken more accurately and more willingly by those who have participated in shaping the decision.

Review Topic 11.1

Company reorganisation usually has the changing of working teams at its centre. What does this tell us about the importance to managers of these teams? What does it tell us about the importance to individuals of these teams?

An advertising campaign will be created by imaginative individuals having brainwaves, but underpinning those creative leaps are a series of meetings and conferences at which ideas are swapped, derided, developed and improved. A clever turn of phrase by a copy writer is turned into a sketch by an artist and sight of the sketch triggers off a further development of the initial idea. The operating theatre of a hospital has in it a group of people all of whom have varying levels and types of skill. The surgeon is at the centre, controlling the operation, but the surgeon cannot complete the operation without the effective and swift co-ordination of all the other skilled people present. When a company is to introduce a new product, the launch is usually preceded by a sales conference at which all those involved in sales promotion, marketing, face-to-face selling and (perhaps) distribution come together to learn what is involved and to generate enthusiasm about the new venture. Many of the traditional problems of tension and disagreement between production and marketing in companies can be traced to the fact that the production people (who were not invited to the sales conference in Majorca) see a new product as a series of headaches while marketing people see it as a golden opportunity. A time-honoured way of overcoming this problem is reorganising employees into product groups, so that the focus of selected marketing and production experts is made the product rather than the function. Taking *everyone* to Majorca is so expensive.

There may be advantages to management interest in team working, but why should individual employees want to work in this way? Although we vary in the degree of our willingness to work closely with others, we each have an inbuilt need to belong to groups with which we can identify and in which we can compare ourselves with other individuals. These needs are not met completely by family and out of work friendship groups, there is a need for work group attachment as well. This can operate at the level of attachment to the industry ('I am in engineering'), to an occupation ('I am an electrical engineer'), to an organisation ('I am with XYZ and Co.'), to a small group ('I am on the design team'), or to a role ('I am the electronics specialist on the design team'). For some people all those attachments will be important, but for most one will dominate the others, and a few people will have very low attachment. It is difficult, for instance, to imagine Beethoven wanting to identify with any working group, yet he was remarkably productive. Every organisation has its share of minor Beethovens.

Katz and Kahn (1978) advocate groups as being an important arena for individuals to find a sense of accomplishment and completion of a task; particularly in those work settings where this cannot be experienced individually, as in many manufacturing processes. This is the main argument behind the movement for autonomous work groups and for quality circles in factories.

> By being part of something beyond the physical self, the individual can achieve a sense of belongingness and can participate in accomplishments beyond individual powers. (Katz and Kahn, 1978, page 374)

TEAMS AT WORK

An initial distinction that has to be made about working in teams is between the *task* that the group has to achieve and the *processes* by which the team members operate. We are here concerned mainly with the processes but only by completing the task satisfactorily is there any justification for considering the process. There is always a danger that the activity of being in the team, with all those other nice people, can be emphasised at the expense of the task, but there is some evidence that a significant basis for the satisfaction of individual team members with their membership is the sense of achievement in producing results. At the same time it is necessary for the team to maintain cohesion while being unsuccessful. Most teams experience failure as well as success and the test of effectiveness may well be the ability to get through the bad times without disintegrating.

Teams differ according to their purpose. The working party, or task force, is a short-term grouping while the work group is fairly permanent and those who are members of the first will also be members of the second, although, maybe, not the other way round. Some teams, such as the board of directors in a company, have decision-making as their prime task; while others, such as autonomous work groups, have the objective of making things by co-operative effort.

CHARACTERISTICS OF TEAMS

Tuckman (1965) suggests that there are clear stages in the growth of relationships in groups of people working together, as shown in Table 11.1, of *forming, storming, norming* and *performing.* People come together and conflict develops between members as they assess each other before they move to the third stage of finding a way of working together. Finally they work well and produce results.

The length of time required for this process varies. For a team that is to be together for a long time, it may take many months because the degree of investment required from each member is so high and the personal risks of failure so great. If the team is convening as a short-term, part-time activity – like the group that is arranging the office party at Christmas – then the individual investment is less, the risks fewer and the mutual tolerance greater so that the process is easily truncated. Individual tolerance of the process varies, so that there is always at least one person who will quickly

Table 11.1 Stages in the growth of group cohesion and performance

Stage of development	Process	Outcome
1. *Forming*	There is anxiety, dependence on leader, testing to find out the nature of the situation and what behaviour is acceptable	Members find out what the task is, what the rules are and what methods are appropriate
2. *Storming*	Conflict between sub-groups, rebellion against leader, opinions are polarised, resistance to control by group	Emotional resistance to demands of task
3. *Norming*	Development of group cohesion, norms emerge, resistance is overcome and conflicts patched up; mutual support and sense of group identity	Open exchange of views and feelings; co-operation develops
4. *Performing*	Interpersonal problems are resolved; interpersonal structure becomes the means of getting things done; roles are flexible and functional	Solutions to problems emerge; there are constructive attempts to complete tasks and energy is now available for effective work

(Based on Tuckman B.W., 1965, pages 384–99)

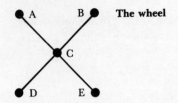

The wheel

All communications have to go through person C at the centre. This network provides quick answers to simple questions, but A, B, D and E are likely to be dissatisfied with their roles.

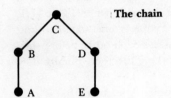

The chain

No one member is able to communicate with all the others. Members of the team are reasonably satisfied with this system of communication, but it can be inaccurate and slow.

The circle

By closing the chain each team member can communicate directly with two others. This provides the highest level of general satisfaction and can be effective for dealing with complex problems.

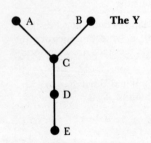

The Y

This combines features of the Wheel and the Chain in a centralised network.

Completely connected network

Each team member can now communicate freely with every other member and all are satisfied with their role. It can be an effective method of dealing with complex problems, but is unsatisfactory for dealing with straightforward matters.

Fig. 11.1 Types of communication network.
(Based on Leavitt, 1951)

make a comment like 'If we don't get something settled soon, we will be here all night'.

A number of experimental studies have attempted to establish which method of communication within a team is the most appropriate. The classic study was that of Leavitt (1951), which is summarised in Fig. 11.1. For experimental purposes members of a small group were given tasks which involved communicating with each other, but they were required to communicate in differing, specific ways. The Wheel and Y networks had a central controlling person in the system, while the others were decentralised with varying degrees of limitation on the freedom with which group members exchanged information. Centralised networks were best for getting simple jobs done and decentralised networks produced better solutions to difficult problems. Centralisation was highly satisfying to person C at the centre, but frustrating for others.

The patterns illustrated each represent a typical situation found in working life. The Wheel is like a regional sales team with four members reporting to a regional manager. The chain is like a department with two executives, B and D, each reporting to a manager C and having personal assistants A and E. The Y is similar to an orthodox chain of command with one person B who is outside and who communicates only with C, as is the case of a key supplier or customer. The Circle and the Completely Connected Network are like discussion groups, with the Circle being an unusual form which is more important from the experimental point of view than because of the frequency with which it is found.

The most effective teams are those which can vary their mode of operation between, say, the Wheel and the Completely Connected Network in line with task requirements. Managers who try to centralise all communication will find resistance from team members, who will lack any sense of involvement in what is taking place. Managers who decentralise everything will miss opportunities through wasting time and team members will come to regard the process as one of all talk and no action. Managers who can achieve a shrewd balance and have thorough, decentralised consideration of matters which can only be dealt with in that way will then find that their team members readily acknowledge the right and necessity of the managers operating in a centralised way for the majority of straightforward decisions and information.

Another classic study was that of Rice (1958). It is interesting that this was conducted in an Indian textile factory; not all our evidence comes from North America. Rice had four main conclusions (pages 37–9).

1. The most productive group, and the one most satisfactory to its members, is the pair; then groups 6–12, with 8 as the optimum.
2. Group stability is more easily maintained when the range of skills is such that all members can comprehend each others' skills; that is they could aspire to acquire them.

Fig. 11.2 Interaction process categories.
(From Bales, R.F., 1950)

3. The fewer differences in prestige and status within the group, the more stable it is.
4. When a member of a work group becomes disaffected and no longer fits in, he should be able to move elsewhere.

Group size is particularly important for teams who need to exchange ideas as too few people are not able to generate sufficient richness of ideas, but too many can lead either to a baffling excess of suggestions or to some more cautious members being inhibited.

TEAM ROLES

R.F. Bales (1950) developed a series of observation categories for studying the process of interaction in small groups. These are shown in Figure 11.2. He found that groups needed both members who were effective in the task area and those who were effective in the social and emotional area. Team members who were task oriented were the most influential and those who were social-emotional oriented were the best liked, but both were necessary for the continuing effectiveness of the group. Bales also differentiated between behaviour in the group that was emotionally positive and that which was emotionally negative.

There are always the conciliators, the antagonists and the neurotics, working alongside the questioners, clarifiers and directors. Neither can succeed without the other and each group member will be partly task-oriented and partly social–emotional-oriented, with one orientation typically dominant.

Belbin *et al.* (1976) carried out a systematic study of management teams and concluded that six roles were needed in effective management teams apart from specialist and functional roles.

His six have now been expanded to eight roles (Belbin, 1981):

1. *Company worker*, who keeps the interests of the organisation to the fore at all times.
2. *Chairman*, who ensures that the views of all participants are heard and who keeps things moving.
3. *Shaper*, who follows particular lines of argument and blends together elements of the contributions from several other members.
4. *Ideas person*, who contributes novel suggestions.
5. *Resource investigator*, who assesses the feasibility of contributions and finds out where and how to obtain the required resources.
6. *Monitor/evaluator*, who evaluates the relevance of the contributions being made and the extent to which the team is meeting its objectives.
7. *Team worker*, who maintains the social cohesion of the group and the discussion process by joking and agreeing with others.

8. *Completer/finisher*, who looks for conclusions and tries to get things done.

Here again we see the importance of task orientation as well as the social-emotional area or team maintenance, but a related aspect of the roles which team members assume is the way in which conflict can develop within the general mode of co-operative team working. As with conflict between management and a collective of employees, this can be constructive or destructive. John Hunt (1979) summarises the possibilities:

> Conflict may:
>   Introduce different solutions to the problem,
>   Clearly define the power relationship within the group,
>   Encourage creativity and brainstorming activity,
>   Focus on individual contributions rather than group decisions,
>   Bring emotive, non-rational arguments into the open,
>   Provide for catharsis, release of interdepartmental or interpersonal conflicts of long-standing.
>
> Conversely, if conflict is destructive, it may:
>   Dislocate the entire group and produce polarisations,
>   Subvert the objectives in favour of sub-goals,
>   Lead people to defensive and blocking behaviour in their group,
>   Result in the disintegration of the entire group,
>   Stimulate win–lose conflicts, where reason is secondary to emotion.
>
> (Hunt, 1979, pages 90–1)

The team leader is always vigilant for the level of conflict in the team. Although the comments of Hunt, above, are directed towards behaviour in face-to-face groups, there is a similar problem with the general, long-term working relationships between team members. They are all to some extent in competition with each other, all likely to feel that they are being left out of important meetings and all likely to mistrust the manoeuvres of their colleagues. This can keep people on their toes and ensure a keen level of contribution, but there is always the risk that the conflict can become destructive and the manager will need then to confront the problem. This is not a favourite job for managers, as it can involve unpleasantness and the outcome is hard to predict. The best guide for dealing with such problems is a publication on interpersonal problem-solving by Richard Walton (1969).

Review Topic 11.2

Think of a group you were with within the last few days, for example:
    a business meeting,
    a lunch group,
    a sports team,
    a seminar, or
    a dinner party.

1. **Who spoke most?**
2. **Who spoke least?**
3. **Who gave most task-oriented conversation?**
4. **Who gave most group-oriented conversation?**
5. **Did you find it a satisfying experience? Why, or why not?**

TEAM DEVELOPMENT

Understanding the ways in which teams work is the best way to working effectively with and through them, as most people have to find a way of working with what there is rather than being able to make changes. For managers, however, who are able to take initiatives to improve their teams, some techniques have been evolved for assisting this process.

Sensitivity training. A controversial method of developing in people an awareness of their impact on others. It is potentially useful to develop an ability of individuals to work in teams and uses group methods to achieve its objectives. The idea is that all of us dissemble in our everyday dealings with others; we smile at people we dislike and restrain critical comments about others, either because we fear retaliation or because it is not accepted behaviour. Sensitivity training forces trainees to be more open in their behaviour towards others and, in the process, become more sensitive to the feelings and attitudes of others. The method is basically to put a group of 8–12 people in a room without any agenda or programme and leave them there for long periods. The lack of structure provides a void which group members try to fill and their comments gradually become more frank. As there is nothing to talk about, they inevitably talk about their relationship with each other. Those who are task oriented or social–emotionally oriented become apparent and everyone comes to a deeper understanding of how he relates to others. The value of this method can be considerable, but the risks are also great. It encourages people to be more open and honest with each other, but has the following drawbacks.

1. It forces many individuals to undergo a personality-humiliating and anxiety-provoking experience from which they might not recover.
2. It strips some people of defenses they badly need and provides them with nothing to replace those defenses.
3. It encourages behavioural modes that are acceptable in the laboratory but unacceptable in most organizational settings.
4. Any benefits accrued from the experience are so short-lived as to make the experience a waste of time and money.
5. It encourages and subtly coerces individuals into revealing aspects about themselves that constitute an invasion of privacy, thus harboring later resentment in participants. (du Brin, 1974, page 424)

Against such a catalogue of drawbacks it is remarkable that the sensitivity training method was used so extensively. It is described here because elements of the method are to be found in many other training approaches.

Organisation development. A term that has been applied to many different approaches, but one of them is to use an Organisation Development (OD) consultant to work with a group of people to improve their collective performance. The group consists of people who *do* work together and the discussion is based on what they have to say rather than on any 'instruction' from the consultant, who is often described as a change agent because this method has so often been used to make working teams more effective at innovation. There will be an agenda, with items such as:

1. Are we each clear about our duties and responsibilities?
2. Are there any areas of overlap? Anything missing?
3. In what ways do we communicate well with each other? In what ways badly?
4. How can we communicate with each other better?

The role of the consultant is to direct the discussion to the agenda and to ensure that it is kept to the way the job is done rather than attacks on individuals and their personal characteristics. This produces candour and constructive discussion, but deflects the behaviours that could be destructive.

This is not a speedy process and it will probably take a number of meetings before all participants are convinced that there will be an improvement. Ideally some everyday working experience is interspersed with the training sessions to put into practice some of the proposals in order to re-examine, in the everyday situation, some of what has been said in discussion. One method is to start with a weekend of discussion and then have two or three follow-up sessions after a few weeks back in the workplace. The consultant should be phased out towards the end of the training period.

COMMITTEE OPERATIONS

Commitees operate in a relatively formal way. There is invariably a chairman and usually minutes are kept. These may be drafted by a secretary during and after the meeting, with the draft then modified by the chairman, but eventually they have to be accepted by all members at the next meeting. The chairman has considerable scope for determining the way in which proceedings are recorded and emphasised, but there is less scope for determining decisions, unless the committee is remarkably compliant. Before a decision is reached it will be framed with some precision, even though it may not be put as a formal motion. Either the chairman will frame it in a leading way – 'Are we all agreed then, that we offer the post to

Smith?' – or it will be put to the meeting as a motion from committee members. The wording is likely to be clarified and tidied up before the committee as a whole votes on it.

One determinant of effectiveness will be the size of the committee. What is appropriate depends on the committee's main purpose. Hare (1981) produces evidence that a membership between six and ten is preferred for problem-solving and making decisions. Fewer members means that there may be insufficient input of information and ideas. More people leads to unwieldly discussion, diverse information input and the inhibiting of the less confident members of the committee. Schwartz (1980, page 342) makes the following suggestions:

> Relatively large committees are desired when:
>
> - A principal purpose of the committee is to inform the members who comprise it.
> - Widely differing talents and experience are needed to make the recommendation or decision.
> - The scope of the committee's activities is very broad. In these cases, however, it may be wise to divide the work into sub-committees.
>
> Relatively small committees are desired when:
>
> - Speedy action is needed.
> - The matter assigned to the committee must be kept confidential. Obviously, the more persons serving on a committee, the greater the chance of information leaks.

Committee effectiveness is also influenced by the nature of the *membership*. There are nearly always some ineffective members who hold their place for political reasons or even as a form of punishment. They are likely to delay, confuse or demoralise the committee as a whole. One of the important matters to be resolved is whether an individual is essential or 'possibly useful'; only the essential should be recruited. The ideal committee member should be interested in its purpose, with relevant knowledge and experience and sufficient time to attend and prepare for meetings. Finally the ideal member should be psychologically equipped for the committee process: able to compromise after reasoned argument, listening as well as talking, but sufficiently resolute to persist in trying to persuade other members to his point of view. In this way his contribution is made and used by the group as a whole in the search for consensus.

The *method* of the committee discussion is basically the exchange of information followed by working on hypotheses. On each issue or item on the agenda members first seek out the facts, even if those facts do not necessarily support their personal cause. This search for information may be aided by information being provided by the chairman or secretary for study beforehand. Nearly all committees have some preliminary documentation of this type, but it will be expanded by verbal contributions from committee members. This will add to what is written or provide interpretation. A committee deciding whether to instal gas- or oil-fired central heating will be provided with the comparative cost estimates, but individual members will have a myriad of questions to put to the various interested members, which could not all be anticipated beforehand. As more and more information is exchanged the committee members build up a shared information base that makes ultimate consensus possible.

Once committee members find answers to all their questions they are reaching a point where decisions could be made, and this decision-making is expedited by exploring hypotheses. The nature of contributions changes. In information exchange the contributions are mainly question and answer, with questions like the following:

> 'Do we know how long it would take?'
> 'Could Fred tell us . . . ?'
> 'Will the suppliers provide . . . ?'

When discussion on a topic moves to hypotheses, the questions become leading.

> 'It seems to me that we have only one course to follow.'
> 'Does this mean that we have to . . . ?'
> 'Would anyone agree with me that . . . ?'

Review Topic 11.2

The Roman poet Ovid (43 BC – AD 17) made the comment 'You will go most safely in the middle . . .' (medio tutissimus ibis).

Does decision-making by committee increase or decrease the desire for safety?

As working on competing hypotheses develops, the chairman will be looking for the most acceptable hypothesis in order to single it out for the committee's consent. When topics are extremely complex, the committee may divide up the work between subgroups of themselves, so that a series of working hypotheses is developed and the committee reconvenes to find a viable amalgram of the contributed part-decisions.

SUMMARY PROPOSITIONS

11.1 The working team is the fundamental unit of organisation and many organisational tasks cannot be achieved by other means.

11.2 All employees can achieve a degree of satisfaction in team working that they cannot achieve by other means.

11.3 A distinction can be drawn between the task of a group and the processes whereby the group deals with the task. Teams need contributions that are both task oriented and social–emotionally oriented.

11.4 Committees formalise the act of groupworking. This is fundamental to the working of any organisation.

11.3 Committees are semi-permanent bodies of which the main purposes are to make decisions and diffuse information.

11.6 Although decisions by committee may be less cost-effective than those made by individuals, they may be bolder, and a committee decision starts life with all the members committed to its success.

11.7 Members of committees compete with each other as well as co-operate. When controlled by the chairman, this improves the quality of the committee's work. *person*

11.8 The main operating method of committees is the exchange of information, working on hypotheses and achieving consensus.

PUTTING IT INTO PRACTICE

Analysing team roles in management groups

Team leaders can make their teams more effective by analysing the roles that team members fill, to see what contributions are being made and what is being left out. This can also provide the basis of developing the contributions and career prospects of individual team members.

Use the matrix in Fig. 11.3 to record incidents of team members' behaviour that you observe in any aspect of team working. The types of activity will vary between teams and the situations in which they are working, but the most common are as follows:

1. Face-to-face (informal).
2. Memorandum.
3. Telephone.
4. Formal meeting.

The matrix is set out with the six roles identified by Belbin and referred to in this chapter. These are on the vertical axis with columns for each team member arranged horizontally. Each of the resulting boxes is divided into

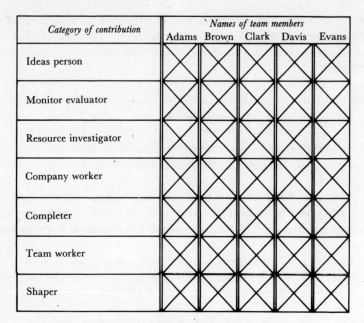

Category of contribution	Names of team members				
	Adams	Brown	Clark	Davis	Evans
Ideas person					
Monitor evaluator					
Resource investigator					
Company worker					
Completer					
Team worker					
Shaper					

Fig. 11.3 Matrix for analysing team members' roles.

four sections, so that the behaviours can be tallied with strokes to record each incident. The sections are as shown in Fig. 11.4.

Incidents should be recorded over a week and at the end of the week you can see both the emphasis of the contributions being made by individual team members and the team roles which are being filled and those which are not. Most people make contributions in a variety of roles but you should also find some who consistently make more contributions in one particular area.

Are there any roles not being filled? Should they be? Who might be encouraged to fill them? (For example, someone who makes an occasional contribution in this area, or yourself?).

This method of analysis is the one we regard as most appropriate for

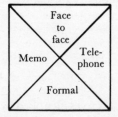

Fig. 11.4 Incidents in team working.

(Based on Belbin R.M. *et al.* 'Building effective management teams' in *Journal of General Management*, 3, 1976, pages 23–9)

management teams, although the methods of Bales and Blake and Mouton (both mentioned in the text) are extensively used.

Interaction guide for committee chair

1. *Before the meeting*

Decide   (a) What the purpose is – decision-making, briefing, problem-solving, generating ideas, or something else.

(b) Whether the meeting is needed, or whether the purpose could be achieved better by other means or at a different time.

(c) What should have been achieved by the end of the meeting.

(d) What your role should be in the meeting – leader, sage, synthesiser, statesperson, spokesperson, or something else.

Review   (a) Minutes of previous meeting, papers for presenting meeting.

(b) Expected attendance and opening positions likely to be adopted by members.

(c) (With secretary) arrangements for the meeting and the distribution of information to members about time, place, etc.

(d) (With individual members) who will introduce different agenda items, perhaps making suggestions about data to be included or aspects to be developed.

(e) The agenda to consider timing and pacing of discussion.

2. *During the meeting*

Introduce   (a) Any new members.

(b) A brief overview of the business to be considered.

(c) The secretary, for apologies and the minutes of the last meeting.

(d) (Progressively through the meeting) each agenda item with a summary statement about the reasons for the topic and general background for the discussion.

Recognise   (a) Members to develop your introduction by inviting them to 'speak to' the agenda item.

(b) Members who want to speak by selecting between those trying to 'catch your eye', so that there is a balance between varying points of view.

(c) Members whose contribution could be important but is not being offered, by asking them to comment.

(d) Members whose *style* of contribution could be timely, such as the member known for his calmness, invited for comment at a time of heated exchanges.

(e) Members whose *authority* of contribution would be useful to move discussion forward, such as the person who initially 'spoke to' an item, asked to offer a hypothesis or propose a motion.

Control and (a) By expediting decision through picking the time when you
facilitate can use your authority with a phrase like, 'I take it that we agree that . . .' without your authority being challenged.

(b) By focusing on disagreements and finding a resolution.

(c) By summarising the state of the discussion and pointing a new direction.

(d) By curbing contributions from members that are irrelvant or too long.

(e) By asking for clarification from a group member of a point that is signalled by the non-verbal behaviour of other members as being puzzling or unacceptable.

(f) By being interested and alert throughout.

(g) By finishing on time.

3. *After the meeting*

Check (a) (With the secretary) that the minutes or notes of the meeting are compiled, agreed with you and circulated.

(b) That those who are to take action know what to do, and do it.

Assess (a) How you could have conducted the meeting better and build that assessment into your preparation for the next.

(b) The appropriate time for the next meeting, material to be prepared for it, and any review of membership to be considered.

Studies and suggestions on chairing appear in Anstey (1965).

Interaction guide for committee member

1. *Before the meeting*

Decide (a) What the purpose of the meeting is (see Chair's list).

(b) What you want to have achieved by the end of the meeting – as a member and as a representative of an interest.

(c) What should your role be in the meeting – sage, synthesiser, delegate, adviser, brake, stimulus, or something else.

(d) Decide whether you could/should be replaced by someone else for this meeting – subordinate, superior, colleague.

Review	(a)	Minutes of previous meeting, papers for present meeting.
	(b)	Action you were asked to take at the previous meeting.
	(c)	(With other individual committee members) their tentative views on agenda items in which you have a particular interest, possibly eliciting support for your own position.
	(d)	Notes you plan to use, papers you are to table, or visual aids to support your contribution.

2. *During the meeting*

Signal	(a)	A wish to speak, by using non-verbal signals to 'catch the eye' of the chair.
	(b)	Reactions to the contributions of others by non-verbal signals – such as nods and frowns.
Ask	(a)	For direction from the chair about points of order or terms of reference.
	(b)	For clarification, from the chair or another member, on information presented.
	(c)	For opinion, suggestion or hypothesis, from chair or from another member.
Offer	(a)	Information for exchange, including prepared presentations asked for by chair before meeting.
	(b)	Opinion, suggestion or hypothesis; either when called for or when mood of the meeting judged to be appropriate.
	(c)	Support for, or criticism of, opinions etc. offered by others.
Seek	(a)	By using social skills to persuade others.
Influence	(b)	By using objectivity and seeking solutions that will be acceptable to others.
	(c)	By avoiding rancorous personal attacks on other committee members that will isolate you from the sympathy of other members.
	(d)	Support and develop the contributions of other members which you regard as constructive and likely to be generally acceptable after modification.
	(e)	By displaying expertise, both on your specialist area and on the general committee documentation and precedents.

3. *After the meeting*

Consult	(a)	With those you represent to advise them of committee decisions and required action.
	(b)	With those you represent about the position you have taken on agenda items and any ways in which this should be modified.

Assess   (a) How you could have participated in the meeting more effectively and build that assessment into your preparation for the next.

(b) The minutes, when they are circulated, and any suggestions you may have for future agenda items. Note corrections needed to the minutes on those items which require action from you.

Administrative drill for committee secretary

(To make this illustration concrete we are assuming a meeting once a month, lasting between two and three hours each time, on Wednesday, day 28.)

Day	*Phase one: minutes and preliminaries*
1,2	Write draft of minutes, including notes of action items.
5	Clear minutes with chair and confirm date of next meeting.
6,7	Type, copy and distribute minutes.
7	Book room for next meeting.

Phase two: agenda

12   Ask committee members for items to be included on next agenda.

16   Discuss order of agenda and inclusion/deferment of items with chairman. Suggested sequence:

(a) Announcements (apologies, introduction of new members, chairman's points).

(b) Minutes of previous meeting and matters arising, where matter involves brief report. Matters arising for further discussion to be separate agenda items.

(c) Items requiring decision but involving little controversy.

(d) Most difficult item.
    (possible break)

(e) Next most difficult item.

(f) Items requiring discussion but not decision.

(g) Easy items.

(h) Any other business.

(i) Provisional date of next meeting.

Phase three: run up

19   Circulate agenda and other papers to members, with note of date, time and venue.

23   Check seating, catering, visual aids.

27   Collate all papers, past minutes, apologies.

28   Attend meeting and take notes for minutes.

REFERENCES

Anstey, E., *Committees: How They Work*, Geo. Allen and Unwin, London, 1965.

Bales, R.F., *Interaction Process Analysis*, Addison Wesley, Reading, Mass., 1950.

Belbin, R.M., Aston, B.R. and Mottram, R.D., 'Building effective management teams', *Journal of General Management*, vol. 2, 1976, pages 23–9.

Blake, R.R. and Mouton, J.S., *Building a Dynamic Organization through Grid Organization Development*, Addison Wesley, Reading, Mass., 1969.

Blake, R.R. and Mouton, J.S., *The New Management Grid*, Gulf Publishing, Houston, 1978.

du Brin, A.J., *Fundamentals of Organizational Behaviour*, Pergamon, New York, 1974.

Elliott, C., 'Making excellence useful', contribution to a conference, *Technical Assistance Overseas and the Environment*, reported in *Royal Society of Arts Journal*, vol. CXXI, no. 5324, 1983.

Gahagan, J., *Interpersonal and Group Behaviour*, Methuen, London, 1975.

Hare, A.P. in Borgatta, E.F. and Baker, P.M., 'Symposia on small groups,' *American Behavioural Scientist*, May/June, 1981.

Hunt, J., *Managing People at Work*, Pan Books, London, 1979.

Katz, D. and Kahn, R.L., *The Social Psychology of Organisations*, 2nd edn, John Wiley, New York, 1978.

Leavitt, H.J., 'Some aspects of certain communication patterns on group performance', *Journal of Abnormal and Social Psychology*, vol. 45, 1951, pages 38–50.

Leavitt, H.J., Dill, W.R. and Eyring, H.B., *The Organizational World*, Harcourt Brace Jovanovich, New York, 1973.

Rice, A.K., *Productivity and Social Organisation*, Tavistock, London, 1958.

Schein, E.H., *Process Consultation*, Addison Wesley, Reading, Mass., 1969.

Schwartz, D., *Introduction to Management: Principles, Practices and Processes*, Harcourt Brace Jovanovich, New York, 1980.

Tuckman, B.W., 'Development sequences in small groups', *Psychological Bulletin*, vol. 63, 1965, pages 384–99.

Walton, R.E., *Interpersonal Peacemaking*, Addison Wesley, Reading, Mass., 1969.

12

THE ORGANISATION OF JOBS AND DEPARTMENTS

The two activities in the title of this chapter are fundamental to the process of management, yet they are not often undertaken deliberately. It is more common for jobs to develop or to be brought into being as a response to some aspect of organisational change, than it is for jobs to be thought out. It is more common for people to be grouped together in a rough-and-ready form of departmental structure than it is for departmental organisation to be thought out to find the best method.

The job of sales assistant in a department store, for instance, has certain characteristics that are dominant because of the demands of customer service and which override any possibility of designing the job in the way most satisfactory to the employee or most efficient in departmental co-ordination and organisation. With many jobs the operating context dictates the main job characteristics and job design can seldom do more than modify existing practice.

Departments in companies usually come into existence as a result of company expansion. At one stage there will be one or two safety officers in a company, each attached to a factory and reporting to the production manager. When there are eight or nine safety officers, they are likely to be grouped together with a safety manager in charge. The method of working in this new alignment will evolve gradually, so that initiatives in organising the members of the department will come in stages rather than being worked out in detail before operations begin.

This chapter contains material on both the design of jobs and the design of departmental organisation, but our opening comment is that most managers will find few opportunities for approaching either task from scratch. Redesign is a much more common activity than design.

THE NATURE OF JOB DESIGN

Job design is the process of putting together a range of tasks, duties and responsibilities to create a composite for individuals to undertake in their work and regard as their own. Some of the job dimensions begin with the reasons for people to be employed in a particular organisation. This can be illustrated by using the example of employees in a department store that was used earlier.

Shop assistants are employed for *product market* reasons. The customer expects some type of sales service, ranging from detailed advice and technical explanation to simple cash-and-wrap operations. This is why shop assistants have to be on view, standing, identifiable and willing to respond to customers' requirements. The *technology* of the product requires cosmetic saleswomen to wear what they sell and those selling popular records and tapes to be able to tolerate sustained high-volume noise. Others are employed for *administrative* reasons and the administrative structure will be the main influence on their jobs, so that wages clerks spend most of their time sitting and doing solo manipulations with figures while buyers spend most of their time not buying at all but filling in forms to get the right balance between materials bought and materials sold.

Others are employed for *social system* reasons and a particular aspect of the social system determines the main dimensions of their jobs. The fire officer wears a special uniform so that people will respond in times of emergency. Catering staff have to fit in with a grossly inefficient timescale of their operations: intense activity around teabreaks and lunchtime.

Part of the management process is to mediate operational constraints and requirements like these in dividing work up between members of the organisation, so that there are a number of composites – or jobs – that employees will be motivated to undertake and are combined in such a way as to produce satisfactory working performance in the co-ordinated effort of the department and the organisation.

Much of the interest in job design has centred round attempts to improve employee satisfaction with the working situation. It is inappropriate however, to regard this type of initiative as only suitable for mass production jobs. Administrative and managerial jobs, especially in large organisations, can be crying out for job design initiatives. Creating opportunities for senior managers can all too often involve limiting the scope of middle and junior managers to such an extent that the initiatives of their seniors are jeopardised. An American study was carried out among forty large organisations that were chosen because they made particular efforts to use their managers effectively, yet:

> Management in the typical organization was characterized by having rather narrow jobs and very tightly written job descriptions that almost seemed designed to take the newness, conflict and challenge out of the job. (Campbell *et al*. 1970)

Table 12.1 An elementary job design matrix

Job	Product market reasons	Technology reasons	Administrative reasons	Social system reasons
Film actor				
Fire officer				
Nurse				
Teacher				
....				
....				

Review Topic 12.1

1. Reproduce the elementry matrix shown in Table 12.1 on a piece of paper.

2. Write in a job dimension in each column against each of the printed jobs and then add in three or four more jobs with which you are familiar, with the dimensions.

3. Are there any of those job dimensions that could be altered to make the job more efficient *and* more satisfying.

Job design sets the individual to work and organisation design sets that work in a departmental, co-ordinated setting.

FACTORS IN JOB DESIGN

John Child (1984) points to three key aspects of the ways in which jobs can be shaped: specialisation, definition and discretion.

1. *Specialisation.* The extent to which a job is clearly identified and different from others, so that there is a clear justification for a person doing it, due to skill, experience or some other distinguishing factor. The reason for this is obviously that it enables the greatest degree of expertise to be developed. The teacher who concentrates on teaching French, rather than on teaching French, physics and woodwork is likely to become more skilled at teaching French because of the specialised development that is then possible. But how specialised should a role be? If the French teacher were also to teach German or Latin, would that enable the development of complementary skills and understanding to produce a generally higher quality of work?

Specialisation develops expertise and expertise produces authority and autonomy, so that the right degree of specialisation enables the job holder to 'own' skills and knowledge in a satisfying way, but if jobs are made too narrow there is the risk of the problem identified by Campbell and his colleagues that we have just seen. Specialisation is not always based on skill, sometimes it is a simple administrative division of duties. Child illustrates this most effectively by contrasting the practice in two companies:

> In one organization . . . 'Peter Jones from Quality or one of his team, and a chap from Engineering – quite often Phil Bond or Jim Dankworth – usually get together on that one. They will sort it out, and call in anyone else, as they think best.' In another organization, you might be referred to page 23 of the procedures manual where it states that 'customer complaints are the responsibility of the Assistant Quality Control Manager – Warranty and Complaints.' This man, you are told, 'has a job description which lays down quite specifically the way he should deal with a complaint, including the maximum amount of expenditure he can incur. Should he wish to spend more, or involve anyone from another Department, he must first refer to the Quality Control Manager.' (Child, 1984, page 25)

The first of those two organisations emphasises skill rather than position and responsibility, with the specialisation not being too precise. It appears more civilised and constructive as a way of running a business, as long as one is looking at it from inside, where individuals can be deployed and appreciated as individuals. Once the interface with the outside world becomes important, then the emphasis on role becomes more logical. The customer telephoning from Land's End to John o'Groats with an urgent complaint would probably begin to foam at the mouth when told about Peter Jones and Phil Bond or Jim Dankworth.

2. *Definition.* The degree to which job boundaries are clearly marked. This is the area of job descriptions, procedures and drills. There will always be a degree of such definition, the managerial problem is again to decide how much. The process of definition has the great merit that the manager has to work out exactly what is required, how it can be done and what the contribution of each team member can be. Ambiguity is lessened and the mission of the individual becomes clearer. Organisational practices can be made identical so that swapping people about is easier.

The overwhelming danger of precise definition is its lack of flexibility and the risk that job holders regard the definitions as challenges to be defied rather than as guidelines for effectiveness. However precise or imprecise the definition the objective should be to define jobs in a way that which makes them 'whole', so that the scope is sufficient for job holders to see assignments through to a completion. They can seldom do all that they would like, but the work needs to have both variety and integration for it to be a coherent, satisfactory whole. This was the direction of many of the job enlargement initiatives that became popular in the early 1970s. The satisfaction of seeing something through is not limited to the job holder; there is a greater satisfaction for the client, whether inside the organisation or outside. Most people have experienced the frustration of being a client in a large, bureaucratic system, like a hospital or an insurance company, where the client feels helpless as the organisational machine grinds through its cycle. Individuals to whom they speak can always answer only some questions and deal with only some requirements before they are passed on to someone else.

In considering job boundaries, the manager needs to think in terms of whole jobs, with a logic and coherence that meets the needs of clients as well as the needs of job holders. The manager must also think in terms of what has to be done, but here it helps to think of what Kellogg (1968) has called 'long term missions', as these will give a sense of purpose and responsibility that is more complete than that of dealing only with the immediate, and it describes the duties of the job holder in a way that produces a clear contribution to organisational affairs.

3. *Discretion.* The degree of autonomy that the job holder enjoys. Effective leadership requires the autonomy of the led, but again the vexing question is to decide how much discretion job holders should have. Discretion leads to responsibility and thoroughness, as the blame for mistakes can not easily be transferred elsewhere. The job enrichment initiatives that have been widely documented (e.g. Wild, 1975) have the deepening of discretion at the heart of the strategy for 'enriching' manual jobs.

Although specialisation, definition and discretion are the main issues in job design, there are one or two commonsense points to add. Where people are employed at the same status in an organisation, doing jobs that are interdependent, it is sensible for them to be of roughly equal complexity, with critical matters also distributed between all posts. It is always useful to look for a combination of duties that fit the logic of the situation rather than a random collection. Some combinations are obvious, like one person doing all that is involved in servicing a motor car, but others are less clear. Consider your experience in eating out at a restaurant. Taking your order, serving your meal and taking your payment are three separate activities; you will have visited restaurants where they are all done by one person and others where they are divided between two, three or more people. It is difficult to say which is the most effective.

RECENT DEVELOPMENTS IN JOB DESIGN

Following the examination of ways to make individual jobs more productive by concentrating on the tasks to be done, recently attention has been directed at other aspects, such as work patterns, autonomy and the orientation of the job itself.

Working life for most people is surprisingly rigid: nine till five for five days a week with a few individual days' holiday at religious festivals and three or four weeks' annual holiday, which must be taken within a twelve month period. *Changing work patterns* enables people to break out of that rigidity and find a more personalised mode. The stimulus towards this has included the desire of some employees with extended families in other countries to spend lengthy periods of leave abroad, and the interest of some potential employees in working part-time, although the mould-breaking development was the introduction of flexible working hours during the early 1970s. This simple practice enables people to vary their actual hours of attendance at work marginally at the beginning and end of the day and is now widespread in clerical and administrative work.

Compressed hours arrangements enable people to work for four and a half, four or fewer days a week by extending the time spent on each day. A further variant is to contract to provide a specified number of hours a year (usually 1700–1750), while the individual enjoys considerable latitude in deciding when to work those hours.

Part-time working is growing rapidly and Syrrett (1983) gives a guide to different methods, including an analysis of how the costs vary between the employment of part-timers and full-timers. After a slow start, there is now growing use of *job sharing*, whereby two people share between them the demands of a full-time contract, so that the employer has the benefit of a full-time commitment and the employees have the flexibility and reduced hours that they prefer.

Clutterbuck (1985) summarises the main recent developments on changing work patterns.

Autonomy is a key feature of the ways in which changing working patterns appeal to individual people at work, but there is a general, slow move in that direction by other means as well. Although hierarchy remains a standard feature of organisation, its form is being gradually modified to give greater emphasis to networking and individuals responsibility. The personal organiser loose-leaf notebook that has become so popular is a symbol of the greater self-sufficiency that many people now find in their jobs.

The *orientation* of the job has also changed so that it is more outward-looking. There have been a number of exercises to train staff in social skills, which have had the effect of orienting people away from preoccupation with the internal affairs of the organisation, pleasing the boss and scoring points off enemies towards positive attitudes with customers.

All of these moves have widened the range of job dimensions that can lead to both personal satisfaction and operational efficiency.

THE NATURE OF DEPARTMENTAL ORGANISATION

Company-wide organisation structures and processes, of the sort we considered in Chapter 9, provide an overall framework and philosophy for the integration of all the jobs in the undertaking. Between that and the ways in which individuals and small groups perform their everyday tasks lies the process of departmental organisation.

> 'Department' designates a distinct area, division, or branch of an enterprise over which a manager has authority for the performance of specified activities. (Koontz *et al.* 1980, page 334)

This is an aspect of organisational practice that has received little attention recently. Company-wide organisation has been much studied and has been the focus of debates about industrial democracy, employee participation and rationalisation in the face of recession. In industrial relations the interest is always in getting to the top, speaking to 'the decision-makers'. In the analysis of company performance, profitability, merger and acquisition there is similarly a focus of interest in overall performance, with the assumption that a Rupert Murdoch, a Michael Edwardes or a Ralph Halpern will produce a miraculous change single-handedly through the overall strategy that is pursued.

There is a different sort of close interest in the individual: the professional, the apprentice, the trainee, the executive. We have received a plethora of advice on how such people should be recruited, selected, trained, paid, developed, appraised, counselled and given enlarged or enriched jobs.

The importance of both these areas is obvious, but sometimes departmental organisation can be more important, even though it is a concept that fails to fire the imagination. It lacks the fascination of the power play of the boardroom and the attraction of the individual's humble hopes and fears, yet the individual employee often finds the greatest frustration in minor aspects of departmental affairs and grand new company strategies can founder through inadequate co-ordination of individual activities, usually euphemised as 'communication problems' or 'the human factor'.

The lack of interest in departmental organisation was demonstrated in an extensive review of research and organisational design by Kilman and his colleagues in 1976, when they found that the process of organising activities in a department was usually intuitive rather than analytical and was likely to express the personality and whims of the 'designer'. They also

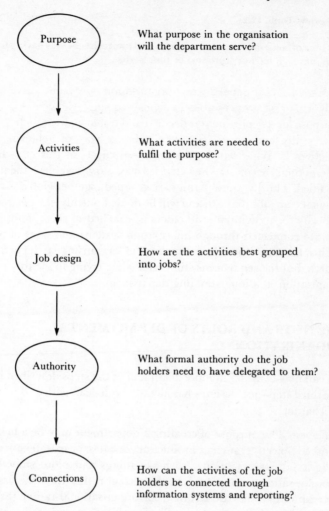

Fig. 12.1 Five steps in departmental organisation.

found that when the pattern of organisation had been designed it was put into operation in a relatively rigid way, allowing little flexibility in practice.

The basis for grouping or clustering activities can be one of several. Most common is *function*, like the safety officers mentioned earlier, who were grouped together because of that specialised interest and identity. Grouping on a basis of *territory* is logical when activities are dispersed, so that a fire station is a unit within the fire service and a ship is a unit of organisation in a shipping company. We also see departments based on common interest in a *product* and others, like night shifts, based on a *time period*.

Review Topic 12.2

Think of some departments you know and categorise them as having their basis in function, territory, product or time period.

Although most departmental organisation may be intuitive rather than analytical, it is easy to establish a logical sequence, shown in Fig. 12.1. First, a purpose for a department is decided and tested against such questions as: 'Is it really necessary?' 'Is there a better way of achieving the same objectives?', 'What will be the knock-on effects of this elsewhere in the undertaking?' Secondly, the activities necessary to achieve the purpose are identified. Thirdly, the activities are grouped together (job design) in ways that make up jobs that can and will be done. Fourthly, the necessary formal authority for individual job holders is attached to them, and, finally, the jobs are connected through information systems and lines of reporting.

This assumes the ideal situation of organising a department from scratch, but the sequence is still useful when trying to identify problems of organisation in a long-standing department.

THE NUTS AND BOLTS OF DEPARTMENTAL ORGANISATION

We can now consider in more detail four of the steps described in Fig. 12.1 (the third step – job design – has already been dealt with at the beginning of the chapter).

1. *Purpose.* The purpose of creating a department may be a basic organisational objective, such as production, or sales, or maintenance, or it may be a purpose of hoping to make things run more smoothly. Much organisational tinkering is of the second rather than the first type: the creation of a new department for organisational rather than business objectives. The regrouping of safety officers, mentioned earlier, is such an example. Another very common creation has been the establishment of a systems department to intercede between the people in the organisation and the electronic monsters that process data. Those who understand the electronic gadgetry are grouped together because of a skill they have in common.

> The search for a basis of classifying activities that leads to the association of those which are similar eventually brings organizers to the skills of people. At first, they may be persuaded that the important element is the object to which labor is applied. But that which results from labor depends on the skills applied to it. After determining what needs to be done and what skills are required, the organizer can then group them under such heads as typing, chemical analysis, process engineering and

accounting. In this way, people who perform similar activities can be grouped in one department, and the advantages of occupational specialization can be realised. (Koontz *et al.* 1980, pages 387–8)

There is always a countervailing argument against the grouping of skills together and in favour of their dispersion. Matrix patterns of organisation go part way towards this dispersion. Once a skill-based department is established there are the risks of separation, aloofness and problems of communication. All the while that the personnel department has one or two of its members who are interested in computing and spend part of their time introducing computer based systems for the personnel function, they are personnel people working with computers. Once such specialists are taken into a systems department and merged with other systems specialists, they become systems people, the personnel department is bereft of that type of expertise and there is the risk that the developing systems will fall into disuse or that new methods developed by the systems department will be not quite what is required. Setting up a new department to deal with something that senior managers do not understand (like computers or new pensions legislation) or something they find unattractive (like dealing with trade union negotiations) may give them an easier time in the short term, but there will be headaches in the long term if there is not a well thought-out organisational purpose.

An alternative to organisation on the basis of skills in common is to group people in departments on the basis of frequent contact. The obvious example is the grouping of typists. If they are all together in a secretarial services department there are the benefits of flexibility, shared facilities – from dictionaries to duplicating machines – specialised supervision and general economies of scale. On the other hand, if they are located individually with the people for whom they type, there are the advantages of easy access for receiving what has to be typed, a wider range of duties, etc.

Creating a new department always brings problems as other departments either resent losing some part of their role or eagerly off-load chores they have been trying to get rid of for years. There are also problems of more communication, more memoranda, more meetings and so on, so any such decision must answer the questions about whether there is a better way and what the knock-on effects will be.

2. *Identification.* Identifying the activities to meet the purpose is largely straightforward when the purpose is to bring together those who have a skill in common, although there will follow arguments about how many typists, errand boys and tea ladies are required.

Organising on the basis of frequent contact can be more difficult as the criteria are less precise, members of staff to be drafted into the new department may wonder whether such a move is in their best interests or whether it represents a veiled demotion, and other managers will be resistant to losing their star team members and over-co-operative in offering the services of people they do not like.

Simon Petch was the son of the chairman of a small printing company that was expanding quickly. He had just joined the company after university and a period of working experience in a larger organisation. He was put in charge of a newly created marketing department to deal with marketing, sales promotion and advertising, although his father would continue to handle sales through agents and two company representatives. Those joining the new department had mixed feelings. Some welcomed the opportunity to be part of a new departure with fresh ideas and working with the man 'who would be chairman one day', while others felt that they were being moved sideways and that their careers and livelihoods were being jeopardised by being used as a training ground for a tyro. The chairman was about to see those who were uncertain and tell them that they would have to do as they were told, but Simon dissuaded him and offered to take a much smaller initial role, dealing only with marketing and leaving sales promotion and advertising to his father. Also he would start by having only two members of staff, both of whom were particularly interested in marketing and keen to work with him. He was very successful and his success brought him onto a number of informal communications networks that had previously been closed to him. Progressively he assumed control of advertising, sales promotion and then all sales, so that within two years he had a 'department' of people readily working with him and smoothly co-ordinated.

3. *Authority*. Allocating authority in departmental organisation is the process of enabling employees to trigger other processes in the organisation by delegating to them authority to act, so that others recognise them as being authorised to act. One familiar method is the job description and its definition of boundaries, but other methods can be simpler and more effective in some circumstances. Being authorised to sign documents is one way of giving power to subordinates. If material cannot be issued from stores until Mr Jones has initialled the docket, then Mr Jones is clearly and effectively given that authority. Knowledge of computer codes, possession of keys to the safe are similar allocations of authority and not to be confused with status symbols, like having a key to the executive washroom.

4. *Communication*. The department organisation is finally made to work by the means of communication between the members. Standard methods are multiple copies of memoranda, meetings and departmental drills specifying the routing of paperwork or other material undergoing transformation. Less obvious is office landscaping, considering how closely people should work together and who should be next to whom.

Those who are constantly swapping items between them, who share a skill and need regular interaction should probably sit together. A set of records to which four different people regularly refer should logically be equally accessible to each of them. There are many ways in which the layout of the working positions of people can aid the communication between them, but this is always limited by the social needs and expectations of employees. Very few people indeed really need an office to themselves and the private office is an impediment to communication, yet the interest in privacy and status is such that many people regard it as a basic requirement.

We can conlude this chapter with an example of the informal integration that is so vital in any department. The pensions department of a large multinational business at one time had to send out 3,500 letters and the particulars on each letter had to be checked. It was not only a very boring job, but also one that took a lot of time. Often such work is 'delegated' to the most humble member of the department, who takes too long to do it, makes mistakes, produces complaints and everybody gets cross. In this company all members of the department did it, working in the last half hour of the working day. It was completed in a week, so that the task was completed quickly. It was also done thoroughly and the members of the department were integrated not only socially through sharing a single task but also all of them thoroughly understood the letter and its implications, so that they were all able to deal with queries that came from recipients of the letter.

Review Topic 12.2

To what extent is the design of departments, jobs and procedures all part of the organisational design? Can an individual manager design his own, or do they all have to comply with overall designs?

SUMMARY PROPOSITIONS

12.1 There is more scope for redesigning jobs than for designing them; and more scope for modifying the organisation of departments than for setting up a complete department from scratch.

12.2 The three key aspects of job design are specialisation to ensure scope for expertise, definition to make clear the boundaries between jobs, and discretion to give job holders autonomy.

12.3 The most common bases for clustering activities to create departments are according to a functional role that job holders share, a territory where people are grouped, a common interest in a product, or the fact that a set of people come together to work at a particular time of day – like a shift.

12.4 The five steps in departmental organisation are deciding the purpose of the department, identifying the activities to achieve the purpose, grouping the activities into jobs to be done, attaching necessary authority to job holders, and connecting jobs together through lines of reporting and communication.

PUTTING IT INTO PRACTICE

Checklist for reviewing the organisation of your department or section

Step 1. The PURPOSE of the department or section
(a) Does it meet a basic business need – like sales or production – or is it intended to make things run more smoothly – like personnel? Is it necessary?
(b) Is it set up on the basis of *output* – like business objectives to be achieved – or on the basis of *inputs* – like people and problems? Are the outputs already being produced elsewhere?
(c) Does the department exist to deal with matters which other managers find uninteresting or unattractive? If 'yes' are the reasons good enough?

Step 2. The ACTIVITIES to meet the purpose
(a) Does the section bring together those who share a particular *skill* or those with a particular *responsibility*?
(b) What activities have to be carried out to meet the purpose?
(c) How many people with what experience and qualifications are needed for those activities?
(d) How many ancillary employees are needed? How can that number be reduced? How can that number be reduced further?
(e) Are all the identified activities needed? Is there any duplication with other sections and departments? Is there a better way?

Step 3. GROUPING the activities
(a) How much specialisation is needed? How will this specialisation affect job satisfaction, commitment and efficiency?
(b) Are boundaries between jobs clearly defined and in the right place?
(c) Will job holders have the amount of discretion needed to be effective?

Step 4. The AUTHORITY of job holders

(a) Do job titles and other 'labels' indicate satisfactorily what authority the job holder has?
(b) Do all job holders have the necessary equipment – like keys, computer codes and information – for their duties?
(c) Do all job holders have the required authorisations – like authorisation to sign documents – that are needed?
(d) Is the authority of any job holder unreasonably restricted?

Step 5. CONNECTING the activities of job holders

(a) Do job holders know what they need to know about the activities of their colleagues?
(b) Are there enough meetings of staff, too few or too many?
(c) Are there enough copies of memoranda circulated for information, too few or too many?
(d) Are job holders physically located in relation to each other in a way that will assist communication between those who need frequently to exchange information?

REFERENCES

Campbell, J.P., Dunnette, M.D., Lawler, E.E. and Weick, K.E., *Managerial Behaviour, Performance and Effectiveness*, McGraw Hill, New York, 1970.

Child, J., *Organisation*, Harper & Row, London, 1977.

Clutterbuck, D., *New Patterns of Work*, Gower, Aldershot, 1985.

Kellogg, M.S., *Putting Management Theories to Work*, Gulf Publications, Houston, Texas, 1968.

Kilman, R.H., Pondy, L.R., Slevin, D.P. (eds), *The Management of Organization Development*, North Holland, New York, 1976.

Koontz, H., O'Donnell, C., Weihrich, H., *Management*, 7th edn, McGraw Hill, Kogakusha, Tokyo, 1980.

Syrett, M. *Employing Jobsharers, Part-timers and Temporary Staff*, Institute of Personnel Management, London, 1985.

Wild R., *Work Organization*, John Wiley, London, 1975.

13

STAFF DEVELOPMENT

The term training is frequently used to refer to the teaching of technical skills to non-managerial personnel, whereas staff development has been used for white collar and management programmes. Staff development is now used in organisations to mean the whole process of identifying training needs, conducting training where necessary, examining individual performance and looking at career development. Some of these are dealt with in the next section but we include here material on training, coaching and dealing with the poor performer. Without developing, the staff organisational effectiveness will suffer as staff become jaded and outdated in their skills.

Coaching and training are both intended to improve a person's working performance, but each involves a different working relationship. The coach is trying to improve the performance of someone who is already competent, while the trainer is trying to bring someone to the level of competence. The most accomplished tennis player needs a coach from whom to receive guidance, criticism and analysis of performance, and that can come from someone who is a less accomplished performer. The child learning to play tennis for the first time has to be trained in the basic techniques and methods of the game, and the accomplishment of the trainer is fundamental to successful instruction.

Both activities are concerned with how people learn, but the nature of the authority required in the coach is not the same as is needed in the trainer. Because of that difference, the approach of the coach is different from that of the trainer and the dependence of the trainee is much greater than that of the person being coached. Although it has received scant attention in the management literature, coaching seems an important activity to discuss in a management book as it is so difficult to isolate what makes a good manager. Effectiveness lies much with individual style, confidence and personality, just as effectiveness in sport lies much with such qualities as touch, timing and a good eye. None of these can be taught *to* people, but coaching may be able to develop them *in* people.

There is a distinction to be drawn between coaching and counselling. Lopez (1968, page 112) points out the danger.

> The supervisor's function is to coach, not counsel. The proper object of *coaching* is to improve present job performance; the proper job of *counselling* is the realisation of potential. The former emphasises *doing*, the latter, *becoming*. If the supervisor attempts to counsel rather than coach, he will indeed do exactly what some critics accuse him of doing: 'play God'.

The counselling relationship involves a great deal of trust and a concern in the counsellor for the wellbeing and personal growth of the client above all else. The manager acting as coach cannot claim that degree of altruism and the person being coached will not be likely to share with him *all* his concerns about the future. Coaching is centred on performance in the job now.

HOW PEOPLE LEARN

As learning is intrinsic to both coaching and training, we need to understand something of the process whereby people learn. It is a subject that has attracted much attention in the training field as well as in schoolteaching. The traditional distinction between cognitive learning, learning skills and developing attitudes was based on the proposition that these were not only three different types of objective but also three different types of process. This has been refined for practical application in adult learning by the CRAMP taxonomy (ITRU, 1976) based on the work of Eunice and Meredith Belbin (1972).

CRAMP divides learning into five basic types.

1. *Comprehension*. Where the learning involves theoretical subject matter, knowing how, why and when certain things happen. Examples would be most of mathematics, the elements of computer programming or the theories of economics. Learning of this type is best approached by methods that teach the whole subject as an entity, rather than splitting it up into pieces and taking one at a time. The lecture is the time-honoured method of doing this.
2. *Reflex learning*. Where the trainee is acquiring skilled movements or perceptual capacities. Effectiveness requires practice as well as knowing what to do and speed is usually important so that the learning process involves constant repetition to develop the necessary synchronisation and co-ordination. An obvious, but extreme, example is juggling, but there are many more common examples, like machining, inspection on an assembly line or computer input.
3. *Attitude development*. Concerned with enabling people to alter their attitudes and social skills. This has been very popular in management

development and centres on the understanding trainees have of themselves. Group methods are typically used for this purpose as attitudes are very difficult to influence and change permanently through instruction although many – like politicians – find it difficult to believe that conversion cannot be achieved by exposition. Socialisation seems more effective.

4. *Memory training.* This obviously deals with people learning information, like the periodic table of chemical elements, and is usually done in the same way as reflex learning with trainees learning parts of the information at a time and then proceeding to the next stage.

5. *Procedural learning.* Very similar to memorisation except that the drill to be followed does not have to be memorised: it has to be located and understood. A lawyer does not have to learn all the statutes and cases, but does need to know where to locate them. If a process plant is run down once a year for annual maintenance, the engineers do not have to memorise the rundown procedure, but they have to know where it is and be able to understand all its stages when it is required.

In practice most forms of training involve more than one type of learning, so that the trainee motor mechanic will need to understand how the car works (comprehensive) as well as practising the skill of tuning an engine (reflex). The car driver needs to practise the skill of co-ordinating hands, feet and eyes in driving as well as knowing the procedure to follow if it breaks down, but the CRAMP analysis helps us to identify the type of learning that is predominating in any particular situation.

Gagne (1975) has examined all processes of learning and identified a chain of eight events which take place:

1. *Motivation.* The learner has to want to learn, and that requires that they want to achieve the product of this learning. A person will be motivated to practise five-finger exercises on the piano because of wanting to achieve the ability to play a Beethoven sonata, which would be the end-product of this learning.

2. *Perception.* The matter to be learned has to be identified and separated from other matters around it, so that it becomes a clear and specific objective.

3. *Acquisition.* The matter being learned is made sense of by being related to other things known by the trainee.

4. *Retention.* The material or skill acquired is retained in the long-term memory and/or the short-term memory. The two-stage process of human learning comprises first the short-term memory in which one holds, for instance, the name of a person to whom one has just been introduced. Secondly, there is the long-term memory to which one transfers those names which one wishes to store permanently. This is an important distinction in learning as some material goes into short-term

memory only to aid understanding at the time and then should *not* be transferred to long-term. An example is the joke in the lecture, which may be remembered at the expense of the point that the lecturer was using the joke to illustrate.

5. *Recall.* The learner has to be able to summon up items from his memory when they are needed.

6. *Generalisation.* This is the ability to apply what has been learned to a wide variety of situations other than the specific situation in which learning has taken place. The skilled motor mechanic will be able to apply the essence of what has been learned to the maintenance of a new model of car that was not produced at the time of training.

7. *Performance.* That which has been learned is now done: the trainee pianist plays the piano, the student writes the examination script, or the embryo salesperson goes out and sells something.

8. *Feedback on performance.* The learner receives some feedback on whether the performance was satisfactory or not. To some extent this lies in the obvious quality of the performance. If the task is to mend a fuse, success or failure is clear, but with most learners some degree of approbation and comment is needed from the coach or trainer, as this can not only incorporate varying degrees of satisfaction and encouragement but also be analytical: what went wrong, how it could have been avoided, what aspect needs more practice, what to do next and so forth.

Review Topic 13.1

Throughout the book we have these review topics. Which one of Gagne's eight events are they trying to help?

A failure in learning can be because of difficulties at any of these eight stages and this sequence applies to all learning, whether of the relatively formal type that is found in training for industrial skills or in an activity like coaching, where the learning may be incidental to some other activity.

TRAINING

We have already seen that training is the process of bringing someone to a level of competence. In most large organisations there is a training department or training officer who has the organisational responsibility for this sort of activity and most managers need no more than a passing understanding of the process that is involved. Figure 13.1 summarises the ASDICE model for training in organisations. This is one of a number that have been developed, and is a basis for the administration of training programmes and courses. The individual manager will not be involved in

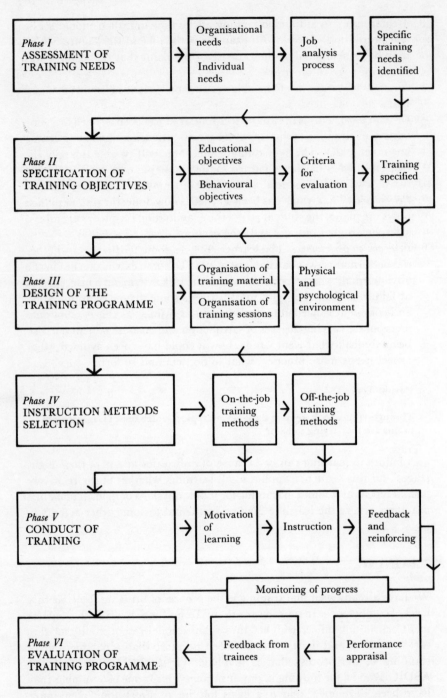

Fig. 13.1 ASDICE: A systematic approach to programme development.
(Based on a more detailed analysis in Torrington and Chapman, 1983, pages 480–1)

all of these elements, but may need to use the framework as a way of approaching an *ad hoc* piece of training that has to be organised with a member of the team.

As a training objective, for instance, the manager will want the trainee to understand the task to be performed and what is required to reach a level of competence. So the manager has to decide how much understanding is needed at the outset in order to provide a satisfactory basis for the training.

In designing the training programme how much should the task to be performed be broken down into components or subroutines to aid learning? When Clive Sinclair introduced the personal computer for use in the home, arrangements had to be made for users to learn computer operation and programming at a distance. What had to be learned was divided up into small packets of information that could be both understand and practised in sequence. Each packet of information, set out in an instruction manual, could be understood by reference either to its own content or what had already been covered. The sequence was as follows:

1.	The computer and setting it up	2½ pages
2.	The keyboard	3 pages
3.	Numbers, letters and the computer as a calculator	3 pages
4.	Some simple commands	2 pages
5.	Simple programming	3½ pages
6.	Using the cassette recorder	3½ pages
7.	Colours	1½ pages
8.	Sound	1 page
9.	What's inside the case	1½ pages

(Vickers and Bradbeer, 1982)

Trainee typists learn subroutines for each hand before combining them into subroutines for both hands together as they use their hands in ways that are relatively independent of each other, with the left always typing 'q' and the right always typing 'p', so that co-ordination of the hands is needed only to sequence the actions. A further aspect of learning to type is to practise short letter sequences that occur frequently, such as 'and', 'the', 'ing' and 'ion'. This sort of practice enables actions to become both automatic and reliable. The amateur typist will often transpose letters or hit the wrong key, writing 'rwong' instead of 'wrong' or 'hte' instead of 'the'. The properly-trained typist will rarely do this because the repeated drills will have made the subroutines automatic and therefore usually correct.

Every person training others has to provide feedback, so that the trainee can compare their performance with the required standard and can see the progress being made. The characteristics of good feedback are immediacy and precision. If it comes immediately after the action, then the trainee has the best chance of associating an error with that part of the performance that caused it, whereas delay will emphasise what was wrong, but the memory of what happened will have faded. Precision in feedback requires the information conveyed to be as accurate as possible and related to what the trainee has done, rather than the results of this action, so that the trainee is able to pinpoint the action that is needed to be remedied and how it can be altered. In teaching someone to drive a car, you may well have the alarming experience of the car lurching forward from a stationary position and then stopping dead. The comment to the trainee driver 'not smooth enough' is unhelpful as it makes an obvious statement about what the car has done instead of a comment on what the driver did wrong. 'Too quick on the clutch' focuses on what the driver did, but probably in language that will be imprecise to the listener. Something like 'You brought the clutch pedal up too quickly with the left foot' would be precise feedback.

Figure 13.1 links feedback and reinforcement, which is praising and underpinning satisfactory performance by encouraging trainees with plenty of positive comment and reward, like giving lumps of sugar to a well-behaved horse. Although this is a useful general rule, it is not a complete explanation of how people learn:

> Learning is *not* fundamentally a matter of gradually strengthening connections but rather an all-or-none event. Thus most modern theorists tend to favour the idea that the individual connection is acquired on a single occasion. . . . The effects of repetition may be to recruit more and more single connections, but each one is learned or not learned. (Gagne, 1975, page 44)

TRAINING METHODS

Recent preoccupation with training methods may have led some people to the conclusion that training would be effective providing that the correct method was selected for a given application. This chapter has already suggested that group methods, for instance, are the most appropriate way of developing attitudes, but that the lecture will be more appropriate for training which involves comprehension as its main purpose. There has, however, developed some reaction against too great a concern about method at the expense of substance. A study conducted among sixty-four students taught by different modes and tested both immediately after the teaching session and again one month later showed no difference in the results achieved by lecturing, case studies and role play or other experiential methods, with the conclusion:

> It appears trainees can learn effectively in a variety of modes, perhaps indeed finding as much or more satisfaction from *what* they are learning than the *way* in which they are trained. (Gale *et al.*, 1982 page 16)

In the generally vague area of management development there is perhaps need for more attention to what it is appropriate for managers to learn.

Table 13.1 Types of learning and training methods

Type of learning	Typical training methods
Comprehension	Lecture Seminar or discussion Film, film strip or video
Reflex	Task Split up into steps Simplification
Attitude	Experimental methods
Memory	Mnemonics Jingles
Procedural	Rules or routines
Varied	Assignments Distance learning

Despite this cautionary note the method of training still has to be appropriate for the purpose to be served. Table 13.1 summarises the methods most suitable for the five sections of the CRAMP listing.

In concluding the section of this chapter about training, we note the current fashion for *self-development methods* as described, for instance, by Pedler, Burgoyne and Boydell (1986). This has much in common with the action learning approach and distance learning, as the focus is on what the trainee knows they need to do, instead of on what someone else believes they should be told. This approach is particularly advocated for management training.

COACHING

In the opening of this chapter we distinguished between coaching and training by describing coaching as improving the performance of someone who is already competent rather than establishing competence in the first place. Further aspects of coaching are that it is usually on a one-to-one basis, is set in the everyday working situation and is a continuing activity. It is gently nudging people to improve their performance, to develop their skills and to increase their self-confidence so that they can take more responsibility for their own work and develop their career prospects. Most coaching is done by people with their own subordinates, but the subordinate positions of the person coached is by no means a prerequisite. What is essential is that the coach should have qualities of expertise, judgement and experience that make it possible for the person coached to follow the guidance.

Examples of coaching incidents are the head of a fashion section in a department store chatting about new lines while putting out the stock with a member of staff, or the foreman working alongside an engineer while changing a gearbox. The coaching process was implicit in the much maligned 'sitting next to Nellie' method of industrial training, whereby a new recruit worked alongside an experienced hand in order to pick up the way of working. This is a valid criticism when used as a method of initial training, as the learner is not able to discriminate between what can be used and what can be disregarded in the performance observed. It is only appropriate when the learner is in a position to make detailed and subtle changes in their own performance: they have the necessary basic skill and knowledge and are merely adding to their repertoire of skills.

Early moves in the United States to integrate black workers in previously all-white workshops used the buddy system of attaching the newly re-cruited black to an experienced, established white worker to act as the buddy during the early days of employment.

Review Topic 13.2

How can a performer be coached by someone who is not as skilled as the performer himself?

It is what is said and how the discussion develops that can turn these pleasant exchanges into constructive coaching sessions. As with most aspects of managerial activity there is no standard method of coaching as the focus of the activity is the person being coached, whose needs and capacities will be so varied. One way managers differ has been described by Schein (1980) when he advanced his theory of the *career anchor*, arguing that every manager has some aspect of his attachment to his work that he will not abandon and which will act as the dominant guiding force in his life. Examples are autonomy, creativity, organisational security, managerial competence and technical competence. If a manager is anchored to the importance of his technical ability, a coach would need to emphasise that and support it while perhaps looking for some modification to another activity like becoming more managerially competent. The coach would never succeed if they were to denigrate the importance of the technical and emphasise the managerial instead.

One of the most difficult judgements in coaching a manager is to distinguish between those aspects of performance that are essential and those that are just a matter of style. Much management training has foundered on the belief of a manager training subordinates that his way of doing things was the only way they could be done.

Stewart and Marshall (1982) have found that managers often reject much of management training as they believe that their own situation is unique and does not fit the generalised analysis of behavioural research. If this applies, then it not only requires a development approach that is specific to the individual, but also makes coaching a particularly apt method.

The essence of coaching is in two activities, delegation and discussion, neither of which will work very well unless accompanied by the other.

1. *Delegation.* One of the least understood words in the management vocabulary. It is *not* giving people jobs to do; it is giving people scope, responsibility and authority. When the legendary James Bond says to a barman, 'A medium dry Vodka Martini – with a slice of lemon peel, no ice, shaken and not stirred; with either Polish or Russian Vodka', he is giving the barman a job to do with no scope for initiative, only the opportunity to perform a skilled task to a precise specification. When Bond's boss, M, says, 'Your assignment, Bond, is to stop Blofeld by any means you know how', he is delegating to James Bond considerable responsibility and authority.

The question we have to ask about delegation is how much scope it gives to individuals to test their own ideas, develop understanding and confidence, and flex some muscles. The more specific the instructions and terms of reference, the less learning will be managed as a result of that activity. With the assignment delegated the individual then starts work with the initiative also of seeking guidance and discussion on progress from the coaching manager, so that action is always in their own hands rather than in the hands of the coach, who will have to exercise a nice judgement on the degree of intervention. Too many interventions and the person being coached leans on the coach and becomes dependent. Too few interventions and the person being coached makes mistakes and loses confidence.

An example of this is the 'shadowing' of hospital consultants by qualified, but junior, hospital doctors and medical students. Initially the junior observes and discusses the case only, but later takes the major role, with the consultant observing and discussing the case. Another example is 'handover time' when a person about to leave a post and the successor are both in the post together for a short time. This period is useful for discussing major issues, for introductions and for demonstrating procedures. It should not be too long a period or the person taking over is less likely to try new methods; they will have become too convinced of the unchallengeable correctness of what exists.

A systematic use of job exchange for training, an extension of the coaching idea, has been developed by Revans (1971) who argues that groups of about six senior managers from a variety of settings can learn a great deal by tackling a particular problem that is currently being faced by one member of the group. Each group member works in one of the other organisations to find a solution to the problem, while all group members meet regularly to discuss their progress – an example of coaching by peers.

2. *Discussion.* Effective coaching discussion depends on a sound working relationship with the coach, whose comments are welcomed rather than resented or mistrusted. The coach can assist by analysing problems and helping to work out alternatives from which choices are to be made. As far as possible criticism is based on facts and not on opinion, and aimed at positive, constructive improvement of the job, not denigration of the job holder. Even reinforcing by praise has to be specific, otherwise it produces a warm glow (and perhaps intensifies a feeling of adoration for the coach) but the warm glow will fade and the praised person is not left with anything on which to build.

The delegation that is involved in coaching involves taking risks:

> No man can be certain that his subordinates will perform well, but the act of giving responsibility should imply confidence that the task set will be achieved. It is unreasonable to expect a man to give of his best if he suspects that his boss, because of his behaviour, does not really expect him to succeed and is only waiting for him to fail before doing the job himself. (Singer, 1974, page 63)

THE POOR PERFORMER

Often training or coaching is undertaken because a team member is not performing well, either not producing enough work or not reaching required standards of work quality. A first step in this situation is to check the facts against requirements in job descriptions, appraisal schemes, manuals and similar yardsticks. If a shortfall can be clearly seen, then the problem is relatively straightforward. Where it is not clearly demonstrable, it is often described in the extremely vague term of 'the wrong attitude'.

A preliminary to attempted corrective action is to consider why the performance is poor (Miner and Brewer, 1976). It may be a *personal quality*, such as physical or mental health, intelligence and ability, motivation, confidence and understanding of the job. Alternatively it could be some aspect of *domestic circumstances*, such as marital breakdown or bereavement. A third possibility is an aspect of the *work group*, such as cohesion, leadership, or personality clashes. Fourthly come *organisational factors*, such as lack of investment, the balance between planning and improvisation, the degree of discipline or permissiveness, poor management and the design of the individual job. There could be a conflict of moral or religious *values* between what the job requires and what the employee regards as right; or there could be *situational* stress because of where the job is located. Lastly there may be lack of *training*.

If one of these is identified as the cause of poor performance, then the obvious strategy is to deal with that specific cause, either by the manager dealing with the matter directly – as with organisational factors, for instance – or by seeking assistance – suggesting a visit to the local marriage guidance council to assist with a marital problem.

The most realistic tactics for a manager seem to be to concentrate on the facts of the performance, to focus on future performance and to set short term objectives for the employee's improvement. Chapter 21 on performance appraisal is relevant to the problem of the poor performer.

SUMMARY PROPOSITIONS

13.1 There are five basic types of learning: comprehension, reflex learning, attitude development, memory and procedural learning.

13.2 All learning has a chain of eight events: motivation, perception, acquisition, retention, recall, generalisation, performance and feedback.

13.3 The appropriateness of training methods varies with the type of learning.

13.4 Training is the process of bringing someone to a level of competence; coaching is improving the performance of someone who is already competent.

13.5 Improving the performance of the poor performer requires analysis to determine the reason for the poor performance.

PUTTING IT INTO PRACTICE

Write a training programme for a friend or relative using the ASDICE model for:

1. Cooking your favourite meal.
2. Looking after your house in your absence.
3. Washing your favourite sweater.

REFERENCES

Belbin, E. and Belbin, R.M., *Problems in Adult Re-training*, Heinemann, London, 1972.

Gagne, R.M., *Essentials of Learning for Instruction.*, Holt, Rinehart & Winston, New York, 1975.

Gale, J., Das. H. and Miner, R., 'Training methods compared', *Leadership and Organisation Behaviour Journal*, vol. 3, no. 3, pages 13–7.

ITRU (Industrial Training Research Unit), *Choose an Effective Style: a Self-instructional Approach to the Teaching of Skills*, ITRU, Cambridge, 1976.

Lopez, F.M. jnr., *Evaluating Employee Performance*, Public Personnel Association, Chicago, 1968.

Miner, J.B. and Brewer, J.F., 'Management of ineffective performance', M.D. Dunnette, *Handbook of Industrial and Organisational Psychology*, Rand McNally, 1976.

Pedler, M., Burgoyne, J. and Boydell, T., *A Manager's Guide to Self-development*, 2nd edn, McGraw Hill, Maidenhead, 1986.

Revans, R.W., *Developing Effective Managers*, Longmans, 1971.

Schein, E.H., *Organizational Psychology*, 3rd edn, Prentice Hall Inc., Englewood Cliffs, New Jersey, 1980.

Singer, E.J., *Effective Management Coaching*, IPM, London, 1974.

Stewart, R. and Marshall, J., 'Managerial beliefs about managing', *Personnel Review*, vol. 11, no. 2, 1982, pages 21–5.

Torrington, D.P. and Chapman, J.B., *Personnel Management*, 2nd edn, Prentice Hall International, Hemel Hempstead, 1983.

Vickers, S. and Bradbeer, R., *Sinclair Spectrum Introduction*, Sinclair Research Ltd, Cambridge, 1982.

14

PERSONAL EFFECTIVENESS

Most advice to managers, like the other chapters in this book, is about how to understand the organisational context one is in, or how to organise other people and materials. At the centre is the manager: how well organised are they personally? Understanding the context and organising subordinates, or the decision-making processes, or the performance appraisal procedures is of little avail if the person taking initiatives is not sufficiently well organised to push those initiatives through to successful completion and to exploit successfully whatever responses are received.

Poorly organised managers are a major impediment to organisational efficiency, slowing things down, producing errors and generating dissatisfaction. Among the clues are the comment 'I just have not had time'. The workload for any manager inevitably varies, from day to day, from week to week and – for many people – from season to season. The manager who 'has not had time' usually is not able to deal with that fluctuation. It may also be that arrears of work are accumulated as a justification for concentrating on those things that are of interest and passing over those that are unwelcome. The manager knows that some of the less interesting things will be dealt with by someone else or overtaken by events, as we saw in Chapter 7. Arthur Brown was a sales manager who enjoyed a deserved reputation as a brilliant salesman and a very nice man. He was also known as not being keen on office work and he had three filing trays on his desk: 'In' 'Out' and 'Too Hard', with the third being used for all those matters that could not be dealt with straight away. A mischievous colleague altered 'Too Hard' to 'Too Dull', and that is all too true for many prevaricating managers.

Another clue is the phrase 'Let's play it by ear'. Here we see lack of preparation, lack of initiative and a mode of operating that is doomed to be responsive to the initiatives of others rather than creating initiatives of one's own. A somewhat similar clue is 'I'm still waiting for . . . (the boss)'. Although some periods of waiting are inescapable, there are occasions when managers await instructions because they are unsure of what to do, or because they believe that having passed a matter to the person next up in the hierarchy, they then forget about it until it returns, because theirs is a dependent role.

Finally there is the clue 'Really? I don't remember that at all'. Managers have to organise their memory and recall to cover a wide range of matters, moving between those matters quickly and effectively. Not for them the purposeful single-mindedness of, say, the sculptor or the research physicist who can concentrate on one task for weeks and in whom absent-mindedness is either a beguiling eccentricity or an indication of absolute, unswerving dedication.

Review Topic 14.1

If you were able to organise yourself better,

1. Do you think your overall management performance would improve?
2. Do you think you would enjoy life more or less?
3. Do you think you would be a more or less stimulating and interesting person to work with?
4. Do you think other (less well-organised) people would become more reliant on you?
5. If you say 'yes' to the last question, in what ways would this enhance, and in what ways weaken, your managerial and administrative effectiveness.

In the next few pages we consider how managers can achieve the type of personal organisation that will protect them from giving these damning clues to perceptive observers, and which can greatly enhance their job performance and job satisfaction. As with other features in the book, we are not advocating the *only* ways in which things can be done, as one person's organisation can be another's straitjacket, but even grandmothers can learn to suck eggs better then they used to.

ORGANISING ONE'S TIME

One method of organising one's time is to analyse how it is spent by using a temporary diary method like that provided at the end of Chapter 4. With such an analysis it is possible to review the proportion of time spent on various activities and to decide whether or not this is how the time should be spent. Various questions are suggested in Chapter 4. Another strategy would be to use Rosemary Stewart's (1982) categories of the demands, constraints and choices of the job to analyse how time is spent. Stewart recommends trying to increase one's choice by rethinking the demands and constraints.

The next step is to decide where changes need to be made, if at all. Are there things being done that could be cut out, or reduced, done differently or delegated? We have found, for instance, several instances of managers keeping careful notes – hand-written in a black book – of figures that are available at the touch of a button on the keyboard of their own computer terminal or workstation. Alternatively there may be some things which should be done and which at the moment are not being done.

The more normal use of the diary is to plan the working day. This is partly an assertion of the individual manager's autonomy, but it is primarily an organising device to fit in various types of meeting. If the weekly marketing meeting takes place at 2 o'clock on Wednesdays and usually lasts all afternoon, that half day is blocked out for other activities. There are normally between one and a dozen such events in a manager's weekly diary: meetings involving a number of people, at a fixed time, mainly at the behest of someone else (no matter how important you are) and these are the immovable blocks in the week, around which other things have to be fitted within the general framework of the working week/day. Although the immovables block out large chunks of available time, they can be used to make good use of what remains. If you need to talk to a colleague who you know to be verbose and indecisive, it may be worth getting the diary out and asking if he could possibly manage 1.30 on Wednesday. . . . 'It's only half an hour before the marketing meeting, so I'll have to be off like a dirty shirt about five to . . . but God knows when the next opportunity would be'.

One factory manager of our acquaintance discovered that the works convener suffered from acute acid indigestion that worsened as meal times approached and was alleviated by eating. Gradually more and more meetings could only be fitted into the diary towards the end of the morning. Although those are two slightly silly examples, they demonstrate how the manager needs to calculate the time needed for different types of meeting and structure the times in the diary according to those estimates. We have already seen that managers spend most of their time talking to other people and these encounters – whether one-to-one or on a larger scale – tend to expand or contract to fill the time available for their completion. If one allows too little time, the meeting is abortive as it has not been possible to deal with the business and if one allows too much time, then opportunities to do other things are wasted.

A refinement of diary usage is to allocate blocks of time to particular activities, just as doctors' surgeries are always at the beginning of the day and in the early evening. Examples of this are doing all the dictation at the beginning of the day, making telephone calls early afternoon (when they are cheaper), reading reports on the train, touring the plant just before lunch. This reinforcement of a habit can make for greater personal efficiency and can make more efficient working relationships with colleagues, who can organise some of their activities to suit. 'We'll ask Charlie. He usually comes by about this time'.

MANAGING THE BOSS

The idea of managing one's boss may sound like a contradiction or a usurping of proper authority, but it is most inappropriate to regard the relationship with the organisational superior as one in which they cope with you and you respond with deference or what the Americans call 'apple-polishing'. It is also insufficient to regard the relationship as one in which the subordinate seeks to comply precisely with what the superior asks for and then awaits further instructions, so that the job is satisfactorily discharged when the wishes of the boss have been met. Virtually all the jobs that people in organisations hold are those in which there are a range of responsibilities, accountabilities and obligations, both formal and informal. Also all jobs require some skill and some initiative, and the more autonomous a job is the less precise is the nature and degree of the supervision provided by the superior.

Very little has been written on this subject, although there is a helpful article by Gabarro and Kotter (1980) that points out that the relationship with the boss is not only crucial but has to be managed. Such management is not political manoeuvring or apple polishing, but consciously working with the boss to obtain better results. Alistair Mant (1983) makes the distinction between binary thinking managers and ternary thinking managers. The first are those who see the relationship as that of master and servant, while the second are those who see the relationship as being of two servants, relating to each other via a third point in a triangular affiliation. The third point is the task on which they are both engaged, the customers they seek to serve or the employees they seek to satisfy. Binary thinkers will find it difficult to see how one can manage one's boss; ternary thinkers will be doing it already.

The process is mainly one of mutual accommodation and adjustment, as the two parties find the most effective way of sharing duties between them. They start from the position that the boss has, for instance, more formal power and access to more extensive information, while the subordinate may have better grapevine information and a more flexible programme of work. To this will then be added the advantages that each has in terms of personal qualities, qualifications and experience. By discussion and getting used to each other both boss and subordinate can improve their joint and individual results, but it needs initiative from both of them; not just from the boss.

From the point of view of the subordinate alone, it has to be remembered that the boss can influence the promotion and career development prospects of the subordinate, and this can inhibit the degree of candour in everyday exchanges. It also illuminates the need for the subordinate to work within the consent, even if only the tacit consent, of the boss in taking initiatives. In this way there will be support in times of difficulty and a greater likelihood that decisions on action are well judged.

Sometimes the boss has to be used to getting things changed. It may be anything from an administrative procedure that is not working or policies about particular clients that need changing to tasks traditionally associated with one's job that no longer seem appropriate. Boursine and Guerrier (1983) make the point that subordinates often assume the boss knows when in fact they do not know what the subordinate's job involves and what is happening within its framework. A useful tactic is to keep the boss advised of what is irritating or frustrating. In doing this, however, it is well to remember the transactional analysis idea. The subordinate is more likely to be successful if the transactions with the boss are adult/adult transactions rather than those of the intemperate child whining to the uninterested parent.

There are also the range of tactics that were described at the close of Chapter 10 on organisational politics: reciprocal support for a patron.

ORGANISING WHAT HAS TO BE DONE

Management jobs inevitably have a delicate balance of long-term and short-term future objectives. Long term considerations are dealt with in our chapter on policy-making and strategy, but there are ways in which managers prepare for short-term eventualities that lie somewhere between the projections of planning and the day-by-day control of diary keeping. In talking with managers during the preparation of this book we have been struck by the difficulty managers have in keeping a number of different issues all in play together. Furthermore this seems to be a growing rather than diminishing problem and was discussed by Kotter (1982) in his study of general managers.

Review Topic 14.2

1. **List five ways in which you manage the relationship with your boss.***
2. **Think of three more ways that you have not yet tried.**
3. **Who benefits from the way you have managed your boss so far?**

* For those who do not currently have a boss in the conventional sense, use the
  example of a parent, a teacher, a sports team captain, leisure activity organiser,
  etc.

One method many managers use is to develop the use of the diary until it almost becomes a timetable. We call this *event anticipation* as people mark in their diary not only the events that are to happen, but also the jobs they have to do in anticipation of those events. A technical manager noted the date of meetings in his diary and then noted three days before the meeting that he had to look through the agenda in order to chase up information or queries. A fashion manager used her diary first to mark the definite dates of fashion shows and similar promotions, and then fixed back in her diary earlier dates for such items as 'contact press office', 'order invitations'. Although this may seem elementary, attendance at any committee meeting shows how few people arrive at the meeting prepared for the proceedings. There are now wallcharts and personal planners commercially available to aid this simple process. For managerial jobs with a strong administrative component and where there is a cycle of seasonal or annual events, the year can be partially mapped out in advance; we looked at the work of one very busy university administrator who had done this several times during the year when the workload was especially heavy. By careful examination she was able to identify a number of jobs that could be done either completely or partly at different times of the year in order to smooth the flow and to improve the quality of jobs done at the peak times.

Similar is the *bring-out system*, long used by private secretaries, in which notes or correspondence about a matter are stored against a date when they will be 'brought out' for review. This avoids the pile of papers on the desk generally awaiting attention or the bulging briefcase which is all too often a sign of a manager who reacts to situations instead of being proactive. A familiar comment by a manager asked about the progress of a particular issue is that 'it is getting near the top of the pile'. This refers to the real or metaphorical pile of papers on the desk and implies that they are being dealt with in strict chronological sequence. Usually they are dealt with only as a result of a query or complaint. With that arrangement everything becomes urgent and other people are always dissatisfied. Jeff Moores is a plant engineer who operated in this way: he dealt with things according to how loudly and often people grumbled at him. It was getting him down, so one week he agreed that he would abandon his standard, defensive, 'I'll get to it as soon as I have time. It's getting nearer the top of the pile.' Instead he said to each enquirer that he would deal with their query at a specified time, often weeks ahead. All the enquirers were satisfied and he suddenly found the breathing space in which he could begin to control his activities and move into a more satisfying and rewarding way of working. The bring-out system can also be used to prevent other people overlooking things which they regard as too hard or unattractive, like the old Jeff Moores before he took hold of his life.

Many managers keep *lists of jobs* to be done. These are typically kept on odd scraps of paper and reviewed morning and night. This is mainly to keep a check on what has to be done, so that things can be brought to mind in the relative calm of the train journey to the office and later reference to the list can prevent them being overlooked in the rush and bustle of the working day. There is a secondary benefit in running through the list at the end of the day, as it makes one realise that something *has* been achieved, despite the feeling of frustration and lost opportunity. We make no comment about those people who remember something to be done that is not on the list, do it, and then write it on the list in order to cross it off! This is essentially a personal, informal activity, and it changes its nature when it becomes an administrative system. A building society manager has a semi-permanent list of all the routine tasks that had to be done in his branch, and either he or his assistant initialled each item when it was done. It included such items as checking each cashier's till randomly each month, sending returns to regional office, and staff training.

Those especially conscious of the problem of getting things to the top of the pile try different ways of *assigning priority*. On the list of jobs, described in the previous paragraph, one or two would have * beside them and some might even have ** to indicate that these were things that should be done first, or that should be done even if some of the others were deferred. Some people use a system of 'must do', 'important' and 'would like to do'. Less effective is to colour code internal memoranda. One local authority manager had an extremely elaborate system of different colour paper for different types of message:

White   – advisory
Pink   – information
Blue   – interest
Yellow – critical for implementation
Orange – needs reply

The idea was that memoranda would be sent on paper of a colour to indicate the attention it should receive, with the urgent matters being dealt with immediately and other matters being dealt with later. This seems to be an extreme of administrative precision that does not quite fit in with the vagaries of human nature. Will white, pink and blue be read at all? Is the coding not reinforcing the idea among managers that they are too busy to read all their paper, when the majority of them can probably cope with it easily? Also, if there is this sort of ascending scale of importance, the lower scales are soon abandoned. In the Foreign Office telegrams are marked 'Most Immediate', 'Immediate', 'Priority' and 'Routine' and much self-discipline is required to ensure that not everything gets the top two markings.

The chief executive of a medium-sized company was anxious that the memoranda that *he* sent should be acted on quickly and he also wanted to spot easily the memoranda that came in to him from his main colleagues, so a system was introduced whereby all the memoranda from his office were on green paper, all those from directors were on blue, and everyone else had memoranda typed on yellow paper. Quite apart from the explicit declaration of differential status, that caused a lot of difficulty, there soon came the problem that important matters typed on yellow paper were sometimes overlooked. To deal with this the colour-coding was modified so that non-directors could have their memoranda typed on pink paper if they were urgent. These were soon christened 'pink frighteners' and people quickly realised that the way to get a response was to write on a pink frightener. Various people were grumbled at for not treating the system properly, but within a fortnight pink frighteners outnumbered the yellow memoranda being typed and the whole initiative failed.

These last two ideas were used by busy people trying to organise their own work, but the methods they chose depended on others organising their work in a reactive, dependent way. Personal reminders, like the list on the back of an envelope, seem much more effective.

ORGANISING PERSONAL RECALL: MAKING NOTES

As managers have to keep in touch with a range of different matters simultaneously, they benefit from being able to recall quickly and accurately information that they have received. Some they retrieve from files, some they remember, but a preliminary to the first and an aid to the second is the ability to take notes. In meetings, while reading journal articles, while telephoning, while talking with colleagues are all occasions when the manager may need to make jottings of material to be used later.

One method is to use shorthand, which enables the writer to record verbatim what someone is saying. Another is to make a tape-recording, but both of these methods are of dubious value as preliminaries to data storage or as aids to recall. The effort of the writer is in getting the record accurate and the effort of the person using the tape recorder is simply to switch on the machine. The understanding and the internalising, or taking in, of the material comes later as an extra job to be done. It is interesting to consider the experience of researchers and students, who are dedicated listeners. The researcher who is interviewing people at some length, and who uses a tape recorder to make sure that nothing is overlooked, will spend approximately four hours in writing up a one hour interview. That is not transcribing it, word-for-word, but writing a summary of what was said, with nuances, illustrations and some interpretation. Nearly all those who use a recorder for this purpose take notes as well, so that the writing up is based on the notes and the personal recall of the interviewer, with the recording being used only to check details. Students often make tape recordings in lectures in order not to miss anything, but seldom do they persist with the practice after a few weeks because the recorder takes away from them the need to be actively listening during the lecture, and the lecture becomes even more boring as a result, with the added tedium of having to listen to it all over again.

The purpose of taking notes is to record what the listener has understood and wants to be able to recall, as well as specific details that enlighten that

Table 14.1 Abbreviations used for note-taking

= is equal to	+ add or and	& and
≠ is not equal to	∴ therefore	∵ because
> greater than	≯ not greater than	n many
♂ male	♀ female	
acs accounts	ca (circa) about	cf (confer) compare with
Do (ditto) the same	e.g. (exempli gratia) for example	etc. (et cetera) and the other things
et seq. (et sequentia) and the following	ibid. (ibidem) in the same place	i.e. (id est) that is
no. (numero) number	non seq. (non sequitur) it does not follow	NB (nota bene) note well
op. cit. (opere citato) in the work cited	Pro tem. (pro tempore) for the time being	sic. so written
stet let it stand	v. (versus) against	VV vice versa

understanding. It is always selective and always interpretive.

In taking notes the manager is summarising as much as possible in as few words as possible. An example is the way in which some people make a note at the back of their diaries of funny stories they have heard so that they can recount them on later occasions. The note is seldom more than a phrase or even a single word, even though the story may take five or ten minutes to relate. The funny story has a pattern, so that a few words are sufficient to recall the entirety. In listening to anything that we are being told, we look for a pattern or interconnection of ideas that we will be able to recall. Each of those patterns then produces a note in the form of a *trigger*, either a word or phrase that will be sufficient to summon up the complete grouping of ideas and data we are recording. In this way the listener is working while listening, structuring understanding and deciding on the triggers.

When it is necessary to record verbatim, there is value in mastering a set of *abbreviations*. Table 14.1 gives a list that is commonly used, but each individual will have a personal set, linked to the context of their own work. In preparing this book, for instance, we have used the following:

Mgt	–	Management
MM	–	Middle management
Gps	–	Groups
F-to-F	–	Face-to-Face
Orgs	–	Organisations

These have been helpful to us, but would be useless to others. There are various ways of adding emphasis in notes. Some words are underlined, or have ** put beside them, as in the personal lists we have already described, but another method is to outline items that are to have a special degree of emphasis. A device available in stationers' shops is a text highlighter. This is a broad-tipped felt pen that can be used to paint a band of transparent colour over a word or sentence, so that it is still legible, but is highlighted. This is much used by people reading reports and memoranda to pick out key words or sections to which they wish later to refer.

ORGANISING PERSONAL RECALL: MEMORY

All of us can improve our ability to recall information from our memory as the potential of the human brain is greatly under-utilised and some individuals who are otherwise perfectly normal are able to recall much more than others. Actors need to memorise their lines and thus develop an ability to recall that is much greater and better organised than that of most other people; some indeed have been able to recall a major Shakespearean role after little more than a single reading. In the 1950s a music hall performer Leslie Welch was known as 'The Memory Man' and his fifteen minute act consisted of answering questions from the audience on sporting events and records.

One widely-accepted theory of human memory is that memorising is a two-stage process: a short-term memory and a long-term memory.

> The difference between them is like the difference between recalling a telephone number you just looked up in the directory and your own telephone number. Your own is stored in LTM along with memories of such items as your name, the words and grammar of the language, addition and multiplication tables, and important events in your life. Except for occasional mental blocking on a word or the name of an acquaintance, these memories are relatively permanent. In contrast, the telephone number you have just looked up, the definition the instructor has given you in class, and the name of the stranger to whom you have just been introduced remain in STM only momentarily. Unless you make a conscious effort to focus your attention on the information, that is, to transfer it to LTM, it is quickly lost. (Hilgard, Atkinson and Atkinson, 1975, page 236)

Recall is summing things up from long term memory and the effectiveness of the recall will be influenced by the way in which items were stored in that memory bank in the first place. Buzan (1977, pages 35–53) provides an excellent summary of this process and the possibility of improvement, but we will here mention only one method of data storage for effective recall, known as the *method of loci*. In this a series of items to be learned for recall are identified in the mind of the learner with familiar, connected locations. The most familiar example being of the shopping list, which is memorised by identifying each item on the list with a room in the house. They are not, however, simply identified with the room, but visualised in it, so that there is a picture of a dozen eggs on the hall floor, a loaf of bread on the dining room table, breakfast cereals on an armchair in the sitting room, and so forth. On entering the shop, the items are easily recalled by summoning up the series of images.

ORGANISING PERSONAL RECALL: FILING

As the amount of information circulating in organisations increases, there is a growing problem of what to do with it after if arrives. Much can be thrown away, either because it did not need to come in the first place or because it will not be needed in the future, but how do you store correspondence, reports and other items in such a way that they can be found when required? The average filing cabinet contains material that will never be looked at again except when you are looking for something else, so that one effective means of filing is to file as little as possible. This can be achieved either by throwing away more, more often and more purposefully, or by relying on other people's files to a greater extent. We realise that some readers will find it difficult to follow this advice. In visiting different organisations it is striking to notice the different number of filing cabinets deployed in operational situations which seem in all other ways to be similar. Some managers are surrounded by filing cabinets while others seem to manage with only one, so filing practice is governed as much by the personality and individual methods of managers as by any objective notion of what is appropriate. One manager we know who is an inveterate hoarder always goes to work between Christmas and New Year when he clears out his filing system.

How do you classify what you decide to keep? Most people operate in a way similar to the short-term memory. Earlier in this chapter we referred to managers who refer to matters 'nearing the top of the pile'; nearly all the managers we have spoken to have a 'pile'. It may be literally a pile of papers on the desk, it may be a bulging briefcase or a dog-eared folder, but it will still have the same characteristics: it contains material that is current and not organised in any particular way. When it ceases to be current, it may be thrown away or filed – transferred to the long-term memory. Once in the filing system, the material is valueless unless you can first remember that it is there, and secondly that you can find it. Both influence how the filing should be arranged.

The most common system of classification is by *subject* and *source*. Some files contain material about a topic, while others contain material received from Mr X or Company A. Other common files are for committees, with all the minutes and papers relating to the Establishment Committee going into a single file. The difficulty of finding material is demonstrated by the way in which many experienced secretaries have a secret 'spare copies' file. It contains copies of all the significant letters and memoranda they have typed in the previous six months. When they are not able to locate an item, they flip hurriedly through their spare copies to find the item or a clue to its whereabouts.

The filing system needs a key. The simplest is a typed list of the files that are kept, so that you remember you have a file on a particular subject; otherwise many of the files are forgotten. If you look in your filing cabinet now you will find that fifteen per cent of the files contain seventy five per cent of the filed material, and twenty five per cent of the files are probably empty or contain only forgotten material. The filing system has to match the needs and mental processes of the user, or it is of little value:

> If possible files should be conceptually organised to fit in with the way the users of the files work. Thus project, case and company file names are likely to satisfy the needs of those concerned with research work, litigation and suppliers respectively. If simplicity and comprehensibility are maintained in this way, staff are more likely to use and rely on the filing system. (Lock and Farrow, 1983, page 827)

SELF-DEVELOPMENT

In this chapter we have reviewed the main ways in which the individual manager can improve the quality of his personal organisation. A more detailed approach to this is to be found in a remarkable book by Pedler, Burgoyne and Boydell (1986) who provide a practical means of self-development. A final consideration is the way in which the managers manage their own careers, so that not only is the here-and-now competence increased, but also the working life meets the ambitions for variety, challenge and reward.

To do this the manager should first realise that 'up' is not the only way to move. In the early stages of a career it may be more judicious to move sideways, so as to broaden experiences and prepare for a move upwards in a different field. Secondly, the attempt to move upwards is one that few can satisfactorily achieve; most people stop going upwards earlier than they would wish. That is the time when so many managers become bored, frustrated or disillusioned, yet the manager who has developed the substance of the current role, rather than always looking beyond it, has the opportunity of deriving satisfaction from doing a difficult job well. Life holds few deeper satisfactions than that.

SUMMARY PROPOSTIONS

14.1 Poorly organised managers are a major impediment to organisational efficiency.

14.2 Time can be managed better by using diary sheets to analyse how time is spent, a future diary to plan the working day and the working week, and to allocate blocks of time daily or weekly to specified activities.

14.3 The working relationship between boss and subordinate is crucial to the effective working of both parties to that relationship, and both of them have to work at managing the relationship.

14.4 Methods of organising the work that has to be done include event anticipation, a bring-out system, keeping lists, and assigning priority.

14.5 The quality of personal recall can be organised in making notes, memorising and filing.

REFERENCES

Boursine, M. and Guerrier, Y., *Surviving as a Middle Manager*, Croom Helm, London, 1983.

Buzan, T., *How to Make the Most of Your Mind*, Colt Books, London, 1977.

Gabarro, J. and Kotter, J., 'Managing your boss', *Harvard Business Review*, Jan./Feb. 1980, pages 92–100.

Hilgard, E.R., Atkinson, R.C. and Atkinson, R.L., *Introduction to Psychology*, 6th edn, Harcourt Brace Jovanovich, New York, 1975.

Lock, D. and Farrow, N., *The Gower Handbook of Management*, Gower, Aldershot, 1983.

Mant, A., *Leaders We Deserve*, Martin Robertson, London, 1983.

Pedler, M., Burgoyne, J. and Boydell, T., *A Manager's Guide to Self-development*, 2nd edn, McGraw Hill, Maidenhead, 1986.

Stewart, R., *Choices for Managers*, McGraw Hill, Maidenhead, 1982.

15

INNOVATION AND CREATIVITY

In the 1970s there was talk about the inevitability of change and its increasing tempo, as well as concern about the unresponsiveness of British industry to its rapidly changing circumstances. Much of the discussion was generated by the influential ideas of Toffler (1970), who argued that change was accelerating to a degree not matched by man's capacity to cope with its challenge. Unless our ability to cope was stepped up, we would suffer from future shock, unable to assimilate and adjust to the changes taking place. Ten years later Drucker (1980) twisted our nerves to a higher pitch by the argument that change had not really begun! Only two new industries emerged in the period from 1947 to 1975: computers, and systemic drugs. In contrast the period from 1856 to 1914 produced a new invention, leading to a new industry, every fourteen to eighteen months. The period after 1975 will see a higher level of innovation:

> The period of fundamental technological change is ahead of us. Unlike the quarter century after the Second World War, it will be a period of structural change rather than one of modification, of extension, or of exploitation. The period ahead will shift technological change to new realms. . . . The 1980s are therefore almost certain to be a period of high technological impact and true innovation. (Drucker, 1980, page 53)

The initial management reaction to this sort of warning was to try to reduce resistance to change among employees, mainly by exhortation. The working assumption was that *we* (the people doing the talking) understand the significance of change and are able not only to cope with it, but also to turn it to our collective advantage. We also happen to be alert, smart, imaginative, and moving with the times. In contrast *you* (those people being talked at) are living in a comfortable, but unreal, fantasy world, and are not aware of how to deal with this crisis. You also happen to be dull, unimaginative, obstinate and behind the times. It was rather like an evangelist warning the congregation of their sins without explaining the means of redemption.

The effect of this approach was unfortunate. For every one sinner who found redemption there were ninety-nine who were confirmed in their ways, having been warned and disapproved of but without any guidance on what to do, nor any realistic glimpse of what the future could hold.

The next managerial response was to try organisational development initiatives. Here the assumption was that change was here to stay and that the way to cope was to develop the organisational structure and the people manning the organisation, so that the organisation would become less formal and rigid, while the members of the organisation became more adaptable and more open with each other. With those two changes it should be possible to evolve new patterns of organisation more appropriate to change. The success of these initiatives varied. Sometimes there was a new lease of life for an organisation and its people, sometimes there was a fresh impetus that did not survive, and in some situations organisational development became a peripheral activity for detached enthusiasts and was swept away in the first cold winds of the economic recession.

Behind this sort of thinking there were a number of inadequacies. Change was 'a good thing' and viewed in an uncritical, unthinking way. Also it was necessary to turn everything upside down to cope with it, so that many people came to believe that anything done differently had to be good and anything that remained the same ought to be shaken up. There was a tendency to make people so insecure that they become defensive and resisted change more grimly. Another problem was that change was seen almost entirely as something to which it was necessary to respond, rather than something to be initiated, and it was usually vague.

Innovation and creativity are terms used not to describe dark forces disturbing our ordered calm, but as interesting activities undertaken by people at work that keep their organisations lively and up to date by exploring possible new activities and changed methods of doing things.

> Innovation and creativity have to do with development, proposal and implementation of *new* and *better* solutions. (Steiner, 1965, page 4)

Proposals have to meet the criteria of being both new *and* better. When colleagues are reluctant to support innovations, it may be because of lethargy and lack of imagination, but it may also be because the proposed innovation is not a very good one, and not a convincing improvement on present practice. The map of underground railway stations in London is a masterpiece of design. Although it has been considerably extended to take account of new lines, the basic design has not altered for fifty years. A recent attempt to introduce a new format was met by such a hostile reception that the original was quickly reinstated.

Other inhibitors of change are cost and acceptance. In many ways it would be more convenient if the British were to drive on the right hand side of the road instead of the left, but the cost of the change outweighs the potential benefits. Decimal currency was initially resisted because of the cost of changing, and because of the difficulty of getting acceptance of the change. Both problems were overcome, so that now it is unusual for anyone to think of pounds and pence and then convert their sum to pounds, shillings and pence. Metrication is taking longer. An interesting example of resistance to innovation is the conventional typewriter keyboard. When Christopher Sholes produced the first typewriter in 1874, the keys used most frequently were deliberately spaced wide apart in order to slow typists down; otherwise the keys would jam. The keyboard layout remains the same a century later, not only on manual and electric typewriters, but also on word processors and computers. It would be completely sensible to change the layout, and simplified layouts are available but not marketed because of the difficulty of changing the habits of millions of typists.

In this chapter we are concerned not with change but with *innovation*, which is the whole process from invention to practice, and with *creativity*, which is the initial phase of generating the new idea, product or approach. Both of these have to be viewed in the light of finding innovations that are better as well as new, and which are thoroughly thought through to verify their practicability, cost and acceptability.

Pavitt (1979) reasons that technical innovation and industrial development are increasingly important for four main reasons. First, because of competition from developing countries who produce an expanding range of standard goods as their industrialisation progresses. Secondly, the taste of consumers and their expenditure level is constantly changing in the advanced countries. Thirdly, we have to consider ways of reducing the consumption of energy and the environment: both scarce and irreplaceable resources. Finally, there are great possibilities provided by the rapid technological changes in fields such as electronics and biochemistry. These may sound like matters for a few leading figures to consider and develop, but an interest in innovation is important for all members of organisations, especially managers, and it is an important approach to the regular, everyday matters as well as the exciting.

There may be a better way of doing things in the department that will save money, or which will be less frustrating for the members of the department, saving wear on their nerves. There may be a better way of meeting customer requirements or enhancing the quality of the product. The interest in quality circles (Bradley and Hill, 1983) is one in a series of initiatives to develop employee interest in quality. Perhaps the most important reason for managers being interested in innovation is that it will prevent them from getting stale. Creativity engenders excitement, innovation presents a challenge. It is a risky business as effort and resources are deflected away from the main task and directed to something new and untried. There is no guarantee of success, but only some innovations pay off, others fail, and others again have quite unexpected results. There have been a number of references throughout this book to the balance between the comforting familiarity of administrative work and the challenge and demand of managerial work, both based on technical work and competence. Innovation is the essence of managerial work, as it is replete with decision-making and creating precedents, and it has the added attraction of being seen as the leading edge of managerial initiative in the organisation: creating the future.

We can now review the main stages of innovation, invention or creativity; dissemination and development of the invention; the consequences of the invention in practice.

INVENTION OR CREATIVITY

Parker (1978) suggests that there are three theories about invention. The *transcendental model* is the theory that invention depends on individual acts of genius. In the *mechanistic model* necessity is the mother of invention in that inventions are produced to meet problems that have arisen. The *cumulative synthesis* model is one where investigation, thought, analysis and discussion are stimulated by individual acts of insight. These insights are not, however, the quantum leaps of the first theory, but a series of insights that illumine the problem and cause progress.

Review Topic 15.1

Think of examples of:
1. **The demand for a new or revised product providing the push to innovation.**
2. **Scientific inventions providing the pull for innovation.**

A continuing academic discussion (e.g. Freeman, 1979) is whether the demand for a new, or revised, product is the push to innovation; or is it scientific inventions that provide the pull for innovation? The practical implications of this question for businesses are important as they centre round the issue of where one should look for innovation. Should a company concentrate its efforts on having sensitive feelers out to pick up changes in the market, like teenage fashion boutiques going to discos, or should it invest in speculative research, like a pharmaceutical company investigating pain? The academic discussion will continue for a long time, but the practical answer to the question seems to be that companies will do both, depending on the particular market and product range in which they are interested.

Whichever of Parker's models one accepts, there is always a small number of people in an organisation who produce a large proportion of the initial ideas to trigger the innovation process. Psychologists have tried to distinguish the characteristics of individuals associated with high levels of creativity. Steiner (1965, pages 7–8) summarises these as follows:

1. *Conceptual fluency*, the ability to generate a large number of ideas rapidly.
2. *Conceptual flexibility*, the ability to discard one frame of reference for another.
3. *Originality*, the tendency to give unusual, atypical answers.
4. *Preference for complexity over simplicity*, looking for the new challenge of knotty problems.
5. *Independence of judgement*, being different from peers and seeing superiors as conventional or arbitrary.

If that listing is accurate, then creative individuals need to be nurtured, as the qualities are unlikely to be warmly welcomed by colleagues and will make it difficult for their possessor to function comfortably in an organisation. They are likely to be regarded as odd and possibly as a nuisance, so they must be identified and their potential contribution channelled effectively.

The organisational setting influences how the creative individual performs, as organisations tend to emphasise an organisational culture and norms: 'There is the right way, the wrong way, and our way'; or 'In this company we all pull together. Team spirit is our watchword.' There may be an emphasis on corporate image through aspects of dress, like the old school tie. Often senior managers in a company all wear the company tie. Organisations acquire a reputation for preferring certain types of skills or personality. Well-known bodies like the armed services or the BBC attract recruits with some potential but other people would never apply. The innovatory organisation needs both to attract and to sustain diverse characters in its ranks as a necessary prerequisite for innovation.

Torrance (1970) provides a classic discussion about creative children and how their inventiveness can be encouraged. Creative adults similarly need to be nurtured within the organisation and reconciled to the fact that the world about them is satisfied with its errors. Here are his suggestions of what one can provide for the highly creative:

1. Provide a refuge.
2. Become their sponsor or patron.
3. Help them understand their divergence.
4. Let them communicate their ideas.
5. See that their creative talent is recognised.
6. Help others to understand them.

Little is understood about the nature of invention, but a great deal of effort has gone in to understanding how it can be stimulated. Here are three ways in which an organisation or a department can make inventiveness among its members more likely (based on Paines, 1970).

First, emphasise the importance of keeping *notes*. Workable ideas seldom leap, honed and finished, into the mind. A stray thought comes into focus for a moment but without any apparent connection with anything else, or at least without a complete connection. It beguiles because of its newness and apparent potential, but will drift away when the telephone rings, or a conversation begins. The moment has passed and the idea is lost. These moments of insight (or flashes of inspiration) have to be written down so that they are captured for future examination. Also the act of writing it down will embed it at least slightly in the mind, which may then work on it without one being aware of it. We are all familiar with the idea of deferring an idea until we have 'slept on it', often finding that a course of action that was uncertain on retiring is clear on waking. Partly this may be the diurnal rhythm of the body that tires in the evening and is rejuvenated in the morning, so that problems lessen as the sun rises; but it is also due to the fact that our unconscious unravels things for us. The philosopher scientist Arthur Koestler (1964) believed that the great acts of creativity happen in periods of rest after working hard on the problem.

Secondly, there is value in setting *deadlines and quotas* for the production of ideas. This ensures that people attempt to find solutions, rather than putting off the problem till later, like Arthur Brown and his 'Too Hard' tray in Chapter 14. Working up new ideas is hard work, and it is all too easy to distract oneself with maintenance activities instead of settling down to wrestle with thinking. One of the authors has over-watered plants and very fat cats!

Thirdly, set aside *a time and place* for generating ideas. As we saw in Chapter 3, managers rarely allow themselves this sort of time, and allow thinking to be squeezed out by the genetic activity of responding to the demands of others before returning home in the evening having 'never stopped'. The technique of brainstorming contrives deadlines, quotas, a time and a place to ensure that idea generation happens. It is not the romantic view of genius as exemplified by Lord Byron moving sadly from one mistress to another while waiting for inspiration to purge his *ennui*, but it does produce results.

Fourthly, check the *housekeeping* of the organisation. Is inventiveness valued and rewarded, or is it regarded as a nuisance? Are there channels by which the inventive can advance, so that nonconformists can have a sense of career growth because of, rather than despite, their unconventionality? Are the channels of communication reasonably open, so that ideas can be expressed and discussed with a view to finding their merit instead of only finding fault? Always there is the need for balance. The organisation devoid of inventiveness and creative thought will wither through lack of nourishment, but the organisation that is taken over by the creative and where the administrators are suppressed, will probably destroy itself.

Review Topic 15.2

The English novelist George Orwell (1903–50) wrote in his most famous work, *1984*: 'Doublethink means the power of holding two contradictory beliefs in one's mind simultaneously, and accepting both of them.'
How is this different from brainstorming?

DISSEMINATION AND DEVELOPMENT OF THE INVENTION

The invention has to be disseminated by informing others about it and making them enthusiastic. It then has to be made feasible and put into practice. If that does not happen, the most brilliant idea will be stillborn. Many academic researchers are criticised for not putting sufficient effort into disseminating the findings of their research to those who could put them to practical use. Ralph Waldo Emerson said that the world would beat a path through the forest to the door of a man who could write a better book, preach a better sermon, or make a better mousetrap. The world will only beat the path if they know the better mousetrap is there – and if they happen to want a better mousetrap.

In an organisational context innovators need first to influence and persuade their immediate circle that the idea is fruitful. This often happens informally in the office or is a regular part of section meetings, as the outline of the idea is tested to see the reaction. It is very difficult to get anywhere with a new proposal without the endorsement of the immediate boss and the constructive criticism of immediate colleagues, who will be the first links in the communications network that will be needed to reach implementation. If this group provides its support and commitment, then the next 'layer' of boss and colleagues have to be persuaded.

Now all the skills of influence and political manoeuvring that are discussed in Part III of this book become important. First the idea has to be understood as a *better* method than what currently operates (See Chapter 19 on how to prepare a case). Then a commitment has to be won to allocate resources needed to explore the possibilities of the idea. This often involves other departments in the organisation and can seldom be ignored. Too often new ideas are adopted by organisations on face value only and are tried out without being properly tested first, and scarcity of resources is the most common pretext. There is no budget provision for committing money to experiments, so either the proposal is implemented straight away or it is passed over.

Most readers will recall at least one instance in their working lives of an organisational change that went wrong (some may not be able to recall one that went right!). Organisational change is one of the types of innovation that is too often put into operation without being thoroughly worked out first. The broad outlines of allocating responsibility between senior managers are discussed extensively and heatedly, but the nuts and bolts and the ultimate feasibility do not receive the same, necessary, exhaustive examination. Senior managers defend such precipitate action by claiming that organisational change has to be forced in order to overcome the resistance and apathy in the lower levels of the hierarchy. To the outside observer, however, it usually seems more like simple impatience and unwillingness to work through the really difficult problems that can be encountered.

Other types of innovation are also difficult to disseminate and Parker (1978, *op. cit.*) suggests some factors that influence the success of getting an invention into practice:

1. Understanding user needs.
2. Paying attention to marketing the product.
3. Developing efficiently; not necessarily quickly.
4. Using outside technical and scientific advice.
5. Having a senior manager responsible for the innovation.

Langrish *et al.* (1972) studied all the companies that had been awarded The Queen's Award for Industry over two years, and identified the following factors that affected success:

1. The top person in the company was outstanding and had authority.
2. There was at least one other outstanding person.
3. The need to be met was clearly identified.
4. The potential usefulness of the innovation was realised.
5. Good co-operation.
6. Resources were available.
7. There was help from government.

Those two lists have points of coincidence that are particularly relevant to the dissemination and development of any sort of innovation. The most ingenious idea will founder unless there is a user need to be met. The user may be a customer; it may be a department within the organisation, part of the administrative process linking supply and demand, or some other gap that can be filled. The need does not have to be known to the potential user, but it does have to be a potential need. There will be a potential need for a better mousetrap among people plagued by mice, but the person who invents playing cards that can be used under water is unlikely to find a queue of customers. It also seems to be an inescapable requirement for the innovator to find a patron. The sluggish processes of organisation have to be stimulated not only by the excellence of the idea and the enthusiasm of colleagues, but also the determination of at least one person holding significant position power in the hierarchy.

Langrish and his colleagues also identified the factors that delayed the development of inventions:

1. Some other associated technology was not sufficiently developed.
2. No market for the idea.
3. The potential of the idea was not recognised by management.
4. Old ideas were embedded and there was resistance to new ones.
5. Resources were not available.
6. There was poor co-operation and communication.

Innovations are not automatically understood and passed smoothly into operation. Dissemination and development are harder to manage than the initial creative stage. Lewis Lehr is Chairman of the 3M company and believes that all members of the organisation have to be attuned to the possibilities of a new idea being a winner.

> The attitude toward new projects or programs can be very significant. In a company where people at any given time are involved in exploring hundreds of potential developments, it is extremely important that top management do not pre-judge the activities and, for example, identify a group of questionable investment projects under the heading, 'problem programs'. Some years ago we did this. It was not until we re-named this list – 'selected opportunities' – that these programs received the attention necessary to eliminate them as problems and re-direct them as opportunities. (Lehr, 1982, page 98)

Invention needs much stimulation and nurture; it is too easy to destroy.

THE CONSEQUENCES OF INVENTION

Like all social action, there are consequences of innovation that are unintended as well as those that are intended, and we have to guard against the assumption, mentioned earlier, that change is automatically desirable. Rogers and Shoemaker (1971, page 71) provide us with three classifications of the consequences that follow innovation.

First the consequences will be functional or dysfunctional, depending on whether the effects are desirable or undesirable. Secondly, there will be direct or indirect consequences, depending on whether it is an immediate response to innovation or a response to the result of those consequences. Thirdly, the consequences may be latent or manifest, depending on whether or not the consequences are recognised and intended.

Advocates of change usually expect functional, direct and manifest consequences, but invariably some latent consequences are indirect and dysfunctional. An important management activity is to anticipate as many as possible of the unintended consequences, without quashing useful innovation.

MANAGING INNOVATION IN THE DEPARTMENT

Some departments in organisations are set up for the sole, or prime, purpose of innovating. It is the business of the research and development department to introduce, test and develop new ideas. Display and advertising departments need to generate new methods of projection and communication, and other departments are specifically intended to seek new business opportunities and to foster new ventures.

For most departments, however, innovation is more a leavening in the continuing operations to keep excess conformity at bay. A steady stream of new ideas and methods is needed to avoid dullness and to ensure that the department is making its proper contribution within the organisation, but too many innovations may destabilise operations. In the chapter about organisational politics we saw how there is a need to strike a balance between openness and political behaviour among managers. Managing innovation is a similar problem of balance. There must be a co-operative, cohesive working group maintaining an efficient operation, but a part of that co-operative effort is always to encourage and nurture individual creativity so that promising ideas are tested and developed in pushing forward the frontier of what is being achieved. *Managerial* innovation and creativity perhaps begins by setting up that equilibrium.

SUMMARY PROPOSITIONS

15.1 Change is not only something to which to respond, but also something to initiate.

15.2 Creativity is the initial phase of generating a new idea, product or approach; innovation is the whole process from invention to practice.

15.3 The main stages in innovation are: invention or creativity; dissemination and development of the invention; the consequences of the invention in practice.

15.4 Inventiveness among organisation members is made more likely by: the use of notes; deadlines and quotas for the production of new ideas; setting aside a time and a place for generating ideas; checking the housekeeping of the organisation.

PUTTING IT INTO PRACTICE

Drill for brainstorming

The technique of brainstorming has been mentioned earlier in the book. Here we suggest a drill for its application in innovation.

Before the session
1. Decide the purpose of the session. Is it:
    (a) To find uses for a new idea?
    (b) To find a better way of doing something? or
    (c) To find a solution to a problem?
2. Make a note of any ideas you have about the subject.

Conducting the session
3. Appoint a note-taker.
4. Ask group members to call out any idea that comes into their heads.
5. Write ideas on blackboard, flip chart or overhead projector, so that all group members can see them.
6. Encourage group members to develop the ideas of others, as well as 'sparking' in different directions.
7. Eschew judgement by anyone in the group. All ideas are valid, however bizarre, and even if they seem to be repeating what has been said already.
8. Generate momentum, so that the group keeps going.
9. Reach a target number – say 75 – ideas in 15–30 minutes.

After the session
10. Classify the ideas generated into five or six groups, possibly adding others that are suggested by the classification.
11. Ask the group to rank the ideas in each classification against questions such as
    (a) How new?
    (b) How relevant?
    (c) How feasible?
12. Decide on action, if any, to be taken to develop preferred ideas.

REFERENCES

Bradley, K. and Hill, S., ' "After Japan": the quality circle transplant and productive efficiency', *British Journal of Industrial Relations*, vol. xxi, 1983, pages 291–311.
Drucker, P.F., *Managing in Turbulent Times*, Heinemann, London, 1980.
Freeman, C., 'The determinants of innovation', *Futures*, June 1979, page 206.

Koestler, A., *The Act of Creation*, Hutchinson, London 1974.

Langrish, J.R., Gibbons, M., Evans, W.G. and Jevons, T.R., *Wealth from Knowledge*, Macmillan, London, 1972.

Lehr, L.W., 'Entrepreneurs, innovation and change', quoted in Wild, R. (ed.), *How to Manage*, Heinemann, London, 1982.

Paines, S.J., 'Education and creativity', in Vernon, P.E. (ed.), *Creativity*, Penguin Books, Harmondsworth, 1970.

Pavitt, K., 'Innovation and industrial development', *Futures*, 1979, page 458.

Parker, J.E.S., *The Economics of Innovation*, Longman, London, 1978.

Rogers, E.M. and Shoemaker, F.F., *Communication of Innovation*, 2nd edn, Free Press, New York, 1971.

Steiner, G.A., *The Creative Organization*, University of Chicago Press, 1965.

Toffler, A., *Future Shock*, Random House, New York, 1970.

Torrance, E.P., 'Causes for concern', in Vernon, P.E. (ed.), *Creativity*, Penguin Books, Harmondsworth, 1970.

PART IV

THE WORKING TEAM

The nucleus of the organisation is the working team of individuals, each of whom has different aspirations, skills and needs. The contribution of each is won through careful arrangements of and for the work that people do. Some of this is done in close collaboration with colleagues, some is done alone. Skilled methods of communication contribute to the effective harmonisation of these diverse activities, but careful initial selection of people – not only to do a particular job but also to join a particular team – is a prerequisite, and performance appraisal that enables rather than passing judgement, can maintain both individual and collective purpose.

16

AUTHORITY, LEADERSHIP AND AUTONOMY

Organisational structure and culture are ways of things getting done: authority, leadership and autonomy are ways of getting things done. When the structure is just as it should be and the culture is carefully aligned to the mission, the people and the context, then the work actually has to be done and management work is getting things done through people in the broad sense of the GROUP analogy set out in the opening chapter. The individual manager gets things done largely on the basis of personal authority, leadership and autonomy. Often managers lack confidence in this aspect of their work more than any other, and seek the endorsement of more senior, powerful people or for clear cut procedural and policy guidelines. However important these may be, they are no more than a background in front of which the manager stands alone, with a distinctive style, personality and approach. The performance of the manager will be improved by understanding how the features of authority, leadership and autonomy mesh together.

Our Chapter 10 on organisational politics dealt with the nature of power in organisations and how managers can increase and manipulate the power available to them. This chapter deals with a specific aspect of how individuals deploy power in relation to subordinates: power made legitimate by expertise or hierarchical position. The three words in the chapter title describe the combination which managers need for effectiveness. Being in authority is a right to control and judge the actions of others. Leadership is the exercise of the power conferred by that right in such a way as to win a willing and positive, rather than grudging and negative, response. Autonomy is that freedom of action which subordinates see as being necessary and reasonable if they are themselves to be effective in their roles.

AUTHORITY

One of the problems of managers being in authority is that their frame of reference is different from that of their subordinates. Partly this is a simple matter of individual difference and partly it is difference in role. After the Allied invasion of Normandy in 1944, there was widespread criticism among senior service officers and politicians of how Field Marshal Montgomery was conducting the fighting round the city of Caen. Supreme Commander Eisenhower came under pressure either to dismiss Montgomery or to issue direct instructions that would require Montgomery to act against his own better judgement. Eisenhower refused, because of his practice of always delegating authority to subordinates and giving them fullest support. Even in an operation that had such detailed planning and extensive information available, Eisenhower realised the importance of being on the spot.

> [Eisenhower] did not have Montgomery's feel of the battle as a two-sided encounter in which he kept the initiative by actions which put the enemy at a disadvantage and kept him at a disadvantage. Eisenhower did not see that by the fighting round Caen the enemy was placing himself in a position from which he would not be able to recover. . . . Eisenhower had rightly delegated command of the land battle to Montgomery: he had wider tasks. (Sixsmith, 1973, page 158)

On a more general level there is a difference in objectives over much of employment. The manager is looking for efficiency, return on capital and trouble-free co-ordination of employee effort, while the subordinate is seeking an agreeable, dignified way of life within the confines of the employment contract. This perennial dissonance between the points of view has been pointed out in relation to the period in eighteenth century England, when workers could appeal to the local Justice of the Peace if they considered their rate of pay unfair.

> The buyers in the labour market operated on the principle of buying in the cheapest market and selling in the dearest. . . . But the sellers were not normally asking for the maximum wage which the traffic would bear and offering in return the minimum quantity of labour they could get away with. They were trying to earn a decent living as human beings . . . they were engaged in human life rather than in economic transaction. (Hobsbawm, 1975, page 222)

Taylorism at the beginning of the twentieth century changed that general wage/employment relationship to a specific cash nexus with a concentration on what would be paid for each of a range of human actions. This was a shift of power as employees lost their control of discretionary knowledge in order to centralise control in the hands of the managers. The long-standing refusal of skilled craftsmen to accept time study and 'the tyranny of the stop watch' has maintained for them a degree of autonomy that is jealousy guarded.

The ideas of F.W. Taylor continue to suffuse much of management thinking but have had overlaid upon them the doctrine of human co-operation advanced by Elton Mayo over forty years. This depends on well-knit human groups and the development of social as well as technical skills.

> Social skill shows itself as a capacity to receive communications from others, and to respond to the attitudes and ideas of others in such fashions as to promote congenial participation in a common task. (Mayo, 1975, page 12)

In considering managerial authority, the juxtaposition of these two innovations is usually misunderstood. Taylor's scientific management is often regarded as the tough but fair way of the old days that was very good as control, but which has now become impracticable; while Mayo's human relations thinking is wishy-washy, undermines managerial authority and leads to dubious practices like underlings addressing managers by their Christian names. In fact scientific management and the cash nexus may well tie down employees to organisational demands as a whole, but can deprive individual managers of effective power over subordinates. The control lies not with the individual manager but with the payment system, so that the employee who has filled the daily quota or who is 'ahead of the clock' may feel under little obligation to the supervisor. The dominance of the control *system* detracts from the legitimacy of the individual manager's authority. When the style changes to 'congenial participation in a common task', that common task is assigned to the working group by an individual manager, and the need for collaboration with other groups in the organisation who are congenially participating in an over-arching common task makes individual group members dependent on a controlling figure to communicate, explain and protect. The manager may resent being called Fred (or, in other situations, have to tolerate being pushed away from the social group so that he is no longer called Fred) but gains, rather than loses, authority in an organisation where social skills are demanded. There is again the problem about different frames of reference. Subordinates look to the manager for authority on which they can rely to act on their behalf, solve problems and offer guidance, while the managers may be looking for deference to them as superior kinds of people.

The majority of the initiatives to develop or alter organisational culture seek to increase the individual's sense of responsibility and involvement by chipping away at unnecessary status differentials like that of 'manager and subordinate', so that the clear distinction between managers and the managed is seldom a valid description of employment categories. Few of us are now either managers or subordinates; increasingly we are both. Every member of the management hierarchy has a boss or superordinate who can prevent or help the manager get things done, and few members of an organisation do not have to get some things done by other people. So we are not here splitting people into categories but discussing two aspects of everyone's role: getting things done through people and people getting things done through you.

Review Topic 16.1

Some managers complain that they have responsibility without authority. Where this happens, what are the consequences?

OBEDIENCE

The authority of managers is underpinned by a predilection to obedience that we all have. Stanley Milgram (1974) carried out a startling series of experiments in the United States, which showed this predilection in a way that many people found disconcerting. Male volunteers were led to believe that they were taking part in a study of memory and learning. They had to administer electric shocks to learners when the learners made mistakes in answering simple questions. The electric shocks became progressively more severe with each incorrect answer. If the volunteer questioned the procedure with the experimenter, who was in charge, he was simply told that he should continue. The range of instructions began as 'Please continue' and went up to 'You have no other choice: you must go on.'

Eighteen different experiments were conducted with over one thousand volunteers, but no matter how the variables were altered the volunteers did as they were told even when administering shocks of 450 volts to a victim begging for release. Some were unwilling to continue, but the majority continued all the way through to the end. It is not quite as bad as it sounds. The shocks were not really being given, the learner was an actor pretending to be on the point of collapse, but the volunteers thought the shocks were real and carried on 'doing their job'. Two samples:

> Mr Batta:
> 'The scene is brutal and depressing: his hard, impassive face shows total indifference as he subdues the screaming learner and gives him shocks. He seems to derive no pleasure from the act itself, only quiet satisfaction at doing his job properly.'

> Mr Gino, speaking at the end of the experiment:
> 'Well, I faithfully believed the man was dead until we opened the door. When I saw him, I said 'Great, this is great.' But it didn't bother me even to find that he was dead. I did my job.' (Milgram, 1974, pages 46 and 88)

Readers of this book will probably not want their subordinates to electrocute their colleagues, but the importance of this study is that it demonstrates a remarkable readiness to obey. Milgram explains this by saying that when people enter a hierarchical system ('someone else is in charge'), those people then see themselves as agents carrying out the wishes of others and put themselves in what he calls an 'agentic state'. Others take the responsibility, so that compliance is not only easy, but also the criterion of satisfaction.

Milgram explains the willingness with which people adopt the agentic state by reference to a series of experiences which virtually everyone undergoes.

1. *Parental regulation.* The experience of almost everyone when young, as parents remorsely issue instructions on a range of matters concerning every department of an infant's life – eating, sleeping, washing, keeping quiet and so on. The one common element in all of these is the implicit 'obey me'.
2. *The institutional setting.* The child emerges from the cocoon of the family into an institutional setting. At school always subordinate, although gradually acquiring seniority in relation to other subordinates. At college and in the early years at work they always have to do things prescribed by others.
3. *Rewards.* Given to those who comply with authority and the disobedient are frequently punished.
4. *Normative support.* Authority is normatively supported as any group or institution is expected, by its members, to have a socially controlling figure.
5. *Justifying ideology.* There is a justifying ideology that supports, or legitimates, the authority of the individual controlling figure. In Milgram's experiments the volunteers came to a university to take part in scientific investigations about learning. Science and education are two powerful sources of legitimacy. Other obvious sources are religious belief and patriotism. Others again are service to the customer, the general good of the organisation and the wellbeing of the employees.

The explanations above have been used to explain such things as the willingness of ordinary people to participate in the slaughter of Jews in Nazi Germany or the massacre of villagers in Vietnam, but political philosophers have long debated the idea that the majority of people *want* to be subservient to a dominant figure or group, who will look after them. This argument runs that people have a choice as humans between freedom and happiness. Freedom involves being responsible and making decisions and judgements. Happiness relieves a person of those 'burdens' as others decide what is right and wrong, what should be done and what should not, so that the individual enjoys freedom from responsibility and the contentment of someone else doing the organisation and making all the difficult decisions. However cynical this sounds it is a recurring theme in art and literature. On a practical level in everyday life we seem to mix issues between those where we want to make our own choices and those where we are happy to leave the choice to others and obey their instructions. The person who campaigns vigorously against government policy on nuclear weapons one day will probably comply unquestioningly with medical treatment for a sore throat the following day. Our willingness to comply varies from individual to individual, but it is there within all of us. A contemporary commentary on this phenomenon is by D.H. Wrong (1979).

Whatever the reasons for obedience, the important lesson for managers is that there is a predilection for those in organisations to comply with instructions from those in authority within the organisational framework. That is the authority of those *in* authority. This can be immeasurably enhanced by those who are also *an* authority, who have some aspect of expertise to make their instructions convincing and welcome. French and Raven (1959) suggest that there are five main bases of power to influence others.

1. A (the person wishing to exercise power) has the ability to control the *rewards* of B (the person to be influenced). Managers control promotions, pay rises, some aspects of fringe benefits, and are important potential sources of praise.
2. A has the ability to *coerce* B by providing punishments. Praise can be withheld, unattractive duties can be allowed to B, who may be rebuked and eventually dismissed.
3. A may have *legitimate* influence because of role. The quality assurance official has the right to examine the work done by others, just as customs officers have the right to open suitcases at national frontiers.
4. *Referent* power is where B wishes to identify with A. An extreme form is seen in the clamorous followers of popular singers, but managers tend to attract a following in organisations, even though the followers may not express themselves with such exuberance.
5. Finally A has authority in relation to B when A has *expertise* which B acknowledges and wants to use. An example we used in the discussion on organisational politics was of the maintenance engineer who can work the miracle of restarting the machine that has stopped, but there are many such examples in every organisation, and this is an authority base that does not depend on hierarchical position. Another example is of the young legal advisor in a large international company, who told the members of the main board of her company that they could not go ahead with the planned sale of a subsidiary for legal reasons. In the hierarchy she ranked low, but her technical expertise was not queried.

From our discussion so far in this chapter it may seem that managers should have no problem in getting others to do things; if people generally are predisposed to obey, then presumably all that managers need to do is to issue instructions and wait for them to be carried out?

Life, of course, is not so easy. The general predisposition to compliance is something of which all managers have to be reminded, but it is not sufficient. Although the majority of Milgram's volunteers complied, 35 per cent did not; also they were being required to carry out a routine task rather than one depending on enthusiasm, imagination or some other quality that cannot be conjured up by simple command. How many managers could tolerate a situation in which they operated by simple decree? They fear that the result will be the corruption of themselves by the power they wield.

LEADERSHIP

The implication behind the notion of leadership is that there is a combination of personal qualities and skills that enables some people to elicit from their subordinates a response that is enthusiastic, cohesive and effective, while other people in the same situation cannot achieve such results. There are two problems about that type of view. First it is often bad for the leaders, who grow an inflated view of their own importance, believing that success lies in who they are rather than what they do. Secondly, it limits the number of people who can safely be put in charge of sections, departments and operations because it emphasises relatively rare qualities of social dominance. It is significant that qualities of leadership are a greater preoccupation among potential leaders than among potential followers. 'I know how to get the best out of them' is heard more frequently than 'He knows how to get the best out of us'. The 'great man' theory of leadership was summed up by the postwar American president Harry Truman:

> I wonder how far Moses would have gone if he had taken a poll in Egypt? What would Jesus Christ have preached if he had taken a poll in Israel? Where would the Reformation have gone if Martin Luther had taken a poll? It isn't polls or public opinion of the moment that counts. It is right and wrong and leadership – men with fortitude, honesty and a belief in the right that makes epochs in the history of the world. (*Wall Street Journal*, 16 December, 1980, page 2)

Studies of effective leaders in order to identify the *traits* of leadership have failed to provide clear cut results and it is now appreciated that there are other factors of comparable or greater significance in explaining leader effectiveness. A review by Davis (1972) shows there to be four general traits related to leadership success, although they do little more than confirm common sense.

1. *Intelligence.* Leaders usually have a slightly higher level of general intelligence than the average among their followers.
2. *Social maturity.* Having self-assurance and self-respect, leaders are mature and able to handle a wide variety of social situations.
3. *Achievement drive.* Leaders have a strong drive to get things done.
4. *Human relations attitudes.* Knowing that they rely on other people to get things done, leaders are interested in their subordinates and work at developing subordinate response.

A more comprehensive understanding requires a consideration of the needs that a particular group of people have of their leader, and of the situation in which the led task is performed.

In 1902 the Scottish dramatist J.M. Barrie wrote a play, *The Admirable Crichton*, in which an English aristocratic family is shipwrecked on a desert island. The authority of the head of the family rapidly disintegrates in this situation and the role of leader is gradually assumed by the one person in the party who has the skills and experience necessary: Crichton, the family butler. Previously his ability and resourcefulness has been recognised with the patronising term 'admirable'; suddenly they become essential. Not born great, Crichton has greatness thrust upon him. On the desert island, his leadership was unchallenged. When the party was rescued, the crew of the ship that found them immediately re-established the norms and values of Edwardian England, so Crichton resumed his tail coat and served his master an excellent breakfast in bed.

As with so many areas of social science investigation, much of the work on leadership over the last thirty years has been to present slightly different versions of explanatory models that are basically very similar but express differing emphasis according to the values of their proponents. So we shall describe just three of these explanations which are mutually consistent and the second depends partly on the explanations in the first.

Fiedler (1967) has developed a *contingency model of leadership effectiveness* in which he argues that any leadership style may be effective, depending on the situation, so that the leader has to be *adaptive*. We thus have a clear difference between this approach and that of the trait theorists, as we are talking of leaders adapting their *style* to the situation. He also appreciates that it is very difficult for individuals to change their style of leadership as these styles are relatively inflexible: the autocrat will remain autocratic and the freewheeling *laissez-faire* advocate will remain freewheeling. As no single style is appropriate for all situations, effectiveness can be achieved either by changing the manager to fit the situation or by altering the situation to suit the manager. Three factors will determine the leader's effectiveness:

1. *Leader–member relations.* How well is the leader accepted by the subordinates?
2. *Task structure.* Are the jobs of subordinates routine and precise or vague and undefined?
3. *Position power.* What formal authority does the leader's position confer?

Fiedler then devised a novel device for measuring leadership style. It was a scale that indicated *the degree to which a man described favourably or unfavourably his least-preferred co-worker (LPC)*.

A person who describes his least-preferred co-workers in a relatively favorable manner tends to be permissive, human relations oriented and considerate of the feelings of his men. But a person who describes his least preferred co-worker in an unfavourable manner – who has what we have come to call a low LPC rating – tends to be managing, task-controlling and less concerned with the human relations aspects of the job. (Fiedler, 1965)

Fiedler then argues that high LPC managers will want to have close ties with their subordinates and regard these as an important contributor to their effectiveness, while low LPC managers will be much more concerned with getting the job done and less interested in the reactions of subordinates. It is then possible to combine all these elements to show how the style of leadership that is effective varies with the situation in which it is exercised. Table 16.1 shows the result of 800 studies which Fiedler carried out, using eight categories of leadership situations and two types of leaders.

High LPC leaders were likely to be most effective in situations where relations with subordinates are good but task structure is low and position power weak. They do reasonably well when they have poor relationships with their subordinates but there is high task structure and strong position power. Both of these are moderately favourable combinations of circumstance. Low LPC leaders are more effective at the ends of the spectrum, when they have either a favourable combination or an unfavourable combination of factors in the situation.

The value of Fiedler's work is that it concentrates on *effectiveness* as it yardstick and demonstrates the fallacy of believing that there is a single best

Table 16.1 Leadership performance in different conditions

Condition	Leader–member relations	Task structure	Position power	
1	Good	High	Strong	Low LPC leader more effective
2	Good	High	Weak	Low LPC leader more effective
3	Good	Low	Strong	Low LPC leader more effective
4	Good	Low	Weak	High LPC leader more effective
5	Poor	High	Strong	High LPC leader more effective
6	Poor	High	Weak	Similar effectiveness
7	Poor	Low	Strong	Low LPC leader more effective
8	Poor	Low	Weak	Low LPC leader more effective

(From Fieldler, 1976, page 11)

way to lead in all situations. It is interesting that the majority of situations he describes appear to call for a generally less attractive type of person as leader, but we should remember that he was examining a range of situations for the purpose of explanation, and that situations which are at the extremes of his continuum may not be very frequent in organisational life. Although this remains the most widely accepted analysis of the leadership process, some people have found rather depressing Fiedler's accompanying argument that individual leaders have little chance of adopting a style which is more appropriate to their situation, so that it is more important to match available managers to a situation than to try changing the individual manager's style. An alternative is to tinker with the situation: modifying the task structure, varying the formal authority or changing the subordinates. The last is the most drastic and is only possible to any significant extent in very few situations. It could, however, transform condition 8 to condition 4.

Some people, especially those concerned with training, cannot believe in the degree of inflexibility that Fiedler found. One person whose ideas on training have been widely influential in the United Kingdom is John Adair.

Adair produces a picture of leadership by arguing that people in working groups have three sets of needs, two of which are shared with all group members, and one being related to each individual.

1. The task to be accomplished together.
2. Maintaining the social cohesion of the group.
3. Individual needs of team members.

These three sets of needs are interdependent:

> If a group fails in its task this will intensify the disintegrative tendencies present in the group and raise a diminished satisfaction for its individual members. If there is a lack of unity or harmonious relationships in the group this will effect performance on the job and also individual needs (cf. A.H. Maslow's *Social Needs*). And obviously an individual who feels frustrated and unhappy in a particular work environment will not make his maximum contribution to either the common task or the life of the group. (Adair, 1982, page 9)

Review Topic 16.2

There is great interest among managers in leadership ideas. Is this solely to justify their idea of their own importance as people deserving larger salaries and bigger cars?

Figure 16.1 shows these three sets of needs, or leadership functions, are expressed as three overlapping circles. This emphasises the essential unity of leadership, so that a single action by a leader may have influence in all three areas.

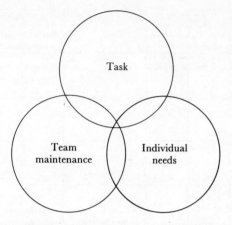

Fig. 16.1 Adair's three circle model of leadership.

This was used by Adair to develop leadership at the Royal Military Academy, Sandhurst, but the methods have been adopted in a wide variety of organisations. They are set out in detail in Adair, 1982.

A well-tried device for identifying leadership style of the individual is the *Managerial Grid* used as an exercise in management development to decide one's leadership style, with the hope that it can be modified at least slightly to become more appropriate to the situation in which one is working.

The Managerial Grid was developed by Blake and Mouton (1969) and identifies *concern for production and concern for people* as the two axes of a grid, illustrated in Fig. 16.2. At the lower left hand corner is a '1.1 management style' which is the style of managers who have a low concern for both people and production, try to stay out of trouble and simply do as they are told. In the upper left hand corner is the '1.9 style' of high concern for people but low concern for production, and so on. The '9.9 style' of high concern with both people and production is the obvious goal.

Grid training requires team members to identify their own management style, as they perceive it themselves, and then as it is perceived by others, so there is an element of sensitivity training thinking in the approach. It is possible to identify the management style composition of any team and either alter team membership to increase effectiveness or enable individual team members to modify their personal style. This emphasis on style rather than personal characteristics is probably the secret of the success that grid methods have enjoyed, as it provides useful criticism of the type that most of us can live with and can hope to modify.

The British writers Wright and Taylor (1984), point out the importance of leaders acting *skilfully* in day-to-day working relationships with people in different roles. Concentrating on the individual leader trying to improve the working performance of a subordinate, they have produced the checklist

Fig. 16.2 The managerial grid.

shown in Table 16.2. This makes the issue of leadership practical rather than philosophical and provides managers with methods of improving their performance.

AUTONOMY

Research and discussion about authority and leadership tend to centre on the role and personality or, more recently, on the needs of groups to have a leadership function exercised on their behalf. These emphases tend to overlook the need of organisation members for autonomy, and the complementary need of organisation to have members who are autonomous. From the point of view of the individual employee, there is a life cycle theory of leadership (Hersey and Blanchard, 1969) which points out that people at

Table 16.2 A checklist for improving work performance

1. What is the problem in behavioural terms? What precisely is the individual doing or not doing which is adversely influencing his or her performance?
2. Is the problem really serious enough to spend time and effort on?
3. What reasons might there be for the performance problem? (See column 1.)
4. What actions might be taken to improve the situation? (See column 2.)

Possible reasons for performance problem	Possible solutions
Goal clarity Is the person fully aware of the job requirements?	Give guidance concerning expected goals and standards. Set targets
Ability Does the person have the capacity to do the job well?	Provide formal training, on the job coaching, practice, secondment, etc.
Task difficulty Does the person find the task too demanding?	Simplify task, reduce work load, reduce time pressures, etc.
Intrinsic motivation Does the person find the task rewarding in itself?	Redesign job to match job-holder's needs
Extrinsic motivation Is good performance rewarded by others?	Arrange positive consequences for good performance and zero or negative consequences for poor performance
Feedback Does the person receive adequate feedback about his/her performance?	Provide or arrange feedback
Resources Does the person have adequate resources for satisfactory task performance?	Provide staff, equipment, raw materials as appropriate
Working conditions Do working conditions, physical or social, interfere with performance?	Improve light, noise, heat, layout, remove distractions, etc. as appropriate

5. Do you have sufficient information to select the most appropriate solution(s)? If not, collect the information required, e.g. consult records, observe work behaviour, talk to person concerned.
6. Select most appropriate solution(s).
7. Is the solution worthwhile in cost–benefit terms?
   (a) If so, implement it.
   (b) If not, work through the checklist again, or relocate the individual, or reorganise the department/organisation, or live with the problem.
8. Could you have handled the problem better? If so, review own performance. If not, and the problem is solved, reward yourself and tackle next problem.

work need lessening task structure as they mature in an organisation, as well as during their maturation as human beings. Most forty-year-olds will find close supervision and direction as irksome as most sixteen-year-olds will find it necessary. From the point of view of the employing organisation, close supervision is time-consuming and expensive, as we saw in the discussion about the optimum span of control. Also many tasks in contemporary organisations cannot be done well without the job holder having full range for personal imagination and responsibility. Bob Ramsey retired in 1981 from the position of Industrial Relations Director at Ford of Great Britain. This is not a company renowned for its weakness and inefficiency, yet Ramsey frequently spoke of employees looking for a better *service* from management. The main work of organisations is done by engineers and salesmen, by designers and analysts, and by many other people with some acquired skill that the organisation needs. Managers enable those employees to do well by the management service they provide in support of the autonomy that is needed for effective individual performance.

AUTHORITY, LEADERSHIP AND THE MANAGER

The basic job of getting people to obey orders is not as problematical as many managers believe, and little skill or personal charm is needed. The reason, however, for the abiding interest of managers in ideas of leadership, motivation and influence is that managers usually seek to do more than bring about simple obedience – they are trying to win a performance. They are trying to enable the members of the group, team or department to produce a workaday contribution to the organisation in commitment, collaboration, imagination, persistence and forbearance. The type of leadership that is effective varies with the situation in which it is exercised, just as the behaviour of team members varies according to the scope which their jobs offer. As with so many other aspects of management, there is no single best way of being in charge of a group of people, but in an increasing range of working situations it seems as if the successful manager is the one who is most thorough in ensuring that the team members have the correct facilities and environment to work. Skilled individuals know what to do, and need appropriate autonomy and services to perform.

Review Topic 16.3

Is the autonomy of individual workers incompatible with the power implicit in organisations?

SUMMARY PROPOSITIONS

16.1 The authority of managers is underpinned by a general human predilection to obey commands from those holding higher rank in the hierarchy of which they are members.

16.2 Tight control of employee performance by incentive payment schemes reduces rather than enhances the personal authority of individual managers in relation to employees.

16.3 Effective leadership depends on the situations in which it is exercised; the main variables being leader-member relations, task structure and position power of the leader.

16.4 A convenient way of understanding what is involved in the leadership of a group is to consider three overlapping needs: the needs of group members to accomplish a task together, the need to maintain the social cohesion of the group, and the needs of the individual group members.

16.5 Increasingly employees – especially those with skills or specialised knowledge – need a style of leadership that acknowledges their need for autonomy in order to make their optimum contribution.

PUTTING IT INTO PRACTICE

The exercise of authority in relation to subordinates sometimes involved a relatively formal disciplinary interview. This is not the on-the-spot rebuke, nor the heat-of-the moment shouting match, but the occasions when the manager feels that there is something wrong with the subordinate's performance, attitude or behaviour that needs to be explored and discussed. For most managers this is the third most dreaded encounter in working life (the second worst is having to dismiss somebody, the worst is being dismissed yourself). The following guide suggests a way of approaching this difficult task.

Interaction guide for the disciplinary interview

1. Before the Interview
Check   1. Facts as they are known and have been reported.
                2. Position in relation to disciplinary procedure and employee's legal rights.
                3. Who will be present. The respondent may wish to be accompanied. You may want to have witnesses available.

2. During the Interview
Begin with   An explanation of the management position, which is based on some unsatisfactory *facts* about the employee's behaviour, not on opinions about those facts.

Ask for   The employee's comments on the facts, including reasons for them and attitude towards what has happened.

Ensure   That you both understand the other's position.

Examine   The shared problem to find a solution. Usually the matter will be resolved by this joint examination.

Persuade   If the matter is not resolved by mutual examination and discussion of the problem, try to *persuade* the employee that continuing the action will not be in their best interests.

Disapprove   If persuasion fails, use *disapproval* of what has happened; either your own personal disapproval, or the reported disapproval of others whose approval the employee wants to retain.

Penalties   If all else fails, deploy *penalties*, either for what has been done or as the inevitable result of repetition in the future.

3. After the Interview

Record   Problems and agreed action.

Take action   If any management action was agreed as necessary, e.g. moving the employee to a different department.

File   Interview notes for later review, especially if there is any possibility of dismissal.

REFERENCES

Adair, J., *Action-Centred Leadership*, Gower, Aldershot, 1982.

Blake, R.R. and Mouton, J.S., *Building a Dynamic Organization through Grid Organization Development*, Gulf, Houston, Texas, 1978.

Davies, K., *Human Behaviour at Work*, 4th edn, McGraw Hill, New York, 1972.

Fiedler, F.E., *A Theory of Leadership Effectiveness*, McGraw Hill, New York, 1967.

Fielder, F.E., 'The leadership game: matching the man to the situation', *Organizational Dynamics*, Winter, 1976.

French, W.L. and Raven, S., 'The bases of social power', in Cartwright, D. (ed.), *Studies in Social Power*.

Hersey, P. and Blanchard, K.H., 'Life cycle theory of leadership', *Training and Development Journal*, May 1969, pages 26–34.

Hobsbawm, E.J., *The Age of Capital*, Weidenfeld & Nicholson, London, 1975.

Mayo, E., *The Social Problems of Industrial Civilisation*, Routledge & Kegan Paul, London, 1975.

Milgram, S., *Obedience to Authority*, Tavistock, London, 1974.

Sixsmith, E.K.G., *Eisenhower as Military Commander*, Batsford, London, 1973.

Wright, P.L. and Taylor, D.S., *Improving Leadership Performance*, Prentice Hall International, Hemel Hempstead, 1984.

Wrong, D.H., *Power: its Forms, Bases and Uses*, Basil Blackwell, Oxford, 1979. Particularly relevant is Chapter 5, pages 84–123. Readers may also like to read Chapter 5 in Book V of *The Brothers Karamazov* by Fyodor Dosteovsky, which is available in many imprints, including that of the Everyman Library, J.M. Dent, London, 1947.

17

MOTIVATION AND INFLUENCE

Much managerial time is spent in winning people round. This is not the same as using power, as was discussed in our chapter on organisational politics, nor is it the exercise of authority in 'the line' as in the last chapter. It is the ability to persuade and to influence, very similar to the art of selling. It is not the manipulation of resources and setting up situations which gives others little choice but to agree, and it is not the working relationship between superior and subordinate behind which there is the implicit assumption that the superior can command the obedience of the subordinate. It is a separate, specialised aspect of managerial work that enables things to get done; an extension of understanding other people and how they are motivated.

Other people do not necessarily see things in the same way that we do. Few comments can be more obviously true. Yet the behaviour and conversation of most individuals suggest that it is a truth we do not readily follow in our everyday lives. We find it difficult to understand how anyone can vote for a political party whose policies are opposed to those of the party we voted for. In industrial relations negotiations it is unusual for the protagonists to see, let alone appreciate, the opposing point of view. Those conducting selection interviews need constantly to remind themselves of the difference in perspective and understanding between themselves and those they interview.

The reason we find it so difficult to adopt a different perspective is that we all need a set of operating assumptions to conduct our daily affairs, and the one we find most comforting is that others see the world around them in the same way as we see the world around us. Recruiting for large organisations, especially recruiting for the management ranks, often follows a routine that selects those who are similar to those already employed. The operating assumption of a common view of the world is then safe. It is further consolidated by induction and training. Those entering the police force have attitudes about authority that are similar and which are reinforced by the process of training in the service. Not everyone outside the police force shares those views. In the electronics company Hewlett Packard there is constant reference to 'The Hewlett Packard way'. This is known, felt and understood by those in the company, without being made explicit. IBM used to have a company song:

> Ever onward, ever onward.
>> We're bound for the top never to fall.
> Right here and now we thankfully
>> Pledge sincerest loyalty
> To the corporation that's best for all.
>> Our leaders we revere, and while we're here
> Let's show the world just what we think of them . . .

There are still many examples of organisations that seek to employ only those who conform to a particular set of values and behaviour, with that conformity being assessed in recruitment, emphasised in induction and confirmed in promotion. Managers in such organisations need to understand individual differences sufficiently for them to identify those who fit the pattern and to avoid those who do not.

A much stronger reason for understanding how individuals differ is the impracticability of any manager seeking to work only with the like-minded. If managers could surround themselves with clones they would get standardised, sychophantic responses to all their initiatives. Different managers may have surrounded themselves with clones of a different type and it is not feasible to people an entire organisation with carbon copies of the model organisation person. Organisations deal with a clientele and the only thing the clients will have in common will be an interest in the organisation's products. As people they will vary enormously. Furthermore the remaking of organisations in their own image is a practice that can lead to criticism of unreasonable discrimination against other, worthy applicants who do not fit neatly into the mould.

Managers spend a large part of their time talking to others and trying to get others to do things. The more they can understand the nature of individual differences, the more effectively they can work with a variety of people.

MANAGEMENT MODELS OF MAN

We all work with a model of man in our heads when we seek to understand others. We behave towards them in line with our beliefs and expect their behaviour to be predictable. The problem is that their model of man may not be the same as ours.

Those who know what their model is are more likely to recognise the occasion when someone else is using a different model. Such recognition not only reduces the likelihood of talking at cross purposes but also increases the likelihood of being able to understand the reasoning behind whatever the other is saying.

Schein (1970) and McGregor (1960) have looked at the models used by managers. Schein (pages 55–76) describes four models that managers use to explain the behaviour of subordinates. Managers holding the *rational-economic* model of man assume that people are primarily motivated by rational appraisal of personal economic needs. The *social* model assumes that people are motivated by social needs, wanting rewarding on-the-job relationships and that they are more responsive to work group pressures than to management control. The *self-actualising* model sees people as both wanting to be, and able to be, mature independent people responsible for their own work. *Complex* man assumes that people cannot be slotted into any of the above categories but have various and complex desires that include all the above and some other needs, not all of which can be met at work.

As usual management thinkers want the best of all possible worlds and advocate the adoption of the fourth model as it includes the other three and rules out any one of them from being taken as the single explanation. Managers believing in rational–economic man can be baffled when they put up wages only to find that labour turnover rises or output falls. Other managers, who adhere to social man thinking, are aggrieved when an employee applies for a better paid job elsewhere, despite the manager's efforts to be nice to him.

Review Topic 17.1

Which are you?
1. **Rational–economic man.**
2. **Social man.**
3. **Self-actualising man.**
4. **Complex man.**
Now ask a friend which *you* are.

McGregor produced what is probably the best known theory about management attitudes to subordinates when he propounded his profoundly simple idea of the theory *X* manager and the theory *Y* manager. He believed that prevailing assumptions among managers about the typical worker were outdated as they did not take account of the education level and psychological maturity of the workforce. What McGregor saw as the prevailing assumption was summed up by theory *X*, which emphasised direction and control in organisations with rigid structures and management styles. In contrast a theory *Y* manager will give people greater freedom, will consult about methods and objectives and will delegate more authority. These theories are summarised in Fig. 17.1.

Theory X

1. The average human being has an inherent dislike of work and will avoid it if he can.
2. Because of the human characteristic dislike of work, most people must be coerced, controlled, directed, threatened with punishment, to get them to put forth adequate effort towards the achievement of organisational objectives.
3. The average human being prefers to be directed, wishes to avoid responsibility, has relatively little ambition, wants security above all.

Theory Y

1. The expenditure of physical and mental effort is as natural as play or rest.
2. External control and the threat of punishment are not the only means of bringing about effort towards organisational objectives. People will exercise self-direction and self-control in the service of objectives to which they are committed.
3. Commitment to objectives is a function of the rewards associated with their achievement.
4. The average human being learns, under proper conditions, not only to accept but to seek reponsibility.
5. The capacity to exercise a relatively high degree of imagination, ingenuity, and creativity in the solution of organisational problems is widely, not narrowly, distributed in the population.
6. Under the condition of modern industrial life, the intellectual potentialities of the average human being are only partially unitlised.

From D. McGregor, *The Human Side of Enterprise*, McGraw Hill, New York, 1960, pages 47–8.

Fig. 17.1 Theory *X* and theory *Y*.

McGregor was widely misconstrued as people, seeking the one right answer to all their problems, interpreted his analysis as replacing an 'old' model with a 'new' one. Theory *X* was wrong: therefore theory *Y* was right. They fell into the trap of believing that there could be only one model of man, whereas McGregor was demonstrating the range of models that could be appropriate and freeing management from the narrow-minded orthodoxy that he found all around him in the 1950s.

MOTIVATION THEORIES

To some extent employees are in control of their behaviour; as are customers, suppliers, shareholders and other managers. Much of their behaviour will thus be *motivated* as they consciously seek to attain certain goals. Internal motives cause people to seek specific outcomes that will satisfy their needs. Just as separate models of man are all partially accurate, so theories of motivation at the moment can only partly explain the mysteries and complexity of motivation.

Needs or motives can be divided into two general categories. *Primary* needs are those relating to basic animal drives such as hunger, thirst, sleep, sex, pain avoidance, recovery from fatigue and safety. Their influence on behaviour is obvious and easy to identify. *Secondary* needs are acquired through experience and vary greatly according to culture as well as the particular experiences of the individual. They are the desires for power, achievement, social affiliation, status and a feeling of personal competence. Satisfying a primary need diminishes or temporarily extinguishes the drive. A hungry person does not feel hungry immediately after a large meal. Secondary needs are not satisfied in quite the same way as meeting a need for, say, recognition is likely to produce a desire for further recognition.

Maslow (1954) grouped needs into a five-step hierarchy, illustrated in Fig. 17.2. The primary needs were physiological and safety. Secondary needs, dealing with the psychological aspects of man, were in three categories: social needs, esteem needs and self-actualisation needs. Maslow contended that individuals tended to move up the hierarchy of needs, and would occasionally move down for brief periods. More significant was that sets of needs came into consideration in sequence, so that until the lowest order needs were satisfied, others were relatively unimportant, but once the lower order needs are satisfied, they lose their potency. A severe headache needs to be relieved before the desire for friendship and affection becomes strong, but once the pain is relieved, then friendship may become important.

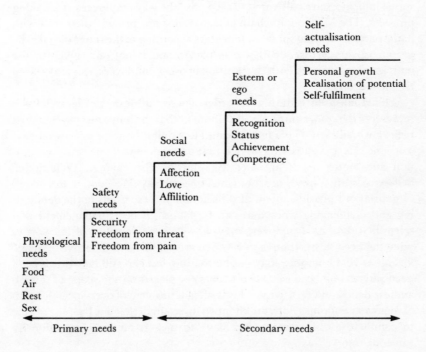

Fig. 17.2 Maslow's hierarchy of human needs.

Employees in western societies generally have their primary needs met (although those unemployed may not) so managers are interested in the secondary needs. Some managers try to eliminate chatting between employees at work on the grounds that it distracts their attention from what they are doing. This can, however, cause output to go down rather than up because this type of social contact is a means of coping with tedious work.

The esteem or ego needs can be met at work because of the opportunities that are provided for doing relatively well when compared with others. Ego needs are interpreted in relative rather than absolute terms. The need can be satisfied by the employee feeling a degree of recognition or status that others have not achieved, or that is now achieved so that comparison is possible with others who have already reached that level.

The athletes raising their arms triumphantly above their heads are asserting their achievement in the feat which they have accomplished. In organisational life there are innumerable ways in which status is marked. Some people have secretaries, while others do not; some wear white coats, while others wear grey; some carry skilled-status union cards, while others do not. Management strategy in relation to these indicators varies. In some organisations much effort goes in to eliminating such status dividers, by ensuring that all eat in the same cafeteria, wear the same uniform and address each other only by their first names. In other organisations the status indicators are cultivated to recognise the way employees are making progress. The Macdonald chain of fast-food shops provide their staff with name badges carrying space for four stars according to the range of tasks the person can undertake, so that this recognition is not only given to the individual to compare with the position of other employees, but is also seen by the customer.

Self-actualisation is the highest order of needs in Maslow's hierarchy as it represents the restless urge to self-fulfilment that the humanist psychologist believe we all have. This not seeking after doing better – or as well as – someone else, but satisfying oneself that one is doing all one can. Recognition and status needs are met by someone else saying, 'Well done!' Self-actualisation needs are met when one can say 'Well done!' to oneself. Organisations provide potential satisfaction of these needs in the demanding and challenging work that can be found in most management and scientific positions. Employees may, however, be deprived of this sort of potential need satisfaction in jobs which are routine and thus give no scope for initiative. Other jobs may not be routine, but can still lack this type of need satisfaction because of limits that are placed on the scope of the job and the denial and creativity. This is often a problem of over-specialisation in management ranks: jobs are chopped up so small that few people are able to complete an assignment and have to pass it on for completion by someone else.

The ranking of these five sets of needs in a hierarchy is based on two important assumptions. First, that a satisfied need is not a motivator and second, that as one set of needs becomes satisfied, then the next set of needs becomes dominant. The implications of this for managers are obvious. It is not worth trying to provide means for employees to satisfy self-actualisation needs if lower level needs have not yet been met. Also it is pointless trying to 'motivate' employees by considering their lower order needs if these are already satisfied. A further dimension is that the level of need satisfaction can vary. A group of managers who assemble for a two-day course, never having met each other before, will initially be much more concerned about the accommodation and catering arrangements than they will be later in the course, when social needs will become dominant, rapidly followed by esteem needs.

Herzberg (1968) developed the Maslow idea of the hierarchy by making a stronger distinction between lower and higher order needs. He described the lower order needs as potential *dissatisfiers*, or hygiene factors, and only the higher order needs were potential *satisfiers* or motivators. He contended that those managing organisations had to get the hygiene factors right, just as an operating theatre has to be clean and a kitchen well-scrubbed. Without those basic satisfactory conditions employees would be dissatisfied. Once the organisation was 'clean', further attention to lower order needs would not enhance employee performance. They can hamper when they are not properly met, but they cannot motivate beyond the level of basic satisfaction. Herzberg listed specific hygiene factors for life in organisations as including:

Company policy and administration
Supervision
Working conditions
Salary
Relationship with peers
Personal life
Relationship with subordinates
Status
Security

Most of these have in common the fact that they are *extrinsic*, coming from outside the person. Herzberg's list of satisfiers or motivators was shorter:

Achievement
Recognition
Work itself
Responsibility
Advancement
Growth

These are generally *intrinsic*, coming from the inside of the person, and are not so easily satisfied. The person who achieves something then wants more achievement; the person who has challenging, interesting work wants more of it to do. This has proved a most popular theory with managers, as it has provided a practical basis for management action: give people scope for achievement, recognition, enriched jobs, etc., and they will work harder, be more content and appreciate the goodness of the manager who made it all happen.

Despite the popularity of Herzberg, based on Maslow, there are some words of caution. Herzberg's research was mainly among engineers and accountants – well educated, middle-class Americans, and other people may have quite different needs and attitudes. Contemporary with Herzberg, a study in a British car manufacturing plant described the *instrumental orientation* of those whose attitudes were examined:

> The workers were particularly motivated to increase their power as consumers and their domestic standard of living, rather than their satisfaction as producers and the degree of self-fulfilment in their work. (Goldthorpe *et al.*, 1968, page 38)

In other words, work for these workers was mainly a means towards another end rather than having intrinsic merit. The attempts by some enthusiasts to revolutionise the quality of working life by introducing motivators to jobs where they have been traditionally absent have usually failed after a brief honeymoon period. Maslow can be criticised for the precision of his stratified hierarchy of secondary needs, as human beings are not as consistent as that, and Herzberg made extravagant claims for the universal applicability of his theory, which have not been borne out in practice for all groups of workers. Despite these reservations, a careful consideration of what both Maslow and Herzberg say provides a very helpful framework for understanding general aspects of motivation.

Review Topic 17.2

The French writer and hostess Madame de Staël (1766–1817) is alleged to have written 'To be totally understanding makes one very indulgent . . .' (*Tout comprendre, c'est tout pardonner*).

As managers try to understand their subordinates are they likely to become indulgent?

Those wanting to delve further into this area are recommended to see the work of Salancik and Pfeffer (1979) for a detailed assessment of the relevance of this research and theorising to organisations.

STEREOTYPING

In trying to understand other people we all, instinctively, use a short-cut method known as *stereotyping*. This is an essential aspect of dealing with others but can also be a straitjacket if we do not use it carefully. If you have lost your way in a foreign city and decide to ask someone for directions, you do not stop the first person you see: you pick out someone from the surrounding crowd who looks to you a potential source of good information. You probably look for someone who is not in a hurry, neither too young nor too old, appearing intelligent and sympathetic. You have a working stereotype of who would be an appropriate person to ask. At work we carry round in our heads a series of stereotypes which influence all our dealings with other people. Some of these are carried over from our general experiences and prejudices, for example:

Scotsmen are careful with money.
Small women are assertive.
Men with long hair are unreliable.

Others are linked to working experience and values:

Shop stewards are bloody-minded.
All engineers think clearly.
Accounts are dull.
Women make good secretaries.

There is seldom time in all working situations to abandon stereotyping as a way of approaching matters, especially in emergencies, where some sort of working hypothesis is needed immediately. The danger of stereotyping is, of course, that people are not treated and understood as individuals but as categories. This is unreasonable to them (and can be unlawful) and it limits the ability of the person who is over-dependent on stereotypes to work with others to the full extent of his abilities and theirs. A special form of this is the *halo effect*, where individuals are judged according to an imaginary halo above their heads. Someone, for instance, who is never late may be pointed out as an admirable employee even though the quality of the work is poor.

Stereotyping often occurs between departments in organisations, so that marketing people are often regarded by others as superficial, flashily dressed and not really doing anything, while production people are seen as earnest, harrassed and socially ill at ease.

Here is a brief summary of suggestions made by Zalkind and Costello (1962) for improving one's ability to perceive others accurately.

1. The better we know ourselves, the easier it is to see others accurately.
2. One's own character affects what one sees in others.

3. The accuracy of our own perceptions depends on our sensitivity to the differences between people.

WINNING CONSENT

Winning consent without having formal authority is becoming more important to managers for several reasons. First, the complexity of organisations increases the number of contacts managers make in which they have no *authority*. In the 1976 study by Rosemary Stewart (described in Chapter 3), 7 per cent of the managers interviewed were in solo jobs, spending a low proportion of time in contact with other people. In our own recent research we have found an increasing number of people in this type of lone, specialist role. Such a person not only has to be constantly persuading and influencing to get things done, but has continually to justify this position. Secondly, managers find their *formal authority* curbed. It is a long time since any but a few managers had the straightforward, unchallenged right to dismiss people, but legislation has gradually reduced that type of authority further, so that the power to dismiss is seldom held by an individual manager in an organisation. Also the power to determine pay rates and pay rises has been gradually impersonalised so that individual managers have only a marginal influence on pay and other financial benefits received by their subordinates. (After extensive consultation we decided, for instance, that there was no place in this book for a section on payment methods.) The development of procedures in organisation has tended to remove the opportunity for managers to act as arbiters and judges in relation to subordinates.

As technology advances and companies diversify, managers find they have *limited expertise* in technical matters and therefore have to depend increasingly on the autonomous competence of others, whether in a subordinate position or not. Nobel Prize winner, H.A. Simon, distinguished between authority and other types of influence:

> The characteristic which distinguishes authority from other kinds of influence is . . . that subordinate holds in abeyance his own critical faculties for choosing between alternatives and uses the formal criterion of the receipt of a command or signal as his basis for choice. (Simon, 1974, page 330)

Winning consent without having authority is a process that assumes the other person will *not* hold his own critical faculties in abeyance and will use his own judgement, accepting responsibility for the outcome.

There are at least three common barriers to this type of interpersonal influence. One is the differences between individuals. The person you want to influence may not like you or trust you. Secondly, the climate of the organisation may be inappropriate. If intensive competition between individuals is encouraged or unavoidable, then political means are more likely to achieve compliance than the more personal methods discussed in this chapter. The third reason is the number of mechanical barriers that can exist. It is difficult to influence the person you never meet and it can be suspect when you try to influence someone where there is a formal organisational barrier between you and that person.

Leavitt (1978, page 127) suggests that we need to consider three factors if we wish to influence another: ourself, the other person and the interaction that is to take place. Handy (1981, page 126) adds to those a need to consider the environment in which the attempts to influence take place.

We need to understand ourself, so that we can consider the reaction of others and their expectations of us individually in our role. In considering the other person we take account of their experience, personality and position. Then we can think of how to approach the interaction between self and other. The environmental points vary. Seating arrangements, for instance, can affect the outcome of conversations. In counselling, career advice and similar discussions it is helpful to have relatively informal seating arrangements without a direct, head-on orientation between self and other. In arguments where there is a direct conflict of opinion, it can help to face each other across a table. Another aspect of the environment is the degree to which influence is achieved in group situations. Most people find it easier to participate in the discussion of a small group (say ten people or fewer) than a large group. It is easier to have a turn to speak and it is easier to win round half a dozen people with different views and expectations than it is to cope with twice that number of varied positions. Large committees struggling with a difficult issue may delegate it to a subcommittee or working party to make suggestions. Unless opinions are strongly polarised on the committee, the small working party should be able to produce recommendations with which all members agree, so that the consequent meeting of the full committee will be faced with a caucus of its members who are committed to the working party proposals, and that degree of commitment will be hard to counter.

ASSERTIVENESS

Assertiveness training is currently popular with women's groups and is designed to develop people's confidence to control their own affairs and involves breaking minor 'rules' of polite behaviour.

Assertiveness training was initially developed in psychotherapy to help people who feel inadequate in their dealings with other people because they are afraid to speak up for what they believe and are not willing to resist when others appear to take advantage of them. Managers are not likely to suffer that degree of social handicap, but the techniques can be useful to develop self-confidence to deal with unfamiliar situations. The method is to work, with a friend or colleague, to identify the type of situations in which one is passive or diffident and then to think out some assertive responses for such a situation, which are practised with a friend and then gradually tried out in real life. This type of role playing has been a familiar part of many management training courses without ever being dignified with the term assertiveness training. Trainee salesmen often role-play with trainers playing the part of difficult customers, and personnel specialists frequently carry out dummy negotiations with tough shop stewards.

There are many situations which few people enjoy dealing with, for example:

1. People talking in the row behind you in the theatre.
2. People who jump the queue.
3. Complaining in a shop about the quality of something you have bought.
4. Going to a party where you do not know anyone.

In organisational life other worries are experienced:

1. Being criticised by a superior.
2. Criticising a subordinate.
3. Advocating an unpopular point of view at a meeting.
4. Being asked to do something you do not feel capable of doing.
5. Asking subordinates to do something that you think they will resent.

The reluctance to criticise underlies the widespread ineffectiveness of performance appraisal, which has been described as 'a good idea gone wrong'. Managers chafe at the chore of filling in forms, but they also resist having to be specific in explaining to subordinates the extent to which their performance is not satisfactory. Apprehension about giving unpopular instructions is probably the most common managerial nightmare and is why managers so often dread situations in which their authority is not clear-cut. What would happen if the subordinate would not comply? In practice the confidence to say 'no' is much more difficult to find and hold to than the confidence to say 'do as I say'.

Review Topic 17.3

Identify one or two situations at work in which you typically feel diffident and think out some assertive responses or initiatives to use in them.

BARGAINING AND EXCHANGE

Call it bargaining, negotiating – even cajoling or bribing in some situations. A agrees with B to give him something in return for desired behaviour. Sweets to a child, tips to the dustman, promotion to the executive are obvious examples.

> Less obvious, but perhaps more common, are friendship and favour, inclusion in a group, approval and status. Exchange methods can follow from any power source, depending on what is offered, but resource and position are the most frequent bases. (Handy, 1981, page 123)

Bargaining covers the explicit as well as the implicit. Occasionally there is an explicit deal, with offer and consideration: 'If you can get the machine repaired by Friday, I'll put your departmental budget higher on the agenda for next week's meeting'. But these are infrequent in transactions within the organisation, as they put on an informal and unofficial basis that which should not require any extra arrangement beyond straightforward request.

More common is the implicit offering of friendship, approval or gratitude if something can be done.

> 'I really have a problem, can you possibly help me . . . ?'
> 'Be a pal and . . .'
> 'You are the only person who could possibly do this . . .'
> 'I always believe in asking the experts . . .'

A similar version of this is to do favours to others, so that there is a scattering of IOUs that can be called in, the bread upon the waters of the Bible. The problems with this type of dealing are first that the 'rewards' offered may have to increase to maintain their value, but also that the exchanges depend on *both* parties being able to reward the other. Offering approval loses its value if your approval is not wanted, so that bargaining works best when the parties to the bargain are roughly equal in their power to reward each other:

> Perceptions of power inequality undermine trust, inhibit dialogue and decrease the likelihood of a constructive outcome. . . . Inequality tends to undermine trust on both ends of the imbalanced relationship, directly affecting both the person with the perceived power inferiority and the one with the perceived superiority. (Walton, 1969, page 98)

The process of reciprocal reward takes a slightly different form when it becomes social exchange in a continuing working relationship between people. Homans (1958) studied the 'traffic patterns' of interaction in groups and concluded:

(a) The more often people interact with each other, the more favourable will be their mutual feelings.
(b) People who interact with each other frequently are more likely to adopt similar practices than people who interact less frequently.

COLLABORATIVE INFLUENCE

When it is important to people to believe in what they have to do, that belief will probably only be reached by participating in the process of deciding what should be done: they will support that which they have helped to create. There is a series of ways to do this, varying in the degree of participation. *Full participation* is the process whereby there is free and spontaneous discussion among members of a group, with the minimum of agenda, so that a collective will emerges from the discussion that will be supported by all members because of the full and frank exchange of views that produced the consensus view. This is not a denial of leadership, as there is a need for summarising, clarification and – ultimately – action, which has to be focused. It is, however, a process which makes the leader answerable to the group.

Consultation is a process which the leader or manager retains the responsibility for deciding what should be done, but seeks a strategy that the responding individual or group will accept. Not always do the respondents have full commitment to such decisions, because they are accepting strategy but they do not have responsibility for the decision that is reached.

A different form is *elite corps involvement*, where members of the organisation are involved in making a decision, but their involvement is based on them being members of an elite group, called in for consultation. As they are specially selected they are flattered and may commit themselves fully to a course of action whether their involvement is by full participation, consultation or simply by being told before other people.

Collaborative influence is often achieved in the most informal ways without any calculation.

> 'What do you think . . . ?'
> 'Any ideas?'
> 'I'd like to have a word with you about . . .'
> 'I'm thinking of . . . but I'm not at all sure that it's right.'

It is also not the sole preserve of those high in the hierarchy winning round those who are lower: it is just as frequently used by those seeking the backing of their organisational superiors.

MANIPULATION

The idea of manipulating other people is generally offensive, with its overtones of puppets and strings. It is, however, an ancient art and does not always arouse disapproval. For most of recorded history the young have indulged in courtship, the result of which is sometimes tears, sometimes frustration, but often a reasonable degree of mutual satisfaction, yet the process of courtship is one of manipulating emotions and cajoling a person to change his or her mind. This is all done against a background of uncertainty about motives. Are the intentions honourable or not?

In the everyday life of organisations consent is often won by manipulation. Leavitt (1978, pages 157–60) summarises the process like this:

1. A is the manipulator; B the person to be manipulated.
2. A's motives are not fully known to B.
3. The relationship between A and B is either established or developed by A to provide a basis of influence; getting B to do what A wants.
4. A exploits dependency of B in the relationship.
5. Dependency of B increased by using emotions such as approval, support, recognition.
6. Influence develops incrementally, by adding bits and pieces as dependency increases.

Described thus, manipulation sounds no more than a confidence trick, but there are many circumstances in which it can be necessary or appropriate. One of the main bases of training is reinforcement through praising the faltering attempts of the trainee in the early stages. This is manipulative in that the trainer is trying to influence the behaviour of the trainee by exploiting the trainee's dependence, using the trainee's need for reassurance. Part of any manager's responsibility is to get others to do things they would not have done otherwise. So a manager will often use manipulation to obtain compliance from someone else towards organisational objectives. The manager who manipulates others simply to advance personal objectives is much more reprehensible.

One form of manipulation is propaganda, which is attempting to build a favourable image by appealing to a large number of people. The methods of public relations are too specialised to have a place in this book, but we can include some comments about public-speaking that is designed to win people round to a particular point of view. To be persuasive the public speaker has to be seen as having some expert knowledge and good intentions. His or her effectiveness will be enhanced by enthusiasm or conviction, and will connect a state of emotional preparedness – engendered at the beginning of the address – with some course of action advocated towards the end of the address. It is important that members of the audience should easily see the connection between the emotional feeling and the prescribed action. This can be helped by graphic illustration and examples.

Argyle and Trower (1979, page 101) suggest that a propagandist should present his case in a certain order:

(a) He makes amiable remarks to establish rapport with the audience.
(b) He arouses guilt, concern or anxiety.
(c) He presents a strong, positive case, showing how the feeling aroused can be resolved by the recommended behaviour.
(d) He deals with any obvious objections.
(e) He draws explicit conclusions and makes recommendations for action.

PERSUASION

Persuasion is talking someone round to your point of view, using the force of argument and the logic of evidence that is deployed to support the argument. This is straightforward and dignified without the worrying suggestions of being devious, as with manipulation, or aggressive, as with assertiveness. It also has the attraction that the outcome will be 'right' as it will depend on the cogency of the argument and people will not comply if not convinced. Personal factors none the less make some people more persuasive than others. Persuaders are likely to be successful only when they are regarded as *credible*, having some track record of effectiveness. Employees find it hard to see a company management as credible if it is not successful in running the business. The persuader must also be *expert*, which is a more precise quality than credibility. It can be attested by qualifications, position or experience, but is a sign of having special knowledge that is seen as relevant and greater than that of the person being persuaded. *Trustworthiness* is important because of the feeling of helplessness that can come from dealing with an expert. The wisdom of the expert makes the person being persuaded conscious of their own ignorance and the need to place themselves 'in the hands' of the expert. So the expert must be trustworthy. The persuader who is *objective* adds strength to the case by being able to see both sides of a question, so that the person being persuaded is able to weigh both and decide. The opposite case has at least been set out, even if it is peremptorily dismissed.

MISCELLANEOUS ASPECTS OF TECHNIQUE

There are one or two aspects of social technique that everybody uses in conversation that can be identified and practised. The practitioner can then become more adept in social exchanges and more successful in winning people round.

1. *Reinforcement.* In our relationships with others we reward some behaviours that they produce; smiling, nodding, making agreeing noises or saying things that convey agreement, pleasure or wonder at the wisdom that is being offered. The effect of this is to reinforce the behaviour that is being rewarded. Equally the withdrawal of rewards prevents behaviours being reinforced. Frowning, not paying attention, yawning, shaking the head or saying things that express disagreement, annoyance or dismay tend to inhibit the behaviour with which they are associated.

   The general effect of reinforcement is to increase the amount of the behaviour that is being reinforced, so that a man rewarded by his wife for taking an interest in the children will continue taking an interest in them and a trainee rewarded by the instructor for producing good work will produce more good work. Despite the general usefulness of this technique, there are two reservations. First, those who are insecure, or anxious, may be so keen on rewards that they will suspend judgement to obtain them, so that the reinforcer is rewarding sycophancy. Secondly, reinforcement is most effective when provided by someone whose acceptance is worth having, so that its effect will not be great unless the personality of the reinforcer or the relationship between the reinforcer and the rewarded person is appropriate.

2. *Reward.* An aspect of manipulative style that is more pervasive than simple reinforcement. It is described by Argyle (1972, page 74) as rewardingness, and deals with the way in which a person becomes relatively popular and influential on the opinions of others. The manager rewards others by being responsive to their needs and interests, responding quickly to requests for information, return telephone calls and assistance. Explanations of why certain things are needed can be a reward, as can suggestions of how problems could be overcome and inviting comments on proposals that are being put forward. This is not quite the same as being permissive or *laissez-faire*, as some core of direction is usually needed. In deciding policy directions, for instance, the manager working with a group of others will not want to direct at the beginning of a discussion as it is important to generate as many ideas and alternatives as possible. So they will do no more than start the conversational ball rolling. Later, however, there will be a need to pull strands of argument together, find a small number of choices for further discussion and focus thinking on those. Later still it will be necessary to adopt a stricter style when discussion moves through decision-making to action.

The essence of being rewarding in one's behaviour is being warm and friendly towards other people, but the way in which the rewards are offered will vary between individuals, as will the way in which they are received. Cheerful exuberance may be interpreted as overbearing; congratulation may be construed as being unctuous; an attempt not to embarrass may be regarded as coldness. Managers also have to exercise control, as they cannot always respond in the rewarding way that the other would like.

In these situations the manager should look for an alternative. The young man in the policy discussion who is advocating a line of action that others regard as haywire will not get his proposal discussed further, but he has to be kept 'in play' to redirect his attention constructively towards the other ideas that are being considered. He therefore has to be rewarded by some alternative such as an agreement to look at his proposal again in three months' time, or a frank acknowledgement that his proposal is very well regarded but too risky for his over-cautious colleagues.

3. *Participation by the other*. A cumbersome phrase to encompass a range of ways in which one sees a matter from the point of view of the other person and so both rewards that person and participates with them in deciding what to do. The main aspect of this is the understanding of a different frame of reference, which is a sociological term to describe a set of basic assumptions that determines behaviour and attitude. This is most relevant on a large scale, and there is the regular example of managers and politicians failing to understand the bloody-mindedness of people who take industrial action at a time when that action will clearly imperil the jobs that the action is intended to protect. The reason is that the people taking the action have a quite different frame of reference, leading to different expectations, priorities and objectives. To them their action is logical and only the management are bloody-minded. Similar differences of view affect what is called 'cashless pay'.

Ray Hughes has worked in a clothing factory for thirty-seven years. On Thursday evenings he receives his weekly wages, paid in cash, approximately £120 after deduction of income tax and national insurance. On the way home he deposits £15 in his Post Office savings account and puts £25 in his back pocket to cover his personal expenditure for the week. He then gives £80 to his wife, who deals with all the household expenditure. He and his working colleagues are resisting a proposal by the management of their factory that they should be paid by cheque. Not only does this involve the inconvenience of cashing the cheque, but it brings nearer the day when a major principle would be lost. Mrs Hughes might find out exactly how much her husband gets paid, and in many families that is a jealously preserved confidence. The management persist in wanting to pay by cheque to overcome the time and expense of handling large amounts of cash, which pose a serious security risk. They point out all the advantages of having a bank account to Ray Hughes and his friends, but the fundamental difference in their frames of reference makes their exchanges a dialogue of the deaf.

On a one-to-one level managers need to think themselves into the position of the person with whom they are talking, to see the topic as clearly as possible from the other point of view in order to make the most of the exchange.

In this chapter we have reviewed some of the ways in which individual managers can get their own way and get things done without having the dubious benefit of formal authority to issue orders. All the comments centre round two aspects of style. First, the confidence of the manager in setting out what he wants, being sure, clear and precise. Secondly, is the ability of that manager to work with the responses and needs of the other person, rewarding, and understanding the other point of view. To be effective, the manager needs not only to understand but also to practise. What we have described here are things that all of us do to some extent every day of our lives, as part of being a member of the human race interacting with others of our species. If we can understand that interactive process better, we can then practise our behaviours and improve our performance.

SUMMARY PROPOSITIONS

17.1 Man has primary needs and secondary needs. Secondary needs are those which have the greatest influence on working behaviour.

17.2 Stereotyping is a necessary mode of behaviour to cope with novel situations but limits a manager's scope for getting the best from himself and others working together.

17.3 Winning consent without having authority is becoming more important to managers because of the increasing number of situations in which they have no authority; their formal authority is curbed or they have limited expertise.

17.4 To win consent managers need to understand themselves, the other person in the interaction and the interaction itself.

17.5 Methods of approaching particular situations include assertiveness, manipulation and persuasion.

17.6 Aspects of style leading to influence include reinforcement, reward, and participation by the other.

PUTTING IT INTO PRACTICE

Next time you want to influence someone, make a list of what is in it for them. Try to think of at least three reasons, from their point of view, for doing it.

Next time you are feeling aggrieved because someone has mistreated or misunderstood you, write down what it is they have misunderstood. Now think what you could have done or said to make their job of understanding you easier. They may of course continue to misunderstand you!

REFERENCES

Argyle, M. *The Psychology of Interpersonal Behaviour*, Penguin Books, Harmondsworth, 1972.
Argyle, M. and Trower, P., *Person to Person*, Harper & Row, London, 1979.

Goldthorpe, J.H., Lockwood, D., Bechhofer, H. and Platt, J., *The Affluent Worker: Industrial Attitudes and Behaviour*, Cambridge University Press, 1968.

Handy, C.B., *Understanding Organizations*, 2nd edn, Penguin Books, Harmondsworth, 1981.

Herzberg, F., 'One more time: how do you motivate employees?' *Harvard Business Review*, Jan./Feb. 1968.

Herzberg, F., Mausner, B., Snyderman, D.B., *The Motivation to Work*, John Wiley, New York, 1959.

Homans, G.C., 'Social behaviour as exchange', *American Journal of Sociology*, vol. 62, 1958, pages 597–606.

Leavitt, H.J., *Managerial Psychology*, 4th edn, University of Chicago Press, 1978.

Maslow, A.H., *Motivation and Personality*, Harper & Row, New York, 1954.

McGregor, D., *The Human Side of Enterprise*, McGraw Hill, New York, 1960.

Salancik, G.R. and Pfeffer, J., 'An examination of need-satisfaction models of job attitudes' in Steers, R.W. and Porter, L.W. (eds), *Motivation and Work Behaviour*, 2nd edn, McGraw-Hill, New York, 1979, pages 66–89.

Schein, E.H., *Organizational Psychology*, 2nd edn, Prentice Hall, Englewood Cliffs, New Jersey, 1970.

Simon, H.A., 'Authority' in Dubin, R. (ed.), *Human Relations in Administration*, 4th edn, Prentice Hall, Englewood Cliffs, New Jersey, 1974.

Walton, R.E., *Interpersonal Peacemaking: Third Party Consultations*, Addison Wesley, Chicago, 1969.

Zalkind, S.S. and Costello, T.W., 'Perception: some recent research and implications for administrators', *Administrative Science Quarterly*, No. 7, 1962, pages 218–35.

18

ORGANISATIONAL COMMUNICATION

The evangelist Billy Graham was due to address a meeting in an American city, but was prevented by a dense bank of fog that lay between his circling aircraft and the airport near to the stadium in which his audience had assembled. The thousands who had gathered to listen to his message could hear the noise of the aircraft engines and Billy Graham lacked nothing in conviction or material for the message he wished to convey, but the bank of fog prevented the message from being conveyed and the response elicited. Those working in contemporary employing organisations often feel a sense of frustration similar to that experienced by the evangelist and his expectant audience.

Most people feel reassured by contact with those making decisions about their destiny. Airline passengers convinced that the aircraft is about to disintegrate and drop them 40,000 feet into the sea will pay close attention to the message relayed over the public address system prefaced by the words '. . . this is your captain speaking . . .'. Being in touch with those who decide gives one a sense of control over one's affairs, no matter how slight this may be. One of the effects of organisation is to distance people from the centre of actions which affect their lives. The rank and file employee, concerned about whether or not his factory is to close, will see that the yes/no decision is to be taken by – say – the board of directors, from whom he is separated by a 'fog' of people and lines of communication that emphasise both his detachment from the decision and his helplessness to influence it.

The irony of the present situation is that the 'fog' has been made denser by brave attempts to penetrate it and to compensate for it: more committees, handbooks, procedures and representatives. For the people waiting in the stadium to hear Billy Graham's message, books, pamphlets, gramophone records and addresses by close associates of the evangelist were not a satisfactory alternative to hearing the message in person. They were merely an incentive to hear the words direct.

In organisational life there is often no satisfactory alternative to face to face conversation, and the substitutes may simply dissatisfy both the senders and the receivers. Managers can feel that dealing with employee representatives makes it harder rather than easier for them to get their messages through to employees, while employees often regard the carefully-minuted proceedings of the works committee as a poor substitute for getting an engineer with a kit of tools to come into the workshop and mend the leaking radiator about which they have been complaining for months.

A further contradiction of the present is that we have problems of communication while having a surfeit of information, which turns the fog into smog! Drucker (1977), as usual, has a trenchant comment.

> The communications gap within institutions and between groups in society has been widening steadily – to the point where it threatens to become an unbridgeable gulf of total misunderstanding.

> In the meantime there is an information explosion . . . the abundance of information changes the communication problem and makes it both more urgent and more difficult. (page 390)

Increasing the amount of information can impair rather than improve communication, as information only becomes communication where there is exchange, with the receiver signalling understanding of the correct meaning by his feedback to the sender. Information output that is not attuned to the needs of the receiver will obscure rather than clarify the receiver's understanding. People in organisations show a general preference for word-of-mouth communication. Mintzberg (1975) found that chief executives spent 78 per cent of their time in verbal communication (page 52). It might be assumed that this was a feature of a very specialised job in the hierarchy, but another study was made among research chemists and engineers, a group of people who, one would assume, spend less time talking to others than chief executives. The findings were that they spent, on average, 61 per cent of their day interchanging facts, information, ideas, attitudes and opinions.

Review Topic 18.1

How do you understand the comment of Peter Drucker quoted here?

If there is preference for communicating by direct conversation rather than in other ways, it is at least debatable whether it is productive to push information into other channels, such as memoranda or announcements on the notice board, unless these are supplementary to the preferred mode of face to face and not a substitute. Equally there are some communications for which a channel such as a formal letter is preferred to word of mouth, like the offer of employment or notice of terms for early retirement.

ORGANISATIONAL COMMUNICATION AND MEDIA

Several chapters in this book deal with specific aspects of communication. Discussion here is therefore limited to one major form, *organisational communication*, which is best defined by distinguishing it from interpersonal communication:

> *Interpersonal communication* is face-to-face. It is person-to-person exchange of information that conveys meaning. *Organizational communication* is the deliberate establishment and use of a system to transmit information conveying meaning to large numbers of people both within and outside the organization. (Carlisle, 1982, page 421)

Organisational communication is not, therefore, all the communicating that takes place in the organisation, but simply that which is a product of deliberate attempts by managers to communicate or enable specific communications within the organisational structure and to the outside environment. In a study to which we refer again shortly, Greenbaum (1974) has suggested that there are four main objectives that managers have for organisational communication:

1. *Regulation* Seeking conformity of employee behaviour with organisational objectives.
2. *Innovation* Seeking to change aspects of organisational functioning in specific directions.
3. *Integration* Maintaining the morale of the work force and developing a feeling of identity with the organisation and its members.
4. *Information* Passing out the mainly factual information that people need in their everyday duties: what has to be done, quality standards, customers' requests, and so on.

The value of this distinction is, of course, that the method of communication will vary according to its objective.

Organisational communication takes place in a variety of ways, using different *media*, and there are some messages that are conveyed unintentionally.

The formal organisational structure

The organisation chart or formal arrangement of working relationships is itself a communication as it tells organisation members important things about their 'place': how distant they are from the centre and what their official status is. The structure is also a prime communications media, as there is an assumption that information will travel up and down it, enshrined in doctrines of responsibility, accountability and reporting, to say nothing of grievance and disciplinary procedures, which invariably nominate stages in the procedure by identifying them with office holders in the structure. Katz and Kahn (1978, pages 440–8) list the main types of up and down communication:

Down	*Up*
Job instructions	Information about selves
Job rationale	Performance and problems
Procedures and practices	Organisational practice and policy
Feedback on performance	What needs to be done
Indoctrination about goals	What should not be done

The formal structure also has lateral as well as vertical connections, which are used to provide communication relating to co-ordination, mutual support and advice.

The informal organisational structure

Behind and between the formal lines is the informal structure or grapevine, through which information passes that has not been officially sanctioned. Although this is not deliberately created, no organisational communication is complete without it.

The grapevine has the advantage of being a spontaneous form of expression, providing the satisfaction of talking face to face, and it can often be both more rapid and informative than official communications. Its operation does not follow the same pattern as the spread of rumours, where the amount of rumoured information increases as the amount of official communication decreases. Davis (1953) and Hage (1974) both found a positive correlation between official and unofficial communication. As the level of official communication goes up there is a fuelling of informal discussion and interpretation of it. Only in extreme cases of information suppression is there a sufficient stimulus to speculation for rumour to grow in order to fill the gaps that the official processes leave.

Davis was also able to identify aspects of how the grapevine works, so that the most common was what he called a *cluster chain*, which is shown in Figure 18.1. The person with the information (1) tells several others (2, 3, 4 and 5). Only some of them (4 and 5) pass on the information, so that the flow of information gradually peters out. Of any group who hear information, there will only be a proportion willing to pass it on. Some will feel constrained, some will forget and others will not bother. Davis found that 81 per cent of the executives in his study had been told the information he was tracking, but only eleven per cent communicated it to others. A later study by Knippen (1974) found that although managers accounted for only a small proportion of the 1970 employees in a grocery store, they were the

= a person with whom information stops

= a person who passes information on

Fig. 18.1 The cluster chain in the informal organisation structure.

source of half the grapevine information and told an average of eight people each; other employees only told four people each.

Word of mouth

Most of the messages passing through the formal and informal organisation structure will be by word of mouth, and we have already seen the preference for this mode of communication demonstrated by research. It is not, of course, only one speaking with one other. It includes interchange face to face in small groups and committees, as well as the rarer address to a large meeting.

Written messages

Written material sometimes stands on its own as a message, so that the monthly statement of pay and statutory deductions is seldom a basis for discussion, unless it is incorrect. Other written material is an adjunct to discussion: the agenda for a meeting, the notice of a claim prior to negotiations, the draft report, the letter confirming an order of material from a supplier '. . . as discussed with your representative . . .'.

It is a form of communication which is used often not to convey information for the first and final time, but as a preliminary to, or confirmation of, some action being discussed. The form can vary from letter to memorandum, from a notice on the notice board to the house journal, from job specification to sales order to instruction manual and many more. It is important that it should be used in circumstances for which it is appropriate. Changes in behaviour are seldom likely to follow from written instructions or particulars only. Pirani and Reynolds (1976) studied aspects of safety training in a Merseyside factory and demonstrated, *inter alia*, the relative ineffectiveness of posters and warning notices in persuading employees to adopt safer working practices.

Review Topic 18.2

Envisage an important decision that you have to make in your organisation that needs to be extensively communicated. What aspects would you communicate formally in writing, what formally by word of mouth, and what would you use informal methods for?

Electronic means

A rapidly developing means of communication is that provided by the advances in microtechnology. In some ways these merely expand the amount of written material, as photocopiers and word processors make it possible to generate an almost infinite number of copies of items. This adds considerably to the volume of information in circulation without necessarily improving communication, and with the possibility of making it worse by overload. This is a problem we consider later in this chapter.

The computer terminal and visual display unit introduce a fundamentally new method of communicating in organisations, with a variety of exciting potentials like the paperless office with the visual display unit replacing the memorandum, but it is difficult to see that the amount of word by mouth communication will decline.

Systems and management objectives

Greenbaum (1974) provides a technique for looking at the variety of systems, or structures, necessary to meet managers' objectives. If, for example, one considers the number of people one wishes to reach and the appropriate media, one can summarise it as in Table 18.1. This type of analysis could also be used to consider other structures, such as formal–informal.

Table 18.1 Media for communication

		Regulation	Innovation	Integration	Information
Face to face (2)	*Oral*	Directions and requests	Superior/ subordinate ideas meet	Selection interview	Induction of new recruits
	Written	Job description and performance standards	Reports on visits, courses	Letter of welcome to new recruit	Memoranda
	Non-verbal	Gesture		Gesture	Demonstration of task to be performed
Small groups (3–10)	*Oral*	Departmental meetings	Problem-solving meetings	Coffee break	Training groups
	Written	Agenda	Suggestions after meeting	Invitation to lunch	Works handbook
	Non-verbal	Pauses, silences	Seating arrangements	Meeting area conditions	Demonstration
Organisation-wide	*Oral*	Meegings of department heads		Address to members of organisation	Mass meeting
	Written	Organisation chart	Suggestion scheme	House journals	Notice board
	Non-verbal	Style of office for organisation member		House style in stationery, etc.	

OVERCOMING PROBLEMS OF ORGANISATIONAL COMMUNICATION

In view of the variety of means whereby information can be passed around, it is of limited use to speak of *designing* a system of communications, but it is helpful to identify some of the problems and review methods of alleviating them.

Formal structure

The flow of information and the effectiveness of communication is affected by the type of formal structure that exists. The first problem is of *size*. In an organisation with a strong central focus, like the entrepreneurial form mentioned in Chapter 9, satisfaction with communication is likely to decrease as numbers of organisation members increase. Structural alteration to split the overall organisation into a number of relatively autonomous units will be more successful than trying to generate more information for dissemination through a monolithic structure.

The problem of *hierarchical levels* has been discussed earlier in this book. In the last quarter of a century numerous experiments have demonstrated the validity of the simple hypothesis advanced by Robert Dubin in 1959, that the smaller the number of communication links in a system, the greater the efficiency of the members of the system in task performance. Every communicator is selective in what he passes on, even if he is only selective in emphasis or inference. One method that reduces this problem is to operate briefing groups, whereby a superior briefs not one but a group of subordinates simultaneously. Through question, answer and discussion the message understood by each subordinate will take on greater similarity and reinforcement than if they had been briefed separately. In turn they brief groups of their own subordinates, and so on. This improves the accuracy of the conveyed message, but eliminating a level in the hierarchy is much more effective.

Many difficulties surround the official *lines of authority and communication* in the organisation. First there is the problem of uncertainty amongst employees about means of access to information or decision. This difficulty was so widespread that legislation was introduced whereby the individual contract of employment now has to specify a person to whom an employee can apply to seek redress of any grievance relating to his employment, but there remain many other matters on which organisation members remain unsure of where to obtain information. A second problem arises when a point of access becomes congested. In the 1960s it could take twelve months for a matter to proceed through the engineering industry disputes procedure, with the result that the procedure was eventually abandoned. Similarly management action may be reserved to too few people, so that decisions are held up because of the non-availability of a key manager to agree or disagree.

Michael Winston was the production manager of a furniture-making plant who had to adjourn a meeting with shop stewards for fifteen minutes in order to sign a handful of release notes for material from stores. A production line of thirty-two people had been idle for an hour and a half because the storekeeper was not allowed to release the material (which was of particular interest to DIY enthusiasts) without Winston's authority. Eventually the foreman persuaded Winston's secretary that the matter was sufficiently important to justify interrupting the meeting with stewards. At home that same evening Winston received a telephone call from his production superintendent, who had been trying to see him for four days about two design draughtsmen who had been offered employment by a competitor but who would stay if there were small adjustments to their pay, which only Winston could authorise.

These problems become less severe when those with centralised authority in their own hands are able and willing to let some of it go, remembering that delegation does not mean giving people jobs to do. It means giving people authority and responsibility. The problem is, however, just as likely to be one of horizontal rather than vertical lines, emphasising the importance of the integrating devices described in Chapter 9.

Social distance

Social distance is the problem that people may limit communication when dealing with someone holding greater prestige or on a higher hierarchical level in the organisation. To some extent the opposite applies also, with those in senior positions feeling inhibited about being candid with those holding more humble posts. Mainly this applies to adverse comments about company affairs. Two salesmen may readily discuss with each other the incompetence of the sales manager and the ineptitude of the marketing policy being followed by the company, but both will feel inhibited about expressing those same views to the sales manager. They feel dependent on his goodwill, which would be jeopardised if they disagreed with him. The much-cherished concept of tenure in British universities has evolved for precisely the purpose of providing lecturers with sufficient security for them to be able to disagree with their professors.

The anxiety to propitiate the person with more power than you have also extends to bad news for which the messenger cannot be held responsible. Cleopatra and her contemporaries were hampered in their military campaigns by their practice of tossing bags of gold to the bringers of good tidings and beheading the bearers of bad, so that the reliability of their intelligence reports were low. Hitler is described as making serious strategic blunders because none of his close advisers dared to tell him bad news for fear of his rage. These are extreme examples, but in every organisation subordinates seek the favour of superiors and are thus inclined to tell them what they like to hear.

Superiors can be restrained from candour with subordinates for fear that the subordinate will lose confidence in the superior. A senior manager will not readily say to a subordinate, 'I have no idea how to deal with this situation' because of a feeling that the subordinate will regard this as a sign of weakness or incompetence.

In our interviews with managers we have frequently heard them comment on how to handle situations where they don't know something. To appear fallible is obviously a minor nightmare for many people. Arthur Tweedle is the manager of a city centre building society branch and has to know how far to go when lending money. One client may ask for much more than is actually needed, while others may underestimate their requirements. In uncertainty about the right course of action he prevaricates and steps away from the decision itself, by saying: 'Well, *we* will obviously have to think about that and let you know'. 'Yes, *I* will be glad to arrange that for you'. In uncertainty it becomes something that *we* will have to think about.

Social distance is desired by superiors and subordinates for certain reasons (authority, for instance) but at the extreme it can seriously impair communication. So some moves to its reduction are needed. One method is to tinker with status symbols, so that they become less inhibiting to those who have not got them. Segregated dining facilities, for instance, not only provide more agreeable and opulent catering for senior members of the organisation, but also cut off those people socially from everyone else by setting them apart at times of relaxation and communion. Another aspect of social distance is territory. People will often communicate more openly if they are in familiar surroundings. One of the authors was interested to observe this aspect of behaviour in a large food-processing plant. The foremen and superintendents all wore white overalls and white straw hats, while the plant manager also wore a white overall but not a hat. The manager used to monitor affairs in the plant by calling each foreman and superintendent in turn into his office to talk in a very informal way about what was going on. He also made frequent tours of inspection of the plant. When entering the manager's office the foremen took off their hats and sat upright in a chair, often on the edge, and said very little that was not called for by the questions that were put to them. The manager changed his routine by incorporating the informal chats with his tours of inspection, so that he called in on the offices of the foremen and superintendents while going around the plant. The foremen did not now take off their hats and were much more relaxed and informative. They were on their own territory.

Intergroup hostility

The contrasted aims and norms of groups in organisations often generate hostility, both between groups and individuals, which can seriously impair the quality of trust and communication between them. It is almost a commonplace that those involved with production are not always in sympathy with those concerned with sales and marketing; and technical personnel typically blame administrators for every misfortune that befalls them. This is a basic problem of organisation and some of the remedies have been examined in Chapter 9. It is necessary to accept the differences and to attempt co-ordination and integration by devices such as committees, co-ordinating departments or individuals. In many cases the difference grows worse through being suppressed. Those in Department A have a minor criticism about those in Department B, which they talk about among themselves but not to those in Department B, to whom they become slightly cool. Those in Department B discuss among themselves the odd behaviour of Department A. Uncertainty and suspicion harden into hostility, even though the substantive cause may be trivial and, if talked about, the suspicion would collapse like a burst balloon. It may therefore be helpful to bring about a confrontation between the two parties to discuss what causes the hostility between them.

Physical setting

Increasing organisational complexity can increase the number of contacts that organisation members need to have with each other, while an increasing number of people in the organisation can make that contact less likely. When a department is set up, it is an elementary move to group those people near to each other, on the assumption that the interaction of their duties and responsibilities make such a juxtaposition necessary, but is it more important than some alternative juxtaposition? Should quality assurance personnel be located in some central corral from which they are sent out into the factory to assure the quality of production, or should they be based in production departments and only occasionally called together with other quality assurers to ensure appropriate standards and incorruptibility? Should typists and word processor operators work together for the benefits of flexibility and variety, or should they be located in the same place as those who generate the words they process?

Often the answer is whichever alternative some individual person regards as preferable, but another method is to prepare a relationship chart, plotting the frequency of communications between individuals.

A similar question is whether people should be segregated in single or double offices, or whether they should share large open plan offices. Where there is frequent communication there is a good case for opening offices up, but office planners and organisation and methods experts have to remember that the social requirements of personnel will triumph over office landscaping plans, if the two conflict.

John Charles was a gifted chief designer of underground locomotives and he worked in a small office adjoining a large drawing office containing twelve draughtsmen. When he wanted something from the drawing office Charles would throw a paper clip against the frosted glass window separating him from the drawing office and his assistant Charlie Johnson would come bustling in saying, 'Yes, Chief'. If Charlie did not hear or see the paper clip signal one of the draughtsmen would say, 'Chop chop Charlie, big chief Charles throw clip'. Inevitably a newly appointed organisation and methods officer heard of the practice and arranged for a small hatch to be placed in the frosted glass so that John Charles could speak to Charlie Johnson direct to attract his attention. In everyday use the hatch would never quite work; it may have been poorly fitted or covered with too much paint, or it may have been that the draughtsmen and Charlie Johnson and John Charles preferred time-honoured methods. Two years later Charlie was still responding to paper clips.

In open plan offices it is amazing how carefully placed filing cabinets are gradually shifted, rubber plants appear, desks move to a different angle and hatstands are mobilised to provide a series of mini-offices in an open plan layout.

Overload

A common reason for managers not communicating with others is that they lack the time. Although this may be partly due to indolence or a failure to acknowledge the importance of communication, the amount of information to be handled is certainly increasing, as has been mentioned earlier. One way of dealing with the problem is to develop specialised scanning skills in reading, and another is to develop delegation, as has already been described as a means of dealing with problems about lines of authority. Few managers, however, can avoid having large amounts of paperwork to deal with, so they have to work out ways of coping with it, such as setting aside a particular period each day – usually at the beginning or the end – for reading, writing and dictating. General Douglas MacArthur never left his office in the evening until all the day's paperwork had been cleared.

ORGANISATIONAL COMMUNICATION IS ONLY AS GOOD AS INTERPERSONAL COMMUNICATION

Whatever initiatives are taken by managers in organisations to manipulate and 'improve' organisational communications, they will only be as good as the quality of the interpersonal communication that is taking place.

> The line-and-box drawings we call organization charts are not the structure of the organization they describe. Structure is the development of relatively consistent patterns of interaction among the members of an organization. These patterns begin to develop when a group of individuals, in response to certain characteristics and needs of the environment, create a system of patterned activities for the accomplishment of a specific task. The process by which these relationships are formed and maintained is interpersonal communication. (Baskin and Aronoff, 1980, page 97)

It is not practicable for employees to develop confidence in a series of procedures or routines. They can only acquire confidence in what those systems produce and in those other members of the organisation with whom they interact. That confidence is built by the substance of what people say and do, but it is also built by a climate in which people feel encouraged to express ideas, make suggestions and question the validity of decisions. Communication and behaviour are so closely connected and interwoven that everything which influences behaviour also influences communication. It is closely related to the particular culture of the organisation.

SUMMARY PROPOSITIONS

18.1 Communication is the most time consuming activity in which managers engage. Improving management usually requires an improvement in communication.

18.2 The fewer the number of communication links in a system, the greater the efficiency of members of the organisation in task performance.

18.3 Managers generally prefer word of mouth communication to other methods.

18.4 The growth of electronic methods of handling information will affect the amount of written communication in organisations, but will have little influence on the amount of word of mouth communicating.

18.5 Only in extreme cases of censorship is the grapevine a substitute for the formal system of communication: normally formal and informal systems complement each other.

18.6 Problems of organisational communication which can be at least partially overcome include those of the formal structure, social distance, intergroup hostility, the physical setting and overload on individual communicators.

18.7 Organisational communication is only as good as the interpersonal communication taking place in the organisation.

PUTTING IT INTO PRACTICE

Drill to study patterns of contact with other organisation members

State one. Draw a personal organisation chart, with yourself at the centre, using □ to indicate job positions and showing the names of those currently holding those posts. The chart should include *formal* relations you have inside and outside the organisation. The circle represents the organisation boundary and your drawing might look something like Fig. 18.2.

Fig. 18.2 A personal organisation chart.

Stage two. On a second chart list all the individuals or groups who can affect how effective you are in your job, but with whom you do not have a formal working relationship included in the first chart. Give both names and positions. The drawing, which may look something like the one in Fig. 18.3, will describe your informal network.

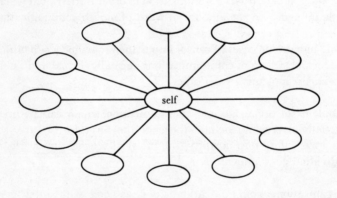

Fig. 18.3 An informal network drawing.

Stage three. (a) Using Table 18.2 rank order the contacts, formal and informal, in their importance to you in getting your job done effectively. (b) Rate each contact on a scale between −3 and +3, according to how helpful the person is to you. (c) What can be done to improve communication with those you have rated between −1 and −3?

Stage four. Is there anyone who should be in your network but is not yet?

Table 18.2 Network action plan

Rank	Contact	−3 −2 −1 0 1 2 3	Improvement by....
1			
2			
3			
4			
5			
6			
7			
8			
9			

REFERENCES

Baskin, O.W. and Aronoff, C.E., *Interpersonal Communication in Organizations*, Goodyear, Santa Monica, Calif., 1980.

Carlisle, H.M., *Management: Concepts, Methods and Applications*, 2nd edn, Science Research Associates Ltd., Chicago, 1982.

Davis, K., 'Management communication and the grapevine', *Harvard Business Review*, Sept./Oct., 1953, pages 43–9.

Drucker, P.F., *Management*, Pan Books, London, 1979.

Dubin, R., 'Stability of Human Organizations', in Haire, M. (ed.), *Modern Organization Theory*, John Wiley, New York, 1959.

Greenbaum, H.W., 'The audit of organizational communications', *Academy of Management Journal*, 1974, pages 739–54.

Hage, J., *Communication and Organizational Control*, John Wiley, New York, 1974.

Hinrichs, J.R., 'Communications activity of industrial research personnel', *Personnel Psychology*, Summer 1964, pages 193–204.

Katz, D. and Kahn, R.L., *The Social Psychology of Organizations*, 2nd edn, John Wiley, New York, 1978.

Knippen, J., 'Grapevine communication: management employees', *Journal of Business Research*, January 1974, pages 47–58.

Mintzberg, H., 'The manager's job: folklore and fact', *Harvard Business Review*, July/Aug. 1975.

Pirani, M. and Reynolds, J., 'Gearing up for safety', *Personnel Management*, Feb. 1976.

19

INTERPERSONAL COMMUNICATION

Communicating with other people is the main activity of managerial life. Mintzberg (1973) was one of many studies that showed managers spending the majority of their working time talking with other people. Some way behind in pervasiveness, but still taking more time than other activities, are reading and writing. To some extent the business of being a communicator is putting on a performance. Erving Goffman (1969) offers us an absorbing account of how all of us are constantly seeking information from each other that is not readily revealed, so that we infer it from a range of clues, like gesture and facial expression. At the same time we are deceiving those trying to obtain the same sort of information from us by the art of impression management, through which we try to create impressions of ourselves that are more favourable than the facts warrant.

One vogue has been the analysis of non-verbal behaviour. If we are constantly seeking from each other information that is not readily revealed, it appears sensible to try to get behind the impression that the other person is trying to convey. The fruits of this labour have been entertaining but of limited value. Most of the conclusions are either of the obvious, such as the observation that actions speak louder than words, or of the trivial, like the fact that men sometimes scratch their heads when puzzled. Other conclusions that have been announced do not carry sufficient reliability to be adopted as guidelines. Once the code of non-verbal behaviour is cracked, then people can fake the signals. Few signals are more general and unequivocal than the smile, which signals friendliness and pleasure at meeting someone, but because we all know that, we can fake the signal and smile warmly at someone even when that is not really how we feel. The welcoming smile can be as meaningless as the accompanying words 'I am pleased to meet you'. Impression management has won again.

There are two aspects of the communication problem that are important to mention, from the plethora of comment on the subject before proceeding to the main sections of the chapter. First is the simple comment about *the frame of reference*. A Frenchman is alleged once to have expressed surprise that all the monuments in London commemorated defeats, because many of the 'glorious victories' for the British have been defeats of the French. Perceptions of an issue will be shaped by the standpoint from which a person views it. When husband and wife separate there will be sharply different interpretations of the reasons for the separation, the truth being somewhere in between. In the words of William Cowper:

> Differing judgements serve but to declare,
> That truth lies somewhere, if we knew but where.

In communication we must always remember that our listener will view the matter differently from us, and we therefore have to write or speak with an understanding of his or her standpoint.

Less familiar is the problem of *cognitive dissonance* which describes the difficulty we have in coping with information that is not consistent with our beliefs. If you believe that wearing formal clothes to work is important, you will not readily accept arguments opposed to that belief. Believing requires commitment by the believer, who metaphorically nails his or her colours to the mast, and information conflicting with the belief is either discredited or manipulated to fit the belief.

People at work have plenty of beliefs that are usually expressed as homespun philosophy and which effect the way they carry out their duties. Here are a few:

There's only one way to do it, and that's by the book.
People will do anything if the money's right.
A machine can never be as good as a skilled person.
The customer is always right.
If I say jump, they jump.
The happy worker is a good worker.
Women are fine doing routine jobs, but they're too emotional to wield authority.

Those may be accurate or misleading as generalisations, but those who express the beliefs will not readily discard them. An opposing point of view will be met by the cognitive dissonance block, not as a deliberate obstruction but as a genuine attempt to understand the unbelievable, to make sense of what sounds preposterous by reinterpreting it to fit the existing pattern of belief. Every manager trying to persuade people of an argument, or even to convey information, has to remember that cognitive dissonance makes it hard for people to understand new information that contradicts what they believe; it is harder still to believe it if it is understood, and hardest of all to take action based upon it.

SPEAKING

It would be unrealistic to suggest how managers should speak to people in their everyday exchanges at work. As we spend a lifetime acquiring and developing this facility, we also develop a high degree of skill at the process. Speaking to groups of people is, however, a much less common activity and one about which many managers are apprehensive, so this section of the chapter considers speaking in public: lecturing, making presentations, offering a vote of thanks, explaining a new procedure to a group of people, addressing a committee, welcoming a party of visitors, or one of the many other occasions when it is necessary to fill the public-speaking role.

Review Topic 19.1

Mr X believes in ghosts and Mr Y does not. Rehearse a discussion between these two in an allegedly haunted house. Which of the comments they produce would you attribute to their different frames of reference and which to cognitive dissonance?

This is a source of power and manifestation of authority. Most of the best known figures of history have been gifted speakers. Demosthenes, Paul of Tarsus, Martin Luther, Lloyd George, Winston Churchill and Adolf Hitler all had an almost mesmeric power over their listeners, although it was not simply a way with words but also a well composed argument that made them effective. Bowra (1970) describes the effectiveness of Demosthenes:

> Demosthenes had no humour, no lightness of touch, but he had extraordinary oratorical power. Appealing to his countrymen to resist the tyrant who meant to overwhelm them, he stated a powerful case . . . driving each point home with relentless force . . . He used all his gifts of argument and persuasion . . . made carefully considered and practicable proposals. (Bowra, 1970, page 144)

Managers do not have the scope of statesmen for their public speaking, but the impact of greater speakers demonstrates the power that lies within the use of the spoken word. Managers may not lead people into battle or initiate sweeping social change, but they can reassure a group of apprehensive employees who are on the verge of industrial action, or gain acceptance for a novel idea, or persuade the members of a committee to back a new proposal because they can produce a convincing case that other people can understand and accept. The emphasis has to be on the way in which the speaker enables the members of the audience to understand. Success is in getting the message understood; not in transmitting it.

Public speaking requires preparation of both the material and the speaker. Adair (1978, page 73) refers to the first systematic exponent of rhetoric, Quintilian, who identified five phases in a speech: an introduction to gain the goodwill of the audience; a statement of the point at issue; arguments to prove the case; refutations of contrary arguments; and a peroration which either recapitulates the main points or appeals to the emotions of the audience. That remains an admirable *plan* for any speech.

In the introduction the audience have to come to the view that the address will be worth listening to and their attention in the later stages can be helped by explaining the framework of what is to come. If the speaker says that the case is going to be supported with three main arguments and it will deal with two opposing points of view, then the audience will listen for three and two.

In arguing the case the speaker has to remember that the aim is to get the audience to understand *ideas* rather than facts. Facts are dangerous as they may remain in the mind more readily than the idea that they are intended to illustrate. The speaker is trying to get understanding of the idea that this product is the one the customer should buy, or that output from the factory has to increase rapidly. The facts (such as the price of the product or the percentage increase in production that is needed) are merely indicators, symbols or measurements of the idea. It is like the recipe for a chocolate cake. There is the picture of the succulent cake, with an account of how it will fit specific occasions and appeal to particular palates, then there is the list of ingredients and instructions. Neither is complete without the other, but the list of ingredients is no trigger to action without the picture.

Ideas can be helpfully linked together by a device that will help listeners to remember them and to see their interconnection. One way to do this is to use key words, especially if they have alliteration or an easy rhythm, like 'planning, progress and prosperity'. Another method is the succinct summary phrase, like 'the wind of change' or 'keep upkeep down'. Where visual aids can be used, a simple system diagram can show the interdependence of ideas being expressed.

Very few people speak well without *notes*, which avoid the dangers of leaving something out, getting a fact wrong, drying up or – most important – wandering from the point. The audience has to work hard to build in their own minds the message that is being conveyed by the speaker. If the speaker wanders from the straitjacket of the message, then they are impeded in trying to hold their own mental picture of the address. The most common form of notes is to use headlines, with the main points underlined and the facts beneath. There may also be a marginal note about an anecdote or similar illustration that would be relevant.

Before speaking the speaker will probably suffer from *stage fright*. This can be useful in putting us on our mettle, sharp and keyed up to produce a good performance, but if the anxiety is too great then the confidence necessary for effectiveness is lost and the audience is more aware of the nervousness than the message. Stage fright can be reduced by deliberate relaxation. On the way to give the address, deliberately walk slower than is usual; concentrate on deliberately relaxing various muscles in the body, especially the ones producing a worried frown on the forehead. Deliberately smiling is relaxing and is also a good mask for nervousness. A simple method of controlling nervous breathing is to breathe in to a steady count of three and out to a steady count of nine; in to four and out to twelve; in to five and out to fifteen. A more elaborate method is advocated by Winifred Marks.

> It is relaxing simply to take several long, deep breaths, filling the base of the lungs and activating the diaphragm. More sophisticated techniques have been advocated, such as holding the nose between thumb and middle finger, with the index finger on the bridge and pressing the nostrils in turn to enforce breathing through each one alternately. (Marks, 1980, page 51)

Making the speech is putting on a performance and the initial impact on the audience will influence their attitude to what is to be said. The speakers need to assert themselves and display confidence in what there is to do: then the audience will begin to believe that it may all be worthwhile. The attention of the audience has to be won and their attention focused. This is done not only by having good and clear introductory material, as has been suggested above, but also by focusing their attention on the speaker. The best way to do this is to look at them, however daunting the members of the audience may appear. The speaker must also convey *vigour*.

> Enthusiasm is contagious. If a speaker wants to convince, he has to believe in the issue himself. His belief helps to get the message across. There is a difference between 'We have to do something about wasted materials', said as the speaker picks lint off his trousers, scans the horizon, stifles a yawn and scratches his head, and 'We have to do something about wasted materials', said with inflection, pausing, direct eye contact and erect posture. (Mayerson, 1979, page 184)

The speaker not only wins the attention of the audience at the outset, but maintains it through the later development of the material:

> Interest and motivation should be sustained throughout by the use of material or examples, which are intrinsically interesting to the audience, dramatic or simply funny. Concrete examples and stories make the material easier to assimilate, but should be subordinated to the main argument. (Argyle, 1972, page 209)

The final point in that quotation is especially relevant to humour. If your preparation reminds *you* of a funny story, which you then tell to the audience, be sure that it will help *them* remember what you are saying. Humour must always illustrate and never distract.

Two general aspects of speaking are *pace* and *language*. Public speaking generally requires a slower pace than normal conversation, which is too quick for the message to be picked up by a number of people simultaneously. Also it is uninterrupted, so that both listener and speaker require more time to cope with forming the ideas for expression and decoding the messages that are received. Variation of pace provides the scope for emphasis and for eliminating the nonsense words that otherwise creep into speech.

When a lawyer was speaking to a lay audience, he frequently used the phrases 'you know' and 'as it were'. Very soon members of the audience were busy noting the frequency and the following coffee break was spent in making comparisons of the different records that were kept. The consensus was that 'you know' occurred every sixteen seconds while 'as it were' came only at forty-seven second intervals. Few people could remember what he had been talking about. Nonsense words and phrases are used automatically to fill the minute gap when the brain has not got the message through quickly enough to the lips. Varying the pace reduces the number of occasions when such gaps occur. Few people avoid jargon, with the danger that some people will not understand. The words used must lie within the comprehension of all if the communication is to succeed. Even when the words are understood, there can be some resentment when it appears that their use is only to display erudition. Is it necessary to use the word 'taxonomy' instead of 'list'? Was it necessary to refer at the opening of this chapter to 'frame of reference' instead of 'point of view'? Many readers will have been irked by the term 'cognitive dissonance', even though it is difficult to find an alternative.

The *peroration* (is that jargon for conclusion?) is as important as the opening. The speaker summarises the points that have been made, reinforces them with the audience and prepares for some positive action by audience members. Among the ways in which this can be done are to tell a story that brings together and illustrates the points that have been made, or to raise a series of rhetorical questions to which listeners can now see answers which they could not see at the beginning, or to make a straightforward statement to show the interrelationship of what has already been said.

Any speech can be enhanced by using *visual aids*, as we remember what we see for longer than we remember what we hear, and we sometimes understand what we see better than what we hear. Visual aids are, however, not a substitute for exposition, and too many can obscure rather than illustrate what is being said.

WRITING

We are all taught to write at school, and some of that teaching appears superfluous in our later working lives as it has a preoccupation with grammatical accuracy or imagery that does not seem appropriate in inter-office memoranda. This may be due to the teaching being unimaginative but it is more probably because at school we are being exhorted to express ourselves; while at work it is important that we get our message across. If our meaning is not clear, it may be misinterpreted. If our writing is vague and muddled, we may be regarded as vague and muddled people. There are many pieces of advice on how to write more effectively, but one of the most helpful is from the advice of Ernest Gowers to civil servants:

> Use no more words than are necessary to express your meaning, for if you use more you are likely to obscure it and tire your reader. In particular do not use superfluous adjectives and adverbs and do not use roundabout phrases where single words would serve.
>
> Use familar words rather than the far-fetched, for the familiar are more likely to be readily understood.
>
> Use words with a precise meaning rather than those that are vague, for they will obviously serve better to make your meaning clear; and in particular prefer concrete words to abstract, for they are more likely to have a precise meaning. (Gowers, 1948, page 91)

Following those three simple rules would improve the quality of most writing, making it easier to understand and giving it greater impact upon the reader. If you look back to the paragraph preceding the above quotation, you can immediately see ways in which Gowers would have improved it. Following his first rule would change the opening to: 'Some of what we learn at school about writing is superfluous . . .'

Following the second rule would take out the words 'preoccupation' and 'exhorted'. Following the third would improve the phrases 'do not seem', 'may be due' and 'may be regarded as'. That paragraph was not deliberately written badly and it is reasonably clear, but writing can always be improved. Here is the rewritten paragraph compared with the original:

Original	*Revised*
We are all taught to write at school, and some of that teaching appears superfluous in our later working lives as it has a preoccupation with grammatical accuracy or imagery that does not seem appropriate in interoffice memoranda. This may be due to the teaching being unimaginative but it is more probably because at school we are being exhorted to express ourselves; while at work it is important that we get our message across.	Some of what we learn at school about writing is not needed in our working lives. Accurate grammar and imagery are not important in interoffice memoranda. At work it is important to get our message across, but at school we are also taught to express ourselves.

That has saved over a third of the words and is easier to understand, but has anything important of the original been lost? The reference to the possibility that teaching was unimaginative has been removed altogether. That takes away that element, but was it worth saying? It was an unnecessary distraction from the main thrust of what was being said. The reference to grammatical accuracy or imagery is now slightly different in the revised version.

While it is always possible to improve a piece of writing by trimming out what is not necessary and following the general guidance of Gowers and similar experts, there is also the possibility that the resultant material is too terse, with rhythm lost. The reader needs not only accurate writing from the writer, but also a style in the writing that makes it comfortable to read. A final comment on the above revision is that the next passage will now need to be rewritten, possibly using more words. The original finishes with the need to get a message across, so that it naturally leads into the dangers of misinterpretation. As revised there is not that natural link as the finish is about school. How would you rewrite the passage to convey the meaning accurately and clearly?

Every piece of writing needs a framework or *outline* before the writing can begin. This makes the subsequent writing clearer as the sequence of main ideas has been thought out beforehand and the writer does not include in one section material that comes more appropriately at a later point. The outline can be constructed by analysing the components of the message we want to convey or the problem that has to be set forth. The components are then subdivided and grouped in a logical sequence. A retailing group was delayed in opening a new store because the local authority refused its planning application. The directors had to decide whether or not to appeal against the decision and asked for a report. The sections of the report were:

1. Introduction
   (a) Initial decision to build.
   (b) Site acquisition and development plan.
   (c) Reasons for refusal of planning application.
2. Alternatives
   (d) Abandon plan, with estimates of costs and lost revenue.
   (e) Appeal without modifications to plan, with estimates of costs, legal opinion on likelihood of success, and time to complete.
   (f) Appeal with modifications, including estimates as in (e).
3. Market research
   (g) Review of latest market research data relating to site.
   (h) Moves by competitors since initial decision to build.
4. Recommendation
   (i) Summary of alternatives with advantages and disadvantages.
   (j) Recommended action.

Before being used, the outline can be adjusted if the sequence does not seem ideal or if additional material should be included. Short pieces of writing, like brief letters and memoranda, are not usually thought out like this, but may be written to a standard formula or according to a simple outline in the mind of the writer. A checklist for report-writing is to be found later in this chapter.

A structural form that helps with the logical development of writing is the *paragraph*, which is the unit of writing for a section of what is to be said. The opening sentence says what the paragraph is about: the topic sentence. This is then developed in following sentences about the single idea or topic that the paragraph represents. The appropriate length of paragraph varies with the type of material being written. The following are some approximate figures:

Understanding Organizations	C.B. Handy	120 words
Management	P.F. Drucker	80 words
Emma	Jane Austen	75 words
Lateral Thinking	E. de Bono	70 words
The Road to Gandolfo	R. Ludlum	60 words
Leader article in popular newspaper		30 words

As paragraphs get longer, the writing becomes harder to read, as we shall see in the next section of this chapter. It is wise to keep to an average paragraph length of under 100 words in reports and less in letters.

The *active* voice is better than the *passive* voice in most instances. Evelyn Mayerson expresses the reasons succinctly for us.

> The active voice is more vigorous than the passive. *The new polyurethane is believed to be superior by the finisher* is a statement made in the passive voice. It is a timid statement. The finisher is hiding his meaning in clouded syntax. Putting the sentence in the active voice – *The finisher believes that the new polyurethane is superior* – makes the statement bolder. We know without question and very quickly who believes what.
>
> The writer makes a direct statement when he selects the active voice. *Leaking is caused when the roof is rained on* is an example of the indirect quality of the passive voice. As with any indirect route, it takes longer to get there. Notice how much shorter the sentence is when rewritten in the active voice: *The roof leaks when it rains.* (Mayerson, 1979, page 307)

A final comment about writing is the piece of advice produced by Winston Churchill in a circular to all Government departments during 1940.

> To do our work we all have to read a mass of papers. Nearly all of them are far too long. This wastes time, while energy has to be spent in looking for essential points.
>
> I ask my colleagues and their staff to see that their reports are shorter.
>
> 1. The aim should be reports which set out the main points in a series of short, crisp paragraphs.

2. If a report relies on detailed analysis of some complicated factors or on statistics, these should be set out in an appendix.
3. Often the occasion is best met by submitting not a full report, but a reminder consisting of headings only, which can be expounded orally if needed.
4. Let us have an end to such phrases as these: 'it is important to bear in mind the following considerations . . .' or 'consideration should be given to the possibility of carrying into effect . . .'. Most of these woolly phrases are mere padding, which can be left out altogether, or replaced by a single word. Let us not shrink from using the short expensive phrase, even if it is conversational.
5. Reports drawn up on the lines I propose may at first seem rough as compared with the flat surface of officialese jargon, but the saving in time will be great, while the discipline of setting out the real points concisely will prove an aid to clearer thinking. (Quoted in Adair, 1978, pages 114–5.)

READING

Being an effective communicator involves not only sending messages effectively, but also improving one's ability to receive messages from others. The managers who can cope with a large volume of incoming memoranda, letters and reports will extend their range of competence and their network.

Quicker reading enjoyed a vogue during the 1960s, when there were a number of courses provided where those attending could increase the speed at which they could both read and understand for an average of 200+ words per minute to nearly double that. Some of the methods were based on false assumptions about how to use our eyes, so that simple increases in speed due to practice and concentration were attributed to using technical aids. Manya and Eric de Leeuw (1965) demonstrated the false basis of these assumptions and produced a manual on how to read both better and faster. Managers need to develop two different skills; first to read some material faster without loss of comprehension, and secondly to read some other material very quickly indeed in order to appreciate the contents superficially before either discarding it or reading it thoroughly.

To read quickly without losing comprehension one has first to suppress a childhood habit: *vocalising*. When we are learning to read, our teachers and parents ask us to read aloud as this is the only way they can easily test our understanding. That habit dies hard, so that many adults subconsciously vocalise the words they read. The lips move silently as the eyes move across the page and the reading speed is thus limited to a speaking speed. If that habit can be broken, the reading speed will increase. The lips are kept firmly shut and the readers push themselves to move along the line quicker, concentrating on *not* sounding the words as they pass. A habit established since the age of seven of eight will not easily be eradicated, so it requires regular practice and concentrated effort.

The second feature of reading more quickly is to persuade the eyes to be more adventurous. Slow readers will move their eyes across the line of print fixing on one or two words at a time and with occasional regressions. This involves the eyes moving and changing focus five or six times in a line of print as the eyes only *read* while they are still. Speed can be increased by practice at reducing the number of eye *fixations*, moving the eye more rapidly along the line to fix on two words at a time, then three, then four.

By combining the elimination of vocalising and reducing the number of fixations per line, the reading speed with comprehension can be increased to double the starting speed. Usually comprehension will improve with quicker reading as the brain is operating at a speed that it can cope with quite easily. Manya and Eric de Leeuw (*op. cit.* page 29) have found an average increase of 60 per cent in reading speed and 10 per cent in comprehension among those taking their courses.

Reducing vocalisation and fixations both involve moving along the line more quickly. This can be aided by using a pencil or finger as a *cursor* moving along the line in front of the eyes. This focuses attention and leads the eyes to move more quickly and smoothly, providing the pencil is moved steadily and quickly. This method is invariably used by people adding a column of figures and is a simple, practical device for increasing normal reading speed.

Reading very quickly to get a superficial appreciation of contents is usually known as *skimming* and requires a different approach from conventional reading. Many people can read as much as they wish of a newspaper in less than half an hour because they read superficially. Most headlines are read, but few of the articles beneath the headlines. Newspapers have many aids for the superficial reader: there are pictures with captions, blocks of type are broken up with headings or inset quotations from the main text, summary tables are used of football results and share prices, and the column of print is narrow, so that it is possible to skim down rather than across constantly. A more advanced method is to scan the first and last paragraphs of a major article for the introduction and conclusion, or to pick up the opening topic sentences of paragraphs.

Review Topic 19.2

Ask someone to prepare two lists of 20 questions, each about the *main* news items on two separate pages of a national newspaper or magazine. Without looking at these lists, read through the first of the pages as quickly as you can using skimming techniques and making a note of the time taken. Then see how many questions you can answer correctly. Repeat the exercise by reading the second page, this time allowing yourself three times as long as you spent on the first page. Then answer the second set of questions.

How much does you success rate alter and what is the significance for your reading habits?

A skimming approach to a book is to see first the title and the summary on the flyleaf, then to look for any information about the author. Already there is the beginning of a framework, which can be clarified by looking through the table of contents and the index. Within five minutes you have a general idea of what the book is about, its weight and range. This may be sufficient for you to decide to discard it; it may be a useful preliminary to reading it thoroughly. Buzan (1977, pages 94–7) has a useful section on this type of reading and later in this chapter we reproduce a summary from de Leeuw.

SUMMARY PROPOSITIONS

19.1 Preliminaries to being effective in communications are: understanding of impression management, the frame of reference and cognitive dissonance.

19.2 Five phases in making a speech are: introduction, statement of the point at issue, arguments to prove the case, refutations of contrary arguments, and a peroration.

19.3 When writing, use no more words than are needed to make your point.

19.4 Material can be read faster and with better comprehension by reducing vocalisation and the number of fixations per line of type. This can be aided by using a pencil as a cursor.

19.5 Some reading can be skimming to obtain a superficial understanding only.

PUTTING IT INTO PRACTICE

Interaction guide for public speaking

Before speaking:
- *Plan the speech* by having an introduction, a statement of the point at issue, arguments to prove the case, refutations of contrary arguments, and a peroration.
- *Distil ideas* for the audience to understand. These will be the core of your message.

- *Ration facts* as they are needed to illustrate and emphasise your ideas; they cannot replace ideas.
- *Connect the ideas* by some device that will show how they are linked: key words, a summary phrase, or a visual aid.
- *Use notes* rather than memory, to provide the framework for the speech and to recall the details.
- *Relax* deliberately, to avoid the tension of stage fright while retaining the verve to win the attention of the audience.

While speaking:
- *Win the audience* by gaining their attention and interest.
- *Ration humour* so that it is used only to illustrate and embellish; never to distract.
- *Vary pace* of speaking so as to provide emphasis, to eliminate nonsense words, and to be interesting for the listeners.
- *Match language to the audience* so that listeners are stimulated to listen, but are always able to understand.
- *Use visual aids* to clarify what is being said, as we remember what we see for longer than we remember what we hear, and we sometimes understand what we see better than what we hear.
- *Use the peroration* to summarise the points that have been made, to reinforce them with the audience, and to prepare for action.

Report writing checklist

1. Before writing
   (a) What is the purpose of writing the report?
   (b) Who will read it?
   (c) How short can it be?

2. Outline
   (a) What exactly is the problem the report is to deal with?
   (b) Into how many subtopics does that best divide?
   (c) What order should those subtopics be in?
   (d) Can that order be improved?
   (e) Will the report, as outlined, meet the purpose described in 1(a)?

3. Writing
   (a) Keep the average length of paragraphs below 100 words.
   (b) Use no more words than are needed to express your meaning.
   (c) Avoid superfluous adverbs, adjectives and roundabout phrases.
   (d) Use words that are precise and concrete rather than vague and abstract.
   (e) Use the active rather than the passive voice.

(f) Make clear the source of any facts used.

(g) Use abbreviations and symbols consistently throughout the report.

(h) Use numbering and sub-headings consistently throughout the report.

4. Reviewing

(a) Does the completed report meet the purpose described in 1(a)?

(b) Is anything missing?

(c) Are any calculations accurate?

(d) Are recommendations thoroughly justified?

(e) Is the action to be taken, or the choice between alternatives, clear?

(f) Is any part of the report likely to offend anyone?

(g) What objections do you expect, and how do you propose to counter them?

(h) Can any possible objections be prevented by rewriting part of the report without reducing its effect?

5. After distributing the report

(a) Have your recommendations been accepted?

(b) In what ways have reactions been unfavourable? Could this have been avoided?

(c) How would you have written the report differently?

(d) How will you write your next report?

Some phrases to avoid in writing

As it were

Be that as it may

Attached herewith is

At the present time

In respect of

I am writing to say

For that matter

In such a manner as to

For the purpose of

He is a man who

In a manner of speaking

Afford an opportunity

Much of a muchness

In the near future

Owing to the fact that

With regard to

Give rise to

Without fear or favour

By and large

Generally speaking

At the end of the day

Arguably

Always remember the advice of William Cobbett (1762–1835):

> Grammar, perfectly understood, enables us not only to express our meaning fully and clearly; but so to express it as to defy the ingenuity of man to give to our words any other meaning than that which we ourselves intended to express.

Punctuation

Comma	Makes a logical division within a sentence:

1. To separate the subject from descriptive words and phrases (Bob Willis, captain of England, waited . . .).
2. To separate clauses (If he wins the toss, England will bat).
3. To separate items on a list (He came in with his bat, pads, gloves and cap).

Semi-colon   Links two sentences which are so closely related that a full stop would be too great a break (Willis did not open the bowling; Botham did).

Colon   Separates an announcement from what is announced (The batting order was as follows: . . .).

Brackets   Used for insertion, additional explanation or oversight (The twelfth man (Foster) brought out drinks).

Apostrophe   Either to indicate a possessive (Gower's batting; Jones's bowling; the men's room).
Or to show a missing syllable in abbreviations (It's Boycott again).

Hyphen   Produces a compound adjective (a well-run single).

Inverted commas   For reported speech or quoted material ('Not out', said the umpire).

Full stop   Used at the end of a sentence which is not a question or an exclamation, after many abbreviations (etc.) and within sets of initials (l.b.w.).

Comprehensive notes on punctuation are in *The Oxford Dictionary for Writers and Editors*, Clarendon Press, Oxford, 1981.

Skimming

(This is an extract from the book by de Leeuw (1965, page 105) summarising how those authors skim.)

1. There is no conscious direction of the eyes.
2. The attention is open and takes in the whole width of the page: we find that words near the margins can easily mask each other.
3. There is a left–right movement to cover the horizontal extent of the page, though sometimes this is so quick that we seem to be going straight down the page.
4. Within this general movement our eyes, as far as we can judge, behave in an extremely erratic manner, darting here and there as words attract our attention. If a word strikes us forcibly we explore the area around it.
6. The speed of skimming varies enormously: say from three to twenty

seconds a page. There often seems to be a combination of fast reading and short skips. Sometimes there is what amounts to an erratic three-line reading.

7. When previewing we combine skimming with sampling.

8. If the meaning is obvious, we skip and skim without compunction, unless we are caught up in the author's mood or take pleasure in the words or situation.

9. If we want to skip and be reasonably sure of our ground, we often read the first few words of each sentence.

10. Gradually we have become more sensitive to less obvious expressions like 'The assumption is', 'In opposition to this', 'The outcome of this', announcing propositions or conclusions; which is a help both in ordinary reading and skimming.

REFERENCES

Adair, J., *Training for Communication*, Gower, Aldershot, 1978.

Argyle, M., *The Psychology of Interpersonal Behaviour*, Pelican, London, 1972.

Bowra, C.M., *Classical Greece*, Time-Life International, New York, 1976.

Buzan, T., *How to Make the Most of Your Mind*, Colt Books, London, 1977.

de Leeuw, M. and E., *Read Better, Read Faster*, Penguin Books, Harmondsworth, 1965.

Goffman, E., *The Presentation of Self in Everyday Life*, Penguin Books, Harmondsworth, 1969.

Gowers, E., *Plain Words*, HMSO, London, 1948.

Marks, W., *How to Give a Speech*, IPM, London, 1980.

Mayerson, E.W., *Shoptalk*, Saunders, Philadelphia, 1979.

Mintzberg, H., *The Nature of Managerial Work*, Harper & Row, New York, 1973.

Torrington, D., *Face to Face in Management*, Prentice Hall International, Hemel Hempstead, 1982.

20

SELECTING TEAM MEMBERS

Few managers are able to pick their own team. A manager moving into a new post is the newcomer surrounded by people who are already established. Except in rare circumstances it is either unethical, unlawful, too expensive, impractical or simply foolish to discard those who are established and replace them with one's own nominees. Selecting team members is, therefore, a quite different activity for the individual manager than it is for the personnel specialist, who is recruiting people for the organisation as a whole.

The personnel specialist has to consider the broad issues such as equality of opportunity, promotion prospects, pension entitlement, closed shops and the degree to which the potential recruit is likely to 'fit' the corporate culture; one development of the late 1980s has been the move to selecting for commitment instead of seeking to develop commitment after appointment. In contrast the individual manager is an occasional selector only, and is concerned much more with the internal dynamics of the working team and the possible working relationship with the person appointed. All those concerned in the selection decision – personnel specialist, individual manager and potential recruit – are concerned that there should be a good match between people appointed and the situation in which they will be working, but each has a different perspective. This chapter is about the decision-making of the individual manager trying to develop and maintain a balanced working team.

The manager selects a few members of his team either single-handed or in consultation with others, but tolerates the vagaries of many others. One could almost say that picking one's own people is an abdication of management, a part of the art being to organise and co-ordinate the contribution of different types of people, including those one does not get on with. This involves managers adapting their style and approach to the varied expectations and needs of others, rather than being able to work only with kindred spirits, hand-picked for their compatibility.

Daniel Greensmith had founded and developed a small printing business, working closely with three colleagues who helped him start the company and who 'grew' with it. When the proprietor of a nearby, slightly larger printing company retired for health reasons, Daniel Greensmith bought the business. The move was welcomed by the managers and staff of the taken-over company, as Greensmith was known and well regarded. To avoid any misunderstanding, a consultant was engaged to advise on the management structure of the combined business and how the senior positions should be filled. Greensmith told the consultant what he was looking for and the consultant advised him about which members of the two companies fitted his specifications. The three loyal lieutenants were appointed to three of the top four posts reporting to Greensmith. Within six months the business was in difficulty, and Greensmith had enough self-knowledge to see why. He explained it to one of the authors as follows:

> I only knew one way to run a business and the three lads who had been with me from the beginning knew no more than I did: they were really just extensions of me. When the merger came along I hired a consultant because I wanted everything to be done fairly, without any feeling of favouritism, but I hired a personnel consultant instead of a business consultant. He was very good at finding out and describing what *I wanted*, but he was not the right person to tell me what the *business needed*. I appointed the people I knew and felt comfortable with, but we were ignorant of the subtleties of the company we had taken over. What I needed was strong, articulate opposition to my new ideas from people who knew what they were talking about, so that the good ideas would have been made better and the nonsense filtered out. What I got was a bunch of yes men.

Review Topic 20.1

In what sense is picking one's own people an abdication of management?

Picking one's own team is a luxury few managers are able to enjoy and it can be a dangerous privilege, leading to the appointment of sycophants instead of creating a robust, balanced group of individuals, working *with* rather than *for* the person in charge.

THE EMPLOYMENT CONTRACT

Notwithstanding the warning of the last paragraph, managers have some part to play in selecting those who join the working team, and this chapter deals with that selection activity.

The approach to selection is to appreciate that selecting people for jobs is a process of setting up an *employment contract* between the individual employee and the employing organisation. This is much more than the legally binding contract of employment which summarises the rights and obligations of the two parties; it is matching two sets of needs and expectations

(Schein, 1979; Mumford, 1972: Torrington and Hall, 1987). It is natural to think in terms of what contribution to organisational success will be made by the employee, although this is seldom thought out very clearly and often centres round narrow, personal preferences of the manager in charge of the section where the appointment is to be made. It is also accepted that individual employees expect certain satisfactions from their employment, but frequently these two sets of requirements are seen as being satisfied independently of each other: the employee gets a salary, some holiday and contributions to a pension scheme in exchange for which personal interest and achievement are set aside in order to accommodate the routine requirements of the employer. Satisfactions for either party are likely to be mainly at the expense of the other.

In reaction against this there are some employment situations where too much is done to satisfy the employee, in such a way that the attempt is self-defeating. The conditions of work are enhanced – more money, longer holidays, free meals, flexible working hours – but nothing is done about the work, which remains an irksome necessity to be tolerated with as much restraint and dignity as possible. The result is often inefficiency, slackness and employees who not only are dissatisfied with their work, but also feel guilty about their dissatisfaction of the paraphernalia of good conditions that surrounds them.

The essence of the employment contract idea is simply that the two sets of needs are not independent but complementary; the employee seeks satisfaction in the work done as well as from the circumstances in which it is done, and employees satisfied with their work will be more secure, more creative, more responsive to customers, more reliable and more efficient. The personnel department can do no more than clear away some of the possible impediments to a good employment contract. It is the individual manager who clarifies the needs of the organisation and integrates those with the needs of the employee, so that both are satisfed by the same processes.

The importance of this approach is that the manager selecting team members has to think just as much about what the appointee is looking for as about what the job requirements are. Both selector and appointee are choosing and it is important to both that each makes a sound decision.

ATTRACTING TEAM MEMBERS

People, working groups and departments acquire reputations and one aspect of those reputations is to influence the number and type of people who want to join the group. All managers are interested in the reputation that they and their departments enjoy. 'A really first-class, very enthusiastic bunch of people' is the sort of label that is likely to attract people seeking that sort of working environment whereas 'It is very well run and the manager is scrupulously fair' conveys a different image that will appeal to different people.

Reputations can be reliable indicators within an organisation, where the grapevine will do its work, but are much less useful as indicators to those outside the organisation, who may be influenced more by stereotypes. One local government official grumbled to us about the difficulty of recruiting people other than those who were looking for 'a safe billet'. She felt that local government had a popular image of being comfortable but dull and this image became a self-fulfilling prophecy as applicants came either because that was what they wanted or because they could not find anything else and thought themselves into the model they expected.

The reputation of the employing organisation in the labour markets is mainly a job for the personnel manager, but other managers can ensure that they are people worth working with and their departments worth working in. They can, however, do little to alter the truth. So they need to declare and embody what they *actually* are and how they really work, rather than generate some artificial picture of what they think will make them 'attractive'.

This process of establishing and sustaining a reputation is similar to the visiposure activities mentioned in Chapter 10. Managers are attracting potential team members in two ways. First, they are attracting the person who is looking for an internal move or awaiting their new posting. In this context reputation can be vitally important. If there is a loosely structured method of career advance, wherein individuals apply for jobs that appeal to them, managers are traders on the internal labour market and will want to create a climate of opinion about who would fit into their department before specific vacancies occur. If movement is centrally controlled, so that individuals are moved between jobs, then the reputation of an individual manager or department will affect the attitude and expectations of the new arrival.

Secondly, managers are attracting potential members by creating recommendations. Existing employees ask if there may be a vacancy for their next-door neighbour, cousin, son, or someone with whom they have worked previously. This remains the dominant way in which new employees are recruited.

INFORMATION SUPPORTING SELECTION DECISIONS

The reputation of candidates and of departments and organisations in which candidates seek openings spreads informally. There are other sources of information, some of which will be available in any selection process.

Application forms. These are nearly always available for scrutiny. Either the candidate is from outside and is completing one with the vacancy in view, or is an insider who completed a form some time previously. The value of this document is that it sets out systematically the basic information about the person being considered. Because of this orderly display it is also the common basis for the selection interview.

Surveying application forms from candidates enables one quickly to pick up and compare a few key points about a number of applicants, such as age, qualifications, current post, salary and location. It is the easiest and most effective method of producing a short list. The way in which information about candidates is displayed in it provides a logical sequence for the selection, or employment, interview. The information is presented in biographical sequence so as to provide a pattern for questioning that is fruitful for the interviewer and coherent to the respondent. Some forms also provide space by each entry for the interviewers to make their own comments.

Curricula vitae. A long-standing practice, which is now becoming more widespread, is for candidates to submit a curriculum vitae (CV). This is often attractive to those who are articulate and experienced, as it enables them to tell their story in their own way, with the degree of detail and emphasis which gives the most positive picture of their track record and potential. It can appeal to recruiters as well because the style and approach of the CV gives a number of individual clues about the candidate which are obscured by the standardised method of the application form.

The shortcomings of the CV are that systematic comparison is difficult and judgements are likely to be based on the more intangible aspects of the application, and on the style rather than substance of the candidate ('I like the look of this one'). The CV writer necessarily uses a grapeshot approach, making every possible point in a very general way rather than tailoring the information to the vacancy.

Letters. Another tactic is to ask candidates to fill in a form but also to write a letter of application, with the form setting out the biographical information systematically and the letter making the case for that particular person being fitted to the specific vacancy. This approach requires clear advice to candidates on what the letter should contain; otherwise there is the likelihood that the letter re-states what is in the form together with self-aggrandizing assertions of little value and at varying levels of self-consciousness.

Job descriptions. May be available in detailed documents, or simply be a picture in the mind of the selector. Usually the written job description is preferred as it sets out what candidates want to know about the job for which they are applying, and summarises for selectors the points against which they are matching those interviewed. It is also argued that the process of producing the job description clarifies for the selector the details of the job to be done.

Candidate specifications. Profiles of the ideal candidate, prepared beforehand on the basis of the job description. This too may be just a picture in the mind of the selector, or it may be a written profile that specifies requirements in terms of qualifications, length and type of working experience, aptitudes, skills and intelligence. The advantage of this is mainly in the short-listing of candidates, comparing application form details with points in the specification. It then has a later role in the examination of the ways in which preferred candidates do not quite meet the specification and deciding which requirements are the most important.

Job descriptions and candidate specifications are the product of *job analysis*, extensively described in many books about organisational psychology and personnel management. Tyson and York (1982, pages 81–94) provides a succinct summary.

Test scores. Sometimes available in larger organisations, or where external candidates are being put forward for consideration by consultants. Easiest to deal with is a test of *skill or proficiency*, such as typing or driving test, which indicates a level of competence by a generally acknowledged yardstick. Tests of *intelligence* are not so easy to use. They measure some of a person's abilities against a standardised indicator, such as intelligence quotient or quartiles of the general population, but there is often resistance from candidates to taking such tests, especially if they are well established in their careers and feel that undertaking such tests is like testing Giotto to see if he knows how to hold a paint brush. A test of this type that is widely used is the Graduate Management Admission Test, which is administered by the University of Princeton and used by business schools in many countries to decide whether or not candidates will be able to cope with their master's programmes. More specialised are tests of *aptitude*, like those used to select prospective trainees for aircrew duties or recruits for engineering apprenticeships. They assess not skill but the potential to develop a skill that depends on some aspect of natural aptitude like manual dexterity or spatial judgement. The most controversial tests are those of *personality*, which claim to produce profiles of human traits and motivation, so that selectors can have a prediction about a candidate's potential for a post that goes beyond an assessment of existing skills, intelligence and aptitudes. A selection of contributions made by Ungerson (1983, pages 96–160) summarises what is currently available.

References provided by previous employers, family friends and Justices of the

Peace are notoriously unhelpful and often misleading. They are now used extensively in the public sector of employment and are almost unknown in the private sector. They are supposed to provide evidence of character, but the self-selecting nature of their nomination by candidates tends to bias their objectivity. Candidates choose reference writers because they think they will provide a 'good' reference, and 'bad' references are extremely rare.

There appears to be a set of coded messages conveyed by the concluding sentence of reference letters, which will usually be one of the following:

'I am delighted to commend Bloggins to you without any reservation . . .'
'I strongly recommend Bloggins as a very well-qualified candidate for the vacancy.'
'I recommend Bloggins to you for serious consideration . . .'

Those three standard recommendations then have the personal embroidery that succeeds in making them difficult to interpret. 'I am delighted . . .' becomes 'I am honoured . . .' or 'I am very happy . . .'. This sounds a flippant comment, but any regular attender at selection panels where references are being considered will notice the tendency for battle-weary members of the panel to look at the end of the reference first. If the remainder is read at all, it is interpreted in the light of that key, closing sentence. References may give an insight into the character of the person writing them, but they tell you little about the person on whose behalf the letter has been written.

Other methods of selection in current use include *bio-data* analysis, which is a systematic examination of the life history of the applicant and scoring certain key features to produce a profile of likely candidates. *Graphology*, *palmistry* and *astrology* are still used in some organisations, although there is no evidence to support their effectiveness. Larger companies increasingly use *assessment centres*, whereby a number of shortlisted candidates undergo a range of selection methods, including group exercises. This has the value that a variety of evidence is collected and a balanced assessment is possible.

THE SELECTION INTERVIEW

Every time someone is selected to join a team, there will be an interview to precede the appointment. Mainly this is for the selector to decide whether the candidate is suitable, but candidates will also be making up their minds whether the move is one that they wish to make or not. Some selection processes seek to rule out the possibility of the candidate deciding against the job as a result of the interview, on the grounds that candidates should have made up their minds firmly and should not waste the time of the interviewers with interviews that may not be needed. Sometimes candidates are asked to declare at the beginning of the interview that they are firm applicants. In other situations travelling expenses are not paid to candidates who do not accept an offer of employment. This is part of the ritual of the selection interview, which is partly an initiation rite. The candidate arrives in his best clothes and is expected to show deference to the interviewers and great keenness to be employed, whilst the selectors are unlikely to wear their best clothes, sometimes demonstrate their superiority by being late or preoccupied with other things, and will never show enthusiasm to employ the candidate – willingness maybe: enthusiasm never.

Review Topic 12.2

Write a reference for someone applying for your job, avoiding outright condemnation or unequivocal enthusiasm. Then show it to a friend and ask if they would be disposed to employ or not to employ the person on the basis of the reference, with their reasons.

Although these ritual elements are inevitable in the selection situation, and their importance should not be underestimated, the purpose of the interview goes much further and has as its main purpose the ability of the selector to decide whether the candidate is appropriate or inappropriate for the post under consideration. How can this be done effectively? The remaining pages of this chapter seek to offer general advice for the occasional interviewer. More detailed guidance is available in, for instance, Fraser (1978) or Torrington (1982).

The setting for the interview. This should be one that is appropriate for a private conversation, so that the exchanges will be frank and constructive. Many people also feel that the setting should reduce the status barriers between interviewer and respondent on the grounds that the interviewer is in the socially superior position of having a job to offer, or not, while the respondent is in the inferior position of wanting the job and being disposed to propitiate the interviewer in order to get it. If the seating arrangements underplay that distinction, then candidates will be more relaxed and more open in what they say. This status reduction can be done by avoiding direct, face-to-face interviewing across a desk and moving to a situation where both participants are sitting at the same height, not directly opposed and without any obvious advantage to the interviewer.

There is a danger in the setting becoming too informal and thus destroying rather than mitigating the ritual elements. The friendly chat over a drink in a local pub may be pleasantly relaxed and the candidate will probably (eventually) become very loquacious, but it is a difficult 'interview' to structure and may disconcert the candidate, who is expecting something more businesslike.

The plan of the interview. This is most easily taken from the sequence of the application form particulars. The development of the questioning is then one that builds logically in the mind of the selector and can be followed constructively by the candidate, who can see how the interview is progressing, rather than feeling that there is some hidden agenda that he does not understand and which consequently worries him. There is one preliminary, setting up *rapport*. At the opening of the interview candidate and selector assess each other and tune in to each other. It is usually done by exchanging words about trivia (some people believe that it rains frequently in Britain simply to provide people with a topic of conversation at the opening of interviews), explaining procedure and plenty of nods and smiles. It also gives the selector an opportunity to sketch out what is to happen and where the interview fits in with the rest of the decision-making process.

After the pleasantries of rapport, there is a change of pace as the interview moves to *information exchange*, and we need to remember that the information is moving both ways, not only towards the selector. If the candidates are from inside the organisation they will know most of the things they need to make up their minds about the post and will probably have just one or two check questions as well as a keen interest in the type of person the selector is. Candidates do not have the benefit of application forms, test scores or candidate specifications of the people with whom they will be working, but they are still keenly interested and try to understand as much as they can during the brief encounter of the interview. The external candidate will have a wider range of uncertainty and more gaps in understanding to fill in; again the interview is the opportunity. Convention says, however, that candidates do not ask selectors questions about their qualifications and ambitions, so they rely on clues and information conveyed unwittingly by interviewers.

The selector has the advantage of being able to structure the encounter as candidates expect to have to respond to initiatives, rather than take initiatives themselves. The first question is important in setting both the tone and direction of the exchange. Consider this very common opening question:

'Tell me, why have you applied for this job?'

Despite its extensive use, it is an ineffective way to begin, as it puts the candidate on the defensive, feeling the need to say the right thing, whether it is true or not. It is also a very difficult question to answer as the reasons for seeking a move are probably varied and hard to summarise. Also some of the common reasons – more money, dislike of present boss, easier travel, more holidays, more security – are the sort of reasons that candidates often feel inappropriate to mention, especially at the beginning, so they speak vaguely about challenge and unfulfilled potential. The interview thus gets underway as a form of verbal fencing, with the candidate wary of the next question. Now consider this, alternative, opening question:

'Could you give me a general outline of your present responsibilities?'

This has a number of advantages. First, the candidate will know the answer and his answer will be full of relevant, valuable information as it relates to what he can do rather than to his subjective evaluation of his motives. Secondly, it is not likely to be regarded with suspicion by the candidate trying to guess what the question is 'really after'. Thirdly, it will provide an admirable starting point as there will be a number of aspects that could usefully be developed further. This is not to suggest that all selection interviews should start with this particular question, but to suggest that questions that are about real facts and events are more sensible and useful than questions that require candidates to speculate or which make them uneasy.

A further development on the interview plan is to take a step back in time to an earlier point in the candidate's career and then move forward to the present, reviewing various developments on the way. This should be done with only one backwards move, if possible, as it is much easier to explain something and to understand something if it is examined as it developed rather than in reverse. Selectors get quite bewildered and candidates become incoherent when asked to explain their choice of degree, *then* their choice of 'A' levels, and *then* their 'O' level performance.

Selectors may find it useful to note key issues and check points. *Key issues* will be two or three features of information from the application form that stand out as needing clarification or elaboration. A particular episode of previous employment may need to be explored to see the range of responsibilities held, the difficulty of the circumstances or the number of subordinates. There may be key issues in the educational record, overseas experience or work in a specific industry that needs to be discussed. *Check points* are details that need to be confirmed, like grades in an examination or dates of appointment.

All of this has to be done in a framework and atmosphere that is not a sceptical cross examination of an evasive witness, but a meeting in which the candidates are *enabled* (not just allowed) to talk about themselves fully, frankly and with relevance to the vacant post. As long as the selector organises and leads the interview, the sort of information flow from the candidate will be much more useful and informative than if the candidate is required only to provide clipped replies to a list of predetermined questions.

DECIDING THE APPOINTMENT

The job of deciding who should be offered the appointment is simple to describe, but less easy to accomplish. It involves deciding first whether there is a good match between the person being considered and the job that has to be done, and secondly whether there is a good match between the group of people among whom the work will be done and the person being considered.

The first of these decisions is the more straightforward and can be based on the self-interest of the candidate, who will not want to get into a job he cannot do, and on the systematic matching by the selector of the job description and candidate specification on the one hand and the information obtained about the candidate on the other. A systematic approach on the basis of good documentation should decide whether someone is appointable or not. The best known aids to this type of decision-making are those of Rodger (1952) and Fraser (1978).

Deciding whether or not the candidate would fit socially is more problematic as it raises all the risks of appointing only 'clones', and the risk of being unlawfully discriminatory. Seear and Pearn (1983) provide comments on keeping within the law. There may be helpful advice from the personnel department if they have run personality tests, but the likelihood of a good match between the prospective new recruit and the other members of the working team is mainly a matter for the selector's judgement.

Consultation with team members can help. The more people who meet the candidate, the more opinions there will be about suitability and the greater willingness to make the match effective, even if individual opinions have been overruled. Information to the candidates can also help. The more frankly they have had problems and opportunities discussed with them, the more prepared they are to make their contribution to a constructive working relationship. Finally, a group of people working together apathetically, poorly organised and critical of their leaders, can undermine the effectiveness of even the most enthusiastic new recruit. A robust, well organised team of confident people who work well together with mutual respect will be able to assimilate some inappropriate appointees without serious trouble. Whereabouts in that spectrum does your team stand?

INDUCTION

Whether new team members come from outside the organisation or from within, the first few days and weeks are an important period of 'reciprocal moulding' as they are fitted into the structure and into the formal framework of relationships. Wise selections are made to work by sensible induction and even unwise selections can be made tolerable by hard work in the early stages of the working relationship.

SUMMARY PROPOSITIONS

20.1 Deciding the types of skill and experience required in a new appointment is more important than pondering the personal qualities of applicants.

20.2 In selection processes both the selector and the appointee are making choices and decisions; it is important to *both* that the other gets what he is looking for.

20.3 The selection interview is partly an initiation rite and the importance of the ritual elements should not be underestimated.

20.4 The most logical and helpful sequence for the selection interview is to review the biography of the candidate.

PUTTING IT INTO PRACTICE

Interaction Guide for the Selection Interview

1. Before the interview

Review	(a) Job description.
	(b) Candidate specification.
	(c) Application forms.
Note	(a) Key issues.
	(b) Check points.
Check	(a) Timetable.
	(b) Interview setting.

2. During the interview

Begin with	(a) Welcome.
	(b) Rapport, through the discussion of trivia, explaining procedure and adopting a relaxed, friendly manner.
Exchange information by	(a) Questioning, e.g. 'Could you give me an outline of your present duties?'.
	(b) Logical sequence, such as working chronologically through the application form.
	(c) Listening and observing.
	(d) Enabling the candidate to be frank and informative.
	(e) Remembering key issues and check points.

At all times	(a) Maintain rapport.
	(b) Keep notes.
	(c) Control the interview.

3. After the interview

Consider the	(a) By reviewing the job information.
person/job	(i) Job description.
match	(ii) Candidate specification.
	(b) By reviewing the candidate information.
	(i) Application form.
	(ii) Interview notes.
	(iii) Test scores (if any).
	(iv) References (if any).

Table 20.1 Recruitment code

Recruiters	Applicants
1. Job advertisements will state clearly the form of reply desired (for example, curriculum vita, completed application form) and any preference for handwritten applications	1. Advertisements will be answered in the way requested (for example, telephone for application form, provide brief details, send curriculum vitae, etc.)
2. An acknowledgement or reply will be made promptly to each applicant by the employing organization or its agent	2. Appointments and other arrangements will be kept, or the recruiter will be informed promptly if the candidate discovers an agreed meeting cannot take place
3. Candidates will be informed of the progress of the selection procedure, what this will be, the time likely to be involved and the policy regarding expenses	3. The recruiter will be informed as soon as a candidate decides not to proceed with the application
4. Detailed personal information (for example, religion, medical history, place of birth, family background, etc.) will not be asked for unless and until it is relevant to the selection process	4. Only accurate information will be given in applications and in reply to recruiter's questions
5. Before applying for references, potential employers will secure the permission of the applicant	5. Information given by a prospective employer will be treated as confidential, if so requested
6. Applications will be treated as confidential	

Taken from *The IPM Recruitment Code*, Institute of Personnel Management, London, August 1980.

    (c) Deciding whether there is a good match or not, and the significant of any 'poor fitting'.

Consider the person/group match
(a) By reviewing results of personality tests (if any).
(b) By consulting with team members.
(c) Guard against unlawful discrimination.

Decide
(a) To whom the job offer should be made.
(b) The terms of the offer.

Notify
(After job offer has been accepted) the unsuccessful candidates.

Drill for recruitment

After extensive consultation, the Institute of Personnel Management published a Recruitment Code in 1980, listing obligations for both recruiters and applicants (see Table 20.1).

Drill for selection decisions

The five-fold framework for selection decisions shown in Table 20.2 was

Table 20.2 Framework for selection decisions

Categories of personal qualities	Names of candidates				
	Adams	Brown	Clark	Davis	Evans
1. *Impact on others*, or the kind of response an individual's appearance, speech and manner calls out from others					
2. *Qualifications and experience*, or the knowledge and skill different types of work require					
3. *Innate abilities*, or how quickly and accurately an individual's mind works					
4. *Motivation*, or the kind of work that appeals to an individual and how much effort he is prepared to apply to it					
5. *Emotional adjustment*, or the amount of stress involved in living and working with other people					

(Based on Fraser, J.M., *Employment Interviewing*, (5th ed.), Macdonald & Evans, 1978)

devised by John Munro Fraser. It is used extensively in companies as a basis for selecting between candidates.

For each candidate score A, B, C, D or E in each box, with A indicating much above average and E indicating much below average for the category. The selector uses this as a way of organising thinking about candidates and then weighs the significance of the scores for the particular vacancy.

REFERENCES

Fraser, J.M., *Employment Interviewing*, 5th edn, Macdonald & Evans, London, 1978.

Mumford, E., 'Job satisfaction: a method of analysis', *Personnel Review*, Summer, 1972.

Rodger, A., *The Seven Point Plan*, Paper No. 1, National Institute of Industrial Psychology, London, 1952.

Schein, E.H., *Organisational Psychology*, 3rd edn, Prentice Hall, Englewood Cliffs, New Jersey, 1979.

Seear, N. and Pearn, M., 'Selection within the law', in Ungerson, 1983 (see below).

Torrington, D.P., and Hall, L.A., *Personnel Management; A New Approach*, Prentice Hall International, Hemel Hempstead, 1987.

Tyson, S. and York, A., *Personnel Management Made Simple*, Heinemann, London, 1982.

Ungerson, B., *Recruitment Handbook*, 3rd edn, Gower, Aldershot, 1983.

21

PERFORMANCE APPRAISAL

When children are at school their performance is monitored and reported upon. Week by week marks out of ten are written in the margins of exercise books, already sprinkled with ticks and crosses. Comments are made about the exercise which has been completed, pointing out any errors and emphasising what has been done well. At the end of each term or school year the general judgement of the teacher on the progress of the child is compressed into a few sentences on the school report. These regularly reported judgements are regarded as essential by the recipients as they give clues to the perennial question: 'How am I getting on?'

When children start work, the reporting stops. It may continue in a different form during apprenticeship or similar initial training, but once the rudiments of the job are learned, feedback on the quality of performance is usually occasional, accidental and ill-considered, especially where there is not an obvious unit of production to be completed. Also there are not the same milestones through the year; life just goes on.

Although we are usually glad to leave school and school reports behind, we still hanker after feedback on our performance in order to feel secure, to have a sense of progress and to enjoy praise. It is only the fear of bad news that makes us uncertain.

In some jobs the 'report' is easily available. The barrister wins or loses a case, the salesman gets a repeat order or sees new business moving to competitors, waiters and waitresses experience the direct response of their customers, possibly reinforced by a tip. Others have a clear quota of work to do, and its completion indicates success. The coach driver finishes the journey, the chambermaid completes the designated number of bedrooms that have to be prepared, a magazine editor completes an edition. But satisfactory completion of the assignment does not answer such questions as 'Could I do better?' 'How?' 'Can I look for promotion?' 'What do I have to do to achieve it?' Also most of those in managerial, administrative and clerical jobs do not even have the satisfaction of regularly completing a quota of work. Many people in such positions provide substitute goals for themselves, so that when the goal is reached they can enjoy the satisfaction of achievement that the continuous nature of their duties denies them. An example is clearing the in-tray. This may provide satisfaction, but is it an appropriate yardstick of effectiveness?

Performance appraisal is intended to overcome the lack of all that is involved in the progress checking system of school examinations and reports: it is intended to provide milestones, feedback, guidance and monitoring. Unfortunately it frequently fails, for reasons we shall see shortly. Readers who have experience of performance appraisal may regard it as little more than an administrative burden placed upon them by the personnel department. Despite this the idea of performance appraisal remains attractive. Hilaire Belloc produced the aphorism 'If a thing is worth doing, it is worth doing badly' and this is a helpful way of considering schemes designed to appraise working performance. The potential advantages are so great that it is worth always trying to make it work, no matter how often the scheme falls short of the thoroughness and fairness that advocates regard as essential. In this chapter we shall not prescribe a system, but will set out to explain the problems and opportunities, the methods that can be deployed and the part that individual managers can play.

TWO APPROACHES TO APPRAISAL

There are two broad approaches to appraisal: the *control approach* and the *personal approach*. The first is the most common, but the second is gaining popularity. Increasingly appraisal schemes have elements of both approaches, but describing them as polar opposites helps to illustrate the key elements.

The control approach starts with an expression of opinion by someone representing the view of controlling, responsible authority in saying something like this:

> We must stimulate effective performance and develop potential, set targets to be achieved, reward above-average achievement and ensure that promotion is based on sound criteria.

That type of initiative is almost always resisted by people acting collectively, despite its spacious appeal. It seems like an inoffensive objective, yet the reaction of those to be appraised will be apprehensive as anxious eyes scan the job ads. Union conferences are full of outrage and individuals collectively assert their feelings of insecurity. This is because people construe the message in a way that is seldom intended: something like this.

They will put pressure on poor performers so that they improve or leave. They will also make sure that people do what they're told and we will all be vulnerable to individual managerial whim and prejudice, losing a bit more control over our individual destiny.

This approach works best when there are clear and specific targets for people to reach, within an organisational culture that emphasises competition. There are considerable problems, like who sets the standards and who makes the judgements? How are the judgements, by different appraisers of different appraisees, made consistent? But it is still potentially useful as a system of keeping records and providing a framework for career development that is an improvement on references and panel interviews. It works best in bureaucratic organisations and the emphasis is on filling in forms.

The personal approach starts with a question in the mind of the individual job holder.

> I am not sure whether I am doing a good job or not. I would like to find ways of doing the job better, if I can, and I would like to clarify and improve my career prospects.

This question is addressed *by* the job holder *to* the job holder. It is not asking to be judged, but seeking to find someone with whom to talk through plans, progress, hopes and fears. Who can help me come to terms with my limitations and understand my mistakes? Where can I find someone with the experience and wisdom to discuss my performance with me so that I can shape it, building on my strengths to improve the fit between what I can contribute and what the organisation needs from me?

This approach works best with people who are professionally competent and self-assured, so that they can generate constructive criticism in discussion with a peer, or in protégé/mentor situations, where there is high mutual respect.

This, of course, is like the crock of gold at the end of the rainbow: very elusive, yet what we all want in all areas of our life. When our children are in trouble, when we don't know whether to move house or not, which car to buy or where to go on holiday, we want to talk the matter through with someone who has expertise and empathy, knowing that we have to decide – even when we wish someone else would decide for us – because we control our own destinies:

There is a view read between the lines of that by those in authority, which is something like this.

> This leads to people doing what they want to do rather than what they should be doing. There is no co-ordination, no comparison and no satisfactory management control.

This approach tends to confront issues and produces searching analysis as well as impacting directly and constructively on performance. It requires high trust, engenders loyalty (which can become dependence) and stimulates initiative. The emphasis is on the face to face discussion rather than on form-filling.

The benefits of this view can be enormous but there are two problems, first the lack of systematic reporting and secondly where are the paragons in whom you can trust?

The bulk of this chapter is written from the standpoint of the first of these two approaches, as it is much more common, but we have drawn the contrast at the beginning so that the reader can have an alternative approach in mind as we set out the stages.

The two essential elements of appraisal are *judgement* and *reporting*. The performance is not simply being measured, as in the completion of a work quota, it is being judged. This obviously involves discretion, worry about bias and the possibility of being quite wrong. This judgement is not, however, made in isolation. It has not only to be made, but also passed on to one or more other people in such a way that the other(s) understand what is intended and take action on it. Those devising performance appraisal schemes devote most of their energies to finding ways of making the judgements as systematic as possible and the reporting as consistent as possible between different appraisers.

Our working definition of performance appraisal is therefore: *The process of judging a person's performance and reporting that judgement.*

ORGANISATIONAL PURPOSES AND PROBLEMS IN APPRAISING PERFORMANCE

Why do organisations seek to appraise the performance of organisation members?

1. *Social Control.* It is first a method of shoring up the hierarchy, confirming the authority of those supervising the activities of others, and sustaining the dependence of subordinates within the cohesive structure of the organisation. 'Big brother is watching you.'
2. *Human resource considerations.* The second consideration is that of maximising the use of human resources. The abilities and energies of employees are an input to the organisational processes, and there is a logical argument for monitoring the performance to see whether the resources are being effectively deployed.
3. *Training.* If employees are to develop their skills and their contribution, they will require periodic training. Appraisal can identify the training that individuals need.
4. *Promotion.* Organisations need regularly to move employees up the hierarchy or across it, and occasionally down. Appraisal can aid the

decision-making involved in determining who goes where, as it can keep up to date knowledge that is held about employee's skills, experience and aspirations. In some large organisations, like the armed services and a number of multi-national corporations, career movements are frequent and involve a regular use of annual appraisals.

5. *Planning*. Associated with promotion considerations are those of preparing for future manpower requirements. Theoretically the regular appraisal process can feed into a manpower inventory, making it possible to pinpoint future skill shortages and to prepare succession plans.

Review Topic 21.1

Consider the five purposes of performance appraisal cited here: social control, human resource considerations, training, promotion and planning.
Are there alternative methods of achieving any of these that would be better than performance appraisal?

Problems

The problems encountered in running schemes of appraisal are formidable, despite constant attempts to build bigger and better schemes that cannot possibly fail.

1. *Paperwork*. Systems always involve a lot of paperwork and documentation which is disliked by the managers who have to carry out the appraisals. There is no escape from the documentation, as an essential feature of appraisal is reporting and schemes invariably include attempts to make both the judgements and the reporting consistent between different appraisers. This involves forms and detailed instructions.

2. *Formality*. The forms and the general paraphernalia introduce an inhibiting feature into the everyday working relationships between managers and their subordinates, who dislike the idea of formal evaluation and prefer a more relaxed, easy-going basis to their working relationship. Reverting to the analogy of the schoolteacher which began this chapter, there is not the same social distance between managers and their subordinates as there is between teachers and their pupils, and managers do not so readily accept the idea of their own responsibility for developing the careers and performances of their subordinates. Performance appraisal thus becomes a burdensome extra to the manager. To the teacher it is burdensome, but central. Managers usually argue that they provide regular, informal performance feedback and evaluation hour-by-hour in the superior/subordinate relationship, so that form filling is irrelevant. This conveniently ignores the benefit of thinking out a

considered view of the whole working performance rather than pointing out errors when they occur. It also does not take account of providing the counselling and training aspects of feedback to the person appraised, which are only likely to register when there is a serious discussion about performance.

3. *Outcomes are ignored.* Managers will not stick with their judgements, so if it is agreed that Ms A should have six months' training elsewhere, the manager may still not find time to send the person. Promotion decisions often are inconsistent with the results of the most recent appraisal, in that the most appropriate person, according to the appraisal forms, is not the one chosen for promotion. This may be due to the promotion decision being irrational, or a need to maintain a necessary political balance by advancing someone's protégé, or of experience and judgement overriding the dictates of the system.

4. *Performance is measured by proxy.* Performance appraisal is used in situations where performance cannot be readily measured, so proxies for performance are often measured instead.

> It may be difficult for me to determine if you are effective at your job; however, I can tell if you are at work on time, if you look busy, if you are pleasant and agreeable, or if you respect authority. While these characteristics may or may not have a relationship to performance, they are frequently easier to measure than performance per se. So, what we often find in organizations is the use of one or more proxies for performance rather than actual measures of performance. The use of proxies by managers, especially inadequate ones, can produce considerable dysfunctional behavior among employees. However, this does not stop managers from using them. (Robbins, 1978, page 209)

5. *The 'just above average' syndrome.* The appraisal carries either an explicit or implicit statement about the general ability and acceptability of the person appraised. Designers of appraisal systems go to great lengths to force appraisers to provide a range of judgements, but there is great reluctance to tell anyone that they are not doing well enough, or to put 'black marks' on paper. There is also a reluctance to tell people that they are outstanding, as this raises expectations that may not be satisfied. There is thus a tendency for most people appraised to be judged as comfortably above average. There is then no demand for remedial action by poor performers and no problem about high flyers asking for more money. The best that this achieves is to prevent the scheme causing too much trouble: the high flyers are frustrated through lack of recognition and the under-achievers leap enthusiastically to the conclusion that they are doing just the right thing.

The unwillingness of managers to face up to unpopular judgements is not because they lack moral fibre or powers of judgement. They are concerned that it will destroy the working relationship between them and the subordinate hearing the bad news, and this is compounded by the preference for informality. A formal structure enables you to be critical. Without that structure adverse criticism is likely to develop into recriminations and vituperation, especially when it is judgement that is being deployed rather than measurement.

6. *Incomplete coverage.* For appraisal schemes to be fair they have to be applied to all employees in a particular cadre, and for schemes to be effective they have to be seen as fair. In operation most schemes fail to achieve complete coverage. In schemes we have looked at, the completion rate has been between 50 and 75 per cent in many cases. This can produce strange side effects and reinforces some of the other problems mentioned so that the scheme is regarded as an administrative burden, dreamed up by the personnel people to give themselves something to do.

Ron Barnes is twenty-five, employed at the British headquarters of a multi-national company based in New York. He has been with the company two years and is a marketing specialist. His main career objective in the short-term is to get 'off reports'; that is he will no longer have an annual appraisal. This is an indication that one has risen above the everyday ranks of managers and administrative staff and been 'noted' for the future. This is a completely unofficial move, but has become established as one of the ways in which senior managers assert their authority and control by undermining aspects of the system that keeps them in power.

Jean Whitehorn is a member of the same company and feels that she is not making progress, but cannot figure out why that should be. Last year all her immediate colleagues had appraisals completed, but she was left out. She asked her immediate manager who explained that 'he had not got round to it' but would do it as soon as he could. He was then suddenly transferred to Rome, so Jean enquired of the management development officer who told her that her erstwhile manager had declined to complete an appraisal on her because 'she wasn't going anywhere'.

Another aspect of complete coverage being lost is in the decay of schemes. Enthusiasts with their careers at stake may succeed in bullying all colleagues to complete appraisals once or even twice, only to be succeeded by someone seeking to try appraisal in a different way and gaining the approval of colleagues by leaving the existing scheme in abeyance for the time being. However, schemes only begin to pay off when they become an established part of the way the organisation functions. Altering them can be as damaging as digging up a plant to see if it is growing.

7. *Ill-informed appraisers and context problems.* A prerequisite for sound appraisal is knowledge by the appraiser of the performance that is being

appraised. Without safeguards, managers may be asked, because of their rank, to appraise members of the organisation whose work they do not know. Alternatively they may be unduly influenced by recent events which are clear in their minds. A trainee health visitor was doing very well until she dropped a baby. The baby was not unduly concerned and passed the matter off with a cynical cough and a weary shake of the head, but all the members of the general public and the nursing profession in the vicinity had a topic of discussion that kept them going for days. 'Did you hear about the trainee who dropped the baby . . . ?' Her end-of-training performance review took place just over one week later and she was asked to repeat the final phase of her training.

The problem of context is how one disentangles individual performance from its context, especially if the scheme is one based on setting objectives.

PERFORMANCE APPRAISAL AND THE INDIVIDUAL EMPLOYEE

Although employees may often contemplate performance appraisal with misgivings, this is usually no more than the type of mixture of feelings that we contemplate on visiting the dentist: we desire the outcome of a 'good report' and helpful guidance, but dread the possibility of bad news. Here are some of the benefits for the individual:

1. *Ability is enhanced.* The person appraised can become a more able performer by emphasising strengths and understanding what changes are needed.
2. *Motivation.* The reassurance and confirmation of encouraging appraisal can increase the level of enthusiasm about, and commitment to, the job that is done.
3. *Career objectives.* In considering career moves and job changes, individuals seek guidance and indicators in making decisions on what to do and where to aim. Performance appraisal can clarify intentions and underpin the confidence needed to take risks or to aim high. It can also temper aspiration to make career objectives more realistic.
4. *Career development.* There should be the advantage for individuals from performance appraisal that they will not only clarify career objectives but also be assisted in reaching those objectives by the outcome of the appraisal process: training will be arranged, moves offered and counselling given.

Review Topic 21.2

1. **For an organisation that you know, write notes of a *management* argument against performance appraisal.**

2. **For the same organisation write notes of a union or employee argument against performance appraisal.**
3. **Write notes that seek to satisfy both sets of reservations.**
4. **Repeat the exercise, but place it in a quite different organisational context.**

Against these advantages, there are the problems that have been referred to already. Subordinates are as inhibited by formality as their managers, bad news is demoralising and will probably be fended off. Also trade unions tend to resist performance appraisal as it breaks down the collective interests of employees, by 'dividing man from man'.

METHODS OF APPRAISAL

Phil Long (1986) reviewed the practice of performance appraisal in 306 organisations and analysed the various approaches used. Table 21.1 summarises the methods in use in the 247 of those organisations that provided copies of their forms; most of them used more than one method.

This table provides us with a useful summary of methods to consider.

Management by objectives. This, or some variant of appraising against results, is now the most popular form of appraisal used after being first advocated by two of the best-known publicists in American management; Drucker in 1955 and McGregor in 1960. The basis of the system is simply to agree, between appraiser and appraisee, a set of verifiable objectives to be achieved over a predetermined future period. By emphasising preset and jointly-agreed targets, the focus is on performance results rather than personality factors. It is less susceptible to appraiser bias or diffidence and less likely to outrage the appraisee. Glueck provides an example of an MBO evaluation report (see Table 21.2).

Table 21.1 Methods of performance appraisal in use

Types of system	Number	Percentage
Results orientated	155	63
Job behaviour oriented	128	52
Personality trait rating	72	29
Alphabetical/numerical rating	68	28
Narrative – free essay	6	2
Narrative – controlled written	108	44
Forced distribution global rating	24	10

(Based on Long, 1986, page 27.)

Table 21.2 MBO evaluation report for salesperson

Objectives set	Period objective	Accomplish-ments	Variance
1. Number of sales calls	100	104	+4%
2. Number of new customers contacted	20	18	−10%
3. Number of wholesalers stocking new product 117	30	30	0%
4. Sales of product 12	10,000	9,750	−2.5%
5. Sales of product 17	17,000	18,700	+10%
6. Customer complaints/service calls	35	11	−84%
7. Number of sales correspondence courses successfully completed	4	2	−50%
8. Number of sales reports in home office within 1 day of end of month	12	10	−16.6%

(From Glueck, 1979, page 217)

This has the appearance of precision and all is performance without any subjective assessment of personality, but to what extent are these achievements and failures absolute and unequivocal? Is the relative success of 5 more important than the apparent failure of 4? The figures only become significant in context, so that the method provides a basis for discussion, it does not provide a neat yardstick of success and failure. This method now is more widely used than all the others, but it can only centre on what can be made reasonably precise and takes no account of circumstances beyond the control of the person appraised.

Job behaviour-oriented. In an attempt to make appraisal more precise and discriminating, some schemes are based on critical incidents which the supervisor is asked to identify over the assessment period as indicating satisfactory or unsatisfactory performance. While being appraised the appraisee has a note kept of each time such a critical incident occurs and at the end of the period the appraiser bases his judgement on the number of satisfactory and unsatisfactory critical incidents. For example, a scheme developed in the public sector had the following critical incidents for relations with members of the public: 'Always keeps clients waiting ten minutes, even when not busy'; 'Often phones other departments for a client who has come to the wrong place.'

This can then be developed into Behaviourally Anchored Rating Scales (BARS) by giving a grading to each critical incident. Although popular among some psychologists because of its potential for precision and accuracy, it has not yet been widely adopted. One great advantage is that in discussions between appraiser and appraisee exchanges can be based on what has actually happened instead of on value judgements. A practical account of the development and use of BARS is in Fogli *et al.* (1971). One development of the method departs from the use of behaviours specific to a job and uses ten standard dimensions: interpersonal relationships, organising and planning, reaction to problems, reliability, communicating, adaptability, growth, productivity, quality of work, and teaching (Goodale and Burke, 1975). This is not a simple reversion to rating, but a move in that direction with the discipline of critical incidents and rating scales.

Alphabetical/numerical rating. There are various methods of rating, but the basis is that the appraiser is presented with a series of performance factors, such as job knowledge, versatility, analytical ability and so on. Each of these is rated with a number or letter in a scale: 1 to 7 or A to E, with A being regarded as outstanding and E as unsatisfactory. In a way it is this sort of rating that has given performance appraisal a bad name and its use has declined sharply. A survey for BIM in 1967 showed this as being the most popular method at that time.

Personality trait rating. This is similar to the above rating method except that it is the person rather than the performance that is judged. Schemes use such factors as drive, initiative, judgement and reliability.

Narrative. This is most similar to the school report and is still used extensively in the armed forces, although in decline elsewhere. The appraiser is asked to write a pen portrait of the person appraised. It has the main drawbacks of the great difficulty of comparing one pen portrait with another and the dependence on the rare skill of pen portrait writing.

Self-rating. This is a growing technique in which the person appraised evaluates his own performance and indicates how he would like to see his job and career develop. So far this is usually used as well as, and not as a substitute for, appraisal by an organisational superior.

CONDUCT OF THE APPRAISAL AND ACCESS TO THE OUTCOMES

Appraisals are usually carried out by managers about their immediate subordinates, but there are other possibilities. Appraisal could be done by *a group of superiors*, as is the practice in some parts of the Civil Service. It depersonalises the process, reduces the likelihood of bias and maintains the easy working relationship between the appraisee and the immediate superior ('. . . I did the best I could, old man, but X swayed the meeting that afternoon . . .'). There may also be more information available about the performance.

Peer rating. This is a very rare practice and requires a high degree of trust and integration in the social group. *Rating by subordinates* is very logical but very rare, although it is often used informally as part of the appraisal process ('. . . one or two of the people in the department have mentioned to me in passing – no names: no pack drill – that you can be a bit heavy-handed sometimes with the younger ones . . .').

An example of formal rating by subordinates that we found was in a research department of a large chemical company. The graduate researchers reported on their section manager's annual assessment form about such matters as generation of ideas, resourcing of development work and encouragement of work. These comments were seen by the section manager's superior.

Outsiders. These can be used either by inviting in someone from outside the organisation completely as an unbiased third party, or by using an internal specialist without departmental affiliation, such as a management development advisor, who appraises everyone. There are obvious snags about this as the appraiser can only have limited knowledge about what performance has been achieved, and will therefore have to base the appraisal either on some form of personality trait assessment or on the grievances of the people appraised, or on both. It is the sort of strategy that could be used as a single event in an organisation where there had been serious dissatisfaction and there was a need to review the career situation with all individuals in a particular cadre as a preliminary to reorganisation or similar initiative. It is not common as a regular event, although the development of *assessment centres* (see Stewart and Stewart, 1981) is a specialised method of taking the whole process of career development out of the line.

A closed system of appraisal is one where appraisals are made and reported without the person appraised knowing what has been said. This removes some of the inhibitions which worry managers making appraisals, as they have not got to justify their comments to the person about whom they are made and do not jeopardise their comfortable working relationships. The obvious drawbacks are that those appraised are full of suspicion, possibly stooping to low tactics to ascertain the contents of their reports. More importantly, the person appraised is denied the advice that might improve the performance. This mode is now unusual, but disclosing the contents also has problems. It makes for 'safe', bland appraisals or for simple avoidance – remember Jean Whitehorn. The approach can be to tell the appraisee what is said, discussing what the report should be and agreeing the wording.

What happens to the appraisals when they are complete? It is a pity if this is regarded as of overwhelming importance, as the most valuable aspect of the procedure is the process of appraisal itself. In that process the two people most concerned with the working performance – the performer and the person immediately responsible for the performance – think about, understand and review what has been happening. That can increase mutual understanding, help to set realistic future targets, develop ability, enhance motivation and meet most of the other payoffs that performance appraisal is supposed to deliver. The next destination of the report is still important for various reasons. Without a destination for the report, the report is less likely to be written and the appraisal unlikely to be carried out. Some organisations use appraisal for career progression organised from a central staffing section and in some there is a centralised training initiative where appraisal reports are used to suggest training and development strategies for employees.

APPRAISAL INTERVIEWING

So far the purpose of this chapter has been to work through the reasons individual managers may decide to participate in a system of appraisal run in the organisation of which they are a part, together with an explanation of the appraisal techniques encountered and the operational problems. This final section deals with an aspect that is an integral part of most organisation-wide schemes, but which can also be used by managers individually when there is no scheme: appraisal interviewing.

This form of interview is not easy to conduct. Randell (1984) conducted a survey in a large pharmaceuticals company and found that managers had difficulty in interpreting the factors contributing to a person's overall performance, such as intelligence and life goals; they were not able to pursue these in interview and did not agree firm recommendations and actions towards improvement. Long describes a widespread reluctance:

> Although most managers acquire a good deal of experience in interviewing techniques during the course of the everyday activities, the performance review discussion still tends to be approached with as much circumspection by the reviewer as by the reviewed. (1986, page 38)

Norman Maier (1976) describes three alternative approaches that are used for this type of interview.

1. *Tell and sell*. The role of the interviewer is that of judge, using the interview to tell the appraisee the outcome of the appraisal and the need to improve. This method is seldom used in appraisals of managers but

can be appropriate for appraisees who have high respect for the appraiser and are insufficiently experienced to have developed self-confidence and the capacity to analyse their own performance.

2. *Tell and listen.* This is a modification of tell and sell. The appraiser is still in the role of judge and is passing on the outcome of an appraisal that has already been completed, but he then elicits the appraisee's reactions, including resentment and disappointment, and this may lead to a change in the evaluation as well as enabling the two to have a reasonably frank exchange.

3. *Problem-solving.* This is a quite different mode of interview. The focus is not the judgement of the appraiser but the growth and development of the person appraised, with the appraiser acting as helper rather than judge. The assumption is that discussing job problems leads to improved performance in that job, and the more skilful the appraiser, the greater the change and improvement that will take place. There is still the need for follow-up and there are problems if the appraisee lacks ideas or has ideas that do not fit in with what the appraiser regards as appropriate. It is important not to be over-optimistic about problem-solving, which sounds ideal. The appraiser will normally be in a hierarchically superior position to the appraisee and this could inhibit the type of candid exchanges that this style of interviewing requires. Also it requires the appraisee to be reasonably confident, secure and knowledgeable about possibilities. If all circumstances are favourable, it is the most appropriate for the appraisal of managers and an outline is given later in this chapter.

PERFORMANCE APPRAISAL AND THE MANAGER

As an organisation-wide administrative system, performance appraisal has a bad name because of its extensive documentation, the time it takes and the way in which the system is seen to rule the participants. Despite the difficulties, the potential advantages are so great that attempts will continue to improve schemes and make them work. Individual managers can run their own, do-it-yourself appraisals of their team members if there is no overarching scheme in which to participate.

There will be a need for preparation, the development of interviewing skill, some record of what has happened and what is to be done, and a willingness to cope with some unwelcome or problematical outcomes. Appraisal interviews of the problem-solving kind are almost certain to produce some improvement, but appraisal of any sort only becomes really worthwhile when it is established and regular, so that those involved see it as a necessary part of their contract with the organisation.

SUMMARY PROPOSITIONS

21.1 Performance appraisal is used in working situations where the achievement of satisfactory performance is not obvious from the nature of the task, and it is the process of judging a person's performance and reporting that judgement.

21.2 Schemes of organisation-wide performance appraisal frequently break down in practice because appraisers dislike the discipline and the amount of work involved, and because appraisees may be apprehensive about the outcome.

21.3 The most widely used current schemes of appraisal are those where the appraisal is related to results achieved. Methods incorporating an element of self-rating by the appraisee are gaining popularity.

21.4 Interviewing is a central feature of appraisal and the problem-solving approach is the most effective, providing that both appraiser and appraisee have the skill and ability to handle this mode.

21.5 Individual managers can carry out performance appraisal among members of their own teams even if there is not an organisation-wide scheme in which to participate, but lasting benefits will only come from making appraisals a regular and thorough feature of the working relationship.

PUTTING IT INTO PRACTICE

Interaction guide for the appraisal interview

1. Before the interview

- Brief appraisee on purpose and form of interview, possibly asking him to complete a self-analysis questionnaire in readiness.
- Review reports, records or other sources of memory-jogging regarding appraisee performance in the period under review.
- Check previous appraisal and outcomes.

2. During the interview

- Begin with rapport, to calm down the appraisee (and the appraiser) who may be nervous due to the significance of the interview. Explain how interview is to be run, reiterating points made in pre-interview briefing.

Table 21.3 A pro-forma worksheet for objectives

Prepared by (appraiser) and (appraisee)
Date of objective-setting ....Date of review ....

Job objectives	Per cent of work time	Measure of results	Target	Date	Results	Date

- Review main facts about performance, without expressing opinion about the facts, but merely summarising as mutual reminder.
- Encourage aspects of performance that are clearly satisfactory, mention them and comment favourably.
- Ask for statement from appraisee about queries or problems, and a statement from appraisee about any dissatisfactions.
  (Talk these out fully with appraisee, adding the appraiser's perspective and opinion *on those points*. Some will be talked out as baseless, some will be seen as less drastic than they first seemed, and some will be confirmed as problems needing attention.)
- Offer comments from appraiser about aspects of performance that he does not regard as satisfactory, but which have not already been mentioned.

- Agree action to be taken – by appraiser and appraisee – to improve future performance and satisfaction.

3. *After the interview*
- Record problems and agreed action.
- Take action on points requiring appraiser action.
- File interview notes for later review.

Drill for management by objectives

Table 21.3 gives an example of a pro-forma work sheet for setting and reviewing objectives:

REFERENCES

Drucker, P.F., *The Practice of Management*, Heinemann, London, 1955.

Fogli, L., Hulin, C.L. and Blood, M.R., 'Development of first-level behavioural job criteria', *Journal of Applied Psychology*, vol. 55, 1971, pages 3–8.

Glueck, W.F., *Foundations of Personnel*, Business Publications, Dallas, Texas, 1979.

Goodale, J. and Burke, R., 'BARS need not be job specific', *Journal of Applied Psychology*, vol. 60, 1975, pages 389–91.

Long, P., *Performance Appraisal Revisited*, Institute of Personnel Management, London, 1986.

MacGregor, D., 'An uneasy look at performance appraisal', *Harvard Business Review*, 1972.

Maier, N.R.F., *The Appraisal Interview: Three Basic Approaches*, University Associates, La Jolla, Calif., 1976.

Randall, G.A., Packard, P.M.A., Shaw, R.L. and Slater, A.J., *Staff Appraisal*, Institute of Personnel Management, London, 1984.

Robbins, S.P., *Personnel: The Management of Human Resources*, Prentice Hall, Englewood Cliffs, New Jersey, 1978.

Stewart, A. and Stewart, V., *Tomorrow's Managers Today*, 2nd edn, Institute of Personnel Management, London, 1981.

PART V

PERFORMANCE MONITORING AND FINANCIAL CONTROL

All management work has within it a control feature. Is the initiative working? Is it costing more or less than we anticipated? Where are we being effective and where are we failing? What information do we need to plan our next initiative?

The core requirement for control is information and the sophistication of management information systems is growing rapidly. Within that information framework each department or section works to a budget and uses administrative procedures to implement and control activities.

The book concludes with a short review of future prospects for the professional manager.

22

MANAGEMENT INFORMATION SYSTEMS

The future of any organisation depends not only on the use made of that organisation's money, material, people and machines but also on the use it makes of information. Too often, however, the NETMA cry echoes around the corridors. NETMA, a phrase invented by the president of a large airline company, stands for No-one Ever Tells Me Anything. Sometimes it is our own fault for not asking the right questions, sometimes it is just a case of the right information not being in the right place at the right time. A well-designed management information system should help to lessen the NET-MA cries, as well as improving the planning, decision-making and controlling capacity of the organisation.

An organisation's information systems are its nerves, without which its operating and maintenance systems would not function. Most organisations have now set computers onto the task, for information technology has increased both the capacity and flexibility of information systems. Computer networks stretch laterally as well as vertically through an organisation, so that staff can access information in relation to other parts of the company independently from senior management.

Terry Lucey (1987, page 2) provides us with a useful definition of an MIS:

> A system to convert data from internal and external sources into information and to communicate that information, in an appropriate form, to managers at all levels in all functions to enable them to make timely and effective decisions for planning, directing and controlling the activities for which they are responsible.

THE NATURE OF INFORMATION

To have an understanding of MIS, it is important to have an understanding of the nature of information flow in organisations. Chaper 18, Organisational Communication, discusses the various formal and informal channels of communication in organisations. Informal information networks are flexible and ideally suited to catering for problems at a local level, so that informal and formal systems both have a contribution to make. Formal systems start off with data. However, data are not information, and information is not necessarily communication. 'Data is (sic) an amount of numeric or quantitative notions which needs to be coded, processed or interpreted in order to become qualitative concepts and ideas forming the basis of information. Even then', says Peter Drucker (1977), 'information is logical, rigid and impersonal – almost the complete opposite of the requirements for effective communication'. Computers issue vast amounts of data, but someone must have the responsibility for checking that they are not only producing useful information, but also that there is a carefully thought out and systematic creation of communication opportunities amongst the various users. The meaning of the information depends on the perceptions, expectations and rules established for its interpretation. The following example illustrates this. The lookout on the boat signals for dangerous rocks by pointing in an appropriate direction. Depending on the perception of the person steering the boat, the lookout could be pointing either to the rock, or in the direction which the boat must be steered to avoid the rock. The signal has a meaning and is information, but there is no reliable communication unless the rules for its interpretation are clear.

We rarely communicate as effectively as we think we do. There are factors such as perceptual bias, distortion of the message, lack of clarity, lack of trust, distance and status which act as blockages. Handy (1981, page 356) admits that, in view of all these blockages, 'it is perhaps worth admiring the fact that any sensible communication takes place at all'.

Levels of information

Bob Tricker, who has done much work on information management in organisations, also considers information to be at various levels (1982, Chapter 2):

(a) Basic data – raw data, facts and figures. These are the building blocks which contain the potential information, but which require processing.
(b) Information as message – aggregated and analysed data and reports. The needs of the potential recipient or user of the message are not identified since this level provides standard information for a multitude of users.
(c) Valuable information. The user derives meaning from the data, increases his/her knowledge, and reduces his/her uncertainty. The individual user's role and expectations are crucial to the meaning derived.

The message that a poll tax per head of population is to replace household rates will have a different meaning for an individual when he or she is a single young healthy wage earner living alone from when he or she is a parent of four young children.

Similarly, the organisation should guard against confusing reports with information. There is little use in providing far more sophisticated information systems and more reports if managers consequently feel less aware of what is going on than they did before.

Review Topic 22.1

'What I need is information and all they give me are reports.' (Tricker, 1982, page 20) How do we turn data into information?

The value of information

The value of information rests upon the results of decisions and actions based on that information. Data are costly to obtain, so that there is a cost/value trade-off, as shown in Fig. 22.1. Value is only acquired via information which is properly communicated and used. It should not be assumed that more information, in more detail and sooner, is always better. Decision-makers rarely have all the information they need, but at some point, as John Adair (1985, page 115) suggests, the search for more information is 'subject to the law of diminishing returns . . . the real limit is the point in a given situation where you judge that the cost in time and money of obtaining more information becomes too high'.

——————— Value derived from improved actions
based on the information

– – – – – – Costs of data handling and processing

Fig. 22.1 The cost and value of information.

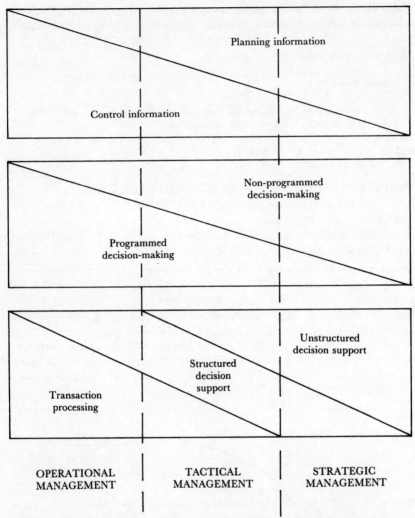

Fig. 22.2 Types of information required at different levels of management.

What makes information relevant

Lucey (1987, Chapter 2) provides us with a guide in the search for what constitutes useful and relevant information.

1. *Timely.* Information should arrive in time for it to be useful, and concerning periods of time which are relevant. Similarly, too frequent or too rapid information may be unnecessary and a waste of resource. For example, information regarding stock levels will probably be required at more immediate and frequent intervals than feedback on research progress.

Table 22.1 Different types of information for planning, control and decision-making

	Level of detail	Timescale	Coverage	Focus
Planning	Patterns and trends	Long time periods	Whole organisation	Insights into future
Control	Detail and precision but also trends	Short time periods	Specific functions or managers	Relating past results to targets
Decision-making	Detailed or broad as required	As appropriate	Everything potentially affected	Future changes

(Adapted from Lucey, 1987)

2. *Appropriate*. Firstly, energy should be put where it matters. Only in important areas should rigorous information be produced. If labour turnover is not deemed to be as critical as, say, a continued supply of fresh ideas into certain parts of the organisation, then information on turnover is inappropriate. Second, information requirements will be different at different levels in the hierarchy (see Fig. 22.2) and in different functions. Shop floor operators and sales staff will require different information from the works manager or the marketing director.

3. *Accurate and of adequate detail*. The level of accuracy must be relevant to the decision level involved. More detail does not always provide a more effective aid to decision-making. (See Chapter 7, Problem-solving and Decision-making.) If accurate detail is required, it must be reliable. Information should always relate to objectives, it must not convey trivial facts. Information to be used for long-term planning purposes will usually be less detailed, and it may be that absolute figures are less important than trends up or down. Table 22.1 shows the different characteristics of planning, control and decision-making information.

4. *Understandable*. Over-complicated information only confuses. The style and format presented to the user by the information designer must be such that energy is not wasted in repeatedly trying to work it all out.

5. *Operational*. Information should be directed towards action, and should be passed to those with authority and responsibility to do something with it, or to those with a legitimate interest. This should include office workers, supervisors, team briefing groups, quality circles, as well as senior managers.

Review Topic 22.2

Tricker has suggested that organisations risk 'paralysis by analysis' (1982, page 20). What can be done to avoid this?

Information and feedback

Information and feedback are inextricably linked. Managers should discuss plans and projects with their subordinates, report the bad news as well as the good, and provide information directly, honestly, and constantly. Beware of paper tigers and treat the organisation as a community of concerned adults, and feedback will follow feedback.

Information, provided in a systematic form, is therefore one of the most useful and powerful tools of which management can make use in the achievement of company objectives through the efforts of employees. One of Peters and Waterman's characteristic attributes of the excellent, innovative companies they studied in the late 1970s was the operation of a 'productivity through people' philosophy. Employees in these companies were all treated with respect and were each seen as a potential source of ideas. Their basic control mechanism was peer comparison – not of the insidious variety, but of the nature of the sharing of general objectives, values and information. Individual, team or unit results were available to and were frequently consulted by everyone throughout the organisation. Whether machine operators or field staff, people had access to confidential operating statistics, or revealing financial figures. 'Information is simply made available and people respond to it', they claimed. (Peters and Waterman, 1982, page 268.)

Indeed, the 1982 Employment Act places an obligation on companies to provide employees systematically with information on matters of concern to them, and to seek a common awareness amongst staff of factors affecting the performance of the company. The Industrial Society is a strong proponent of the practice of *team briefing*, where employees have decisions affecting their jobs or conditions of employment explained to them face to face by their immediate boss in a systematic communication drill, rather than in a memo from the director. At shopfloor level, information of local relevance should comprise at least two thirds of the information passed on the briefing session. Briefing sessions should have an individually prepared written brief, a briefing folder should be kept, and notes should be taken, in order that the passing on of items of information is not casually left to chance. The four main groups of subjects covered in briefing sessions concern the four P's – progress (how the section is doing), people (joiners, leavers, internal moves), policy (recruitment and training, safety, output and productivity, terms and conditions), and points for action (priorities in the coming period). See Garnett (1983) for more details of team briefing.

The passage of information is thus an essential part of the decentralisation of decision-making in organisations. An organisation can strengthen its lateral resources by moving the decision-making down to where the information exists, rather than taking information up to the point of decision. This will invariably result in conflict but, as Galbraith says,

(1977), this is a good thing since it results in a greater sharing of information, more contact with the problem, the voicing of preferences and the seeking of new alternatives. As we stated in Chapter 7, Problem-solving and decision-making, good quality information can lessen uncertainty.

There is, of course, an enormous potential for the abuse and manipulation of information in organisations, since its communication is seldom either totally objective or neutral. However, the danger of the immoral use of information is lessened if that information focuses on results – on the effect of actions rather than the effort put into them; that is, on effectiveness rather than on efficiency.

Information overload

Organisations with a high degree of uncertainty in what they do, either because of increased competition or technical change, diversification, the large division of labour and hence number of specialist departments, or an increase in performance standards, normally find they have to handle a vast amount of information in order to lessen that uncertainty. Computers especially have increased our capacity to generate information and there has been an information explosion. Overload can be avoided in various ways. Galbraith (1977) suggests that organisations can deliberately select one of various strategies to reduce information overload. These are as follows, and they fall into two groups.

1. Reduce the need for information processing through:
   (a) Seeking to lessen demands from the environment by managing, manoeuvring or influencing relationships with the environment (e.g. ensuring access to scarce resources, making use of media to influence the environment, seeking co-operation with others in the environment, searching for new environments).
   (b) Reducing performance levels and therefore the amount of information processing required.
   (c) Creating self-contained tasks, with a reduced division of labour and reduction of cross-functional specialists.
2. Increase capacity to process information by:
   (a) Investing in vertical information systems, for example by employing assistants, computers, etc, so that information is collected and redirected to appropriate places in the hierarchy.
   (b) Creating lateral resources, decentralising decision-making by allowing direct contact between people who can share problems, or by forming short-term teams or task forces to resolve issues via interdepartmental problem-solving.

Many of these strategies have a 'cost'. For example, with (e), greater amounts of management time has to be spent in group processes, and more integrating or liaising roles may be required. The organisation must, however, make a choice between these five. Not to decide, says Galbraith, is to fall back upon reduced performance levels, option (b), as a means of reducing information overload.

Review Topic 22.3

Drucker (1977, page 396) says 'An overload of information leads to information blackout. It does not enrich, but impoverishes.' How is overload avoided?

Restrictions in the knowledge market

In some organisations, there exists an almost complete absence of lateral communication systems and structures. People are totally absorbed with mending their own fences so that their peers in other parts of the company are irrelevant. There are various reasons why information is hoarded rather than shared. Rosabeth Moss Kanter, in her study of innovating companies, cites four groups likely to restrict the flow of information. Firstly, there are the 'time servers' who have virtually retired on the job and who neither receive nor seek information. Second, there are 'defensive cliques' who restrict information to prevent the threat of change. Thirdly, there are 'mutual-aid-and-comfort' groups, who are settled into a comfortable routine and resent their more ambitious colleagues. Finally, there are 'coalitions of the ambitious', who keep information in their own hands to monopolise power, (Kanter 1984). The opening up of the 'knowledge market' in organisations, where information is exchanged openly both through formal and informal channels and support is freely given, gives rise, as we have mentioned in Chapter 5, The management functions of the business, to 'airwaves for innovation'.

There also exists the fact that most managers, understandably, prefer to get their information from people rather than machines like computers. Stewart (1986) suggests that this is largely because most managers do not know how to make the best use of computers. There is a debate about whether those lower in the hierarchy who are now familiar with computers will continue to make use of them when they reach senior management, or whether computers can contribute little to top management. We would contend that Management Information Systems are of use, albeit a different kind of use, at all levels in the hierarchy, (See Fig. 22.2).

KEY PRINCIPLES OF MANAGEMENT INFORMATION SYSTEMS

Having described in some detail the nature of information flow in organisations, it is now appropriate to have a look at some of the key principles of

Management Information Systems. It is only when an understanding is gained of these issues that we can go on to examine practical steps concerning the design, implementation and operation of such systems. This section will look at the various types of information system and their purposes and we will examine specific uses that various parts of the organisation can make of them.

Types of information system

Management Information Systems did exist before computerisation, but more often than not it has been the introduction of computers into a company which has prompted an examination of the way information is handled. Now, an MIS being operated without the aid of information technology, even in the smallest of organisations, is highly unlikely, even inconceivable. There are various types of system which will be incorporated into a total MIS – and it is this combination of all the elements in a combined package which can potentially turn a random collection of functional data bases into a centralised information system. They can broadly be described as follows (adapted from Lucey 1987, Chapter 15).

1. Office support systems, such as electronic mail, word processing, micro-computers, VDUs and computer networks, which provide assistance with day-to-day office functions concerning data storage and reference, telecommunications, computing and text handling. We will not describe these in detail here but would comment that the transformation of office work by information technology is influencing the availability and type of information used by managers.
2. Data processing systems, such as accounts, payroll, production control, stock control, which record, process and report on day-to-day activities within the organisation. These types of systems were the first to make use of the power of the computer and they are the building blocks upon which an MIS is built.
3. Decision support systems, such as spreadsheets, forecasting techniques, decision models, linear programming, statistical analyses, which are intended to provide management with assistance in planning and decision-making. The user is able to interact with them and, unlike DP systems, managers develop and communicate with the systems them-selves via their own terminals. Such systems provide support for the manager – they do not replace his or her judgement. There is a large range of software packages available in this area, and new ones are being developed all the time.

More detail on all of these can be found in specialist texts on management information systems or information technology, e.g. Lucey (1987), Tricker (1982), or Rank Xerox (1982).

Review Topic 22.4

A decision support system is a co-ordinated collection of data, systems, tools and techniques by which an organisation gathers and interprets relevant information and turns it into a basis for action. Go to your local technical bookshop and find out how many 'off-the-shelf' software packages, for example, spreadsheets or decision models, are the subject of new user-guides. Are they mainly in the financial field, or the marketing field, or in other areas?

Purpose of information

It will be seen from the above that a management information system can provide information to assist with planning, control and decision-making at all the various levels in the organisation, whether operational, tactical control or strategic management. See Figs 22.2 and 22.3 for a reminder of how information requirements fit in with these classic conceptions of organisation and strategy.

Information for planning concerns the longer term direction of the organisation, aims and policies – the *strategy*; Information for controlling and evaluating is concerned with how to carry out the overall strategy – the *tactics*; Information for doing is that concerned with the day to day execution of activities and short term decisions – the *action*.

As stated before, the value of information must be judged against how useful the information is in planning, controlling or doing.

The use of MISs in different functions

In Chapter 5, The management functions of the business, we have described the four main elements of an organisation's activities as being Finance, Operations, Marketing and Personnel. A management information system will be able to connect all these activities in a networked system whereby information in a central data processing unit can be accessed by every part of the organisation, thus ensuring consistency in the treatment of historical, current and estimated data. The same data concerning, for example, sales figures over the past quarter may be used in the warehouse stock control system, fed into the financial control system, used by the graphic designer in the publications unit, called up on the public relations word processor, as well as being used in the marketing department. See Fig. 22.3 for a diagrammatic representation of data flow between different sections of a centralised manufacturing organisation.

The following gives some of the more specific areas of operation and application of an MIS in relation to particular functions within the company, mostly at the tactical, middle management level. It is probably worth at this point glancing back at the definition of an MIS set out at the beginning of this chapter.

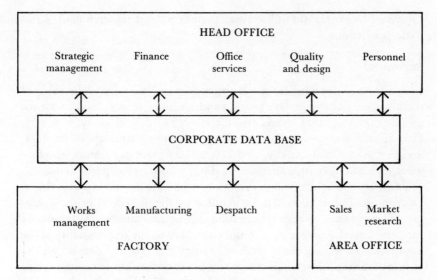

Fig. 22.3 Information network in a manufacturing organisation.

Finance

Aggregated information is supplied to other functions concerning costs and budgets, analyses of contribution and profitability, investment appraisal, profit forecasts and cash flow statements. Data input involves internally generated figures relating to production and operations, sales and marketing, and salaries and wages, and external figures regarding rates of inflation, price indices, government legislation and trade projections.

Production and operations

Information made available for operations control relating to distribution, warehousing, stock control, manufacturing, maintenance, forecasting and scheduling, and product design. Data concerns order quantities, demand levels, inventory levels, turn-round times, transport activity and costs, throughput levels, machine breakdown, work-in-progress figures, scrap rates.

Marketing

Information is produced mainly for use by management in relation to the progress of activities within marketing such as sales force management, orders and enquiries, advertising campaigns, market analyses, selling costs, credit control. Internal data used includes sales, despatch figures, call data, advertising costs and response figures, entertainment and travel expenses. External data utilised may include market research figures and trade predictions.

Personnel

Information is provided for use by management generally in the areas of recruitment, training, salary progression, promotion, age and experience profiling, employment trends and turnover, health and safety, pensions. Data used concerns employment data, training returns, appraisal data, accident statistics internally, and external employment trends, employment legislation, comparative salary data, pension fund performance.

There is, of course, often an overlap between the functions of the above. Distribution information may be handled by the marketing or the operations departments; salaries information may be generated by the finance or the personnel departments; material costs may be the responsibility of the production or the accounts sections. Sometimes this will depend on the nature of the business, the degree of autonomy of the different sections, and how much centralised planning and decision-making is performed. A useful MIS will ensure that information flows equally throughout the organisation, across functional boundaries, upwards and downwards, making information generate centrally available to those who need it, and incorporating local feedback into the system. There are many activities of an MIS that are not mentioned here, and new ones are being developed all the time.

Again, it should be remembered that the value of the information produced on an MIS is its effect on planning, decision-making and problem solving activities of the organisation. In general, information that is merely of casual interest is of little value, and just occupies time and space which would be better utilised elsewhere. Similarly, it must be born in mind that the information provided by an MIS is not a replacement of management judgement. Schumacher (1973, page 200) says 'The best decisions will still be based on the judgement of mature non-electronic brains possessed by men who have looked steadily and calmly at the situation and seen it whole. "Stop, look, and listen" is a better motto than "Look it up in the forecasts".'

Review Topic 22.5

Philip Kotler has said of the importance of strategic management: 'There are three types of companies. Those who make things happen. Those who watch things happen. Those who wonder what happened'. (1980, page 63) In what areas can a management information system assist production, finance personnel and marketing management in making theirs the first type of company, rather than the last?

THE DESIGN, IMPLEMENTATION AND OPERATION OF AN MIS

Developments in information technology have opened up new opportunities for better control, reduced data-processing costs and increased speed of information handling. However, it is important that management is not seduced into choosing a certain type of information system on the basis of the attractiveness of the technology.

As in other areas of the organisation, there should be an information strategy, well thought out, formulated, administered and monitored. Formal communications systems in organisations can have an effect on the structure of the organisation, the style of management and the overall direction of the company. The management consultant, Arthur Putnam, has suggested that a successful business information system is regarded as the 'nervous and response system' of the organisation. The system must therefore be designed and developed to be the servant of the organisation's managers, who should be encouraged to voice their needs and commit themselves to obtaining the system they require (Putnam, 1980). An information systems strategy is an equal partner to other organisational strategies such as those for finance and investment, or markets and products, or recruitment and training. It is more than just a plan for the use of computers, since it involves a greater understanding and interlinking of organisational processes, management functions, planning and decision-making processes, control principles, and the nature of communications and information flow. Many of these issues we have covered in the previous sections of this chapter, or in other parts of this book.

Review Topic 22.6

Why is an information systems strategy as important as a marketing or financial strategy?

It is now appropriate to look at how an organisation would go about the process of introducing an MIS. This should be done in three steps: assessment, choice and implementation.

The assessment of MIS requirements

This stage involves gaining an understanding of the information currently existing in the organisation. A useful thing to be carried out initially is an information audit. Uncertainty in the organisation is the difference between the amount of information required to achieve organisational goals and the amount of information already possessed in the organisation. An audit should establish two things, firstly where the gaps are and secondly how the information already possessed is handled. Companies can seek

WHAT RECIPIENT
DOES WITH THE
INFORMATION

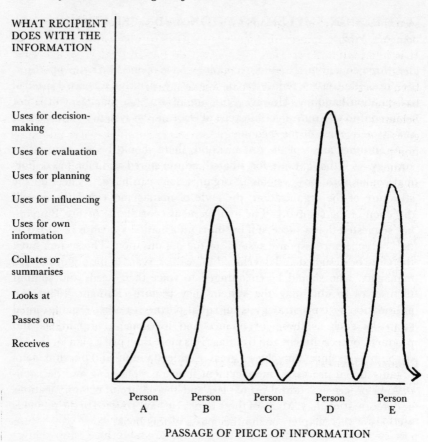

Uses for decision-
making

Uses for evaluation

Uses for planning

Uses for influencing

Uses for own
information

Collates or
summarises

Looks at

Passes on

Receives

Person A   Person B   Person C   Person D   Person E

PASSAGE OF PIECE OF INFORMATION

Fig. 22.4 The level of usage of information.

outside help on a survey of this kind if they wish. Organisations such as the Advisory, Conciliation and Arbitration Service (ACAS) and the Industrial Society, as well as commercial management consultants will undertake an audit of information in organisations. During this process, the objectives of the organisation should be reviewed, the strengths and weakness of internal resources should be identified and the opportunities and threats of external issues should be recognised. (Here we come across again the familiar SWOT analysis already mentioned in connection with marketing strategy in Chapter 5, The management functions of the business.)

One way to look at the way information is used is to examine the flow of certain identified pieces of information and plot their progress. This can be done by listing the various recipients of the information along the bottom axis of a graph and showing along the vertical axis the use to which that information is put. See Fig. 22.4 for an example of this. Too often it may be seen that the level of usage hovers near the bottom axis, with no real use being made of the information during its passage through the organisation. It is information flows such as this that do not add value, which once identified can be shortcircuited, redesigned or eliminated. The method has been used successfully in a variety of major industrial organisations, and is based on a technique called 'information profiling' developed by Christian Schumacher. His technique is no more than applied common sense, but gives a powerful visual representation of tortuous and inefficient information paths.

Another way to analyse the organisation's existing information system is to ask the following questions:

1. Does the information it provides satisfy the needs of individuals?
2. Does it enable people to have access when and where required?
3. What would be the effect of losing the information?
4. Is the information based upon data of sufficient accuracy and in a form that can be readily interpreted?
5. Is it easily updated?

Once the existing systems are evaluated by an information audit of this sort, the needs of the new information system are more easily identifiable.

Choosing a management information system

This next stage concerns identifying and evaluating the options available in deciding the shape and nature of the MIS. An integrated management information system, combining electronic data processing, decision support systems and logistical techniques, will probably have four or five primary sub-divisions. The following have been suggested (Putnam 1980):

> Order entry forecasting, marketing and scheduling:
> > Customer orders, quotations, forecast materials requirements, invoices, sales analyses, engineering specifications.
> Material control and capacity planning:
> > Parts lists, inventories, requisitions, purchase orders, accounts payable, costs, requirements planning, distribution.
> Production control:
> > Stocks, scheduling, workloads, costs, payroll, manhours.
> Accounting control:
> > Costing data, final costs, income and balance sheet information.
> Personnel planning:
> > Recruitment targets, training plans, salary and pension costs, appraisal data.

These sub-divisions provide information for use by the various functions of the organisation, some details of which were listed earlier in this chapter. The weight given to each part of the above will depend on the nature of the organisation's business, its technology, and its corporate strategies.

The right computer system is one which will deliver the greatest improvements in productivity possible for the investment being made, and which will not become obsolete in the reasonable future. These criteria can be satisfied if a system is chosen which accurately reflects the exact nature of the task, the size of these tasks, the quantity of information to be accessed and transferred, the degree of planning flexibility required to extend the system in the future if necessary, and the available budget in relation to costs and benefits to be gained.

Unfortunately, there is no simple checklist of features to be adopted in order to produce the perfect MIS. Good communication between management and information specialists, both with a real understanding of the principles of information systems, will make the task of developing an appropriate system much easier. As with all decisions, alternative choices have to be identified based on the information gathered during the previous stage, an evaluation has to be made, and a final path chosen. Fairbairn's 'Ten-point plan' for the selection of a system runs as follows:

  (i)   Needs are defined.
 (ii)   Alternatives to computer applications are examined.
(iii)   Quantities in relation to file size, time scales and access requirements are defined.
 (iv)   Software is explored.
  (v)   Hardware alternatives are considered.
 (vi)   Software and hardware are evaluated.
(vii)   Expansion capability is considered.
(viii) Suppliers are compared.
 (ix)   Support and maintenance is considered.
  (x)   Installation is scheduled.

(Fairburn, 1982)

The complexity of information technology in relation to the hardware, software, interrelated processes, documentation and program development, and the increasing number of suppliers and systems available, precludes us from describing specific systems in this book. There is a variety of sources of advice available. Details of many of these may be found in publications such as the Department of Trade and Industry's *Technical Services for Industry*.

The Government has also established Microsystems Centres in various parts of the United Kingdom in collaboration with the National Computing Centre, which offer training and consultancy as well as impartial advice and guidance, with no commercial links with the trade. The British Computer Society in London is a source of information on information systems, and there are other such professional associations. Commercial consultancy is not cheap, but compared to the cost of getting the MIS wrong, it may be worthwhile.

Implementation of an MIS

Many organisations, especially large ones, will have a management services section. This consists of information, communication and computing specialists grouped in a central service division, for the specific purpose of providing an advisory and consultancy service to managers at all levels in the company. Such a group would have a vital role in seeking out new ideas, introducing new techniques and smoothly implementing changes to the information system within the company.

The introduction of a sophisticated communication system in an organisation may be met with scepticism or resistance. It is often the lack of top management involvement at the outset which is a key reason for the failure to develop systems which meet operating criteria. Substantial top management attention is needed at the start since the MIS network cuts across all departmental boundaries. The time and cost taken to install and convert existing equipment and programs is often underestimated: programming is a specialised technical task, installation of equipment involves satisfying space and structural requirement in offices, and there may have to be a period for the parallel running of old and new systems. Training must be provided for personnel at all levels in the organisation, both before and after the introduction of a new information system.

Apart from commitment from top management, there are other criteria for success. A management information system must be understood by the manager – it must be simple, easy to communicate with, and inspire confidence in its output. It must also be perceived as useful – it must be complete in key areas, logical, easy to update, and controllable. Einstein once said, 'Everything should be made as simple as possible, but not simpler'.

PROBLEMS AND IMPLICATIONS

Many difficulties are encountered by organisations with management information systems, no matter how sophisticated the computer equipment used. Many of the reasons for the failure of MISs to provide management with the information needed have been mentioned during this chapter. These and others are listed below for ease of reference.

1. Lack of support from top management.
2. Absence of management involvement generally with the design of the MIS.
3. Deficiency of knowledge of computers and computer applications amongst managers.
4. Mistaken application of computers and computer systems.
5. Too great an emphasis on low-level data processing applications.

6. Lack of understanding by information specialists of the requirements of management.
7. Insufficient attention to the assessment, choice and implementation stages of MIS design.
8. Absence of an information systems strategy.
9. Insufficient sharing of the philosophy behind the MIS, and little training in its nature and use.
10. Misuse of the information system in the area of control.

Lucey (1987) also says there is an inevitable human reaction to change brought about by a new system. People have fears about their status and job satisfaction, they are unsure about changes in organisational boundaries, they distrust systems analysts as well as computers, and they see the new system as a criticism of previous performance. Dr Schumacher states that the 'very exactitude (of computers and computerised problem-solving devices) is a sign of the absence of human freedom, responsibility and dignity' (Schumacher, 1973, page 199). In order that these fears are allayed, it is necessary at all stages to involve personnel concerned from the beginning, encourage suggestion, contribution, communication and co-operation, make clear statements about job security and organisation changes, and demonstrate that job satisfaction will improve due to the elimination of certain routine work.

Review Topic 22.7

In the matter of decisions about the supply of eggs and bacon, the hens are involved but the pigs are committed. What factors might determine the different levels of concern and participation regarding the introduction of a management information system in an organisation?

There are potential problems, too, with the operation of the information system. These may include crises such as fire or flood, loss of power, theft, malfunctioning of equipment or systems, or difficulties such as accidental human error, deliberate misuse, sabotage or fraud. Checks and balances need to be built in to the use of equipment and programs to minimise these eventualities, both on a technical and a human level.

The organisation also needs to guard against an information system becoming a misused power tool. There is no doubt that information is vital to the exercise of power. 'Disclosure' has become a politically charged concept. There is power not only in what information is released, but in the ability to deprive people of information, especially where that information could be open to challenge or critical in determining the outcome of controversial issues. The 'gatekeeper' function of certain individuals or groups can lead to the control of information being used to increase spheres of influence, whilst the distortion or withholding of information is a common tactic in organisational conflict. Some of these issues are discussed in Chapter 10, Organisational Politics and in Chapter 16, Authority, Leadership and Autonomy.

The Data Protection Act of 1984 in Britain is intended to limit the potential for misuse of personal information processed on a computer. Areas of exemption include personal data held for the purposes of tax, payrolls, accounts, criminal records, consumer credit and research. A management information system may make use of personal information for training, promotion or manpower planning purposes, and managers should be aware of their legal responsibilities and obligations in this respect.

The introduction of a management information system is not, therefore, a simple or straightforward matter. There are plenty of potential pitfalls. But with careful planning, commitment and time, together with a positive and confident organisational environment, the organisation is likely to perform better with than without a management information system.

SUMMARY PROPOSITIONS

22.1 An understanding of the flow of information in organisations is essential to the understanding of management information systems.

22.2 Data is not necessarily information, and information is not necessarily communication.

22.3 Information has a cost and a value. Information must be relevant and its value lies in subsequent results and actions, and not in the information itself.

22.4 Information, feedback and devolution of decision-making are intertwined in an organisation: they can spiral upwards or downwards.

22.5 Organisations have the ability to control the quantity of information and the way information is handled, by either reducing the need for information processing or increasing the capacity of the organisation to process information.

22.6 A management information system is a combination of data processing systems, office support systems and decision support systems. Each function in an organisation can make specific use of these various elements in its planning, decision-making and controlling activities.

22.7   An information system should serve the organisation, not take control of it. An information systems strategy should reflect and develop the corporate plan.

22.8   The three steps in the introduction of a management information system are assessment of requirements, making the choice, and implementation.

22.9   The introduction of a management information system in an organisation is rarely straightforward, but problems can be anticipated and overcome.

PUTTING IT INTO PRACTICE

Corporate communications – what happens?

The order in which most employees actually get information about the progress of the company and issues affecting their jobs is as follows:

1. The company newspaper
2. Local briefing meetings
3. The grapevine
4. Their immediate boss
5. The company noticeboard

The way they would prefer to get this information is as follows:

1. Their immediate boss
2. Briefing meetings
3. Department meetings
4. The company newspaper
5. The company noticeboard
6. Staff committees
7. The grapevine

There is some place for the grapevine in the informal information system of an organisation, but on the whole people would prefer to receive their information in a less random, haphazard fashion, whilst still receiving it personally. A vacuum will inevitably be filled by rumour.

Designing a short training course on MIS for managers

Imagine you work in the management services department of an organisation and have been asked to prepare a one day course for a group of senior managers to inform them about the principles and philosophy of management information systems.

The outline structure of the day might look as follows:

1. The objectives of an MIS in relation to the planning and decision-making activities of the organisation, and the need for information to have a value.
2. How an MIS might be applied in this particular organisation, and to particular functions within it.
3. The three stages of designing, choosing and implementing a new system, and the nature of management involvement during these stages.
4. Summary of training requirements and feedback structures for management and other levels in the organisation.
5. Suggested timetable for implementation.

The contents of an information systems strategy

A written strategy statement might include the following sections:

1. An abstract summary of information systems philosophy, in the context of organisation structure and management style.
2. The nature and purpose of the strategic plan.
3. Description of the current status of information flow in the organisation, and the existing use of computer hardware and software.
4. The projected requirements, purpose and objectives of an integrated information system, as viewed from the users' perspective.
5. The means of fulfilling these requirements, with an examination of the technical and organisational implications.
6. The method and timescales for implementation, together with specific implications in the areas of finance and manpower.
7. How the effectiveness of the system will be evaluated, and how value-for-money will be judged.

REFERENCES

Adair, J., *Effective Decision-Making*, Chapter 10, Pan Books, London, 1985.
Drucker, P.F., *Management*, Chapter 30, Pan Books, London, 1979.
Fairbairn, D., Chapter 10 in Rank Xerox, 1982, below.
Galbraith, J.R., *Organisation Design*, Chapter 3, Addison Wesley, Mass., 1977.
Garnett, J., *Team Briefing*, The Industrial Society, London, 1983.
Handy, C.B., *Understanding Organisations*, Penguin Books, Chapter 11, Harmondsworth, 1981.
Kanter, R.M., *The Change Masters*, Chapters 3 and 6, George Allen & Unwin, London, 1984.
Kotler, P., *Marketing Management*, 4th edn, Prentice Hall, Englewood Cliffs, New Jersey, 1980.
Lucey, T., *Management Information Systems*, 5th edn, DP Publications, Eastleigh, Hampshire, 1987.
Peters, T.J. and Waterman, R.H., *In Search of Excellence*, Harper & Row, New York, 1982.

Putnam, A.O., *Management Information Systems*, Pitman, London, 1980.
Rank Xerox, *Brave New World?*, MacDonald, London, 1982.
Schumacher, E.F., *Small is Beautiful*, Chapter 16, Blond & Briggs, London, 1973.
Stewart, R., *The Reality of Management*, Chapter 10, Pan Books, London, 1986.
Tricker, R.I., *Effective Information Management*, Chapters 2 and 7, Beaumont Executive Press, Oxford, 1982.

23

DEPARTMENTAL BUDGETARY CONTROL

Planning, control and evaluation are major aspects of the task of managing. Much of this activity concerns non-financial questions, such as the achievement of product quality, the provisions of employee welfare facilities, or the performance of sales staff. Other objectives can more easily be expressed in financial terms, and it is the process of translating the expected investment of capital and personnel into financial budgets and the operation of these budgets that concerns us here. As with any control device, budgets set standards and facilitate the measurement of performance against these standards, using results and feedback. Corrective action for any deviations can then be considered. Budgets are the expression, in quantitative terms, of plans for the future, and it is with planning that the budgeting cycle begins (see Fig. 23.1).

THE PURPOSE OF BUDGETS

There are three important purposes served by the budgeting process. Firstly, the preparation of the budget is a *planning* device; it imposes a duty upon members of departments to quantify their targets and performance levels objectively. Individual departmental plans are interlocked with each other so that they then become a co-ordinated and comprehensive plan for the whole organisation. Without planned targets, departments' operations lack direction, unexpected problems occur, and results are meaningless. Too often, the pressures of the moment drive out the importance of looking to the future. An objective approach, whereby organisational and departmental goals are considered, together with the means of achieving these goals, indicates that budgeting is being used as a serious planning tool.

Secondly, the budget acts as a *controlling* and *motivating* device by expressing expected performance levels which then provide criteria for the judgement of departmental performance. Progress can be compared with the targets to see whether plans are being fulfilled. If monitored expenditures

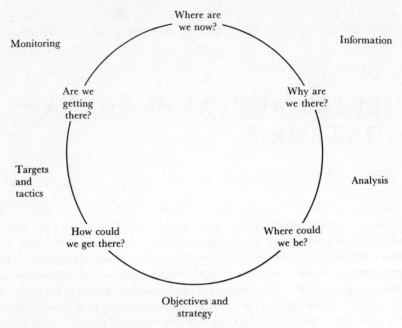

Fig. 23.1 The budgeting planning cycle.

are different from budgeted levels, whether below or above, the manager is alerted. The budget acts as an early warning device as well as highlighting areas where performance is better than expected, and time and attention can thus be directed to finding out the reason for either underperformance or performance in excess of targets. If possible, the responsibility for the budget must be allocated to particular managers, and these managers use actual results to guide them towards the production of the desired results. It is considered that comparisons with past performance are less valid than comparisons with budgeted performance, since the former perpetuate the inefficiencies of the past, and ignore unrealised potential and intervening changes in technology, competition and economic environment (Horngren, 1982). (See also methods of preparing budgets later in this chapter.) Budgets of course are only a guide towards the achievement of planned objectives. They should not be regarded as a straitjacket, and like all control mechanisms should be flexibly and reasonably applied by departmental management.

Thirdly, the budgeting process promotes *communication and co-ordination*. A departmental budget highlights operational relationships both within and outside the department, and can help people to broaden their outlooks to include those of others. Equally important, it provides a framework for feedback, as well as clarifying working relationships and responsibilities. It also requires the understanding and support of top management in departmental affairs and aims.

Review Topic 23.1

Horngren (1982) suggests that 'Budgets must be respected but not revered'. Where do we draw the line between serious adherence to budgets and persevering with them indiscriminately?

THE USE OF RESOURCES

An organisation has various resources – time, people, space, equipment – as well as finance. Whether the organisation is labour intensive or capital intensive, it is the way in which finances are deployed that determine the effective use of the other resources. Employing expensive scientists, for example, becomes a nonsense if the research department is deprived of funds and materials for investigation and experimentation. Investing in complex, high technology machine tools is absurd without extra money being spent on staff training. Failing to pay attention to those items which make the principal investment more effective is not only negligent, it may have a profound effect upon the future of the organisation. A positive view of the use of resources will lead to them being properly controlled and exploited, and providing a sense of ownership will lead to thoughtful use. In this way, it should not be possible to put the blame for deficiencies in the system onto lack of resources *per se* – rather it is lack of management of those resources which is at fault.

Organisations also develop a resources culture. Managers handling budget forecasts should be aware that estimates may well be based on what is perceived to be likely to be granted. There are organisations which have a culture which encourages improvement and innovation, and those where there is a background of conditioning against extravagance. In addition, we may come across comments such as 'Our estimate (for stationery, manpower, extra market research, or whatever) is always cut back, so we will put in for more than we actually need.' It is the job of management to be aware of, and if necessary, to change this culture, in order to make it more positive and objective.

The way the budgeting process is conducted should ensure that the organisation's finances become a reason for doing things, not a justification for not doing things. The following section details some departmental budgeting methods.

THE BUDGETING PROCESS

The nature of budgets

As stated above, budgets begin with those who devise future plans and forecasts. Obtaining the commitment of all members of the organisation to departmental objectives and plans is vital. Individual members on whom the budget is imposed, and who do not have an active part in its drafting, are likely to pay it little attention or will abuse its control function. Budget preparation and planning should be carried out at working level, therefore, and it is only when all the budgets have been passed up the line that they are then formed into a company-wide policy and passed back down the hierarchy, with head office issuing divisional budgets, divisions issuing departmental budgets, departments issuing sectional budgets, and so on down to a personal level.

Richard Coleman is a divisional accountant and has described to us the broad steps in his budget procedure:

1. He and his colleagues prepare their plan and send it to headquarters.
2. Headquarters responds with guidelines such as 'We are not happy with an expected profit of £10 million in two years; try for £11 million' or 'Administration costs should be 19 per cent not 20 per cent of the budget'.
3. Richard responds by agreeing with some points and resisting others by further justification.
4. Headquarters agrees the divisional budget.
5. Richard now 'cascades' the same process down to the departments in the division.

Steps 2 and 3 may be repeated several times before 4 is eventually reached, but Richard finally has not only a series of financial yardsticks against which divisional performance will be measured, but also a substantial degree of latitude: autonomy to exercise discretion and initiative within an agreed framework. The reason for the protracted negotiations is to ensure that the framework is acceptable to those operating within it, so that they cannot claim an unreasonable budgetary constraint as a reason for failure.

> Management control is a systematic effort to set performance standards with planning objectives, to design information feedback systems, to compare actual performance with these predetermined standards, to determine whether there are any deviations and to measure their significance, and to take any action required to assure that all corporate resources are being used in the most effective and efficient way possible in achieving corporate objectives. (Mockler, 1972, page 2)

Tying people down precisely will always be likely to produce resistance or defensive behaviour unless the details of the controls are worked at to make them mutually acceptable as a framework. Budgets should ensure that everyone sees, understands and works towards the goals and central drives of the organisation.

The variety of plans made by an organisation is reflected in the range of budgets that are in use. These fall into two main types, capital budgets and expense budgets.

1. *Capital* budgets are estimates of expenditure on things like new equipment or new buildings. These are regarded as assets of the organisation, rather than expenses.
2. *Expense* budgets cover the material and labour needed to achieve the forecast production and/or sales activities of the department. These are the everyday running costs of the organisation, and at a company level may include other overheads such as interest on loans. Whether the latter are regarded as departmental expenses or not will depend on the treatment of cost allocation within the company (see the later section on Profit and Cost Centres).

Some organisations set a minimum figure on items of expenditure to be included in capital estimates, but this is often a question of administrative convenience rather than logic. As capital and expenses expenditure are treated differently by the inland revenue (the latter being a legitimate deduction from tax liability, while only the annual depreciation on capital expenditure is tax allowable), it is important that expenses should be correctly located, otherwise unnecessary costs are incurred.

In addition, alongside these there may be *cash budgets*. The organisation must have the cash resources to meet its commitments as they fall due – it has to be able to pay its suppliers, creditors, employees and shareholders. Income and expenditure are not constant over the year, and highlighting discrepancies should help to smooth out the occasions when there is either a cash surplus or a deficiency of cash. There is little point in formally estimating costs for operational activities if the organisation then runs out of cash funds for financing these activities. A cash budget emphasises that departments create the need for cash, as well as bring in cash, through their activities.

These three types of budget – capital, expense and cash – are built up on the basis of *operational budgets*. These are estimates of how many widgets will be made and sold, or in the case of service organisations, how many students will be taken in, hospital patients treated, legal cases handled, meals served, or guests accommodated. The more unstable supply and demand movements are, the more difficult and important accurate forecasting becomes, and the more elaborate the forecasting procedures will need to be. There are many formal trend analysis and prediction techniques in use in organisations, of both a quantitative and qualitative nature. (See

Torrington, Weightman and Johns, 1985, Chapter 43 for a description of some of these.) Sometimes, however, these may be rejected for a more entrepreneurial approach with the acceptance of the consequent risk, or alternatively for a bit of simple guesswork. If the decision is of a short term nature and can be changed with little expense, then the use of sophisticated forecasting techniques is merely a waste of time and effort. Sometimes objectivity is completely discarded, and advocacy and political negotiation prevail instead. However they are drawn up, these operational budgets are the ones which are translated into the flow of finance in and out of the organisation.

Budget forecasts are normally prepared along the same divisions as the functional organisation of the company, so that there will be budgets for the manufacturing section, for the marketing section, and for the administration, personnel and finance sections. Whether labour and service costs are budgeted for by the department in which they are incurred, or by the central service department, will again depend on the company's policy regarding the allocation of costs. Within these functional budgets, there will be departmental budgets. All these separate forecasts are then co-ordinated into the company's *master budget*, when the system can be viewed as a whole. Alternative forecasts are considered, and restraining factors are taken into account. The period covered by the budget is not always one year, but may be three months or five years. A longer-term budget will contain more uncertainties than a short-term budget, of course. Two types of budgets which may be long term or striving to cope with the uncertainty of the long-term future are as follows:

1. *Life cycle budgeting.* This is used where it is unreasonable to expect financial commitment to last a short period, for example capital projects, complex retraining programmes or research. The financial estimates are prepared over the whole life cycle of the activity, and will assume the continued success of the project.
2. *Flexible budgeting.* This requires a series of different budgets to be prepared depending on the particular scenario painted, perhaps according to different inflation rates, or changes in the availability and price of a basic feedstock, or different performance levels. This can sometimes make it easier to use the budget as a controlling and evaluating device, since it is based on what actually happens in the environment, rather than a compromised guess.

All control through budgets requires the determination of *key result areas*. These are aspects of the organisation that produce the performances on which everything else depends. The obvious key result areas are sales, output, stock levels and cash position, but each individual organisation will have one or two that are special to its setting or to its mode of operation. One organisation may have 10 per cent of its sales volume taken up by the sales of one product which produces 50 per cent of the gross profits. Television companies watch the viewing levels of their programmes very carefully. A car manufacturer may have one department where a strike or other form of industrial action would have repercussions elsewhere in the organisation far greater than would be assumed. Identifying these key result areas makes it possible for managers to monitor closely a selected number of performance indicators whilst allowing maximum discretion elsewhere.

The preparation of budgets

Departmental managers or functional heads will at some time find themselves faced with decisions about how to go about formulating their budget estimates, or dealing with any special or one-off funds that may be allocated to their sections. With the latter, their aim should be to extract the maximum value from their finances. Two extreme approaches are the departmental head who makes all the allocation decisions without any sharing of the problem with his or her staff, or an open departmental finance committee which debates the issue in great detail. Brian Knight, an acknowledged authority on finance in education, describes four possible strategies (Knight, 1983, Chapter 8).

1. *Benevolent despotism.* Here staff in the department may be consulted about their individual or section requirements, but much of the money is actually allocated on a grace-and-favour basis, rather than based on real need. This method can be effective, but is open to unfair wheeler-dealing and persuasion.
2. *Open market or zero-basing.* Here estimates and justifications are submitted for each and every item making up the request. This method is quite searching, since there is no dependence on the previous year's budget. The modest and realistic estimates tend to lose out to the aggressive and artful ones here, unless the justification for each item is carefully examined.
3. *Creeping incrementalism.* This simply sorts out allocations by adding an amount for inflation equally to the previous period's allocations. This method takes no account of changing needs or new developments, and also perpetuates any previous inequities in distribution.
4. *Formula approach.* Here budget estimates and allocations are based on factors such as the number of students, number of overseas visits or number of new products, with perhaps some weightings applied to certain elements. Each 'unit' receives an amount of finance which is pre-determined and applicable across the whole section or organisation. This method can be quick, once the initial weighting and factors are agreed upon, but tends to err on the conservative and unadventurous side.

All these methods have their good and bad points, and most organisations will probably use a combination. Some are useful due to their simplicity. Others, for example 3, mean that the budget is no more value than are past results for judging performance against, and indicate that the budget is not being used as a serious planning device. Ideally, as mentioned earlier, the budget estimates should be prepared using an objective, task-orientated approach (see Putting It Into Practice), which considers departmental goals and the ways of achieving goals. Such 'rule of thumb' measures like 1 or 3 will generally not produce a useful budget.

The operation of budgets

This section could perhaps be called 'good housekeeping', and concerns what goes on after the negotiating of the budget is over, and the spending starts. Ideally budgets should be spent as soon as possible after the beginning of the budgeting period to minimise the effects of inflation, but this is obviously not possible for ongoing expense items, such as additional stock or salaries, and rash buying should in any case be avoided. *Value-for-money* should always be born in mind – if the organisation insists on certain suppliers being used, but the section head knows the supplier down the road will do it more cheaply, then this should be discussed, and agreement reached on action. It may transpire that there are reasons other than price, for example reliability or efficiency, why another supplier has been nominated, and these factors can add their own value.

Departments should also complain bitterly if their accounting function insists rigidly on allowances being completely spent-up by the end of the budgeting period. Knight calls this a 'medieval practice' (1983, page 122). It risks making spending itself more important than gaining value from the budget. Some organisations we have come across not only prevent the division from keeping its underspend, but they also reduce the following year's budget by a similar amount, so imposing a double penalty. Obviously, extremes of underspending will ring warning bells, but allowing departments to carry forward unspent balances prevents the frantic activity or spending on trivial items that often occurs at the end of the financial year. It also allows departments to save up for some particular but unexpected change in priority arising in a few months time. Similarly, there should ideally be some facility for allowing occasional overspending for legitimate requirements. As stated earlier, the budget is not a straitjacket, it is a guide, and should be flexible not rigidly applied. A large credit or debit balance at the end of the financial year should, of course, be avoided since if the budget has been objectively prepared, this indicates bad management of the budget.

Another tool of flexible budget management is *virement* – a term more commonly used in the public sector – which means the transfer of finances from one heading to another, within the budget as a whole. If handled with care, but not to excess, this can assist departments or individuals within it who find that their needs have changed over time. It should not be so easily granted that it prevents budget planners from not taking the initial task seriously, knowing that changes can easily be made in future months. Normally, requests for virement will have to be accompanied by a detailed justification.

The most that some members of the department will be conscious of the budgeting monitoring process may be the use of the departmental key or counter to use the photocopying machine, or the need to get their section head's signature on a request for a petty cash advances, or the periodic check-up that all the capital items listed as being in the possession of the department are still present, or the occasional reminder that if possible long personal phone calls or sending private mail through the company system should be avoided, or the notice on the board about switching lights off and turning off taps . . . and so on. These are the signs of 'good housekeeping' in an organisation – it shows that someone, somewhere is paying some attention to the value the organisation or department is deriving from its budget. But departmental management should seek to ensure that this is not the only type of involvement with the budget which members experience. Staff need to have some sense of *ownership* of resources. If people have been involved in the budgeting process from the beginning, they are more likely to be interested in its progress, and to share some of the responsibility for its success.

Evaluation of the budget

When the next year's budgeting planning cycle restarts, questions must be asked on the effectiveness of the previous period's spending. It is not enough simply to record an under or overspend, since this tells us little about spending patterns within different sections of the budget. If the department has a large training budget, for example, the department should examine whether the money was well spent, whether some other way of spending it would have given more value (perhaps on external rather than in-house courses, or located in Chester rather than London), and whether the pattern of spending achieved departmental training objectives. This will, of course, involve discussion between various members in the department. Similar questions can be asked for each budget heading, including hardware and equipment, consumable software and stationery, and expenses such as travel and entertainment.

BUDGETS, RECORDS AND COMPUTERS

Keeping records is part of the feedback process for the effectiveness of plans and budgets. Records are needed to measure the contribution made by departments or sections, as measured against expected performance. Without a record of how many bandage packs have been issued this month, it is not only difficult for the hospital administrator to know how many to order, it is also difficult to determine when to argue for more funds for bandages, or at what point funds should be diverted from bandages to laundry. Similarly, personnel departments need records of those off sick or working overtime, so that the correct pay calculations may be made. The computer has made a large impact on record keeping and filing, overcoming some of the drudgery and routine. The computer can store so much information and retrieve it with such ease that there is a risk that records may be expanded unnecessarily.

There is a danger that the keeping of records becomes a burdensome administrative activity that is neither accurate nor useful, with the activity becoming an end in itself. One high-tech company we worked in had a system of wall charts on which engineers recorded the number of hours spent on each of several different parts of a project and on each project for different clients. The reason for recording this information was to provide a basis to work out costings for future projects. In practice, however, the records were made nonsensical by the fact that engineers often had to spend more time on an assignment than was anticipated. It would have been sensible to record the extra hours against the project that had been underestimated. In fact the engineers were asked *by their managers* to record the extra hours against a different project where there was still space on the chart, as they did not want to give the impression that they had estimated incorrectly in the first place. Nor did they want it to seem that they had lost control of the operation! This is an extreme example of how individuals make nonsensical those records that prescribe their activities too closely. There is particular suspicion of records that are maintained so that an individual manager can keep personal control of the activities of subordinates rather than the records needed for organisational control. To avoid these problems, we suggest three simple rules.

1. Records should be justified in terms of the stated task of the department or organisation.
2. Records should be entered on simple forms.
3. Records kept should only be those essential to running the unit.

Review Topic 23.2

Why was the use of wall charts (described on this page) made nonsensical and how could the problem have been avoided?

The impact of the computer on managing is varied, but one of the significant innovations has been the spreadsheet, which is probably the most popular piece of computer software among managers. The first of what have now become known as spreadsheets was Visicalc (1980), although that has been followed by many others both simpler and more elaborate. The financial spreadsheet is a computer program that provides a display of data relating to income and expenditure over a period of, say, twelve months. Each item of information is metaphorically in a box, with the boxes arranged in rows and columns. The row is the category of information running across each of the twelve months and the column is of the different categories of information for a single month. The computer program then enables a series of calculations to be made that link one box to another, one row to another or one column to another. In this way it is possible to enter in the figures of expected income and expenditure for the forthcoming twelve month period and then calculate the effect of changing different variables. One can, for example, change one feature of income in month one and ask the computer to calculate the effect of that single change on all the following months, making all the necessary additions, subtractions and other calculations so that there is still a calculated figure for each row and each column with all the cumulative effects accounted for. This helps the initial budget preparation to be more carefully worked out by considering a wide range of possible strategies. It also makes it possible to assess quickly each month what the effect of that month's performance will be over the remainder of the year. Table 23.1 shows a typical spreadsheet format.

In many organisations now, data for financial computer decision-making

Table 23.1 A typical spreadsheet format

	January	February	...
Sales	42,000	42,840	
Cost of sales	28,560	29,131	
Gross profit	13,440	13,709	
Less:			
Wages	7,800	7,800	
Rent	2,050	2,050	
Other	1,500	1,800	
Total expenses	11,350	11,650	
Trading profit	2,090	2,059	
Less Interest	800	850	
Net profit	1,290	1,209	

systems are fed in at source, which does away with some of the tedium of manual input. An example of this which most of us will have come across is the supermarket checkout till, where a barcoding pen or some other electronic device instantly records the fact that a particular item of stock has been purchased, at what time and at what price. The information generated in this way can be used not only for stock re-ordering routines, but also for sales analysis, examination of product margins, turnover levels, etc. By connecting computerised systems with the operational and record-keeping systems of the organisation, the potential of electronic hardware is truly realised. (See Chapter 22, Management Information Systems, for more discussion on this.)

PROFIT AND COST CENTRES

As discussed at various points earlier, organisations will vary in their allocation of accounting responsibilities to individual departments. There are various spheres of responsibility.

- *Cost centres.* Costs are assigned to the section where the items incurring those costs are consumed (this may be different from where those costs are first incurred).
- *Profit centres.* Both revenue (income from sales or the provision of services) and costs are made the responsibility of departmental management. A profit centre will probably have its own profit and loss accounts to use in future planning activities.
- *Investment centre.* A further extension of the above where not only expenses and income are made the responsibility of the department, but also the management of the assets of the department. Such a centre would have its own balance sheet, showing the total resources invested in the department. The most important concept in all these is that the responsibility for all the expenses connected with running the department should be located at the point of consumption.

The use of profit or cost centres is a means of providing autonomy to departments or sections of a business at the same time as providing a basis for management control of operations that are decentralised. One method is to set targets for a division or department in terms of profits or costs that have to be achieved and then to measure the results obtained. It is thus a form of management by objectives using a single criterion of success and – at least theoretically – providing those in the cost or profit centre with greater scope for deciding how their objectives are to be reached. It is also a different form of using key result areas than have been mentioned earlier.

Review Topic 23.3

How can the use of profit or cost centres provide both autonomy to departments and a basis for management control of decentralised operations?

In practice individual managers seldom enjoy the complete autonomy that the use of profit centres implies. Organisations are entities, no matter how attractive is the idea of decentralising, so that managers in individual cost or profit centres have to work within quite tight limitations. If there is a national agreement on wages and salaries, managers in the cost centres will have to accept that constraint all the time that the agreement is accepted. Managers will also be required to use some central services, even if they do not want to, as there are economics of scale for the organisation as a whole in working this way.

Central overheads, like head office and general service departments, can be apportioned between cost centres or regarded as separate, but problems arise if a department that is a cost centre wants to reduce its overhead burden by not using a central service department such as personnel, purchasing, computing, public affairs or management services. A manager may review the use made by his centre of management services and decide that his level of use is so low that he could make a useful saving by doing without the services altogether or using the occasional services of a consultant. Although there has long been reluctance to encourage competition for internal services, some organisations have begun turning central service departments into cost centres that have to survive by selling their services to client departments within the company and in competition with suppliers of similar services from outside the organisation. The next step can be to close the central service department altogether and depend on outside suppliers.

A necessary feature of cost or profit centres is to determine the prices at which goods and services are transferred from one department to another. One option is to use an open market price, so that the internal client pays the same price for internally supplied goods and services as he would pay for those same services supplied from outside. If, however, the internal client is free to buy externally as well as internally, then the internal supplier is at a considerable disadvantage as he does not have the same freedom to sell his services. It is therefore more common for some lower value to be determined, but the precise level is problematical.

The reason why managers in senior positions use the device of profit or cost centres is to try and make the organisation as a whole more efficient, by providing control information on unit performance, and to provide job satisfaction for subordinate managers, by supplying feedback on the progress of their operations. If they are to achieve both objectives the degree of competition between cost centres has to be kept at a healthy level, without allowing it to become so strong as to be destructive.

FINANCIAL STATEMENTS

Budgets are planning, decision-making and monitoring instruments. They are different from an organisation's statements of financial activity in the previous period. However, past accounting information, in the form of balance sheets, profit and loss statements, and source and use of funds statements, is necessary to help in the prediction of future events. In most organisations, these statements are produced as summaries of the organisation as a whole, rather than for individual departments, but departmental management will benefit from some understanding of their structure and purpose. In very large organisations, where the organisation is structured along profit and investment centre lines (see section above), individual departmental or functional statements may be produced. The information contained in such statements helps to identify trends and relationships, major changes which have occurred, and strengths and weaknesses in the organisation. Such statements are snapshots of the financial structure of the business at a given time, and for this reason may not be representative of the average position of the business over a longer period. Managers should, therefore, exercise judgement as to how they use financial statements in the analysis of the business. The following is a brief description of the nature of the three main types of final accounts. More detailed information can be gained by reading specialist financial texts, for example Harvey and Nettleton 1983, or Wood and Townsley 1983.

The balance sheet

The balance sheet discloses the property and possessions of a business together with its internal and external debts and obligations. These are known as the capital, liabilities and assets of the organisation.

Those which are tangible and measurable by cash values can be arranged on a balance sheet to show the financial situation of the organisation at a specific time. Table 23.2 shows a simplified balance sheet. Current assets are those such as cash and marketable securities that could be turned into disposable cash at a reasonably predictable value within a relatively short time. Fixed assets show the monetary value of the company's plant, equipment, property and other items used to produce its goods or services. After liabilities have also been listed, the company's net worth is calculated by subtracting total liabilities from total assets.

Examination of the balance sheet focuses mainly on capital structure and the use of working capital, that is the excess of current assets over current liabilities. Some questions that the individual manager, rather than the accountant, might raise after studying the balance sheet might be as follows:

Table 23.2 A simple balance sheet

Assets			Liabilities		
		£000			£000
Current assets:			*Ordinary share capital*		5,492
Stocks	4,784		*Reserves:*		
Debtors	4,865		Capital	706	
Marketable securities	324		Revenue	2,631	3,337
Cash	102	10,075	*Ordinary shareholders' equity*		8,892
Less Current liabilities:					
Creditors	3,133		*Long-term liabilities:*		
Bank overdraft	1,430		Debentures	2,552	
Taxation	803		Loans	1,424	3,976
Dividends	367	5,733			13,196
Net current assets		4,342			
Fixed assets:					
Land and buildings	3,312				
Plant and machinery	4,675	7,987			
Investments		867			
		13,196			

1. What action are we taking regarding old or obsolete equipment?
2. Do we have too much money tied up in stock?
3. Are we offering too much credit to customers?

The profit and loss statement

The profit and loss statement (sometimes called the income statement) aims to set out how much income has been generated from capital in a given period of time. It helps determine the significance of different revenues and expenses in relation to profitability, and to isolate any changes in circumstances. The profit and loss statement should encourage the manager to question such things as the amount of fixed and variable costs incurred by the department, how effective spending has been (for example, on research or new technology), and how factors such as competition or labour relations may be affecting income and profitability.

The flow of funds statement

This can also be called the sources and uses of funds statement. It shows how much new wealth has been made available during the period (for example, through injections of new capital, business loans, sales of assets, and operating income), and how this new wealth has been invested in the business, whether in the purchase of new assets, repayment of loans, tax payments or operating losses. It will highlight changes in the cash position of the business. This is a particularly useful tool in budget forecasting for the estimate of future cash flows.

It is important to ensure that financial statements are objective, verifiable and consistent, and internal audit procedures are regarded as an effective tool of financial control in this respect. It must be emphasised that financial statements such as these do not in themselves provide the answers to management questions. They are a starting point towards more detailed investigation, and are a highly useful part of analysis and planning decisions. There are many systematic analytical devices concerning financial information, including the use of ratios to examine profitability, capital structure, cash flow and the use of assets.

THE HUMAN SIDE OF BUDGETING

Behavioural considerations are important in all areas of management. The effectiveness of accounting information and control systems depends on how they affect behaviour. If the original targets are too tight and highly difficult to achieve, budgets are unlikely to be a motivating force. Neither will they motivate if they are too slack to constitute any sort of challenge. Moreover, what might be a challenge for a young section leader may be a discouraging objective for an older one. Glautier and Underdown (1986) suggest that

> The budget process alone is not sufficient to maintain adequate management control. Too often, organisations tend to expect results from budgetary control and fail to recognise its behavioural implications. As a result, pressures are created leading to mistrust, hostility and actions detrimental to the long term prospects of an organisation.
>
> Human nature being what it is, individuals may be tempted to use a variety of techniques to influence the budgeting process, for example, the withholding of information until very late to highlight its importance, the overstatement of requirements, and unhelpfulness in the provision of information to the budget compiler. (Appleby, 1987, page 206)

There are also likely to be certain entrenched group attitudes about finance questions. Departmental staff and managers are heard to make comments like these:

1. The company budget is a bottomless pocket.
2. It's their money, not mine.
3. There is always a magic wand in the last resort.

4. I'm not paid to be an accountant.
5. Electricity costs are not my business.
6. Our section is special.

The accounting section staff may, on the other hand, have attitudes such as these:

1. We must not set a precedent.
2. You cannot use that, it is in the wrong pot.
3. They could not run a fish stall.
4. They should do it for love.
5. Beat the scroungers.
6. Keep to the rules.

(Adapted from Knight, 1983, Chapter 7)

A head of department may have to explain more than he or she thinks necessary to individual members of the department if the budget is to be an effective motivator. Time and effort should be devoted to providing opportunities where discussion can take place and where queries, worries or feedback can be shared. This can, for example, be done by means of management by objectives techniques where personal targets can be set in line with budgeted goals, or during the progress section of team briefing sessions. (See Chapter 21 Performance Appraisal, and Chapter 22 Management Information Systems for discussion of these techniques.)

Review Topic 23.4

Organisations are developed, not through systems, but through people. How does human behaviour in organisations affect departmental budgetary control?

SUMMARY PROPOSITIONS

23.1 Budgets are tools for management control of organisational performance.

23.2 The main functions of budgets are as planning, controlling, motivating, communication and co-ordination devices. They are guides to management, not straitjackets.

23.3 Different types of budgets are capital, expense, cash, operational and master budgets. There are also long-term budgets known as life cycle or flexible budgets.

23.4 Rule of thumb budget preparation methods indicate that the budget is not being used as a serious planning tool.

23.5 Good housekeeping procedures go hand in hand with good budgeting procedures.

23.6 Computers have taken away much of the drudgery of financial record-keeping, but care is needed to prevent the proliferation of unnecessary records.

23.7 Control is made more effective by identifying key result areas, and profit or cost centres.

23.8 Budgeting procedures need to affect behaviour to be effective as control mechanisms, therefore some awareness of human behaviour and organisational culture is useful to the manager. Success is dependent on whether those operating the budget system accept it.

PUTTING IT INTO PRACTICE

Practical problems of forecasting for operational budgets

Operational budgets are the basis of capital, expense and cash budgeting activities. There are many difficulties in forecasting levels of activity for these budgets, including the following:

1. The preparation of estimates of inflows and outflows of materials, products and services is time-consuming, and often imprecise in nature.
2. Assessment of demand rates, selling prices, growth rates, the life of assets, yields of plants, maintenance costs and interest rates is a difficult task, and wide margins of error occasionally have to be expected and tolerated by management.
3. Errors in forecasting are often not due to inexperience, but unresolved uncertainties in the environment.
4. Innovations where the future market potential was initially grossly underestimated include computers, robots, polythene and PVC. Ones where success was overestimated include the airship and Concorde. Market success is a more difficult thing to estimate than likely development costs.

A task-orientated method of departmental budget preparation

1. Forecasts covering departmental activities in physical terms are prepared by individual departments, using the planning cycle illustrated in Fig. 23.1.
2. All departmental forecasts are checked by senior management to ensure their compatibility with each other and with organisational objectives.

3. Individual forecasts are expressed in financial terms, using any organisational and economic guidelines which may be appropriate, for example inflation rates. Decisions are taken at this stage to maintain or cease certain operational activities, bearing in mind the financial costs and benefits involved.
4. These financial forecasts are again scrutinised by top management, or by the budget committee. Decisions are made regarding their acceptability in line with organisational objectives, and a master forecast is drawn up.
5. After formal approval of the master forecast by the board, each department's forecast becomes its budget and becomes an instrument of departmental control.

Practical recommendations for management in budget control

1. The success of the budget control system depends on you, the managers, not on the clerk in the accounts department. But don't forget to discuss it with the bursar – he or she is a useful systems educator within the organisation.
2. Do not avoid decisions which must be made at your level, but communicate them to your subordinates.
3. Get draft budgets prepared at the lowest possible level of management, and make sure everyone's subordinates are included in the discussions.
4. Decide beforehand what variances you will allow before intervening. Show interest, not intervention. If budgets are not met, this does not necessarily imply fault. If you point the finger accusingly, budgets will be met but will not be innovative.
5. Discuss within your departments what records are desirable from a line management point of view, and what from a data-processing point of view, and try to merge the two. Resist attempts to be supplied with too much information, and review the situation periodically.
6. Show enthusiasm and respect the responsibilities of members of your staff. Do not display mistrust or exert undue pressure. Tackle the task of budget control as a team.

(Adapted from Hofstede, 1968, Chapter 15)

REFERENCES

Appleby, Robert C., *Modern Business Administration*, 4th edn, Chapter 6, Pitman, London, 1987.

Glautier, M.W.E. and Underdown, B., *Accounting Theory and Practice*, 3rd edn, Pitman, London, 1986.

Harvey, D.A. and Nettleton M., *Management Accounting*, Mitchell Beazley, London, 1983.

Hofstede, G.H., *The Game of Budget Control* (Chapter 15), Tavistock, London, 1968.

Horngren, C.T., *Cost Accounting: A Managerial Emphasis*, 5th edn, Prentice Hall, Englewood Cliffs, New Jersey, 1982.

Knight, Brian A., *Managing School Finance* (Chapters 7 and 8), Heinemann, London, 1983.

Mockler, R.J., *The Management Control Process*, Prentice Hall, Englewood Cliffs, New Jersey, 1972.

Torrington, D., Weightman, J. and Johns, K., *Management Methods*, (Chapter 43) IPM, London, 1985.

Wood, F. and Townsley, J., *Managerial Accounting and Finance*, Polytech Publishers, Stockport, 1983.

24

PROCEDURES FOR ADMINISTRATIVE ACTION

Procedures are the life blood of any organisation, yet are scarcely ever discussed. Many books on general management extend over more than 500 pages but the term 'procedure' does not appear in the index. The reason they are ignored is that they are dull. The reason they are important is that it is by the use of procedures in organisations that things get done. Exciting decisions may be taken, creative ideas may be developed, new products may be conceived, but all of them depend on organisational procedures for things to get done.

In some organisations one major procedure is the key determinant of success or failure, like the procedure for booking seats in an airline, or order processing and despatch in a mail order company, but in all organisations procedures are essential to success; they get things done. Three universal examples are post, pay and minutes. When post is delivered to a company, a procedure is operated. There are two stages of sorting, as some letters and packages will be addressed to individuals, but others will be addressed simply to the company, or to the general manager, and will require opening so that a decision can be made about where they should be routed. Sometimes records are kept of the arrival of particular categories of mail and many companies stamp the date and time of arrival on the envelope so that any subsequent queries can be dealt with. After sorting there is distribution to the various depatments and offices within the organisation where the mail is to be dealt with. Then there is a reverse procedure whereby outgoing mail can be collected, franked and taken to the post office.

When new employees join an organisation there is a procedure for getting them on the payroll: the right rate of pay, the right arrangements for routing the pay, the correct deductions and so forth. After meetings there is a procedure for disseminating the minutes and preparing for the next meeting.

Managers' lives are dominated by procedures and much of their creative energy is spent in trying to circumvent them or expedite processes through them. A popular managerial self-image is of the person who can 'beat the system' or 'get things done without waiting for procedures which always take such a hell of a long time'. The idea of procedures is such anathema to most managers that many readers will have passed over this chapter entirely! There are obviously many occasions when procedure is not appropriate – like the apocryphal story of the man in the burning building who could not find the right requisition form for a fire extinguisher – but the impersonal, dead hand of administrative routine is the best way to put into practice the majority of the decisions taken within organisational structures. Managers need, therefore, to consider and design procedures with consummate care, so as to save money, so as to save time, and so as to run a successful operation.

Review Topic 24.1

What types of decisions in organisations are best implemented by the impersonal, dead hand of administrative routine?

THE PURPOSE OF PROCEDURES

> Procedures . . . establish a customary method of handling future activities. They are truly guides to action, rather than to thinking, and they detail the exact manner in which a certain activity must be accomplished. Their essence is chronological sequence of required actions. (Koontz, O'Donnel and Weihrich, 1980, page 166)

The relationship to policy is one needing some elaboration. A *policy* is a general statement of intention.

1. Wherever possible we will purchase component parts from British rather than foreign suppliers.
2. We are going to switch our advertising from television to national dailies.
3. We are going to discontinue manufacture of . . .
4. We are an equal opportunity employer.

Each of those statements requires to be 'sold' to members of the organisation before it can become effective, not only for them to be advised, but also for them to be convinced that the policy is appropriate, so that they will put it into practice with enthusiasm and thoroughness. The policy statements also, however, need procedures to make them work. If British rather than foreign suppliers are to be used, there will need to be a modification of the administrative routines operating in research and design, development engineering, production engineering, purchasing and production scheduling.

Procedure is the link between policy and practice, and policies that fail may be poor decisions or good decisions that people elsewhere in the organisation never understood, but most often they are good decisions that foundered because there was no procedural follow-through.

The reasons for using procedures are first *to reduce the need for future decisions*. This is like the cookery recipe. A chef does not say to himself, 'How should I bake a cake?' and then work it out by trial and error or even from first principles: he uses a recipe, a routine that has worked before and will work again. The personnel manager needing to fill a vacancy for a clerical assistant will similarly use a 'recipe' or standard operating procedure. This not only has the advantage of speed in implementation because the decision-making has been done before, it also provides the opportunities of efficiency through practice and a modest amount of de-skilling. The smooth procedure can be operated by those with less skill than the decision-maker and procedure inventor, just as a million cooks can use one of Mrs. Beeton's recipes.

The second value of procedure is *consistency*. Most operations that are to be repeated benefit from being repeated in the same way, particularly when they involve other people who have to respond to the operation. Customers gradually become familiar with an organisation's procedures and practices, so that they waste less of the organisation's time if all organisation members treat them consistently. Organisation members become accustomed to a routine of departmental practice and are able to develop smooth interaction and swift handling if the method remains the same. Herein lies one of the great problems, as well as an advantage, of procedures: they are very difficult to alter and those who use them will abandon them only under duress. This is well illustrated in the field of industrial relations, where not adhering to procedure is the most heinous of crimes.

Thirdly, procedures should provide *autonomy for members of the organisation*. Without procedure as a guideline, people have to await decisions from others. They have to be told how to do things as well as what to do, so that they remain dependent with little scope for individual action. Procedure authorises and informs. Individual members of the organisation know what to do and how to do it. In uncertainty they may ask a colleague, but they can 'look it up'. Good procedure always provides scope for individual decision and action to interpret the rules in particular situations. The importance of close management attention to devising procedures is shown by the frequent problems that occur when they are poorly conceived or inappropriate. Poor procedure can be worse than no procedures at all as it is only the experts who can cope with them – usually through custom and practice – so that the relatively inexperienced are not authorised and informed, they are made dependent on the experts.

A final main advantage is that procedure is a means towards *management control of operations*. The delegation that was implicit in providing the autonomy mentioned above means that managers can turn their attention to other things, confident in the system that will keep things moving in the right general direction. There will be fewer requests for information and guidance, fewer complaints and errors, fewer worries about the minutiae of organisational life. At the same time as providing freedom from control for individual members of the organisation, procedure provides effective control of operations to the management generally.

TYPES OF PROCEDURE

There are four types of procedures generally found in contemporary organisations: task performance, planning and expenditure authorisation, information and co-ordination, and mutual control.

Task performance procedures. These are among the most common.

> How does the part get fabricated? How are the books kept? How are the products priced? In terms of quantity of words, probably most of any given recorded standard operating procedure consists of specifications of methods for accomplishing whatever task is assigned to an individual member or subgroup of the organisation. (Cyert and March, 1963, page 103)

The ability of the engineering craftsman to work to drawings is an ability to work to procedures. Other examples are the job description, which describes a job partly in order to explain to job holders what to do and how to do it; the training manual, which is used by the new recruit to acquire a knowledge of the routine which the job involves; the list of operations that are run through in closing down a plant; fire drill for evacuating the premises in cases of emergency.

Some task performance procedures are brought to the organisation by trained, newly-recruited personnel. The typist arrives knowing the procedures involved in producing a page of accurate typescript, the electrician arrives knowing how to wire a plug. Many of the tasks to be done in the organisation depend on task performance drills that are learned elsewhere, but there is a further set – for all personnel – that is specific to the organisation in which they are carried out. The typist knows how to type, but does not know where to obtain supplies of paper and envelopes, where to put outgoing mail for despatch, nor a whole series of procedures relating to house-style, number and destination of copies and so on. The accountant charged with pricing a product to ensure a proper return needs to know not only good practice in the accountancy profession and a technique for making the calculation, but also the organisational practice on credit in order to establish the appropriate criteria for the calculation.

An important subset of task performance drills are those concerned with changing the rules and coping with new situations. An example is the introduction of legislation that presents new problems. Legislation on the payment by employers of statutory sick pay was a simple idea that spawned innumerable one-day seminars, training packages and computer programmes to explain it to managers. However, what was being 'explained' was not the law, but devices for changing organisational procedures in task performance so that organisational members did their routine operations in a different way. It was the daunting nature of *that* task that caused the managerial anxiety.

Planning and expenditure authorisation procedures. Mostly the domain of senior managers, but minor authorisations are replicated at all levels of the organisation. Although long-range, corporate planning is not as comprehensive an activity as the writers of management books would have us believe, there is always some amount of planning which seeks to set goals and targets for achievement. The plan specifies not only the ultimate destination but also the intermediate steps to be reached on the way. A marketing plan would, for instance, specify not only a target market share of x by a stated date, but also steps of 25 per cent of x to be achieved by an earlier date, 50 per cent of x to be achieved six months later and 75 per cent to be reached six months after that.

Any such plan is based on untested assumptions and is therefore theoretical, so it is not as tight and specific as the task performance procedure, but provides a more general operating framework that is susceptible to change and updating as circumstances evolve. The way in which the plan is given influence over the behaviour of organisation members is by allocating resources and authorising expenditure. The retailing organisation that has a plan to double its number of outlets in three years will not see any action until resources are allocated and expenditure agreed, but once the personnel director is authorised to recruit 700 more staff in each of the next three years and the marketing director is allocated £x million in each of the years to acquire and convert premises, then the plan becomes more than a possibility: it become a requirement for those two executives to implement the proposals.

> The budget in a modern, large-scale corporation plays two basic roles. On the one hand it is used as a management control advice to implement policies on which executives have decided and to check achievement against established criteria. On the other hand, a budget is a device to determine feasible programs. In either it tends to define – in advance – a set of fixed commitments and (perhaps more important) fixed expectations. Although budgets can be flexible, they can not help but result in the specification of a framework within which the firm will operate, evaluate its success, and alter its program. (Cyert and March, *ibid.* page 111)

We are concerned here with the procedures of planning and expenditure authorisation, rather than with planning methods, and the procedures of planning are unusual in the participative nature of their generation. Agreeing on the budget and setting operating plans are nearly always collaborative acts in which a range of interests are reconciled to obtain consensus support for the programme. Key aspects of procedures are thus the meetings at which plans are agreed and any possible power of veto which an individual, or another committee, might deploy; the timing of such meetings and the source of initiatives for consideration. Procedures for expenditure authorisation are of two kinds. Setting the overall budgets is aligned with the planning agreements and probably follows the same procedures precisely, but authorising items of expenditure against budget is an activity delegated to officers who have task performance rules for this procedure. Spending the company's money is not just being allowed to do it because your proposal has been accepted by the senior management team, but following the drills which check that the expenditure is in accordance with another set of rules on proper organisational behaviour.

Information and co-ordination procedures. These have a less precise objective in that organisations can limp along without them, but performance is generally improved if people know what is going on and feel that they are kept in touch. Typically information flows in from the outside of the organisation to the apex of the organisation pyramid or to well-identified other places in the hierarchy. The method of passing information on to other members of the organisation will lie in procedure, so that there is some semi-automatic means whereby dissemination takes place, rather than dependence on the individual recipient to take thought and decide on dissemination.

Review Topic 24.2

The procedure for salesmen claiming expenses in a large chemical company was elaborate. Four authorising signatures were needed plus two separate clerical checks. The time from claim to settlement was usually between 16 and 20 working days. An internal consultant devised a different procedure that needed only one signature and one clerical check. The time from claim to settlement would drop to 5–8 days. There were no objections to this new arrangement, but four months later it had not been implemented. Why do you think this was?

Among the procedures found for information and co-ordination are the use of minutes of meetings, which are often circulated to a wider group than just those who attended the meeting at which the minutes were taken. A common refinement is to include a note as to who is expected to take action on the decisions made at the meeting. Another procedure is the checklist of recipients of memoranda, so that a manager will have two or three standard routine lists for passing information onwards. Notice boards are a potentially useful means of distributing information, but a procedure is needed to make it an effective means: who is responsible for putting items on the board and removing them? What items are appropriate, bearing in mind that all have to be read and understood in a very brief timespan? How long should items be displayed? A procedure which deals with these questions can make good use of a notice board system.

Mutual control procedures. Those which enable the employing organisation and the individual employee to exercise a degree of control over each other. Grievance and discipline procedures are the main example, as the parties to the contract of employment have a series of procedural steps available to them so that they can limit the action of the other.

> Joint regulation seeks to reconcile the interests of viewpoints of management and employees by a process of negotiation but it begins with the recognition that there are such differences of interest and view point and that there is sufficient strength behind them to make the quest for agreement necessary and desirable. Agreed procedures establish a *modus vivendi* reflecting the interests and strength of the parties. (Singleton, 1975, page 5)

These industrial relations creations should not only be seen as ways in which action is prevented or made more difficult, they also *authorise* certain actions by managers and others. Discipline procedures, for instance, specify who has the authority to make relevant decisions, the circumstances which would justify those decisions and the means whereby a decision would be implemented.

PROBLEMS AND SOLUTIONS

Procedures present problems as well as opportunities, the most difficult of which is their dullness.

> Managers often fail to obtain the interest and support of top managers in the tedious and unromantic planning and control of procedures (Koontz *et al.*, op cit., page 769)

That is difficult to resolve, but has to be recognised. Another problem is that *they inhibit change.* When they eventually become operational and everyone is used to them, they provide a comfortable, secure routine, an aspect of organisational maintenance where people can feel at home with the familiar. This is much like the way in which managers move from management to administrative activity, when the management work gets too hectic. There is always the risk that procedure becomes custom and practice and as immutable as the laws of the Medes and the Persians.

Overlapping and duplication cause problems when each section of the organisation has its own procedures that do not quite coincide with those of other sections. Purchasing has procedures that are not quite the same as Accounts and both are quite different from those in Engineering. The varying emphasis is necessary as accountants have different responsibilities from buyers. The problems come when the overlapping or duplication becomes too great.

A less obvious problem is when procedures are used to try and solve problems that require a *policy solution.* Just as procedures are needed to put policy into practice, policies are needed for procedures to be effective. The personnel manager in a small textile company was anxious to eradicate racial discrimination from personnel practice within the organisation and made a number of procedural adjustments to this end. Standardised forms of words to be used in job advertisements were devised, instructions were given to telephonists about handling telephone enquiries, short-listing arrangements in the personnel office were altered and various other methods of preventing unfair discrimination were introduced. He failed, however, to explain these moves to anyone outside the department and was accused of high-handedness and deviousness by his colleagues. He also found that the procedural devices did not work: checks on advertisement wording were overlooked, departmental managers disagreed with short lists and there was a formal complaint to the Commission for Racial Equality. All of this was due to a lack of policy decision and commitment. The policy decision was made only in the personnel manager's mind, being neither discussed with, nor communicated to, anyone else. The telephonists and personnel staff did not fully understand the reasons for the changes they had been asked to make and other managers did not understand what was being done. Once the policy was clear, sold and accepted, the procedure worked well. Procedure can only deal with organisational problems for which a procedural solution is appropriate.

Procedure has all the inherent risks of *rigidity.* In producing a standard way of doing things, there is the danger that it is regarded by some as the only way of doing things. Grievance procedures nearly always specify that aggrieved employees should raise their dissatisfaction first with their immediate organisational superiors. This is for a number of very good reasons, such as to prevent the immediate superior being bypassed and to ensure that the matter will be resolved as quickly as possible and by the people most closely involved. Carried to an extreme that could be interpreted as prohibiting an employee talking to a more senior manager about anything. When organisational change is needed, the rigidity of procedures can prove too much for the enthusiasm with which the change is sought.

A common problem is the *complexity* of procedures. This is where the procedural steps are intended to eliminate any discretion at all. Such procedures are difficult for people to remember and to understand, so that they may be used only by – literally – following the book. They are also a challenge to the ingenuity of people who resist the lack of scope for personal judgement and interpretation. An example is in safe working procedures, which are regularly ignored by skilled and experienced operators who have sufficient skill and knowledge to do, safely, what would be highly dangerous for others.

To overcome these difficulties those designing procedures should always aim for *simplicity*, so that they can be readily understood by those who operate them and those who are affected by them, allowing scope for interpretation to suit particular circumstances. Procedures should also be as *few* as possible, so that there is less to remember and so that the degree of overlapping and duplication is limited. Also a new procedure should not be introduced unless it is deemed as really necessary. To be necessary a series of future incidents has to be likely so as to require some thought-out decisions in advance. Producing a procedure to deal with a situation that occurs seldom but with similar results is useful. Producing a procedure to deal with a situation which occurs seldom and with very varied results is pointless. A sombre example of the first is a procedure for dealing with attendance at funerals of those who die while in the employment of the organisation – who attends the funeral, how much time off, with or without pay, in company cars or not, etc. An unbelievable example of the second is 'Procedure for the Golden Jubilee of the Monarch', found to be still available in the head office of an insurance company.

Procedures should be tested to see if they meet their *objectives*. A hospital was receiving a number of complaints from patients' relatives, so a complaints procedures was set up. This had the unfortunate effect of lengthening the time taken to deal with complaints and increasing their number. We have to make sure that procedures have not only an internal logic, but also that they do what they are set up to do.

Procedures must have the *before and after* stages of policy and communication. There must be a policy for the procedure to implement, even if it is only the implicit policy of established practice, and all affected must know what the procedure is. 'Knowing' is not the same as 'being told about'.

Monitoring can prevent procedures becoming obsolete and inefficient. Not only must they be communicated, they must also be monitored in operation to make sure that they are being worked properly and that there are no unintended effects that should be smoothed out before too much damage is done.

PROCEDURAL METHOD

There are four methods of producing procedures: task logic, modelling, checklist and flowcharting.

Symbol	Meaning	Example
◯	Operation	Filling in a form
☐	Inspection	Checking accuracy of previous operations
⇨	Transport	Item passes to another person or section
D	Delay	Item awaits further operation
▽	Storage	Item is filed or stored

Fig. 24.1 Symbols used in flowcharting.

Task logic. This is the method of work study and associated techniques, whereby the logic of the task to be accomplished dictates a sequence of actions or activities to be carried out in task performance. This method is not dealt with in this book, but a standard reference is Larkin, 1969.

Checklist. The checklist method is to set up a series of check questions as a basis of formulating the drill. Such a list could be derived from the sections of this chapter.

Modelling. A method much used with industrial relations procedures. A typical procedural system is devised as a model that could be used, with modification, for a wide variety of similar situations. At the end of this chapter there is a model of a grievance procedure.

Flowcharting. The most sophisticated method is flowcharting, which is a simplified form of systems analysis. This is appropriate for those administrative drills that consist of a lengthy system of interrelated activities, possibly involving several different departments and certainly involving a number of different people. It can sometimes be elaborated from its basic linear form into a network analysis. Figure 24.1 shows the symbols used in flowcharting and Figure 24.2 gives an example of a flow chart.

There is a danger in regarding procedures as dull and not requiring managerial time and attention. The organisation without satisfactory procedures can rarely operate effectively unless it is in an unusually favourable business situation. Any organisation can be hamstrung if its procedures get out of control. The need for swift action and consistent decision-making has to be balanced against the need for managerial initiative and employee creativity.

Fig. 24.2 Flowchart of procedure for settling expense claims.

SUMMARY PROPOSITIONS

24.1 Procedures are the link between policy ('what we would like to happen') and practice ('what is happening').

24.2 Reasons for using procedures are to reduce the need for decision-making in the future, to ensure consistency, to provide autonomy for members of the organisation and mangement control of operations.

24.3 Types of procedure are task performance, planning and expenditure authorisation, information and co-ordination, and mutual control.

24.4 Problems with procedures are that they can inhibit change; overlapping and duplication; providing the wrong solution to a problem requiring a policy solution; rigidity and complexity.

24.5 Problems can be overcome by having few, simple procedures; meeting objectives with before and after phases and monitoring.

24.6 Methods of procedure are task logic, checklist, modelling and flowcharting.

PUTTING IT INTO PRACTICE

Outline model for grievance procedure

Statement of intent
The purpose of this procedure is to enable individual employees of . . . employed in . . . to obtain satisfaction of grievances which they have about their employment. It provides a framework for the employee to voice his dissatisfaction and seek improvement. It is separate from the disputes procedure for resolving matters relating to employees collectively in their relationships with the management.

Step 1 (Preliminary)
The dissatisfied employee discusses his complaint with his immediate superior and serves notice that he would like his case heard at the next stage if he has not received a satisfactory reply within . . . days.

Step 2 (Hearing)
The dissatisfied employee duly presents his case to a more senior manager (position to be specified). The reason for this being that this manager will be able to take a more dispassionate view of the matter than the immediate superior and will have the benefit of a broader range of responsibility to judge potential problems in meeting the employee's requirements.

Step 3 (Appeal)
If still not satisfied the employee may take his case to appeal within . . . days of the hearing. This will be with a more senior manager or committee (position to be specified) or

external arbiter, invoking greater authority to examine the first two decisions.

If the employee is still not satisfied he has no further recourse within this procedure.

REFERENCES

Carter, R., *Business Administration*, Heinemann, London, 1982.

Cyert, R.M. and March, J.G., *A Behavioural Theory of the Firm*, Prentice Hall, Englewood Cliffs, New Jersey, 1963.

Koontz, H., O'Donnell, C., Weihrich, H., *Management*, 7th edn, McGraw Hill, Kogakusha, Tokyo, 1980.

Larkin, J.A., *Work Study, Theory and Practice*, McGraw Hill, London, 1969.

Singleton, N., *Industrial Relations Procedures*, HMSO, London, 1975.

25

THE FUTURE AND THE
PROFESSIONAL MANAGER

Few aspects of understanding are sought more eagerly than a look into the future. For centuries people all round the Mediterranean consulted the oracle at Delphi before embarking on any major enterprise. The tragedy of Macbeth is heightened by his reliance on the prophecy of the three witches – using such odd methods as eye of newt and toe of frog, wool of bat and tongue of dog – that he would not be vanquished until Birnam wood be moved to Dunsinane. Today large segments of national newspapers are taken up with predictions based on the position of the stars and planets, and whether it will rain before breakfast. Having heard our favourite prediction, we then do not exactly ignore it; we interpret it in the way that suits us. Macbeth met his end at Dunsinane, King Croesus went to war against Cyrus of Persia when the Delphic oracle told him that the war would lead to the destruction of a mighty kingdom. Croesus assumed that the kingdom to be destroyed belonged to Cyrus; in fact it was his own.

As we conclude this book with some thoughts about the future, we do so realising that we are probably wrong and that whatever we say readers will interpret it in the way that suits them, emphasising and remembering what they like and ignoring what they dislike. We also realise that some people, browsing in bookshops and libraries, will glance at only this chapter before putting the book back on the shelf. So, with some misgivings and with feet firmly on the mantelshelf, here we go.

DECENTRALISATION AND AUTONOMY

The trend towards decentralisation of organisations and individual autonomy will continue. Operational units will be smaller and more manageable by having more scope delegated to them from the centre and less emphasis on conformity to a single pattern. This is not always possible, especially where consumer preference is important. Retail banks cannot vary their operational patterns much as their interconnection is a major feature of their working, but gradually operational units of all types are gaining more independence for their operations. This provides more managers with more scope. Just as management by objectives was a popular attempt to isolate the activities of individual managers so that they could see their performance in isolation from collective performance, so there is growing a more real independence as accountability, responsibility and autonomy are made more feasible through managers being required to conform to organisation-wide norms on a relatively narrow range of activities only but with considerable scope to run the undertaking in their own way.

In Chapter 3, we drew a distinction between the nature of managerial work in senior mangement posts and those in top and middle management. The decentralisation trend could lead to more people having senior management responsibilities and opportunities. This type of professional autonomy makes the idea of the *professional manager*, with skills suitable for a number of different situations, a more feasible proposition for the future than it has been in the past. Accountancy and marketing skills have become professionalised and transferable, but managerial skills have been more organisation-dependent due to the 'middleness' of most managers. That could now be changing. Two widely-publicised reports (Handy, 1987; Constable and McCormick, 1987) advocated professional qualification for all managers and moves are underway to establish specific management competences against which preparation for management posts can be assessed.

This is accompanied by an expectation of greater autonomy among those who do not see themselves as managers. Autonomous work groups received great publicity and scrutiny because they broke the mould of supervision. The pre-existing assumption had been that people at work needed supervision to keep them from idleness and to avoid their individual efforts being uncoordinated. By the basically simple tactic of getting (or letting?) work groups to organise themselves and exercise their own responsibility without the yoke of close supervision, it was demonstrated that tight control is not always necessary. Although the speed of movement varies, the general development of autonomy is growing apace, so that the professional manager will be increasingly concerned with a management team or departmental team of other professionals or quasi-professionals, wanting to know what is required of them and then wanting to be left alone to get on with it.

THE MANAGERIAL ELITE

In many ways managers as a social grouping are growing apart from those with whom they work. It is not their social origins, upbringing or schooling that makes the difference, but the approach to the job. Most of those at work find their weekly hours slowly reducing, their annual days of holiday increasing and their age of retirement dropping. Paid employment may still be the central organising feature of our society and occupation may still be the main determinant of social status, but for many people work is not as focal as it was and *some* of our human needs are now met not through work but through the twin anodynes of television and do-it-yourself. If even slightly fewer needs depend on paid employment for their satisfaction, then employees become marginally more amenable and less prickly because it means less to them.

For managers it is different. There is a continuing preoccupation with correct dress and correct manners. Smart suits and self-coloured ties are still *de rigueur* for men, and women maintain a distinctive convention of dress, even if they are not quite so hidebound. Manners, or styles of behaviour are also distinctive, so that some outside observers regard management as being no more than games-playing and posturing. Although this is an exaggeration in most instances, and is much reduced by decentralisation and autonomy, one of the conventional behaviours is 'commitment'. Managers are expected to be enthusiastic and thoroughly committed to their jobs and their careers in a way that would nowadays seem slightly odd in many other occupational groups. This, of course, is a standard attribute of the professional in other fields. For managers it involves a willingness to travel considerably, day-by-day or week-by-week, so that it must be possible on one day to take the 6.30 a.m. train to London, returning at midnight and on another day to fly to Bahrain for a week. Domestic commitments and family responsibilities do not fit easily into that sort of operating style. For most managers it also involves mobility, which presents a different set of domestic difficulties.

Review Topic 25.1

Few managers appear relaxed and their lives are characterised by constant bustle, as we saw in Part I of this book, with hectic travelling a familiar feature of the managerial life-style. To what extent do you think this is:
1. **Setting a pace for everyone else to follow?**
2. **Inevitable due to the demands of the business?**
3. **Putting on a show, to convince people (and themselves) that they deserve to be well paid?**
4. **Unnecessary?**
5. **A result of management appealing mainly to people who are hyperactive?**
6. **Changing?**

Total preoccupation of this type is relatively easy and attractive to the young and independent. It is tolerable to the married, but problematic for those with families – especially women. Women at the professional managerial level in business have found much improved opportunities in the last decade and have fared better than semi-skilled and clerical women, but for most of them success is gained at the expense of family life. The

28-year-old woman manager who is wondering whether or not to have a baby for the first time will realise that her neighbours who are doctors, barristers, schoolteachers, civil servants, lecturers and solicitors will find it much easier to return to their professional careers as young mothers than would she. It seems to be easier for those who bear their children while they are in their late teens or early twenties and who then begin the assault on the male-dominated bastions of management in their later twenties.

SOCIAL RESPONSIBILITY

The crude, over-simplified view of management – all that matters is making profits – produces some scepticism among onlookers when managers speak of being socially responsible. Sir James Goldsmith was proud to declare his opposition to the idea of social responsibility:

> Entrepreneurs come in all shapes and sizes. They straddle every class and every system of education. The common theme that links them all together is sound judgement, ambition, determination, capacity to assess and take risks, hard work, greed, fear and luck. The most dangerous entrepreneur is the self righteous one who preaches morality and pretends that he is doing it all for the good of others. (Goldsmith, 1980, pages 185–6)

That sort of view would be echoed by many trade union representatives, who believe that they would be better judges of social responsibility than managers, who should concentrate on being efficient while socially responsible behaviour was imposed upon them by legislation, public opinion or trade union power.

Despite this managers are concerned to behave as human beings and to exercise some social responsibility greater than balancing the books. Even those entrepreneurs whom the reader will have in his mind at the present moment, and who epitomise exactly what Goldsmith was describing, do not operate in a vacuum but via organisational and management processes; they work with other people and those people will seldom share their single-mindedness.

There is a wealth of social problems that need the attention of business managers, because the appropriate initiatives cannot readily come from elsewhere. One is some initiative about unemployment, especially hard-core unemployment. We do not have solutions to offer here, but clearly employment comes from employers and managers, no matter how much politicians may nudge, exhort and manipulate. An associated matter is that of equal opportunity. The number of disadvantaged groups grows and the degree of their disadvantage increases. Age for age unemployment among blacks is much higher than among whites. The number of blacks who break out from the lower levels of employment and enjoy the wider prospects of white-collar and management positions remains few. Apart from the privileged minority in managerial posts, the position of women in employment is weak in relation to men. They are still largely found in a narrow range of 'women only' jobs with poor rates of pay and limited opportunities, although the female participation rate in employment is higher in Britain than in most of our competitor countries and the unemployment rate among women is lower than for men. Both blacks and women have received much attention and legislative support in recent years, but the employment prospects of disabled people and those who have served terms of imprisonment have attracted less interest and remain gloomy.

A different aspect of concern about unemployment is its effect on the young and the old. The general level of anxiety about unemployment among school leavers is such that there have been a series of quite costly initiatives to mitigate that problem. The Youth Training Scheme that began in 1983 shows signs of potential long-run success. It can, however, only defer the time when those who have been trained seek employment. Job opportunities for the young may mean the loss of employment for those who are older. Workforce reductions are easiest when those who go are volunteers, and many of the job losses in the public sector of employment and in the larger private organisations have been achieved by early retirement, sometimes as young as fifty years of age. In other situations whole organisations and whole industries have closed down, making jobless all employees regardless of age. Here the re-employment prospects for those of forty-five or more have been very poor indeed.

A different aspect of management responsibility is the ecological worry, where business is criticised as much as governments. Technological advance not only accelerates the rate at which we use up our natural resources, such as fossil fuels and iron ore, but the processing of those resources pollutes our delicately balanced ecology and is increasingly resisted. The rain forests of South America have been called the world's lung, yet their extent is being rapidly reduced. We have widespread problems of acid rain, frequent explosions at chemical factories and the occasional calamity like Seveso. Those major problems are reproduced on a smaller scale in many localities and overall hangs the constant fear of a Chernobyl-style nuclear accident.

AGE

Managers will respond to two different challenges relating to age. First will be the age of the customers. The decline in the fertility rate in Western countries has been accompanied by steadily growing life expectancy so that the mean age of the population is rising. We have already seen how managers supplying goods and services have exploited the adolescent market and, more recently, the market among the 'mature young' in their twenties and thirties but without family commitments. An expanding market will be among those of advancing years.

Within organisations, however, the situation will be different. At the beginning of this chapter we suggested that decentralisation and autonomy could lead to more managers requiring senior management rather than middle management skills. We have also referred to the shake-out of employment among those who are older. In our interviews with managers while preparing this book we have been struck by how young managers are. This is not just a version of the hoary old comment about policemen getting younger as you get older, it appears to be a clear trend of significant management responsibility to come to younger people.

Partly this is a result of early retirement and similar shake-out strategies. If the 'old' people in the organisation are in their late fifties instead of in their early sixties, then the age balance shifts, so that the 'middle aged' are 40 instead of 48 and the 'young' are 25 instead of 30. Another reason is the growing significance of new technology, especially the computer, which seems to be best understood and developed by those in their teens and early twenties. Also the need to be committed, that we have mentioned, is easier to sustain while young.

The idea of giving real responsibility to young people has been a commonplace for decades, even though it has not often been seen in practice. Now it is becoming more common, but what happens to older managers? In times of expansion the answer is easy: the organisation grows and more people are constantly needed to feed growth. If organisations are getting smaller, or remaining small, that answer will not work. The alternative is that managers move down the hierarchy as well as up. At the moment that sort of move is almost unknown, partly because of the concern with status and partly because of the concern with income level and pension level. The manager at forty is anxious to maximize earnings because of family responsibilities with children and ageing parents. The manager at fifty plus develops an anxiety to maximize his or her final salary, so as to boost the pension. This can produce a number of undesirable effects. One is the managers who are 'counting the days' until retirement but have to cling grimly to jobs they no longer really want to do, just to maintain the pension. Another possibility is the department or business that stagnates for years because the person in charge is in the run-up to retirement and does not want any innovation or change. A third problem is that of the managers who keep going at full throttle in the closing stages of employment, only to find the sudden change to the different pace of retirement very hard to take.

It is unrealistic to think simply of moving people out of the organisation as they get older. First this can be extremely expensive and secondly it reduces the all-round capability of the management, which needs the contribution of older people as well as those who are younger.

Shakespeare's seven ages of man distinguish between the soldier and the justice:

> . . . a soldier, . . .
> Jealous in honour, sudden and quick in quarrel,
>   Seeking the bubble reputation . . .
> And then the justice . . .
>   Full of wise saws and modern instances.

For effectiveness, management seems to need both sets of qualities. Traditionally the 'soldier' is junior to the 'justice'. Perhaps the time has come for that to change, but we have to find a way of doing this that will ensure the effective contribution of both.

One development that may increase the tendency for people to move down as well as up the hierarchy is the recent emphasis on performance-related pay in professions long opposed to such a principle. In the civil service and in teaching, for instance, certain incentive payments have been introduced that have to be earned – or at least justified – regularly, so that incremental pay scales do not lead everyone inexorably to the top of the earnings league. Personal, portable pensions are a recent innovation that can be attractive to the young and mobile. If this practice becomes widespread it could further weaken the tendency for people to move up the hierarchy, but never come down.

INTERNATIONAL OPERATIONS

Despite decentralisation, organisations are getting bigger, so that the multinational is a feature of western societies that concerns some because of the considerable power that such companies are able to wield and concerns others because of the difficulty such companies have in innovating. With the improvements in communications, almost all organisations now operate across national boundaries. If there is not a branch of the business overseas, there will certainly be overseas selling and buying and observation of technical developments.

Underlying this development of the international dimension is the interdependence of western countries and the developing economies of the world. The British buyer of a British washing machine may not realise that the machine may have been partly manufactured in Korea, partly in the Philippines, partly in Italy and only assembled in Britain. The Third World has long looked to the developed countries for technical expertise and investment, even though they have been exploited in the process. More recently the developed countries have shifted manufacturing into developing countries, not in order better to supply *those* markets, but in order to have cheap manufacturing to supply western markets. Pay rates have been low, industrial action unlikely and increased automation has made it possible to produce high quality components.

This transfer of manufacturing operations could lead to a situation where the western nations become more dependent on the developing countries than they have been in the past.

THE COMPUTER

One great uncertainty is the influence of the computer. We have plenty of predictions and mostly these are prophecies of what the computer and the microprocessor *can* do and then logically developed to produce a picture of what *will* happen; manufacturing will progressively be taken over by robots, rapid transfer and manipulation of data, the paperless office, people working from home instead of coming into a centre, and so forth: the golden age of the post-industrial society. Our questions about this are first the extent to which the possible will become reality and secondly to wonder what will be done to make up what the computer will take from us.

Managers have long had the opportunity to spend more of their time, and make more of their decisions, by rational planning and operational research methods than in fact they do. There continues to be a preference among managers to spend their time talking with people and to make their decisions as a result of discussion and shrewd judgement. Will managers now begin to eschew face-to-face discussion in favour of face-to-terminal decision-making, or will they continue to confer and keep busy while others feed to them an ever-increasing flow of processed information requiring interpretation, evaluation and further discussion.

Research findings suggest that managers work the way they do at least partly because they like it that way.

> The manager actually seems to prefer brevity and interruption in his work. Superficiality is an occupational hazard of the manager's job.
> Very current information (gossip, hearsay, speculation) is favoured; routine reports are not.
> The manager clearly favours the . . . verbal media, spending most of his time in verbal contact. (Mintzberg, 1973, pages 51–2)

How significantly will managers allow this pattern of working to change and how great will the influence of the computer on managerial work actually become?

Apart from managers, there is then the question about how everyone else will make up for what the computer takes away. If there is a general tendency for people to work at home, taking their terminal with them, how popular will that turn out to be? It is over a century since the household ceased to be the central productive unit and the men, and later the women, began to spend a large part of their waking hours at a different social centre – the factory, shop or office. To be housebound has become a blight. We can see how it used to be:

> In 1810 the common productive unit in New England was still the rural household. Processing and preserving of food, candlemaking, soap-making, spinning, weaving, shoemaking, quilting, rug-making, the keeping of small animals and gardens, all took place on domestic premises. Although money income might be obtained by the household through the sale of produce, and additional money be earned through occasional wages to its members, the United States household was overwhelmingly self-sufficient. . . . Women were as active in the creation of domestic self-sufficiency as were men. (Illich, 1981, pages 111–2)

Since that time we have dismantled, or allowed to wither, all the social mechanisms that supported that self-sufficiency, and developed the social institution of the workplace as the arena for many of our human needs, like affiliation, interaction, team working and competition. If we are about to reverse that trend, we need different arenas to meet those needs.

On a less dramatic level, there is the slightly isolating nature of the work that computerisation produces. The individual employee is not one of many in a crowded workshop, but one of a few scattered around a mass of busy machines. The clerical employee spends more time gazing at a computer terminal and less talking to colleagues. What employee behaviour will this engender and what attitudes will be associated with that behaviour?

CONCLUSION

In this concluding chapter we have suggested a few possibilities for the future. There are many more and some readers will already have read the best known set of prophecies by Toffler (1980). His predictions and ours may be no more accurate than that of the man who predicted the end of the world at 11.01 a.m. on the 6th November 1882, but they are offered here as they sustain our belief that managers progressively need to develop a personal survival kit that will enable them to be effective in a wide variety of situations, becoming less organisationally dependent and more self-sufficient.

We see the stereotype of the future manager as being younger, better-paid and more autonomous than those of today. To succeed they will need to be mobile and bright. More of them will be women and most will have a strong specialist skill in either accountancy, marketing or a technological area. All of them will need organisational knowledge and a set of operational managerial skills of the type that we have described in these pages. Finally they will need individual flair, imagination and application.

Management is a science: successful management is an art.
  Good luck!

REFERENCES

Constable, J. and McCormick, R. *The Making of British Managers*, British Institute of Management, Corby, Northamptonshire, 1987.

Goldsmith, J., 'Entrepreneurs, innovation and change' in Wild, R. (ed.), *How to Manage*, Heinemann, London, 1982.

Illich, I., *Shadow Work*, Marion Boyars, London, 1981.

Mintzberg, H., *The Nature of Managerial Work*, Harper & Row, London, 1973.

Toffler, A., *The Third Wave*, Morrow, New York, 1980.

AUTHOR INDEX

SUBJECT INDEX